1000 CHURCHES TO
VISIT IN SCOTLAND

ST NINIAN'S CATHEDRAL, PERTH

KILARROW PARISH CHURCH,
BOWMORE, ISLE OF ISLAY

GARNETHILL
SYNAGOGUE

THE CATHEDRAL OF
THE ISLES, CUMBRAE

PITLOCHRY
BAPTIST CHURCH

BUCCLEUCH & GREYFRIARS
FREE CHURCH

ST MARY AND ST FINNAN CHURCH,
GLENFINNAN, INVERNESS-SHIRE

NICOLSON SQUARE
METHODIST CHURCH

CATHEDRAL CHURCH
OF ST LUKE

KELSO QUAKER
MEETING HOUSE

1000 CHURCHES TO VISIT IN SCOTLAND

Illustrated by John R Hume

Published on behalf of
SCOTLAND'S CHURCHES SCHEME
by
NMS ENTERPRISES LIMITED – PUBLISHING
National Museums of Scotland, Chambers Street, Edinburgh EH1 1JF

Text © Scotland's Churches Scheme, 2005
Illustrations © John R Hume, 2005
Maps © Jim Lewis, 2005

ISBN 10: 1-905267-00-2
ISBN 13: 978-1-905267-00-2

British Library Cataloguing in Publication Data
A catalogue record for this book is available from the British Library.

Designed by Mark Blackadder.
Typeset in Columbus and Gill Sans.

DIRECTOR
Dr Brian Fraser BA PhD FIPD

Office: Dunedin, Holehouse Road, Eaglesham, Glasgow G76 0JF
Telephone: 01355 302416   *Fax:* 01355 303181
E-mail: fraser@dunedin67.freeserve.co.uk
Website: http://churchesinscotland.co.uk
Registered Charity Number: SC 022868

FRONT COVER PHOTOGRAPH
St Magnus Cathedral, Kirkwall, Orkney. *Photograph:* Crown Copyright © Royal Commission
on the Ancient and Historical Monuments of Scotland

BACK COVER PHOTOGRAPHS
Top left. Quaker Meeting House, Edinburgh. *Photograph:* © A Stewart Brown
Top middle. Lyne Kirk, Borders. *Photograph:* © A Stewart Brown
Top right. Crichton Memorial Church, Dumfries. *Photograph:* Crown Copyright © Royal Commission
on the Ancient and Historical Monuments of Scotland
Bottom left. Stobo Kirk, Borders. *Photograph:* © A Stewart Brown
Bottom right. Our Lady of Sorrows, South Uist. *Photograph:* Crown Copyright © Royal Commission
on the Ancient and Historical Monuments of Scotland

SPINE PHOTOGRAPH
All Saints', St Andrews. *Photograph:* Crown Copyright © Royal Commission
on the Ancient and Historical Monuments of Scotland

Printed in Scotland by Bell & Bain Ltd, Glasgow.

CONTENTS

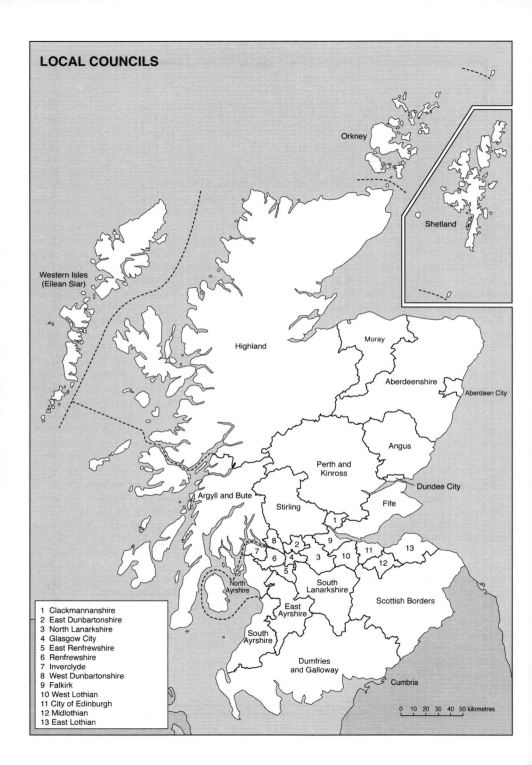

LOCAL COUNCILS

Orkney

Shetland

Western Isles
(Eilean Siar)

Highland

Moray

Aberdeenshire

Aberdeen City

Angus

Perth and
Kinross

Dundee City

Fife

Argyll and Bute

Stirling

North
Ayrshire

South
Lanarkshire

East
Ayrshire

Scottish Borders

South
Ayrshire

Dumfries
and Galloway

Cumbria

1 Clackmannanshire
2 East Dunbartonshire
3 North Lanarkshire
4 Glasgow City
5 East Renfrewshire
6 Renfrewshire
7 Inverclyde
8 West Dunbartonshire
9 Falkirk
10 West Lothian
11 City of Edinburgh
12 Midlothian
13 East Lothian

0 10 20 30 40 50 kilometres

HOW TO USE THIS GUIDE

Entries are arranged alphabetically by council and then by locality. The number preceding each entry refers to the map at the beginning of each section. The denomination of the church is shown on the last line of each entry, followed by the relevant symbols:

    ♿   Access for partially abled

    ☉   Hearing induction loop for the deaf

        Welcomers and guides on duty

    📖   Guidebooks and souvenirs

    wc   Toilet for the disabled

    ®   Inventory completed by Church Recorders

        Features for children/link with schools

    ☕   Refreshments

    wc   Toilets on premises

    A   Category A Listing

    B   Category B Listing

    C   Category C Listing

Category A: Buildings of national or more than local importance, either architectural or historic, or fine little-altered examples of some particular period, style or type.

Category B: Buildings of regional or more than local importance, or major examples of some particular period, style or building type which may have been altered.

Category C: Buildings of local importance, or lesser examples of any period style, or building type, as originally constructed or altered; and simple traditional buildings which group well with others.

The information appearing in the gazetteer of this guidebook is supplied by the participating churches. While this is believed to be correct at the time of going to press, Scotland's Churches Scheme cannot accept any responsibility for its accuracy.

SCOTLAND'S CHURCHES SCHEME

Serving Churches of all denominations in Scotland

AIMS AND PURPOSES

1.

To promote spiritual understanding by enabling the public to appreciate all buildings designed for worship and active as living churches

2.

To advance the education of the public in history, architecture and other environmental subjects through the study of historic church buildings of all denominations in Scotland, their contents and environs

3.

To encourage co-operation among the churches themselves and between them and their local communities

4.

To publish details of churches open to visitors through a handbook *Churches to Visit in Scotland* as a guide for visitors, and to encourage support for the churches visited through donations, especially for specific appeals

5.

To receive donations for churches, in particular or in general, in order to provide when requested advice on the care and reception of visitors and the provision of historical and other information

6.

To promote the common purpose of mission through the ministry of welcome for visitors, tourists and pilgrims

FOREWORD

A Thousand Years – A Thousand Churches:
Ten Years of Scotland's Churches Scheme

A thousand years of surviving church buildings? Not quite yet. A thousand churches in the handbook? Yes! Ten years of Scotland's Churches Scheme? Yes, yes!

In this 21st century we will celebrate the 1000th anniversary of Brechin Round Tower which is part of Brechin Cathedral – a Scheme member. Within the last few months the 1000th church joined us and in this year of grace 2006 we most certainly celebrate ten years of our Scheme. Surely this near coincidence of achievement is, at least, a good excuse for a party and a party in which many branches of the Christian Church and Judaism can all join as equals – perhaps the happiest example of wholehearted cooperation between religious bodies we yet have. For we have in common a faith in a living, loving, forgiving God, and a real desire to share with others the places in which we worship Him. Hospitality to strangers, and to those in need, is at the heart of our shared beliefs. Through the Scheme we can not only welcome people to our beloved churches, but also share our experiences, and enjoy the company of others of like mind in a way that transcends denominational and even faith differences. We can, too, be challenged and enlarged in our thinking by those with different perspectives. Welcoming strangers brings with it the chance to be surprised and blessed by the different and unexpected.

The division of time into days and years has a logic in the alternation of day and night and in the order of the seasons. That into decades, centuries and millennia presumably derives from our having (usually) ten fingers and ten toes. Though to an extent arbitrary, there is no doubt that the beginning of a new century, a new millennium, or even a tenth – or fortieth – birthday marks a watershed in the lives of individuals, groups and even of whole societies. But though these anniversaries are convenient milestones for marking our individual or collective journeys through the years, they have a habit of constraining our thinking about the past. Does not the relegation of 1999 and earlier years to 'the last century' give them a sense of the dead and gone, of irrelevance to now, which is misleading?

'Now' is merely the pivot between the past and the future, and 'New' has an inevitable transience, as does 'Modern'. Our belief is in a God without beginning or end, so to us 'now' is rightly a moment in a long sequence of lives lived in that belief. Our ancestors' belief in an eternal God and their disposition to come together to worship Him in permanent buildings has allowed the truths and duties of our respective faiths to be transmitted to us in a particular way, complementing oral tradition, written texts and iconography.

The implication of this is that places of worship have real and enduring value as statements of belief, and as evidence of how successive generations have sought to share and to communicate that belief. That is at the heart of their importance. Their form, furnishings and detailing are part not only of changing patterns of belief, but also of non-verbal communication of those patterns: the languages of art and of architecture and buildings are as valid in communicating as those of writing, speaking and of music, and can be as powerful, or even more powerful. The little stone churches of the 12th century and their greater contemporaries speak of the mystery of God. The soaring building of the high Gothic tells of aspiration amid growing prosperity.

DALMENY PARISH CHURCH (ST CUTHBERT'S)

The experimental church of Burntisland is evidence of shared worship round word and sacrament, and some 17th-century buildings strongly suggest that cultural, economic and family ties with northern Europe were more important than those with England and its church. The many simple 18th-century churches are evocative of a thriving rural

DYKE PARISH CHURCH

society, and of the physical and spiritual focal point of the preaching of the Word. Their large town and city counterparts tell of great mercantile and craft congregations, gatherings of people never hitherto brought together in such large numbers. Other 18th-century buildings remind us of growing diversity of opinion within the Christian polity, of dissent about relationship between Church and State, of continuing loyalty to beliefs officially marginalized by the established church since the Reformation, and of the migration of other forms of church from south of the Border.

By the end of the 18th century the design and scale of church buildings were being used to express shades of belief and of denominational aspiration in a very explicit way, and throughout the 19th and early 20th centuries the architectural languages being used

KIRKCUDBRIGHT PARISH CHURCH

became more insistent and more complex. Classical churches often expressed rationality, and frequently opposition to the undue influence of the State on church government. Gothic at first expressed the idea of

ST CUTHBERT'S PARISH CHURCH, SALTCOATS

continuity with the pre-Reformation church, but eventually became so accepted as an appropriate style for church buildings that as an external treatment it lost much of its original expressive meaning, and was embraced by most Christian denominations. In the late 1880s, however, the Ecclesiological Movement breathed new life into both Gothic and into the 12th-century Romanesque, with architects responding to more open briefs to create some of the finest worship spaces, visually speaking, ever built in Scotland. Some of the design solutions drew on English Arts and Crafts style; others harked back to Scots prototypes, mainly of the 12th and 15-16th centuries. The phenomenon was not confined to the Lowland cities: architects in all of Scotland's cities, and in some of the larger towns demonstrated a feeling for historical sources while at the same time creatively responding to up-to-date ideas about worship practice. During this period, too, migrations of

LOWSON MEMORIAL CHURCH, FORFAR

Jews, Roman Catholics and Anglicans into Scotland brought variety and a new richness into existing and new patterns of religious expression.

The discontinuity exemplified by the Gothic Revival of the earlier 19th century was echoed in the inter-war period of the earlier 20th century. This was a time, after the tragedy of the First World War, for reappraisal, and a measure of retrenchment, culminating in the reunion of most of the Church of Scotland in 1929. Comparatively few churches were built during this period, and most of those that were were constructed of brick. This lent itself to round-arch construction, and hence to the Romanesque style, which with its intimate, almost cosy, spaces was reassuring at a time of economic and political uncertainty. Of the few architects that looked beyond cosy practicality, Jack Coia and A G R Mackenzie stand out, creating buildings with a timeless quality, which look outside Scotland for inspiration and symbolise new beginnings.

GARNETHILL SYNAGOGUE

KING'S PARK PARISH CHURCH

The Second World War not only marked the end of this uneasy period, but led to a period of physical austerity and visionary socialism, which in Scotland was not primarily atheistic: indeed many Scots responded positively to the asceticism and altruism which emerged as unlikely outcomes of the conflict. At first the most basic of buildings were put up to serve the new housing areas which were physical expressions of the largely Christian socialism of the period, and then reinterpretations of pre-war diluted Gothic emerged. Jack Coia's firm again broke the mould with the French inspired St Paul's Glenrothes, which released an extraordinary flood of creativity. Many of the liturgical, constructional and architectural ideas embodied in these churches were frankly experimental and some quickly failed, but there was no good going back to tradition, at least for the time being. When the time came for another phase of retrenchment, in the 1970s and '80s, it was a new kind of conservatism that emerged, a domestic system-built one, reflecting a loss of confidence in the outward expression of worshipping communities. Though mitigated since then, the residue of that approach is still with us in the new churches constructed in the last few years. It is noteworthy that confidence in new worship-space design is much more apparent in the buildings erected by the Muslim community within the past few years. There are real opportunities for cultural as well as spiritual exchanges within the multi-faith society which Scotland is becoming.

ST PETER IN CHAINS, ARDROSSAN

Now we have the within the Church of Scotland, a questioning of the role of buildings within that communion. It is right that conventional wisdom be challenged, and the relevance of many older buildings to the life of the Church in the 21st century be questioned. However, one must be aware of the danger of throwing the baby out with the bathwater. The success of Scotland's Churches Scheme over the past ten years is evidence that love of buildings – of a wide range of types and periods – is an expression of love of God and of neighbour, and that buildings as places in which to give and receive hospitality and spiritual support are deeply embedded in the human psyche. If, as many

ST PAUL'S CHURCH, GLENROTHES

believe, a kind of 'Re-formation' – a rebirth – of the churches is needed, it is unlikely that it can be achieved without new and inspiriting buildings, and without retaining, in love, the best buildings from all periods of the past. These are a vital part of our inheritance from those who before us knew and loved their God and their neighbours, and are thus as much worthy of our love and respect as exciting new expressions of what it is to be 'Church' in the 21st century.

And so a thousand years, a thousand churches, and ten years of Scotland's Churches Scheme. All the religious bodies in the Scheme recognise festivals –'milestones' if you like – as important aspects of and encouragement to worship. So let us celebrate this milestone in humility, but also joyfully, and pray for the fruitful continuance of the warm cooperation and hospitality which is at the heart of Scotland's Churches Scheme.

SCOTLAND'S CHURCHES SCHEME

LOCAL REPRESENTATIVES

Mrs Elizabeth Beaton, *Moray*
Mrs Margaret Beveridge, *East Lothian*
Mrs Jane Boyd, *Glasgow*
Mrs Mary Canavan, *North Lanarkshire/Glasgow*
Mr and Mrs Robert Cormack, *Orkney*
Mr Michael Dunlop, *Galloway*
Miss Joan Fish, *South and East Ayrshire*
Mr Sandy Gilchrist, *Tweedale/Clydesdale*
Mrs Deirdre Howie, *Edinburgh/Midlothian*
Mrs Lyndall Leet, *North Highland*
Mr Norman MacGilvray, *North Ayrshire*
Ms Atisha McGregor Auld, *Western Isles*
Mr Norman G Marr, *Aberdeenshire*
Mr Ian Milne, *Inverclyde*
Mrs Ann Moohan, *Renfrewshire*
Dr Ramsay Napier, *Shetland*
The Rev John Paton, *Argyll & Bute*
Mrs Mary Reid, *Borders*
Mr Louis Stott, *Stirlingshire*
The Rev J W Scott, *Dumfriesshire*
Mr Robert Tait, *Falkirk/West Lothian*
Mr Andrew Thackrey, *Edinburgh*
The Rev Malcolm Trew, *Fife*
Dr Anne Weatherhead, *Angus/Dundee*

DIRECTOR

Dr Brian M Fraser

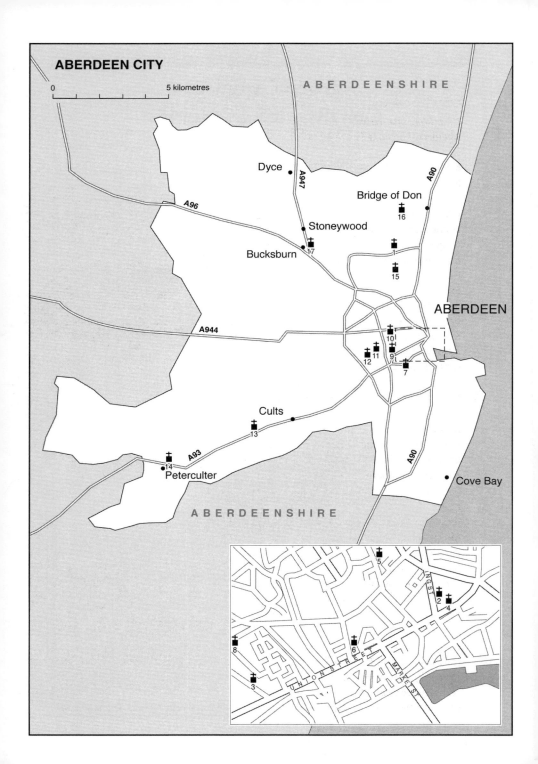

ABERDEEN CITY

0   5 kilometres

ABERDEENSHIRE

Dyce

Bridge of Don
16

Stoneywood
17
Buacksburn

1
15

ABERDEEN

10
11
12
9
7

Cults
13

Peterculter
14

ABERDEENSHIRE

Cove Bay

5

2
4

8
6

3

ABERDEEN

Local Representative: Mr Norman Marr, 63 Devonshire Road, Aberdeen AB10 6XP (*telephone* 01224 322937)

1 ST MACHAR'S CATHEDRAL

NJ 939 008

The Chanonry, Aberdeen

Church website: www.ifb.net / stmachar

Fourteenth to 16th-century nave with unique heraldic ceiling and fortified west front. Interesting monuments, stained glass. Ruined transepts. 3-manual organ by Willis 1892/97, rebuilt Rushworth & Dreaper 1928/56 and Mander 1973. Peal of eight bells. Sunday Services: 11.00am and 6.00pm *Open daily 9.00am-5.00pm. Recitals programme information, telephone 01224 485988*

CHURCH OF SCOTLAND ♿ ⚯ ⚸ 📖 **A**

ST MACHAR'S CATHEDRAL

2 ST ANDREW'S CATHEDRAL

NJ 945 065

King Street, Aberdeen

Church website: www.cathedral.aberdeen.anglican.org

Built by Archibald Simpson 1817 and altered and enhanced by Sir Ninian Comper 1939-45. Gold burnished baldacchino over the high altar. National memorial to Samuel Seabury, first Bishop of America consecrated in Aberdeen in 1784. Interesting roof heraldry depicting American states and Jacobite supporters of the '45 rebellion. Stained glass. Sir John Betjeman described it as one of Aberdeen's best modern buildings. Organ by Bruce of Edinburgh 1818, rebuilt and enlarged by Hill, Norman & Beard. Daily Services: Tuesday Holy Communion 8.30am; Wednesday and Saints' Days Holy Communion 10.00am. Sunday Services: Holy Communion 8.00am; Sung Eucharist 10.45am; Choral Evensong 6.30pm (July and August, Evening Prayers (said) 6.30pm) *Open May to September, Monday to Saturday 10.00am-4.00pm*

SCOTTISH EPISCOPAL ♿ wc ⚸ 📖 ☕ **A**

ST ANDREW'S CATHEDRAL

3 THE CATHEDRAL OF ST MARY OF THE ASSUMPTION

NJ 937 061

Huntly Street, Aberdeen

The principal church of the Roman Catholic Diocese of Aberdeen, built in 1860 by Alexander Ellis. Spire and bells added in 1877, designed by R G Wilson. Contains religious artefacts by Charles Blakeman, Gabriel Loire, Ann Davidson, Felix McCullough, David Gulland and Alexander Brodie. The organ is a rare example of the work of James Conacher, Huddersfield, 1887. Off Union Street. Mass Times: Saturday Vigil 7.00pm; Sunday 8.00am, 11.15am, 6.00pm

Open daily, summer 8.00am-5.00pm, winter 8.00am-4.00pm.
Also Aberdeen Doors Open Day. Clergy House at 20 Huntly Street
ROMAN CATHOLIC   **B**

THE CATHEDRAL OF ST MARY OF THE ASSUMPTION

4 ST PETER'S CHURCH

NJ 942 065

Chapel Court, Justice Street (off the Castlegate)

By James Massie, 1803-4; gallery added 1815 and façade finished 1817 by Harry Leith. Within the courtyard is the residence occupied since 1774, including, in the 18th century, the Vicars Apostolic of the Lowland district: Bishop James Grant and Bishop John Geddes. Services: Saturday Vigil 6.00pm; Sunday 11.00am; Weekdays as announced

Open Tuesday and Friday 9.30am-2.00pm,
or by arrangement, telephone 01224 621581.
Doors Open Day – September each year
ROMAN CATHOLIC **B**

ST PETER'S CHURCH

5 ST MARGARET OF SCOTLAND

NJ 942 067

Gallowgate, Aberdeen

Church website: www.stmargaretsgallowgate.netfirms.com

Completed in 1869, the spacious sanctuary includes many fine examples of the work of Sir Ninian Comper, including the chapel of St Nicholas, the first building he designed and with the original stained glass. His style is mainly Early English with elements of Byzantine and Renaissance. Memorial garden. Just north of Marischal College. Sunday Services: Parish Mass 10.30am, Evensong 6.00pm

Open Tuesday mornings. Other times, telephone Canon Nimmo 01224 644969,
or A Allan 01224 872960. Gallowgate Festival Saturday in early August
SCOTTISH EPISCOPAL **B**

6 KIRK OF ST NICHOLAS

NJ 941 063
Back Wynd, Aberdeen
Church website: www.kirk-of-st-nicholas.org.uk
The 'Mither Kirk' of Aberdeen dates from the 12th century. The present building is largely 18th and 19th century. The west end 1755 by James Gibbs, the east end by Archibald Simpson 1837. The church contains the Chapel of the Oil Industry, and the 15th-century St Mary's Chapel. West Kirk: 3-manual organs by Willis 1881/1927; East Kirk: organ by Compton 1933; St John's Chapel: organ by Brewsher & Fleetwood 1825. The carillon of 48 bells is the largest in Great Britain. Seventeenth-century embroidered wall hangings. Situated in Aberdeen city centre. Sunday Service: 11.00am, also July and August 9.30am; Daily Prayers: Monday to Friday 1.05pm.
Open May to September, Monday to Friday 12.00 noon-4.00pm, Saturday 1.00-3.00pm.
Other times, on application to the Church Office 10.00am-1.00pm, telephone 01224 643494
CHURCH OF SCOTLAND   ♿ wc ☺ ⬦ ⬦ **A**

7 FERRYHILL PARISH CHURCH

NJ 939 054
Junction of Fonthill Road and Polmuir Road, Aberdeen
Church website: www.ferryhillpc.org.uk
Designed by Duncan McMillan for the Free Church 1874. Early Gothic style with a tall square bell tower with octagonal spire. Side galleries added in 1896 were reduced in 1994. Contains several fine windows by James McLundie, A L Moore and others, including a number removed from the former Ferryhill North Church. The sanctuary was re-ordered 1994, and new porch and foyer 2000, by Oliver Humphries. The memorial Chapel incorporates the 51st (Highland) Divisional Signals War Memorial, the Piper Alpha and Steele memorial windows, both by Jane Bayliss and Book of Rememberance. Allen organ. Small museum in the basement. Sunday Service: 11.00am (10.00am in July and August); see notice boards for evening and weekday services and musical events

FERRYHILL PARISH CHURCH

The Church and the Foyer Coffee Shop are open 9.30am-11.30am, Monday to Friday, 9.30am-12.00 noon on Saturday. Other times, telephone 01224 580025 or 01224 589465
CHURCH OF SCOTLAND ♿ wc ☺ ⬦ ⬦ **B**

8 DENBURN PARISH CHURCH

NJ 936 059

Summer Street

The buildings incorporate the *Chapell of Ease* (William
Smith 1771), one of the few surviving buildings in
Aberdeen constructed of Loanhead granite. The
frontage and elegant arcaded interior date from 1878.
Organ: 3-manual by Wadsworth 1893. The great Irish
preacher and character Dr James Kidd ministered here
from 1802-34. The church houses the model ship
Agnes Oswald and an interesting 17th-century edition
of the Bible. Sunday Service: 11.00am
Open by arrangement with Mr Marr 01224 322937,
or Mr Innes 01224 312426
CHURCH OF SCOTLAND ♿ wc ② ⎸ (by arrangement) 📖 **B**

DENBURN PARISH CHURCH

9 GILCOMSTON SOUTH CHURCH

NJ 935 059

Union Street, Aberdeen

Church website: www.fgilcomston.org

Sandstone and granite building by William Smith 1868.
Spire added in 1875 and rebuilt in 1995. Stained glass by
David Gauld, Douglas Strachan and Jane Bayliss. Oak
screen and choir stalls. Binns pipe organ 1902. A hundred
yards from west end of Union Street. Sunday Services:
11.00am and 6.30pm; Tuesday (fortnightly) 12.45pm;
Wednesday 7.30pm; Saturday Prayer Meeting 7.00pm
Open by arrangement, telephone Mr John Glibborn 01224 873919
CHURCH OF SCOTLAND ♿ ② wc **C**

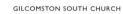

GILCOMSTON SOUTH CHURCH

10 ROSEMOUNT CHURCH

NJ 933 069

120 Rosemount Place, Aberdeen

Traditional church 1870 converted to multi-purpose
Celebration Centre in 1984. Ground floor accommodates
Sunday worship, weekday activities and coffee lounge.
Gallery houses 'Jonah's Journey' – children's museum.
Situated close to two municipal parks. By road or by bus 22
from lower end of Union Street. Sunday Service: 11.00am
Open all year (not public holidays), Monday to Saturday
10.00am-12.00 noon, Sunday 2.30-4.30pm (except July)
CHURCH OF SCOTLAND ♿ wc ② ⎸ ☕ **C**

ROSEMOUNT CHURCH

11 THE CHRISTIAN COMMUNITY

NJ 919 056

8 Spademill Road, Aberdeen

Situated in the west end of Aberdeen, this small church was built in 1991, by Camphill Architects, to house community facilities as well as priest's office and vestry. Simple interior in lilac wash lit by four flanking windows; the altar is lit only by candles. Oak candle holders, altar and pulpit. Altar painting by David Newbatt, a local artist. Sunday Service: Act of Consecration of Man (Communion) 10.30am

Open by arrangement with Mr William Milne, telephone 01224 647609

CHRISTIAN COMMUNITY   👨‍🦽 wc

THE CHRISTIAN COMMUNITY

12 ST MARY'S CHURCH

NJ 929 060

Carden Place, Aberdeen (between Skene Street and Queen's Road)

Church website: www.beehive.thisisnorthscotland.co.uk/st-marys-aberdeen

The variety of granites and patterned roof tiles earned it the nickname 'The Tartan Kirkie'. To a design by Alexander Ellis and the Rev F G Lee, dating from 1864. The east end sustained severe damage during an air raid in April 1943. Reconstructed 1952. Altar triptych by Westlake (c.1862) in the crypt. The church is home to a Samuel Green chamber organ, built in 1778. Display of historical photographs in the choir vestry (1905) adjoining church. Sunday Services: 8.00am and 10.15am; Tuesday 7.00pm; Wednesday 11.00am; Thursday 7.00pm

Open by arrangement, telephone the Rector 01224 584123

SCOTTISH EPISCOPAL wc 🔈 **A**

13 ST DEVENICK'S BIELDSIDE

NJ 882 025

North Deeside Road, Bieldside

Church website: www.stdevenicks.org.uk

Pink and grey granite church, designed by Arthur Clyne and opened in 1903. Organ (Wadsworth) installed in 1910: 'best specimen of its kind by Wadsworth ever placed in Aberdeen or for a considerable distance round about.' North transept completed in 1959 by building of Lady Chapel, which seats 24. West gallery and foyer added 2000. Sunday Services: 8.30, 10.30am and 8.00pm; Thursday 10.30am

Open by arrangement, telephone the office 01224 863574

SCOTTISH EPISCOPAL 👨‍🦽 wc 🔈 📖 🎅 **B**

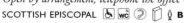

ST DEVENICK'S BIELDSIDE

14 PETERCULTER PARISH CHURCH

NO 594 996
North Deeside Road, Peterculter, Aberdeen
Church website: www.culterkirk.co.uk
Prominently sited on the main road, this
church was built in 1895 and has a recent
extension built in 1995 providing a meeting
place. Extensively refurbished in 2001, it now
offers a multi-purpose sanctuary which can be
used by the local community.
Sunday Service: 10.30am
Open Thursday and Saturday mornings,
or by arrangement with the church office,
telephone 01224 735845 (mornings only)
CHURCH OF SCOTLAND   🚹 wc wc 🕐 ☕

PETERCULTER PARISH CHURCH

15 THE CHAPEL OF THE CONVENT OF ST MARGARET OF SCOTLAND

NJ 941 074
17 Spital, Aberdeen
The chapel, built in 1892, is one of the earliest works of Sir Ninian Comper, son
of the Rev John Comper, Rector of St John's Church in Aberdeen, who in 1863
had invited sisters from St Margaret's Convent, East Grinstead, to work with him.
The furnishings, fittings and windows were also designed by Sir Ninian, and
executed in his workshop. The oak panelling over the stalls was a thank offering
after the Second World War. On left hand side of road from Mounthooly
roundabout to the Old Town. Services: Vespers 5.30pm (Thursdays 5.00pm); Daily
Eucharist at varying times. Please telephone 01224 632648 for exact information
Open by arrangement. Apply at front door of convent.
Chapel may be viewed through grille in west porch
SCOTTISH EPISCOPAL 📖 **A**

16 ST COLUMBA'S PARISH CHURCH

NJ 935 104
Braehead Way, Bridge of Don
Church website: www.st-columbas.org.uk
St Columba's Parish Church is shared with the local Roman Catholic congregation.
The most notable feature is a steel cross at rear of the church.
Sunday Services: 10am and 6.00pm
Open by arrangement, telephone Mr Wilson 01224 703672
CHURCH OF SCOTLAND 🚹 wc 🕐 🚹 ☕

ST COLUMBA'S PARISH CHURCH

17 NEWHILLS CHURCH

NJ 876 095

Bucksburn, Aberdeen

Church website: www.newhillschurch.co.uk

The present church was built in 1830 to a design by Archibald Simpson, near to the site of the original 17th-century church (now part of the graveyard). Painted coat of arms of the patron, Lord James Hay of Seaton, and the Earl of Fife and several modern banners add colour to the interior. Sunday Services 10.30am and 6.00pm (not July and August)

Open Monday to Friday, 9.00am-1.00pm

CHURCH OF SCOTLAND   🚹 wc ⊘ ⚲ 🕯 (by arrangement) **C**

NEWHILLS CHURCH

ABERDEENSHIRE

Local Representative: Mr Norman Marr, 63 Devonshire Road, Aberdeen AB10 6XP (*telephone* 01224 322937)

18 HOWE TRINITY PARISH CHURCH, ALFORD

NJ 577 151

110 Main Street

Church website: www.howetrinity.org.uk

Built in 1867 as Alford Free Church and substantially reordered in 2001 by William Lippe to mark the union of Alford, Keig and Tullynessle & Forbes. Renovations include reorientation of chancel to the long wall; pews replaced with chairs; creation of glass vestibule. Set of engravings showing the parable of the Sower in modern form and stained glass window of the Burning Bush by Jane Bayliss. Sunday Service 10.00am *Open by arrangement with the Minister, telephone 01975 562282*

CHURCH OF SCOTLAND ♿ 🚻 👂

HOWE TRINITY PARISH CHURCH, ALFORD

19 ST TERNAN'S CHURCH, ARBUTHNOTT

NO 801 746

On the B967, 3 miles from Inverbervie

Almost certainly a St Ternan cult church long before it became a parish church by the late 12th century. The chancel dates from the early 13th century, the Arbuthnott family aisle and the bell-tower from the late 15th century and the nave is medieval or earlier but has been much altered. The church was gutted by fire in 1889 and reopened in 1890 with the nave and chancel restored as at the time of consecration in 1242; architect A Marshall Mackenzie. One manual and pedal organ by Wadsworth 1890, a 'small but resourceful instrument'. The unique Arbuthnott Missal, Psalter and Prayer Book (now in Paisley Museum) were transcribed and illuminated in the Priest's Room above the Arbuthnott Aisle between 1497 and 1500. For Services, see local paper and notice board *Open all year. Refreshments in Grassic Gibbon Centre in village*

CHURCH OF SCOTLAND ♿ 👤 A

ST TERNAN'S CHURCH, ARBUTHNOTT

20 ST PALLADIUS or AUCHENBLAE PARISH CHURCH

NO 726 784

Auchenblae, near Laurencekirk

Built by John Smith 1829 as Fordoun Parish Church
on a site known as Kirkton of Fordoun. Religious
site since 7th century. St Palladius died and reputedly
buried here. Celtic stone in vestibule. Memorial to
first Protestant martyr George Wishart (born at Mains
of Pittarrow in old parish of Fordoun) in graveyard.
Seating in nave replaced 1990. Stained glass rose
window. Sunday Service: 11.00am, excluding first
Sunday of month

Open by arrangement, telephone Rev Catherine Hepburn
01561 340203
CHURCH OF SCOTLAND ♿ 📖 **B**

ST PALLADIUS or
AUCHENBLAE PARISH CHURCH

21 BANFF PARISH CHURCH

NJ 689 638

High Street, Banff

Built in 1789, Andrew Wilson architect and
builder, with tower added in 1849, William
Robertson. Chancel added and interior altered
in 1929. Stained glass. Small chapel created at
rear of church in 1994. Pulpit, font, communion
table and stained glass in chancel all gifted in
1929. Other furnishings from Trinity & Alvah
Church, united in 1994. Beside St Mary's car
park. Sunday Services 11.00am and 6.30pm
Open mid June to August, 2.00-4.00pm.
CHURCH OF SCOTLAND ♿ ⓘ 🚻 ☕ **A**

BANFF PARISH CHURCH

22 ST MARY'S CHAPEL, BLAIRS

NJ 883 009

On B9077, 4 miles south of Aberdeen
Church website: www.blairs.net

The building, designed by Richard Curran of
Warrington, was opened in 1901; unusual interior design
is due to the fact that it is a former collegiate chapel.
The walls originally had painted decoration, but in 1911
were lined with marble. At the same time were added the
reredos and baldacchino in carved wood with its figures
of the Scottish patron saints, Andrew and Margaret. The

ST MARY'S CHAPEL, BLAIRS

church also has fine stained glass windows. Sunday Service: 9.00am. The Blairs Museum (adjacent to the chapel) is open from May to October (12.00-4.00pm) *Open Monday, Tuesday and Thursday 10.30am-2.00pm. Saturday and Sunday by arrangement, telephone 01224 869424*
ROMAN CATHOLIC 🚻 ⌂ **A**

23 BRAEMAR CHURCH

NO 1591
Behind the Braemar Mews
The inspiration for the building of this former Free Church in 1870 was the Rev Hugh Cobban. Unusually, he was buried in the church, behind the pulpit. Four lancet stained glass windows with lilies, a branch with fruit and a tree with palms. Some interesting tapestry banners, described as 'living pictures'. Sunday Service: 10.00am
Open 9.00am-9.00pm, April to October
CHURCH OF SCOTLAND ② ⌂ **c**

BRAEMAR CHURCH

24 ST PHILIP'S, CATTERLINE

NO 869 789
Church website: www.nmearnssec.org.uk
St Ninian was reputed to have landed at Catterline. The present building, designed by Charles Brand, dates from 1848 and was built on the site of an earlier church, retaining its historic graveyard. The

ST PHILIP'S, CATTERLINE

style is Early English. The interior has been recently refurbished. Off A9 between Montrose and Stonehaven and near Dunottar Castle. Sunday Services: 10.15am
Church open daily
SCOTTISH EPISCOPAL 🚻 **c**

25 CHAPEL OF GARIOCH

NK 716 242
In centre of Chapel of Garioch village
The present church, dating from 1813, was built on the site of a 12th-century church. Subsequent changes include a chancel built out from the north wall and the impressive stained glass window. Of particular interest are the baptismal basin of 1742,

CHAPEL OF GARIOCH

the mosaic plaque and the A-listed gateway in the west wall of the churchyard, dated 1626. Sunday Service: see notice board or telephone for information
Open by arrangement with Keyholder Mrs Whewell 01467 681543 or Mrs Stannett 01467 681207
CHURCH OF SCOTLAND 🚻 wc ② ⌂ **B** (church) **A** (gateway)

26 CRATHIE PARISH CHURCH

NO 265 949

On A93 Ballater-Braemar

Queen Victoria laid the foundation stone in 1893, the church opened 1895. Cruciform design by A Marshall Mackenzie. The church stands on a hill overlooking the ruins of the 14th-century church and the River Dee. Memorial stones, plaques and stained glass commemorate royalty and ministers. Fine Iona marble communion table and 17th-century oak reredos. Sunday Service: 11.30am

Open April to October, Monday to Saturday 9.30am-5.00pm; Sunday 12.45pm-5.00pm

CHURCH OF SCOTLAND ⟨⟩ ⎰ ⬠ **B**

CRATHIE PARISH CHURCH

27 ST JAMES'S CHURCH, CRUDEN BAY

NK 069 356

Chapel Hill, Cruden Bay, 1½ miles from Cruden Bay
Church website: www.saintmaryandsaintjames.net

The tall spire of St James's can be seen from miles around. Designed by William Hay in 1842. The font is from the chantry chapel, built after the battle between the Scots and the Danes in 1012. Sunday Service: Family Communion 9.30am

Open daily 10.00am-dusk

SCOTTISH EPISCOPAL ♿ ⟨⟩ **B**

ST JAMES'S CHURCH, CRUDEN BAY

28 ST MARY ON THE ROCK, ELLON

NJ 958 301

Craighall, Ellon, on A90/A948 at south end of the town
Church website: www.saintmaryandsaintjames.net

A superb example of the work of George Edmund Street, built in 1871 to incorporate chancel, nave, narthex and spire. Floor tiles by Minton. Good glass, including windows by Clayton & Bell on the north side of the nave, Lavers & Barreau on the south side, all dating from the 1880s, and by Jane Bayliss 1996. Sunday Service: Early Eucharist 8.30am, The Eucharist 10.30am

Open daily 10.00am to dusk

SCOTTISH EPISCOPAL ♿ ⟨⟩ **A**

ST MARY ON THE ROCK, ELLON

29 FINZEAN CHURCH (BIRSE AND FEUGHSIDE)

NO 617 924
Finzean, near Banchory
Small mission church. Includes former congregations at Birse and Strachan. Between Banchory and Aboyne on South Deeside Road.
Sunday Service: 11.00am
Open by arrangement, telephone 01330 850329
CHURCH OF SCOTLAND **B**

FINZEAN CHURCH (BIRSE AND FEUGHSIDE)

30 FOVERAN PARISH CHURCH

NJ 985 241
One mile south of Newburgh on A975
Built 1794, organ apse added 1900, interior refurbished 1934 with pews and fittings from the demolished Foveran United Free Church. Number of items from medieval church (since disappeared): early 15th-century Turin Stone, 17th-century bust of Sir John Turing, Queen Anne hourglass attached to pulpit and font using carved medieval column. Various monuments including bronze plaque to painter and etcher James McBey, born nearby.
Sunday Service: 11.00am (shared with Holyrood Chapel, Newburgh)
Open by arrangement, key available from the Manse, or from Newburgh Post Office during opening hours
CHURCH OF SCOTLAND  **B**

FOVERAN PARISH CHURCH

31 FETTERCAIRN PARISH CHURCH

NO 651 735
Fettercairn near Laurencekirk
Built in 1803 and with a steeple added in 1860, the building was completely refurbished and extended in 1926. The interior has interesting stained glass and locally made furnishings. Sunday Service: 9.30am
Open by arrangement, telephone the Minister 01561 340203
CHURCH OF SCOTLAND  wc **B**

FETTERCAIRN PARISH CHURCH

32 FRASERBURGH OLD PARISH CHURCH

NJ 998 671

The Square, Fraserburgh

Present building dates from 1801, with a church on
this site since 1572. The pulpit is one of the highest
in Scotland and the superb memorial window
designed by Douglas Strachan 1906 was gifted by
Sir George Anderson, Treasurer of the Bank of
Scotland, in memory of his parents. A front pew in
the south gallery is marked as the place where
Marconi, pioneer of wireless telegraphy,
worshipped during his stay in Fraserburgh.
Untouched Forster & Andrews 2-manual organ of
1892. Sunday Services: 11.00am and 6.00pm
Open daily July and August
CHURCH OF SCOTLAND [symbols] C

FRASERBURGH OLD PARISH CHURCH

33 GLENBERVIE PARISH CHURCH

NO 766 807

Glenbervie, near Stonehaven

Built 1826 and preserving original design
and features. Oil lamps electrified. Stones
preserved and sheltered. Grandparents of
Robert Burns buried in old kirkyard. Sunday
Service: 11.00am, first Sunday of month
Open by arrangement, telephone 01561 340203
CHURCH OF SCOTLAND [symbols] B

GLENBERVIE PARISH CHURCH

34 ST MARGARET'S CHURCH, HUNTLY

NJ 528 402

Chapel Street, Huntly

Octagonal church with impressive classical front façade
built 1834. The architect was Bishop James Kyle in
collaboration with William Robertson. Spire 80ft with
fine toned bell. Altar piece and other paintings from
the Gordon family of Xeres, Spain 1840. Restored
1990 by Doric Construction, Aberdeen. Organ by
Peter Conacher 1871. Sunday Service: 9.45am
Open by arrangement, telephone
Mr W McKay 01466 792409
ROMAN CATHOLIC [symbols] A

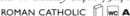

ST MARGARET'S CHURCH, HUNTLY

35 ST DROSTAN, INSCH

NJ 630 281

Commerce Street, Insch

Alexander Ross 1894. Agreeable rustic
Gothic in red granite with sandstone
dressings. Red-tiled roof with broach-spired
wooden bellcote. Font 1892, and screen
1904. Church is on road from Insch railway
station to town centre. B992 off A96.
Service: second and fourth Sundays, Sung
Eucharist 10.00am

Open by arrangement, telephone Mrs Mitchell,
Greenhaugh, Rannes Street, Insch 01464 820276

SCOTTISH EPISCOPAL **C**

ST DROSTAN, INSCH

36 BERVIE PARISH CHURCH, INVERBERVIE

NO 830 727

43 King Street (in centre of town)

Built in 1836 by architect John Smith, with elegant
clock and bell tower. Two stained glass windows
originally from United Free Church. Lawton pipe
organ 1904. To mark the millennium, new doors
were fitted to the inner vestibule/sanctuary. Doors
fitted with stained glass overlay panels depicting
significant local landmarks/buildings, including
the church. Sunday Service: 11.30am

Open by arrangement, telephone Mr W Beattie,
39 King Street 01561 361256, or 9 Farquhar Street
01561 362728

CHURCH OF SCOTLAND ♿ ⓘ 🚾 **B**

BERVIE PARISH CHURCH, INVERBERVIE

37 KING DAVID OF SCOTLAND EPISCOPAL CHURCH, INVERBERVIE

NO 828 733

Victoria Terrace

Small, simple church with very pretty interior. Shared with the local Roman
Catholic community. Sunday Service: 9.30am Holy Communion; Saturday:
Roman Catholic Mass 6.30pm

Open daily 9.00am-4.30pm

SCOTTISH EPISCOPAL

38 SKENE PARISH CHURCH, KIRKTON OF SKENE

NJ 803 077
Quarter mile off A944 Aberdeen-Alford
Road, 9 miles from Aberdeen city centre
The church was built in 1801, architects
William and Andrew Clerk, and
contains stained glass by Blair & Blyth.
Sunday Service: 11.15am
Open by arrangement, telephone the Minister
01224 743277 or the Beadle 01224 743534
CHURCH OF SCOTLAND [♿] [wc] [🔊] **B**

SKENE PARISH CHURCH, KIRKTON OF SKENE

39 LONGSIDE PARISH CHURCH

NK 037 473
Inn Brae, Longside
Impressive rectangular building by
John Smith 1836. The west gable is
capped by a bellcote. The adjoining
old parish church, a roofless ruin, dates
from 1620 and is accessed through a
lychgate of 1705. Some notable
monuments in the graveyard. Services:
Sunday 11.30am, 2nd Sunday 6.30pm
Open by arrangement with the Minister,
telephone 01779 821224
CHURCH OF SCOTLAND [♿] [🔊] [♀]
B (Old Parish Church) **A**

LONGSIDE PARISH CHURCH

40 ST JOHN THE EVANGELIST, LONGSIDE

NK 039 473
Peterhead Road, Longside (at east end of village on main road)
Built 1853 to a design by William Hay. A large building with many fine features,
including saddle back tower, stained glass by Chance and one by J Hamilton
depicting St Margaret of Scotland. Superb reredos of Caen stone with figures and
scenes from the Bible. On display are many rare items belonging to the Rev John
Skinner of Linshart, Rector for 65 years (1742-1807), also known as Tullochgorum,
poet and writer. Sunday Service: 10.00am
Open May to October, 8.30am-6.00pm, or via contact in entrance porch
SCOTTISH EPISCOPAL [♿] [wc] (in hall) [🔊] [📖] **B**

41   MACDUFF PARISH CHURCH

NJ 701 643

Church Street, Macduff

Church website: www.macduffparishchurch.fsnet.co.uk

Once used to guide boats to safe haven, this white box kirk of 1805 high on the bluff above the harbour was transformed in 1865 by architect James Matthews of Aberdeen into a magnificent Italianate landmark, with notable stained glass windows and a lovely three-storey tower with a lead-domed roof and cupola above. Galleried interior, most of the fittings dating from 1865. Magnificent views. Nearby stand the town cross and an anchor, symbolic of the message of the church. Sunday Services: 11.00am and 6.00pm

Open by arrangement,

telephone 01261 832316

CHURCH OF SCOTLAND & ? wc **B**

MACDUFF PARISH CHURCH

42   ST TERNAN'S, MUCHALLS

NO 891 921

Muchalls, by Stonehaven

Church website: www.nmearnssec.org.uk

Simple country church with attractive chancel. The oldest church building in the Diocese of Brechin, built 1831-70. Sunday Service: 10.30am Holy Communion

Open daily

SCOTTISH EPISCOPAL wc ? ?

43   HOLYROOD CHAPEL, NEWBURGH

NJ 999 253

Main Street, Newburgh

Built in 1838 as the original Newburgh Mathers school; converted as Chapel of Ease for Foveran Parish Church 1882. Clock Tower added 1892, interior refurbished 1907, including pitch pine roof in imitation of St Laurence, Forres. Named in honour of the original medieval chapel of the Holy Rood and St Thomas the Martyr in Inch Road, Newburgh – all that remains of this is the Udny Family Mausoleum in the Holyrood Cemetery. Sunday Service: 11.00am (shared with Foveran Church)

Open by arrangement, key available from the Manse, or from Newburgh

Post Office during opening hours

CHURCH OF SCOTLAND wc ? **B**

HOLYROOD CHAPEL, NEWBURGH

44 ST MATTHEW & ST GEORGE, OLDMELDRUM

NJ 812 279

North end of village on A947

Ross & Joass 1863. Pleasing granite Early Decorated with striking chequered voussoirs to west window. Octagonal spire alongside the simple nave and chancel. Tendril-like freestone tracery is carved with real freedom. Stained glass by Hardman records the Life of Our Lord. Intricate Arts & Crafts monument to Beauchamp Colclough Urquhart of Meldrum. Sunday Service: Sung Eucharist 11.30am

Open by arrangement, telephone the Rector 01651 872208

SCOTTISH EPISCOPAL & **B**

ST MATTHEW & ST GEORGE, OLDMELDRUM

45 DEER PARISH CHURCH, OLD DEER

NJ 979 477

Old Deer village

Built 1789 as a simple rectangular church with Venetian windows to the east and west. The front porch with tower and spire were added in the late 1890s to a design by Sir George Reid PRSA. The pulpit table and font are by A Marshall Mackenzie 1898. Willis pipe organ of the 1890s. Stained glass windows in memory of George Smith, local benefactor who emigrated to America and the Rev Dr Kemp, the minister from 1899-1953, and his wife. Sunday Service 10.30am

Open by arrangement, telephone

Mr Wishart 01771 623582

CHURCH OF SCOTLAND & wc ? Ů ů ☕ **B**

DEER PARISH CHURCH, OLD DEER

ST JAMES THE GREAT, STONEHAVEN

46 ST JAMES THE GREAT, STONEHAVEN

NO 873 857

Arbuthnott Street, Stonehaven

Church website: www.nmearnssec.org.uk

The nave was built by Sir Robert Rowand Anderson in 1877 in Norman/Early English style. The chancel was added in 1885 and the narthex and baptistry in 1906 by Arthur Clyne. Baptistry glass by Sir Ninian Comper 1929. Elaborately sculptured reredos by Gambier-Parry of London. 2-manual organ of some merit by Wadsworth 1881/85. Off south side of Market Square in Stonehaven.

Services: Sunday 8.30 and 10.30am; Wednesday 10.30am

Open daily

SCOTTISH EPISCOPAL [♿] [📖] [wc] **A**

47 ST CONGAN'S, TURRIFF

NJ 722 498

Deveron Road, Turriff

Elegant church by William Ramage 1862 with a red, slender Gothic western tower. Mural tablet of Bishop Jolly who is depicted in the east window. Beautiful stained glass. Oak rood screen, pulpit and lectern are the important ornaments. A short distance away are the ruins of the medieval church whose elaborate belcote of 1635 survives. Services: Sundays 11.00am (winter), 10.30am (Easter to end-October), Wednesdays 10.00am

Open by arrangement with the Assistant Priest, telephone 01888 562530

SCOTTISH EPISCOPAL [♿] [👁] [👤] [📖] [wc] [☕] **B**

ST CONGAN'S, TURRIFF

TRINITY CHURCH, WESTHILL

48   TRINITY CHURCH, WESTHILL

NJ 833 072

Westhill Drive, Westhill (off A944 Aberdeen-Alford Road)

Built 1981 by Stock Brothers. Ecumenical and multi-purpose. Extension completed in 2003. Services: Roman Catholic 9am; Church of Scotland 10am; Scottish Episcopal 11.15am.

Open most of week, check with Minister, telephone 01224 743277

INTERDENOMINATIONAL & wc &

49   ALL SAINTS', WHITERASHES

NJ 855 235

On A947, 3 miles south of Oldmeldrum

Gothic style nave and chancel built by James Matthews in 1858. Windows by Sir Ninian Comper of saints chosen for the Christian names of the Irvines of Drum and Straloch. Service: first Sunday, Evensong 3.00pm

Open by arrangement, telephone the Rector 01651 872208

SCOTTISH EPISCOPAL & (one step) **B**

ALL SAINTS', WHITERASHES

50 ALL SAINTS', WOODHEAD OF FETTERLETTER

NJ 790 385

1½ miles east of Fyvie

Early English aisleless nave and chancel by John Henderson 1849. The fine tower with the slated broach spire was added in 1870. Described by Pratt in Buchan as 'one of the finest examples of a Scottish village church'. Crosses and a sheaf of arrows from Fyvie Priory are incorporated in the walls. The altar and reredos are from St Margaret's, Forgue. Organ by David Hamilton of Edinburgh, recently restored by Sandy Edmonstone.

Sunday Service: 10.15am

Open by arrangement, telephone Mrs Cleaver, Gowanlea, Woodhead 01651 891513

SCOTTISH EPISCOPAL ♿ B

ALL SAINTS', WOODHEAD OF FETTERLETTER

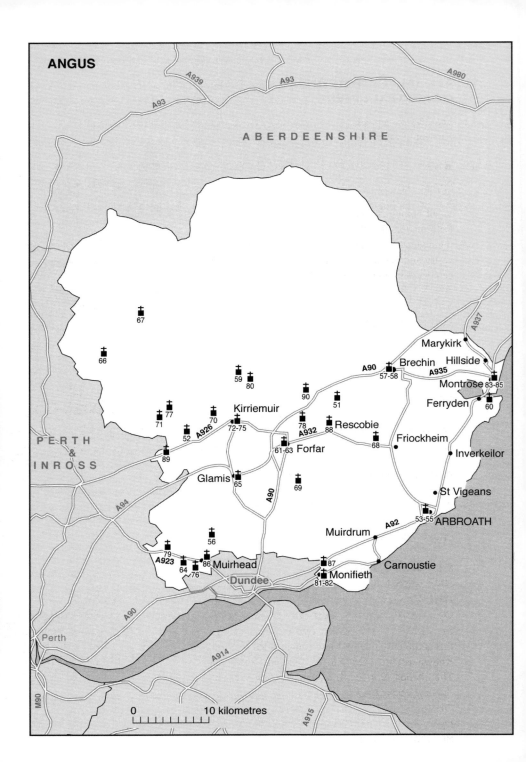

ANGUS

Local Representative: Dr Anne Weatherhead, Newton Park, 59 Brechin Road, Kirriemuir (*telephone* 01575 572237)

51 ABERLEMNO PARISH CHURCH

NO 523 555

Five miles east of Forfar on B9134

Small oblong church re-built 1722 on the site of Pre-Reformation church, was extended to a T-plan in 1820 and remodelled in Gothic style in the late 19th century. The vestry and galleries were added in 1856. Famous 8th-century standing stone in kirkyard (covered in winter months). Pre-Reformation stone font was brought into the church in 1992. Sunday Services: 10.00am or 11.30am, contact the Minister on 01241 828243 for details

Open during daylight hours

CHURCH OF SCOTLAND 🦽 wc (only available during services) 📖 **B**

ABERLEMNO
PARISH CHURCH

52 AIRLIE PARISH CHURCH

NO 313 515

Kirkton of Airlie

Stands on a site where the Gospel has been preached for over 780 years. The present simple building was completed in 1783. The interior was renovated in 1893 using pitch pine and an addition added to accommodate the pipe organ and choir. Pre-Reformation relics; the oldest gravestone is dated 1609. Sunday Services: 10.30am, united service with Glenisla, Ruthven, Kilry, Lintrathen and Kingoldrum. At Lintrathen 6.30pm in rotation

Open by arrangement, telephone Mr G Bruce 01575 530243

CHURCH OF SCOTLAND 🦽 wc 👂 **A**

AIRLIE PARISH CHURCH

53 ST JOHN'S, ARBROATH

NN 645 411

Ponderlaw Street, Arbroath

Opened for worship by the Rev John Wesley on 6 May 1772. Built in the octagonal style favoured by Wesley, this is the only one of these churches left in Scotland. Known as the 'Totum Kirkie'. Vestibule added 1883. The Lifeboat Window is a memorial to the loss of the Lifeboat *Robert L Lindsay* and six crew members in 1953. Old Manse adjacent to church. Sunday Service: 11.00am

Open by arrangement, telephone Mr Nicoll 01241 875172

METHODIST 🦽 wc 📖

ST JOHN'S,
ARBROATH

54 ST THOMAS OF CANTERBURY, ARBROATH

NO 638 406

Dishlandtown Street

Church website: //sites.ecosse.net/stthomas

Church opened for worship 1848, designed by
George Mathewson of Dundee. Romanesque design
with aisled nave and chancel. The front is a miniature
replica of St Augustine's gateway at Canterbury.
Unique 1-manual and pedal organ by Postill of York,
*c.*1860, recently rebuilt. Services: Saturday Vigil Mass
6.30pm, Sunday Mass 10.30am

Open daily 9.00am-6.00pm

ROMAN CATHOLIC ♿ wc ② ☕ (after Sunday Mass) **B**

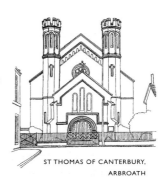

ST THOMAS OF CANTERBURY,
ARBROATH

55 ST VIGEAN'S CHURCH, ARBROATH

NO 583 446

St Vigean's, Arbroath

Dedicated to St Vigean (or Fechin), Irish saint, died
664. Church rebuilt in 12th century, but not
dedicated until 1242. Some 15th-century alterations;
19th-century restoration with lovely stained glass
windows. Largely unaltered since. Organ by
Harrison 1875. Sunday Service: 11.30am

Key available from house opposite church main gate.

St Vigean's Museum also open

CHURCH OF SCOTLAND ② 📖 ☕ wc **A**

ST VIGEAN'S CHURCH, ARBROATH

56 AUCHTERHOUSE CHURCH

NO 342 381

Kirkton of Auchterhouse, 1 mile east of B954

Built 1630 with stone from earlier churches of 1275
and 1426. Partially rebuilt 1775. Chancel and nave
with tower at west end. Burial vault at east end.
Interior completely renovated 1910. Gothic chancel
arch lends character and dignity. Three impressive
stained glass windows, medieval octagonal font,
stool of repentance and 18th-century clock. Linked
with Murroes and Tealing. Situated on south side of
Sidlaw Hills. Sunday Service: 11.00am (1st and 3rd
Sunday of the month), 9.30am (2nd and 4th)

AUCHTERHOUSE CHURCH

Open by arrangement, telephone John Skea 01382 320257, or Heather Heggie 01382 320305

CHURCH OF SCOTLAND ♿ ② wc **B**

57 BRECHIN CATHEDRAL

NO 595 601
Church Lane, Brechin
Church website:
www.brechincathedral.org.uk
Founded in the 11th century, the
round tower of that date is of Irish
inspiration. Thirteenth, 14th and
15th-century medieval architecture
underwent major restoration in 1900-2
supervised by J Honeyman
(Honeyman, Keppie & Mackintosh).
Special features include the 12th-
century font and a collection of
Pictish sculptures. Stunning 20th-
century stained glass by Henry
Holliday, Gordon Webster, Douglas
Strachan, Herbert Hendrie, William
Gauld, Hugh Easton and the firm of

BRECHIN CATHEDRAL

William Morris. The cathedral also contains the largest group of William Wilson
windows in Scotland. Sunday Service: 10.30am. Wednesday 1.00pm
Open most days all year 9.00am-4.00pm, with hosts in summer months (and guides by
special arrangement outwith these times). Afternoon teas in church hall, alternate Thursdays
2pm. Brechin Caledonian Railway nearby. Historical artefacts in Brechin Library. Brechin
Town Trail. Pictavia. Angus Pictish Trail
CHURCH OF SCOTLAND [♿] [wc] (100 yards) ⊘ ⌂ ⓘ ⓘ **A**

58 ST NINIAN'S CHURCH, BRECHIN

NO 600 603
Bank Street
Tall simple church of 1875 in Normandy
Gothic, distinctive of the architect William
Leiper. Small octagonal spire on the left of
the front gable. Interior enlivened by stained
glass and murals. Services: Sunday Mass
10.00am, Tuesday and Thursday 10.00am
Open by arrangement, telephone Mrs Josephine
McMahon 01356 622840
ROMAN CATHOLIC **B**

ST NINIAN'S CHURCH, BRECHIN

59 CORTACHY CHURCH

NO 396 597

Church website: www.gkopc.co.uk

Cortachy Church was built by the 7th Earl of Airlie,
the sole heritor, in 1828 on the site of a previous
church. The architect was David Patterson. It has a
magnificent setting overlooking the river South Esk.
The gallery gives the church a seating capacity of
300. Inside there are memorials to the 9th and 12th
Earls and against the east gable is the Burial Aisle of
the Airlie family. Sunday Service: 10.00am,
excluding 5th Sunday of month

CORTACHY CHURCH

Open by arrangement with the Glens and Kirriemuir Old Parish church office,
telephone 01575 572819

CHURCH OF SCOTLAND ⏣ ⌖ **B**

60 FERRYDEN UNITED FREE CHURCH, NEAR MONTROSE

NO 718 567

Bellevue Terrace, at east end of Ferryden village

Opened in 1935 to meet the needs of families from the fishing community who did
not adhere to the 1929 union of churches. An annual sea service continues to be
held on the second Sunday in November. A small building, which accommodates
70. Sunday Service: 6.00pm; praise service with hymns from the Sankey Hymnal,
1st Sunday

Open by arrangement with Minister 01674 673772 or Session Clerk 01674 674410

UNITED FREE CHURCH ⌖

61 LOWSON MEMORIAL CHURCH, FORFAR

NO 465 509

Jameson Street (at east end of Forfar,
off Montrose Road)

Church website: www.lowson-memorial.org.uk

A gem of a church designed by A Marshall
Mackenzie 1914. In the style of late Scots Gothic,
cruciform in shape with five-bay nave, aisleless
transepts and a one-bay chancel. Built of a ruddy-
hued local stone. Low central tower and squat
spire. Wooden wagon roof. Excellent stained glass,
Douglas Strachan. Sunday Service: 11.00am

Open Monday to Friday 9.30am-4.30pm all year

CHURCH OF SCOTLAND ♿ ⌖ ⬦ ⌖ **A**

LOWSON MEMORIAL CHURCH, FORFAR

62 ST JOHN THE EVANGELIST, FORFAR

NO 458 507

71 East High Street, Forfar

Built on the site of an earlier church, the
present building was designed in Early English
style by Sir R Rowand Anderson and
consecrated in 1881. The broach spire intended
for the tower was never built. Panelling and
redecoration of the roof by Sir Matthew
Ochterlony, late 1940s. Altered in 1975 by Dr F
R Stevenson to provide Lady Chapel and
vestries. The font has traditionally been
associated with St Margaret and Restenneth

ST JOHN THE EVANGELIST, FORFAR

Priory. 3-manual pipe organ by Conacher of Huddersfield. Stained glass by Charles E
Kempe and Septimus Waugh. Queen Elizabeth The Queen Mother was confirmed in
the church. Historic graveyard predates present church. Sunday Services: 8.30am and
11.00am, weekdays as announced

Open daily, summer months 9.00am-4.00pm, winter months 9.00am-2.00pm

SCOTTISH EPISCOPAL ♿ (on request) ♻ wc **B**

63 ST FERGUS'S, FORFAR

NO 453 498

96 Glenogil Terrace, Forfar

Opened 1963 to replace original 1946 parish church on the High Street.
Stations of the Cross designed by local artist William Cadenhead. Patron St Fergus
was an 8th-century bishop who travelled across the east of Scotland.
Sunday Service: 11.00am

Open by arrangement with Parish Priest 01307 462104

ROMAN CATHOLIC ♿ ♻

64 ST MARNOCK'S CHURCH, FOWLIS EASTER

NO 322 334

In centre of Fowlis Easter, 1 mile west of Liff

Church website: www.muirhead-church.members.beeb.net

Constructed 1453 and notable for the oak board paintings of the Crucifixion and
of saints dating from the same period and rood screen doors from the 15th century.
Stained glass commemorates the Gray family which founded this collegiate church.
Cross-slab gravestone in graveyard. Sunday Service: 10.00am alternate months

Open by arrangement with the Minister 01382 580210 or Session Clerk 01382 360478

CHURCH OF SCOTLAND ♿ wc ☗ **A**

65 ST FERGUS CHURCH, GLAMIS

NO 386 469

Kirk Wynd, Glamis

Church website: www.stferguskirkglamis.co.uk

Present church built 1792 on site of church
dedicated to St Fergus 1242. Substantially altered
and beautified 1933. Classic bell tower and spire.
Seventh-century Celtic stone in manse garden and
Well of St Fergus nearby. Category B kirkyard with
interesting stones. Strathmore Aisle (category A)
built in 1459 by Isabella Ogilvy on death of her
husband Patrick Lyon, 1st Lord Glamis. United
with Inverarity. Sunday Service: 11.30am

Open daily

CHURCH OF SCOTLAND 🦽 🏠 WC **A/B**

ST FERGUS CHURCH, GLAMIS

66 GLENISLA PARISH CHURCH

NO 215 604

Lovely rural setting at the head of Glenisla.
Small oblong Gothic building with belfry
and session house. Sunday Services:
10.30am, united service with Ruthven,
Airlie, Kilry, Lintrathen and Kingoldrum.
At Lintrathen 6.30pm in rotation.
4th Sunday; Songs of Praise ✴

Open by arrangement, telephone 01575 560260

CHURCH OF SCOTLAND 🦽 WC ☺ ☕ **C**

GLENISLA PARISH CHURCH

67 GLEN PROSEN CHURCH

NO 328 657

Glen Prosen, Kirriemuir

Church website: www.gkopc.co.uk

Present church built 1802, paid for by local inhabitants,
ensuring continuous worship in the glen for nearly 400
years. Special features include wood carvings by Sir
Robert Lorimer and war memorial porch with rare
slated cross. Sunday Service: 1st and 3rd Sundays 12.00
noon; Songs of Praise for Guide Dogs for the Blind:
April to September, 1st Sunday of month 6.00pm

Open daily, access via vestry door

CHURCH OF SCOTLAND **B**

GLEN PROSEN CHURCH

68 GUTHRIE PARISH CHURCH

NO 568 505

Half mile north of A932, 7 miles east of Forfar
Present church was built in 1826 to a Telford
design. The 15th-century Guthrie Aisle is
beside the church. Two stained glass windows:
'The Good Shepherd' (1920), Dickson family
and 'The Sower' (1976), Guthries of California.
Sunday Services: 10.00am or 11.30am or
6.30pm; contact the Minister on
01241 828243 for details
Open at all times
CHURCH OF SCOTLAND 🦽 📖 **B**

GUTHRIE PARISH CHURCH

69 INVERARITY CHURCH

NO 460 440

Inverarity, eastern boundary of village, B9217
Church website: www.stferguskirkglamis.co.uk
Church built 1754 with recent impressive
renovation. Kirk Bell by Peter van dem Heim
dated 1614, cast in Holland. Gable porches
added 1854. Modern church/community hall
next to church. Sunday Service: 10.00am
Open by arrangement, telephone Mr A L Ingram
01307 840223
CHURCH OF SCOTLAND 🦽 [wc] **B**

INVERARITY CHURCH

70 KINGOLDRUM PARISH CHURCH

NO 334 550

There has been a church in Kingoldrum since
earliest times. A carved stone coffin lid found
in the churchyard dates to 12th or 13th century.
The present church is a small oblong Gothic
church with a pinnacled belfry and projecting
porches of 1840. Pews and panelling were the
gift of Betty Sherriff, in memory of her
husband, and the pulpit fall in memory of her
parents. Sunday Service: 11.00am
Open by arrangement, telephone 01575 574727
CHURCH OF SCOTLAND 🦽 **C**

KINGOLDRUM PARISH CHURCH

71 KILRY PARISH CHURCH

NO 246 538

Stands in a valley on the edge of the hills at
the entrance to Glenisla. Sunday Services:
10.30am, united service with Glenisla, Airlie,
Ruthven, Lintrathen and Kingoldrum. At
Lintrathen 6.30pm in rotation
Open by arrangement, telephone 01575 560260
CHURCH OF SCOTLAND 🅰 wc ⓐ ☕ **C**

KILRY PARISH CHURCH

72 KIRRIEMUIR OLD PARISH CHURCH

NO 386 539

Bank Street, Kirriemuir, behind shops
Church website: www.gkopc.co.uk
Ninth-century stones were found when the church
was rebuilt on this earlier Christian site in 1788 to
a design by James Playfair, father of William
Henry Playfair. The steeple was completed in
1790. The 17 stained glass windows include the
Last Supper, a memorial window to Violet Jacob,
and windows by William Wilson. Interesting
kirkyard, the earliest stone dating from 1613. In
centre of the town, behind Bank Street's shops.

KIRRIEMUIR OLD PARISH CHURCH

Sunday Services: 9.00am and 11.15am
Open Monday to Friday 10.00am-12.00 noon and 1.30-3.30pm
(call at office if door locked); Saturday 10.00-4.00pm (June to August)
CHURCH OF SCOTLAND 🅰 ⓐ 📖 ⓘ **B**

73 ST ANDREW'S CHURCH, KIRRIEMUIR

NO 386 535

Glamis Road, Kirriemuir
Late Gothic style church (originally the South United
Free Church) with a 60-ft tower by Patrick Thoms
1903. It replaced an earlier church (the South Free
Church) built in 1843 for those who left the South
Church (across the road) at the 'Disruption'. In the
grounds are the headstones of the Rev Daniel Cormick,
first minister of the South Free Church and of the Rev
A Duff, minister of the South Church. Linked with
Oathlaw and Tannadice. Sunday Service: 11.15am
Open daily 9.00am-5.00pm
CHURCH OF SCOTLAND 🅰 ⓐ

ST ANDREW'S CHURCH, KIRRIEMUIR

74 ST MARY'S CHURCH, KIRRIEMUIR

NO 383 544
West Hillbank, Kirriemuir (north side of the town)
Gothic revival church by Sir Ninian Comper
1903 built to replace classical church of 1797
destroyed by fire. Stained glass by Comper and
William Wilson. 2-manual tracker organ,
Hamilton of Edinburgh 1906. Sanctus bell 1741.
Conspicuous red sandstone bell-tower. Sunday
Services: 1st, 2nd and 3rd Sundays 10.00am
Sung Eucharist; 4th Sunday 10.00am. Matins,
11.30am Said Eucharist; 5th Sunday 10.00am
Family Service; 11.30am Said Eucharist:
Wednesday 10.00am
Key at Rectory, 128 Glengate,
or 91 Glengate, Kirriemuir
SCOTTISH EPISCOPAL **A**

ST MARY'S CHURCH, KIRRIEMUIR

75 ST ANTHONY'S, KIRRIEMUIR

NO 383 543
St Mary's Close, Kirriemuir
Rectangular red sandstone church by local Architect James F Stephen, opened
1987, replacing earlier wooden church. Dedicated to St Anthony of Padua.
Semi-circular seating and red granite altar. Stained glass, stations of the cross and
statute of St Anthony by local artists. Sunday Service: 9.30am
Open during daylight hours
ROMAN CATHOLIC ♿ wc

76 LIFF CHURCH

NO 333 328
Church Road, Liff
Church website: www.muirhead-church.members.beeb.net
Built 1839 to a design by William MacKenzie of Perth, to replace an earlier
structure. The style is English Gothic with a 108-ft stone spire. Inside is a
horseshoe gallery. Four stained glass windows by J & W Guthrie of Glasgow.
Organ 1880 by Alexander Young. Old priest's house, now a ruin, in neighbouring
garden. Sunday Service: 10.00am alternate months
Open by arrangement with Session Clerk 01382 360478 or the Minister 01382 580210
CHURCH OF SCOTLAND **B**

77 LINTRATHEN PARISH CHURCH

NO 286 546

Beautiful wooded setting near
the banks of Lintrathen Loch.
Small oblong Gothic church of
1802, remodelled and extended
to T-plan in 1875.

Sunday Services: 10.30am, united
service with Glenisla, Airlie, Kilry,
Ruthven and Kingoldrum. At
Lintrathen 6.30pm in rotation
Open by arrangement,
telephone 017575 560267
CHURCH OF SCOTLAND ♿ ② 🖵 **B**

LINTRATHEN PARISH CHURCH

78 ST MARGARET'S CHURCH, LUNANHEAD

NO 476 522

Carsebarracks, Lunanhead; on B9134, 1 mile east of Forfar

Built in the planned village of Carsebarracks on the site of an earlier chapel in
1907 by the builder/architect William L McLean of Forfar as a gift of Mrs Susan
Helen Gray of Bankhead House in memory of her husband. Stained glass window
of the Crucifixion by A D Fleming of London 1913. Mural by Miss W M Watson
of Edinburgh 1909. On the B9134, one mile east of Forfar. Service: 1st and 3rd
Sundays, excluding July and August 2.00pm
Open by arrangement, telephone Mr Orrock 01307 468156
SCOTTISH EPISCOPAL

ST MARGARET'S CHURCH, LUNANHEAD

79   LUNDIE CHURCH (ST LAURENCE)

NO 291 366
In centre of Lundie village
Church website: www.muirhead-church.members.beeb.net
Belonging to the Priory of St Andrews, the medieval church was dedicated to St
Laurence. It was restored in 1892, when the porch and bellcote were added, the apse
removed and the Duncan Mausoleum converted into a vestry. Framed texts from the
Psalms and Lord's Prayer were affixed in 1892. A stained glass window depicting St
John looks south with a War Memorial on the north wall. The Reformer, Paul
Methven, administered the Sacrament in 1558. Sunday Service: 9.00am
Open by arrangement with the Minister 01382 580210 or Session Clerk 01382 580145
CHURCH OF SCOTLAND **A**

80   MEMUS CHURCH

NO 427 590
Church website: www.gkopc.co.uk
Memus Church was built as the Free Church of
Tannadice in 1843 in an outlying part of the
parish. It is a plain rectangular building free of
external ornamentation apart from the bellcote.
The internal furnishings are of very fine pitch
pine. The church had only two ministers in
103 years. Sunday Service: 10.30am, 1st and
3rd Sundays
*Open by arrangement with the Glens and Kirriemuir
Old Parish church office, telephone 01575 572819*
CHURCH OF SCOTLAND **B**

MEMUS CHURCH

81   HOLY TRINITY CHURCH, MONIFIETH

NO 499 327
High Street, Monifieth
Black and white half-timbered style
building by Mills & Shepherd 1909.
Originally intended as church hall, adapted
to church. Pleasant sheltered garden. Buses
from Dundee to Monifieth, Carnoustie and
Arbroath stop outside. Sunday Services:
8.00am, 10.30am
Open daily
SCOTTISH EPISCOPAL   **B**

HOLY TRINITY CHURCH, MONIFIETH

ST BRIDE'S, MONIFIETH

82 ST BRIDE'S, MONIFIETH

NO 499 325
6-8 Brook Street, Monifieth
Church website: www.catholic-forum.com/churches/stbrides
The original church was established in 1880 in a converted cottage, which became
the hall when the new church was built in 1983. A light airy building, it was
designed by Brocks Bros of Leeds. Stained glass by Gail Donovan. Services:
Monday to Friday in St Bride's 10am; Saturday 9.30am; Wednesday in St Mary's
Home 6.30pm; Saturday Vigil Mass 6.00pm; Sunday 10.30am and 6.15pm
Open daily 8.30am-7.30pm
ROMAN CATHOLIC 👨‍🦽 ⊘ ⛪ wc

83 MONTROSE OLD CHURCH

NO 715 778
High Street, Montrose
Built 1793 by John Gibson with a 'lovely flying-buttressed spire (J Gillespie
Graham 1832) which is Montrose's town-mark' (Colin McWilliam, *Scottish
Townscape*). Sunday Service: 11.00am, also last Sunday 6.30pm
Open June to August, Monday to Friday 2.00pm-4.30pm
CHURCH OF SCOTLAND 👨‍🦽 ⊘ ⛪ **A**

84 ST MARGARET'S, MONTROSE

NO 716 581
23 Market Street
Opened 1886. Font by David Lamb. Painting of St Margaret for 900th anniversary
in 1993. Services: Sunday Mass 11.30am, Monday, Friday, Saturday 10.00am;
Eucharist Tuesday and Thursday 10.00am
Open 7.30am-6.00pm; entry restricted to back of church
ROMAN CATHOLIC 👨‍🦽 wc **B**

85 KNOX UNITED FREE CHURCH, MONTROSE

NO 716 582

Mill Street, junction with John Street

Neo-classical church with Ionic portico 1829 by William Smith of Montrose.
Opened 1851 as Mill Street United Presbyterian Church, as St Luke's United Free
Church in 1900, closed 1953 and reopened as Knox's United Free Church in 1954.
Stained glass depicting the gospel stories of St Luke. Carved wooden pulpit and
reredos. Sunday Service: 11.00am

*Open by arrangement with Church Officer, telephone 01674 671598. Annual Thanksgiving
Service 2nd weekend in October (flowers and themed exhibition)*

UNITED FREE CHURCH   🦽 wc ②

86 MUIRHEAD OF LIFF

NO 342 345

149 Coupar Angus Road, Muirhead of Liff
Church website: www.muirhead-church.members.beeb.net
After the Disruption in 1843, the church was built
with stones given and transported by local farmers. In
1960 it was re-conditioned and in 1997 the vestry and
choir-room were converted into a hall and a new
vestry and toilets added. Sunday Service: 11.15am
*Open by arrangement with the Minister 01382 580210 or
Session Clerk 01382 580145*
CHURCH OF SCOTLAND 🦽 wc ② C

MUIRHEAD OF LIFF

87 MURROES AND TEALING CHURCH

NO 461 351

Murroes, near Broughty Ferry
T-plan church by William Smith 1848 on a site
occupied by a church for 750 years. Church records
from 1202. Interesting gravestones and coping on
churchyard wall carved with texts in English, Latin
and Greek. Interior is simple and relatively original.
Pews with doors, four impressive stained glass
windows in south wall and small pipe organ in
gallery. Former coach house and stables restored
to provide hall, chapel, kitchen and toilet facilities.
Linked with Auchterhouse. Sunday Service:
9.30am and 10.45am alternate Sundays
*Open by arrangement, telephone
Gordon Laird 01382 350242*
CHURCH OF SCOTLAND 🦽 ②

MURROES AND TEALING CHURCH

RESCOBIE PARISH CHURCH

88　RESCOBIE PARISH CHURCH

NO 509 521

Three miles east of Forfar on B9113

Built 1820 to a Telford design incorporating a 17th-century mural monument in the south wall. Very fine oak ceiling. Single-manual pipe organ by Millar of Dundee. Sunday Services: 10.00am or 11.30am, contact the Minister on 01241 828243 for details

Open by arrangement, telephone the Minister 01241 828243

CHURCH OF SCOTLAND 　 ♿ **B**

89　RUTHVEN PARISH CHURCH

NO 286 489

Ruthven Parish was first noted in 1180. The present red sandstone church of 1859 is the fourth on this site overlooking the River Isla. Two ancient stone crosses in the west wall, a ship's bell marked *The Enterprise WW 1735,* and the Royal Warrant appointing John G McPherson Minister in 1874 are of interest, as is the adjoining graveyard with headstones dating from the early 17th century. Annual Music Festival mid June weekend. Sunday Services: 10.30am, united service with Glenisla, Airlie, Kilry, Lintrathen and Kingoldrum. At Lintrathen 6.30pm in rotation

Open by arrangement, telephone 01828 632558

CHURCH OF SCOTLAND 　🕯 📖 **C**

RUTHVEN PARISH CHURCH

90 TANNADICE CHURCH

NO 475 581
Four miles north of Forfar on B957
Church website: www.standrews-kirriemuir.org.uk
Present church by John Carver built 1866 on site of previous buildings and
sympathetically extended 2003. Place of Christian worship since 7th century.
Monastery recorded in 1187 and Kirk of Tanatheys consecrated by the Bishop of
St Andrews 1242. Union with Oathlaw 1982. St Columba and St Francis windows
at west end of church 1976 in memory of 2nd Lord Forres of Glenogil. Former
Oathlaw war memorial windows on north wall, by James Ballantine 1923 and Neil
Hamilton 1949. Sunday Service: 9.45am
Key available at Post Office 9.30-11.30am; or by arrangement,
telephone Mrs Davidson 01307 850345
CHURCH OF SCOTLAND Ⓓ wc C

TANNADICE CHURCH

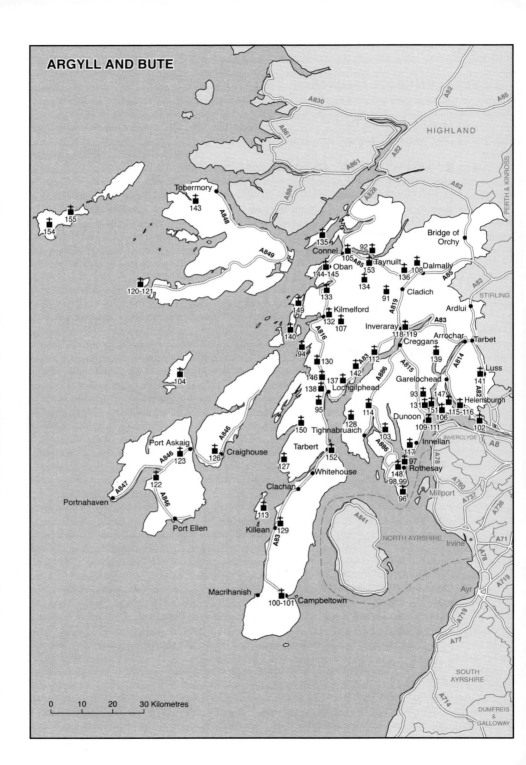

ARGYLL AND BUTE

ARGYLL & BUTE

Local Representative: The Rev John Paton, Muasdale, by Tarbert
(*telephone* 01583 421249)

91 ST JAMES' CHURCH, ARDBRECKNISH

NN 072 212
Church website: www.scotland.anglican.org/argyll
Built 1891, stone interior with fine series of
monuments and excellent windows. Bells rehung
1991. Grass churchyard overlooking Loch Awe.
Sunday Service: in summer 11.00am, 3.00pm;
Eucharist on 3rd Sunday of the month (winter).
Linked with St John's Cathedral, Oban
Open daylight hours in summer
SCOTTISH EPISCOPAL

ST JAMES' CHURCH, ARDBRECKNISH

92 CHURCH OF THE HOLY SPIRIT, ARDCHATTAN

NM 971 349
Church website: www.scotland.anglican.org/argyll
Built 1886. Fine First World War memorial incorporating the three banners of
Scotland, England and Ireland. Ardchattan crucifix on south wall. Stone pedestal
font and ancient stone stoup. One mile west of Bonawe Quarry, beside Loch Etive.
Sunday Service: 2nd Sunday 12.15pm. Linked with St John's Cathedral, Oban
Open by arrangement, contact Mrs Colquhoun, The Ferry House, Ardchattan
SCOTTISH EPISCOPAL

93 ARDENTINNY

NS 188 876
Shore Road, Ardentinny
Simple oblong kirk of 1838-9 with three tall
windows each side. Gabled front with gabled
porch and arched bellcote at apex. Pulpit with
sounding board decorated with finials. The
church contains the memorials to the men of
HMS Armadillo, the wartime Royal Navy
Commando Unit who trained in Ardentinny.
Sunday Service: 2.30pm
Open daily
CHURCH OF SCOTLAND **B**

ARDENTINNY

94 CRAIGNISH PARISH CHURCH, ARDFERN

NM 805 042

South side of Ardfern village on B8002

Attractive Georgian-style building of 1826 with hipped roof and harled masonry walls. Simple rectangular plan with vestry to rear, front façade dominated by a pediment and short tower. Lancet windows have fine fenestration. Symmetry in front and side elevations maintained by trompe-l'œil windows. Inside, a fine tiered presenter's box and pulpit. Sunday Service: 10.00am

Open at all times

CHURCH OF SCOTLAND ♿ ⊘ **B**

95 ARDRISHAIG PARISH CHURCH

NR 854 852

Tarbert Road, Ardrishaig

Gothic tower-fronted nave church of 1860 with low semi-octagonal transepts and vestibule added 1904. The octagonal castellated stage of the tower and the sharp spire were added in 1868. Edwardian Art Nouveau patterned stained glass in all windows. Sunday Service: 11.00am

Open by arrangement with the Minister, telephone 01546 603269

CHURCH OF SCOTLAND ♿ ⊘ wc

ARDRISHAIG PARISH CHURCH

96 KINGARTH & KILCHATTAN BAY CHURCH, ISLE OF BUTE

NS 100 552

Kilchattan Bay, Kingarth

Built in 1894/5, this Gothic style kirk stands on the site of an earlier building which started life as a mission station after the Disruption of 1843. The Kirk has a long and proud ancestry, Christianity having reached Bute through St Catan in the 6th century and the first post-Reformation minister having been inducted to Kingarth in 1572. Sunday Service: 1.00pm (most Sundays)

Open July and August, Friday 2.00-4.00pm

CHURCH OF SCOTLAND wc ⊘ ⌕ **B**

97 ST NINIAN'S, PORT BANNATYNE, ISLE OF BUTE

NS 078 674

Shore Road, Port Bannatyne

Designed by William F McGibbon in 1885/6, a plain but dignified church with off-set square bell tower. The Romanesque columns which support the pointed arch arcaded aisles lend solidarity to its height. Memorials to Henry Robertson Bowers of the ill-fated Scott expedition and the 12th Submarine Flotilla.

Sunday Service: 9.30am (most Sundays)

Open July and August, Friday 2.00-4.00pm

CHURCH OF SCOTLAND [wc] ⌀ B

98 ROTHESAY HIGH KIRK, ISLE OF BUTE

NS 086 637

High Street, Rothesay

Designed by Adam Russell and built in 1796, this is the third church on this site, the first of which served for a period as Cathedral of the Diocese of the Isles. Remodelled by John Russell Thomson in 1905-6 with U-plan gallery, pitch pine dado and oak pulpit flanked by organ pipes and six stained glass windows by Stephen Adam and D Hamilton.

Sunday Service: 11.15am (most Sundays)

Open July and August Friday 2.00-4.00pm

CHURCH OF SCOTLAND [wc] ⌀ ⎕ B

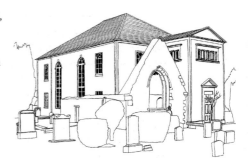

ROTHESAY HIGH KIRK, BUTE

99 CRAIGMORE ST BRENDAN'S, ROTHESAY, ISLE OF BUTE

NS 098 653

Mount Stuart Road, Rothesay

St Brendan's was built in 1889, architect David A Crombie. In 1973 fire destroyed the whole building, save the tower. The architect Miss Margaret Brodie, prepared plans for a new building, completed in 1975. It is in stark contrast to its predecessor; with the pinnacled Perpendicular Gothic tower in front of the unadorned modern shallow nave gable. No regular Sunday Service

Open July and August, Friday 2.00-4.00pm

CHURCH OF SCOTLAND [wc] ⌀

100   HIGHLAND PARISH CHURCH, CAMPBELTOWN

NR 720 201

New Quay Street, Campbeltown

'To be causewayed with whinstone and paved with hewn flags. The lock on the front door to be of 20/- value and the rest to have snecks and wooden bolts': the instruction of the architect George Dempster of Greenock, for a new church, built for the Highland, Gaelic-speaking, congregation of the area, and completed in 1807. Harled rubble with red sandstone dressings, an oblong with

HIGHLAND PARISH CHURCH, CAMPBELTOWN

rectangular stair towers at each end of the front. Three galleries. The planned belfry was not large enough for the heritors, so a steeple was built; it has been rebuilt twice since, the casualty of lightning strikes. Allen Renaissance organ, 2000. The organ screen bears a memorial to the fallen of the Second World War.

Sunday Services: 11.15am and 6.30pm, except July and August

Open daily

CHURCH OF SCOTLAND ⓓ **B**

101   LORNE AND LOWLAND CHURCH, CAMPBELTOWN

NR 718 206

Longrow, Campbeltown

Church website: www.lorneandlowland.com

Built in 1872 to the design of John Burnet, historically called The Longrow Church. Classical, influenced by Italian Renaissance style. Its bell-tower is a well known landmark. Two stairways lead from the entrance foyer to a horse-shoe gallery. Fine plaster ceiling. Pulpit 1895.

Sunday Services: 11.15am

Open July to August, Monday to Friday 11.00am-4.00pm; other times, telephone Mr Robert Young 01586 552601

CHURCH OF SCOTLAND ♿ ⓓ ⌨ **C**

LORNE AND LOWLAND CHURCH, CAMPBELTOWN

102   CARDROSS PARISH CHURCH

NS 345 775
Station Road, Cardross
Church website: www.cardrossparishchurch.org
Church founded 1225 on west bank of River Leven and
rebuilt in village 1640. Present building 1872. Stained
glass windows, Sadie McLellan 1972, embroidered
panels, Hannah Frew Paterson 1981, woven silk
hangings, Sarah Sumsion 1990, and engraved glass
windows, John Lawrie 1992. Peal of six bells
augmented to eight for the Millennium. A82 from
Glasgow; half-hourly train service from Glasgow
Queen Street. Sunday Services: 9.30am and 11.00am;
June, July, August 10.00am only
Open Monday, Wednesday, Thursday and Friday mornings, or
by arrangement, telephone Mrs S McLatchie 01389 841509
CHURCH OF SCOTLAND 🦽 ⑨ wc **B**

CARDROSS PARISH CHURCH

103   COLINTRAIVE CHURCH

NS 045 735
Erected 1840 by Mrs Campbell of Southhall as a chapel of ease, part of
Inverchaolain parish. Became a Free Church in 1843, United Free in 1900 and
returned to the Church of Scotland in 1929. United with Kilmodan Church.
Spectacular views over Kyles of Bute. Sunday Service: 10.00am or 11.30am,
alternating monthly with Kilmodan
Open daily
CHURCH OF SCOTLAND 📖

104   COLONSAY PARISH CHURCH

NR 890 941
By Scalasaig ferry terminal
Built by Michael Carmichael 1802 on a site of
a medieval chapel and close to a Bronze Age
burial site. Neighbouring former Parochial School
is mentioned in John Buchan's *Island of Sheep*.
The church originally had galleries at both ends,
accessed by extramural staircases. Attractive
wooden ceiling. Sunday Service: 11.30am
Normally open at all times. For assistance,
telephone Kevin Byrne 01951 200320
CHURCH OF SCOTLAND **B**

COLONSAY PARISH CHURCH

105 ST ORAN'S CHURCH, CONNEL

NM 914 343

Gothic Revival cruciform church of 1888
with lancet and pointed traceried windows,
gabled porch and a central tower with
corbelled parapet. Good interior with open
timbered ceiling. Fine collection of 20th-
century glass by various artists. Beautiful
views up Loch Etive from garden. On A85.
Sunday Service: 10.30am
Open during daylight hours
CHURCH OF SCOTLAND 🦽 ⊘ 📖 ⚲ **B**

ST ORAN'S CHURCH, CONNEL

106 CRAIGROWNIE CHURCH, COVE

NS 224 810

Church Road, Cove, near Helensburgh
Daughter Church of Rosneath, opened 1853.
Architect David Cousin, enlarged by
Honeyman & Keppie 1889. Organ by James
J Binns of Leeds. Various examples of
stained glass including J Benson, S Adam,
Mayer & Co. Frescoes by the sisters Doris
and Anna Zinkeisen of the four Evangelists.
Nearby Church Hall in a former church

CRAIGROWNIE CHURCH HALL, COVE

designed by Hugh Barclay 1858, with
windows by F Hase-Hayden, A Webster, A McW Webster and others.
Sunday Service: 10.00am in 2006, and 11.30am in 2007
Open by arrangement with the Minister, telephone 01436 842274
CHURCH OF SCOTLAND 🦽 wc ⊘ ⚲ 🖳 (by arrangement) **B**

107 DALAVICH CHURCH

NM 968 124

15 miles from Taynuilt
The building dates from about 1770. Linked
with Muckairn and Kilchrenan. A small bell-
tower built on the gable to celebrate the
Millennium. Sunday Services: 10.00am,
2nd and 4th Sundays of the month
Open by arrangement, MacIntosh,
1 Dalavich, by Taynuilt
CHURCH OF SCOTLAND ⊘

DALAVICH CHURCH

108 GLENORCHY PARISH CHURCH, DALMALLY

NN 168 275

On A85, 25 miles east of Oban

Church website: www.loch-awe.com/community/glenorchychurch.htm

Octagonal Gothic church with square tower by James Elliot 1810. Twenty-six clan chiefs of the Macgregors lie buried under the entrance to the church. Fine stained glass window of 1898. Major restoration 1988-91. Fourteenth- and 15th-century grave slabs with interlaced floral designs in burial ground. Sunday Service: 9.00am

Open during daylight hours

CHURCH OF SCOTLAND ♿ wc 🚹 A

109 DUNOON BAPTIST CHURCH CENTRE

NS 171 770

9 Alexandra Parade, Dunoon

Formerly the American servicemen's YMCA. The centre welcomes all visitors to the beautiful Cowal Peninsula. Browse in the well-stocked Christian book and gift shop. Sample excellent coffee and home baking with a splendid view of the Clyde estuary. Next to Tourist Information Centre and five minutes from the pier. Sunday Services: 11.00am and 6.30pm

Open Monday to Saturday 10.00am-4.00pm

BAPTIST wc ♲ 🚹 ☕ A

110 THE HIGH KIRK, DUNOON

NS 173 769

Church Square, Dunoon

Church website: www.dunoonhighkirk.org.uk

The present building probably stands on the site of a much earlier church which until 1688 was the Cathedral Church of both the Roman Catholic and Episcopalian Bishops of Argyll. Towards the end of the 18th century the building became dilapidated and was demolished, the stone being used to build Gillespie Graham's Late Decorated Gothic Revival church of 1816. The belfry tower was added in 1839 and the church was lengthened and widened by Andrew Balfour in 1909. Chancel window 1939 by Douglas Hamilton. Gravestones of the 13th and 17th century in the kirkyard. Sunday Service: 11.00am; mid-week service Wednesday 10.30am

First Thursday to Saturday in August, Flower Festival. June to September inclusive: exhibition (history and memorabilia), Monday to Saturday 10.30am-4.00pm. Other times open by arrangement, telephone Mr James Brogan, Church Officer 01369 702241

CHURCH OF SCOTLAND ♿ wc ♲ 🚹 ☕ B

THE HIGH KIRK, DUNOON

ST JOHN'S CHURCH, DUNOON

111 ST JOHN'S CHURCH, DUNOON

NS 172 769

Argyll Street, Dunoon

Church website: www.stjohnsdunoon.org.uk

A magnificent nave and aisles kirk by R A Bryden 1877 built to supersede the
original Free Church of 1843. Normandy Gothic spired tower. Galleried 'concert
hall' interior. Raised choir behind central pulpit. Three-manual pipe organ by Brook
& Co 1895. Interesting stained glass including windows by Stephen Adam and
Gordon Webster, also Lauder Memorial. Sunday Services: 10.15am and 6.30pm
(last Sunday of the month)

Open June, July, August and September, Monday to Friday 10.00am-12.00 noon. September
Sunday concerts at 3.00pm (last 3 Sundays in September), includes organ recitals, visiting
choirs, etc; contact 01369 830639

CHURCH OF SCOTLAND   🚻 🚾 ② 🍴 📖 ☕ **A**

112 CUMLODDEN PARISH CHURCH, FURNACE

NS 014 994

Built in 1841 by local mason, David Crow, to a
design by James Nairn of Balloch. Interior
redesigned 1894. Contains an early Christian cross-
shaft showing a bearded figure, 8th or 9th century,
removed from Killevin Burial Ground. Stained
glass 1924 by William Meikle & Sons, Glasgow.
Sunday Service: 10.30am, 4th Sunday 11.00am
Open by arrangement with the Minister,
telephone 01499 500288

CHURCH OF SCOTLAND 🚾 **C**

CUMLODDEN PARISH CHURCH, FURNACE

113 GIGHA AND CARA PARISH CHURCH, ISLE OF GIGHA

NR 643 481

Ardminish

Built 1923. Designed by architect minister Donald MacFarlane Windows by Gordon Webster. First minister Dr Kenneth MacLeod, author of 'The Road to the Isles'. Stone baptismal font from Kilchaltan Church. Sunday Service: 11.00am

Open at all times

CHURCH OF SCOTLAND 🚻 📖

☕ (at village hall, 2.00pm Wednesdays)

GIGHA AND CARA PARISH CHURCH, ISLE OF GIGHA

114 KILMODAN CHURCH, GLENDARUEL

NR 995 842

Clachan of Glendaruel on A886

A Georgian T-plan church of 1783 on site of an earlier church of 1610. Completely restored in 1983. Segmental-arched windows; lofts in the three arms. Two long narrow communion tables. Memorial to Rev John MacLaurin and his two famous sons (Colin, author of *MacLaurin's Mathematical Theorem*). Bus and post bus from Dunoon. United with Colintraive. Sunday Services: 10.00am or 11.30am, alternating monthly with Colintraive

Open daily

CHURCH OF SCOTLAND 🚻 (nearby)

KILMODAN CHURCH, GLENDARUEL

115 ST MICHAEL AND ALL ANGELS, HELENSBURGH

NS 292 825

William Street, Helensburgh

Built by Robert Rowand Anderson in 1868 in French Gothic style. Tower with peal of eight bells added in 1930. Richly decorated interior with oak chancel screen and elaborately carved Austrian oak north porch screen. West porch screen 1996 of light oak and engraved glass by James Anderson. Alabaster and mosaic reredos against encaustic tiling. Organ originally by August Gern, foreman to Cavaille-Coll. Fine sculpted

ST MICHAEL AND ALL ANGELS, HELENSBURGH

west portal nave and chancel capitals. Good stained glass by Clayton & Bell, Shrigley & Hunt, Adam & Small, and Barraud & Westlake, with five windows by C E Kempe including fine rose window in west façade. Located 800m west of Central railway station, off Clyde Street. Services: Sunday 8.00am, 10.15am and 6.30pm; Tuesdays 10.30am; Wednesdays 7.30pm

Open daily 9.00am-5.00pm

SCOTTISH EPISCOPAL ⬛ ② ⬛ **A**

116 THE WEST KIRK OF HELENSBURGH

NS 295 825

Colquhoun Square, Helensburgh

Victorian Gothic building of 1853, W H & J M Hay, restored after disastrous fire in 1924 by Robert Wemyss, with a porch by William Leiper. Impressive panelled interior, with fine woodwork and half-timbered ceiling. Organ by Hill, 1894, rebuilt Hill, Norman & Beard. Exceptionally fine stained glass including memorial windows to Andrew Bonar Law, one-time Prime Minister, and

THE WEST KIRK OF HELENSBURGH

to John Logie Baird, inventor of television and son of the Manse in Helensburgh. Hill House (Charles Rennie Mackintosh) is one mile away. Sunday Service: 10.00am May to August, 11.00am September to April

Open daily all year 9.00am-5.00pm; and with guides June to August, Monday, Wednesday and Friday 2.00-4.00pm. Exhibition summer months

CHURCH OF SCOTLAND ⬛ ② ⬛ ⬛ ⬛ **B**

117 INNELLAN PARISH CHURCH

NS 152 707

7 Matheson Lane, Innellan

Built of local whin rubble in 1852 and expanded in 1867 and again in 1887. Fine stone pulpit from 1887 re-ordering. The central stained glass window is a version of Holman Hunt's 'The Light of the World' which glows whatever the lighting conditions. The church is best known for its association with George Matheson who ministered for 18 years from 1869 during which time he wrote 'O Love that wilt not let me go'. Sunday Service: 11.30am

Open by arrangement with the Clerk to the Congregational Board, telephone 01369 830554

CHURCH OF SCOTLAND ⬛ ②

INNELLAN PARISH CHURCH

118 ALL SAINTS CHURCH AND BELL-TOWER, INVERARAY

NN 095 085

The Avenue, Inveraray

Church website: www.scotland.anglican.org/inveraray.htm

Gothic-style church built 1885 in local red granite, designed by Wardrop and Anderson of Edinburgh. Many of the interior furnishings given by Niell Dairmid, 10th Duke of Argyll. Belltower, in Gothic revivial by Hoare & Wheeler, built 1923-31 as a memorial to Campbell dead of First World War and previous wars. Peal of ten bells by John Taylor of Loughborough, 1926. Exhibition in entrance to ringing chamber. Sunday Service: Scottish Episcopal 2nd Sunday 3.00pm. Roman Catholic 12.30pm every Sunday

Open daily, early April to end September

SCOTTISH EPISCOPAL 📖 **B** (Church) **A** (bell-tower)

119 GLENARAY & INVERARAY PARISH CHURCH, INVERARAY

NN 096 084

Church Square, Inveraray

Designed by Robert Mylne in 1792 to house two congregations, English and Gaelic. A solid wall separated the two. Gaelic portion converted to church hall 1957. Chamber organ by David Hamilton of Edinburgh 1840s. Sunday Service: 11.15am

Open July and August on request at Church exhibition and sale in Church Hall at rear of Church

CHURCH OF SCOTLAND **A**

GLENARAY & INVERARAY
PARISH CHURCH, INVERARAY

120 IONA ABBEY

NM 287 245

Isle of Iona

On the original site of St Columba's monastery, c.563. St Columba's Shrine dates from the 9th century, most of the present buildings from around 1200. The massive restoration of the Abbey Church was undertaken by the Iona Cathedral Trust, who own the buildings, and was completed in 1910. The Iona Community now occupy the monastic buildings which they restored under the leadership of the Rev Dr George MacLeod. Historic Scotland care for the Abbey and associated monuments. Beautiful Augustinian nunnery, 12th-century ruin, Reilig Odhrain (Royal burial ground), 'Street of the Dead', imposing standing crosses and one of the largest collections of early Christian carved stones in Europe. Ferry from Oban

to Mull, by bus/car to Fionnphort, pedestrian ferry to Iona. Services: Sunday
10.30am and Monday to Saturday 2.00pm, March to October; also Monday to
Saturday 9.00am all year
Open at all times (Historic Scotland)
INTER-DENOMINATIONAL [wc] 🍴 🚪 ☕ **A**

121 IONA PARISH CHURCH

NM 285 243
Isle of Iona
A Thomas Telford church of 1828.
Pews, pulpit and communion table
realigned in 1939. Former Manse of
same date now a heritage centre with
picnic area adjacent. Ferry from Oban
to Mull. Bus/car to Fionnphort for
ferry to Iona. Sunday Service: 12.00
noon. Short Service: Tuesday 1.00pm
and each weekday in high summer
Open daily
CHURCH OF SCOTLAND **B**

IONA PARISH CHURCH

122 KILARROW PARISH CHURCH, BOWMORE, ISLE OF ISLAY

NR 312 596
At the top of Main Street
Church website: www.theroundchurch.org.uk
This 18th-century church, known as 'The Round Church', was built by Daniel
Campbell of Shawfield and Islay in 1767 at a cost of £1000. Bowmore is a
'planned village' for those of the village of Kilarrow who were not directly
involved in the work of Islay Estate, mainly
agricultural workers and weavers. The two-
storey circular body of the church has a main
central pillar 19 inches in diameter, possibly of
hemlock oak, harled and plastered. Above the
coved ceiling is a radial king-post roof truss
into which eight major beams are jointed.
The gallery was added in 1830, increasing its
capacity to 500. Extensive renovation has
been carried out in recent years. Linked
with Kilmeny. Sunday Service: 11.30am
Open daily all year, 9.00am-6.00pm
CHURCH OF SCOTLAND [♿]
🍴 (during summer months) ◔ 🚪 **A**

KILARROW PARISH CHURCH,
BOWMORE, ISLE OF ISLAY

123 KILMENY PARISH CHURCH, BALLYGRANT, ISLE OF ISLAY

NR 353 636

Church website: www.kilmenychurch.org.uk

KILMENY PARISH CHURCH,
BALLYGRANT, ISLE OF ISLAY

Kilmeny Parish Church is situated in sheltered wooded grounds which are at the moment being developed. The present church was remodelled in 1828 to plans by Thomas Telford and stands about 400m north east of its medieval predecessor. There is evidence of a number of early Celtic Church foundations within the parish boundary, and nearby is the famous Finlaggan site, adminis-trative centre of the Lords of the Isles. The church has been the recipient of some fine gifts, the most recent being an organ donated by the Caol Ila Distillery Company during their 125th anniversary in 1996. The interior has recently been upgraded with confortable seating both on pews and padded chairs. Linked with Kilarrow. Situated above the main Port Askaig/Bowmore road. Sunday Service: 9.45am

Open July to August, Thursday 10.30am-12.30pm and 2.00-4.00pm

CHURCH OF SCOTLAND [wc] 🍴 📖 ☕ **B**

124 ST KIARAN'S, PORT CHARLOTTE, ISLAY

NR 257 594

On A847, midway between Bruichladdich and Port Charlotte

Church website: www.stkiarans.co.uk

Constructed 1897 and designed by Peter McGregor Chalmers. In Romanesque style in rubble stone dressed with red sandstone. Conical roofed apse. Centenary tapestry on display. Sunday Service: 11.30am

Open at all times

CHURCH OF SCOTLAND [♿] [wc] ✍ 📖 Gaelic spoken **A**

125 PORTNAHAVEN PARISH CHURCH, ISLAY

NR 168 523

In centre of Portnahaven village

Church website: www.stkiarans.co.uk

A Telford Parliamentary kirk built 1828 by William Thompson. T-plan with north, east and west galleries. The symmetrical south front has two tall four-centred arched windows and two doorways. Legend has it that one door is used by Portnahaven residents exclusively, the other door by residents of nearby Port Wemyss. Sunday Service: 10.00am

Open at all times

CHURCH OF SCOTLAND [♿] Gaelic spoken **A**

126 JURA PARISH CHURCH

NR 527 677

Craighouse, Isle of Jura

The harled church was built in 1776. Pennant in his
Voyage to the Hebrides (1776) says 'land in Jura, at a little
village, and see to the right on the shore the church,
and the minister's manse'. Alterations 1842 and 1922.
Superb photographic exhibition of 'Old Jura' in
gallery behind the church. Sunday Service: 11.30am
Open at all times

CHURCH OF SCOTLAND 🔾 wc ⓘ 📖

JURA PARISH CHURCH

127 KILBERRY PARISH CHURCH

NR 741 620

Lergnahension, 12 miles from Tarbert on the B8024

The church was built in 1821. A plain oblong
building, galleries on three sides, later alterations
provided an internal stair and removed the
original external access. Sunday Services:
fortnightly, summer 10.00am, winter 2.00pm
Open all year during daylight hours

CHURCH OF SCOTLAND 📖 **B**

KILBERRY PARISH CHURCH

128 KILFINAN PARISH CHURCH

NR 934 789

On B8000 Tighnabruaich to Strachur

A place of worship since 1235. Gothic 1759, including the earlier Lamont Vault of
1633. Stones of interest. Sunday Service: 12.00 noon
Open all year

CHURCH OF SCOTLAND **B**

129 KILLEAN & KILCHENZIE KIRK, A'CHLEIT, KINTYRE

NR 681 418

A83, 1 mile north of Muasdale

The church, 1787-91 by Thomas Cairns, is set on a rocky promontory out to sea.
White harled with round arched windows. Belfry added 1879 by Robert Weir. The
pulpit, in the long west wall, is a First World War memorial with Celtic style
carving and faces a large laird's loft. Beside the pulpit is a marble monument of
1818 to Col Norman Macalister. Sunday Service: 11.15am
Flower Festival mid July. Open daily

CHURCH OF SCOTLAND 🔾 ⓘ wc (on request) **A**

KILLEAN & KILCHENZIE KIRK, A'CHLEIT, KINTYRE

KILMARTIN PARISH CHURCH

130 KILMARTIN PARISH CHURCH

NR 836 993

Kilmartin, by Lochgilphead

On the site of earlier churches, the present building opened in 1835. The architect was James Gordon Davis. Three interesting memorial panels from the 18th and 19th centuries to members of the family of Campbell of Duntroon. The church has two outstanding crosses, with explanatory panels provided by Historic Scotland. The kirkyard contains the mausoleum of Bishop Neil Campbell and medieval tomb slabs. Extensive views over Bronze Age burial cairns.

Services: see local paper and notice board

Open April to October, 9.30am-6.00pm

CHURCH OF SCOTLAND   🦽   ⊙   **B**

131 KILMUN PARISH CHURCH, ST MUNN'S

NS 166 821

Kilmun, A880, 6 miles from Dunoon

On the site of a Celtic monastery, overlooking Holy Loch. Tower of 15th-century collegiate church. Present building dates from 1841, by Thomas Burns with interior remodelled by P MacGregor Chalmers in 1899. Important stained glass by Stephen Adam and Alfred Webster. Water-powered organ by Norman & Beard 1909. Ancient graveyard with fine 18th-century carved stones. Mausoleum of Dukes of Argyll, Douglas vault. Grave of Elizabeth Blackwell, first lady doctor.

Sunday Service: 12.00 noon

Open May to end September, Tuesday to Thursday 1.30-4.30pm (last tour 4.00pm). Other days and times throughout the year by appointment. Groups welcome. Telephone Valerie Gilles 01369 840342. Benmore Botanic Gardens (RBGE), two miles, open April to October

CHURCH OF SCOTLAND   wc   ⊙   ⫯   ⌷   ⊑   **B**

KILMUN PARISH
CHURCH, ST MUNN'S

132 KILMELFORD PARISH CHURCH

NM 849 130

At junction of A816 and road to Loch Avich

Small attractive building of 1785, re-roofed 1890. Oblong plan with gable front with birdcage belfry and 8-spoked wheel window over pointed arch entrance. Plain tall interior with open timber roof. Balcony with spiral stair with barley-sugar balusters. Pulpit box. Sunday Service: fortnightly 12.00 noon (alternates with Kilninver)

Open all the time through vestry

CHURCH OF SCOTLAND ♿ C

133 KILNINVER PARISH CHURCH

NM 825 217

At junction of A816 and B844 to Seil

Simple country church of 1793 by John Clark, mason, of Oban; oblong in plan with birdcage belfry. Radically reconstructed 1892 when porch and vestry added and windows altered. Panelled rear gallery and pitch pine pulpit box. Christian worship recorded at Kilninver in 1200s. Sunday Service: fortnightly 12.00 noon (alternates with Kilmelford)

Open by arrangement with Fabric Convenor, 01852 200588 or telephone 01852 316272

CHURCH OF SCOTLAND C

134 KILCHRENAN PARISH CHURCH

NN 037 229

The building was built in 1770 on the site of an earlier church dating back to the 12th century. Some stones from that church have been incorporated into the present building. There are interesting tombstones in the graveyard including that of Cailean Mor in 1294. Linked with Muckairn and Dalavich. Sunday Services: 10.00am on the 1st, 3rd and 5th Sundays of the month

Open during daylight hours

CHURCH OF SCOTLAND ♁

KILCHRENAN PARISH CHURCH

135 ST MOLUAG, CLACHAN, ISLE OF LISMORE

NM 861 435

'The Cathedral of Argyll' was built in
late 14th to early 15th century and
attributed locally to 'The Roman' or
'An Roimhanach'. Six stained glass
windows, two modern by Mitton.
Eight medieval carved slab-stones,
said to be of the 'Loch Awe' school
and recumbent carved stone within
the building. Traditional Baptismal
font is carved in a natural rock
surface. Exhibition on 800 years of
Christianity on Lismore

Open at all times

CHURCH OF SCOTLAND [wc] [] (by arrangement) []

ST MOLUAG,CLACHAN,
ISLE OF LISMORE,

136 ST CONAN'S KIRK, LOCHAWE

NN 116 268

On A85, 22 miles east of Oban

Church website: www.loch-awe.com/community/stconanskirk.htm

A labour of love built 1907-30 by Walter Campbell of Innis Chonain, architect.
An astonishing building, mostly in Romanesque style, although Walter Campbell
'did not allow himself to be trammelled by orthodoxy'. A show piece in Argyll
which attracts 80,000 visitors a year. Overlooking Loch Awe in a place of great
natural beauty. Popular for weddings. Sunday Service: 10.00am

Open during daylight hours

CHURCH OF SCOTLAND [&] [wc] [] A

137 LOCHGAIR PARISH CHURCH

NR 922 905
Originally Mission Church of Glassary Parish.
Built 1867 to a simple oblong design. Half-
octagon box pulpit centred between blind lancets.
Services: 1st and 3rd Sundays 3.00pm, 2nd
Sunday of the month; Gaelic Service: 3.00pm,
5th Sunday 6.30pm
Open during daylight hours
CHURCH OF SCOTLAND wc **C**

LOCHGAIR PARISH CHURCH

138 CHRIST CHURCH, LOCHGILPHEAD

NR 860 884
Bishopton Road, Lochgilphead
Church website:
www.scotland.anglican.org/lochgilphead.htm
Church and adjoining rectory designed by
John Henderson 1850-51. Nave-and-chancel
church with an arch-braced nave roof. Organ
chamber built 1887-8 to house the organ by
William Hill & Son 1876. Sunday Services:
9.00am (except 1st Sunday) and 11.00am
Open during daylight hours
SCOTTISH EPISCOPAL ♿ (ramps available) ② **B**

CHRIST CHURCH, LOCHGILPHEAD

139 LOCHGOILHEAD & KILMORICH PARISH CHURCH

NN 198 015
Lochgoilhead, A83 Arrochar–Inveraray, top
of Rest and Be Thankful, B828 and B839
into village
Dedicated to the Three Holy Brethren,
the church is first mentioned in papal
letters of 1379. It was rebuilt in the
18th century incorporating the medieval
walls. Many features of interest.
Sunday Service: 10.30am
Open by arrangement, telephone Mr F West
01301 703378. Church Fair in August.
Coffee mornings depending on local weather
conditions
CHURCH OF SCOTLAND **B**

LOCHGOILHEAD & KILMORICH PARISH CHURCH

140 KILCHATTAN KIRK, TOBERONOCHY, ISLE OF LUING

NM 743 104

Toberonochy, Isle of Luing

Kilchattan Kirk was built in 1936 and houses a beautifully carved, floor-standing wooden lectern and two wooden offering plates donated by Latvian ship owners to mark the rescue efforts of the islanders when one of their ships foundered in a storm on the island of Belnahua in 1938. Just beyond the school on the road to Toberonochy. Sunday Service: 11.30am, except last Sunday in month 3.15pm

Open all year

CHURCH OF SCOTLAND [wc] ⓐ

141 LUSS PARISH CHURCH

NS 361 929

This picturesque church, the third built on this site on the banks of Loch Lomond, with its beautiful stained glass windows and uniquely timbered roof, featured frequently in TV's 'Take the High Road'. The ancient graveyard has 15 listed ancient monuments. Luss Village, off A82. Sunday Service: 11.45am

Open daily from 10.00am

CHURCH OF SCOTLAND **B**

LUSS PARISH CHURCH

142 LOCHFYNESIDE PARISH CHURCH, MINARD

NR 978 962

Good example of a corrugated-iron church by Speirs & Co of Glasgow, 'Designers and Erectors of Iron and Wood Buildings'. Stained glass window by Sax Shaw 1984. Pulpit of ancient ash from Crarae estate, designed by Ilay M Campbell. Service: 12.00 noon except 4th Sunday

Open by arrangement with the Minister, telephone 01499 500288

CHURCH OF SCOTLAND

LOCHFYNESIDE PARISH CHURCH, MINARD

143 KILMORE CHURCH, DERVAIG, MULL

NM 432 517

Dervaig

Opened in June 1905 on the site of an earlier church, architect Peter McGregor Chalmers. Simple exterior with 'pencil' tower. The interior is in the Arts & Crafts style and features a painted apse and characteristically plain but beautiful pulpit and communion table. Significant stained glass by Stephen Adam. Sunday Service: 2.00pm

Open at all times

CHURCH OF SCOTLAND [♿] [wc] ⓐ ⌂ **C**

KILMORE CHURCH, DERVAIG, MULL

144 CATHEDRAL CHURCH OF ST JOHN THE DIVINE, OBAN

NM 859 304
George Street, Oban
Church website:
www.scotland.anglican.org/argyll
The cathedral is a small part of the
projected building, consisting of chancel,
crossing, nave of one bay and one
transept by James Chalmers 1908,
attached at right angles to existing church
by Charles Wilson and David Thomson,
giving an extraordinary building
internally. Tall reredos on a Scottish
theme with painting of Ascension set in

CATHEDRAL CHURCH OF
ST JOHN THE DIVINE, OBAN

the West Highlands by Norman Macdougall. Vast hovering bronze eagle. Choir
stalls in form of Celtic graveyard. Much Iona marble and terrazzo.
Sunday Services: 8.00am, 10.15am; Wednesdays 11.00am
Open daily
SCOTTISH EPISCOPAL wc ⊘ 📖 **c**

145 ST COLUMBA'S CATHEDRAL, OBAN

NM 855 307
Corran Esplanade, Oban
Church website: www.dioceseofargyllandtheisles.org
Built between 1932 and 1958, St Columba's Cathedral is the principal Church of
the Roman Catholic Diocese of Argyll and the Isles. Designed by Giles Gilbert
Scott in the neo-Gothic style,
of highly distinctive, lofty,
pink granite. The tower soars
above the Esplanade. High
timber reredos with intricate
Gothic fretwork, designed by
Scott and carved by Donald
Gilbert. Services: Saturday,
Vigil Mass 7.00pm; Sunday,
Mass 10.30am
Open dawn to dusk
ROMAN CATHOLIC ⊘ **A**

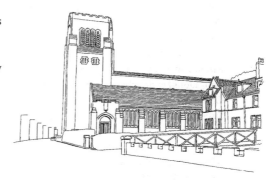

ST COLUMBA'S CATHEDRAL, OBAN

146 ST COLUMBA'S, POLTALLOCH

NR 816 965

Poltalloch Estate, by Kilmartin

Church website:

www.scotland.anglican.org/kilmartin.htm

In the gentle parkland of ruined Poltalloch
House (William Burn 1849), St Columba's was
conceived as a private chapel but built as a
church with congregation and incumbent. Built
1852 to a design by William Cundy of London
in Early English style with leafy carvings and
pointed arches. Complete set of stained glass
by William Wailes. Organ by Gray & Davison
1855. Two Whitechapel Foundry bells. Three
misericord seats. Sunday Services: 1st Sunday
9.00am, 3rd Sunday 3.30pm

Open Daily

SCOTTISH EPISCOPAL **B**

ST COLUMBA'S, POLTALLOCH

147 ST MODAN'S PARISH CHURCH, ROSNEATH

NS 255 832

A814 to Garelochhead, then B833 to Rosneath

There has been a church at Rosneath since the time of St Modan *c.*AD 600-50, the
present building, 1853, is by architect David Cousin. The bell from the earlier
church, and now on display in the present building, was made by Ian Burgerhuis
in 1610 and was rung as a summons to arms during the 1715 Jacobite rebellion.

Two-manual organ by Hill 1875. Queen
Victoria's Bible was gifted by Princess
Louise. Reredos of ten commandments by
W A Muirhead and The Last Supper by
Meredith Williams, carved by Thomas
Wood. Mural of St Modan by Mary
Ainsworth 1995. Stained glass by Clayton &
Bell, Douglas Strachan, Stephen Adam &
Co, Gordon Webster, Crear McCartney.
Sunday Service: 11.30am in 2006, and
10.00am in 2007

Open by arrangement, telephone the
Minister 01436 842274

CHURCH OF SCOTLAND

☕ (by arrangement) **A**

ST MODAN'S PARISH CHURCH, ROSNEATH

148 TRINITY PARISH CHURCH, ROTHESAY, ISLE OF BUTE

NS 089 645

Castle Street, Rothesay

Opened as the Free Church in 1845. Designed
by Archibald Simpson in severe Gothic with a
square tower surmounted with a slender spire.
The interior, in contrast, is softened by the
warmth of the hammer-beam roof and
colourful stained glass windows, a triple lancet
First World War memorial by Oscar Paterson
and, adjacent to the pulpit, the Second World
War memorial by Gordon Webster. Only
Church of Scotland church in the centre of
Rothesay. Sunday Services: 11.00am and
6.30pm, 1st Sunday of the month
Open by arrangement with Mrs O'Neile,
telephone 01700 502900
CHURCH OF SCOTLAND ♿ wc ◔ **B**

TRINITY PARISH CHURCH,
ROTHESAY, ISLE OF BUTE

149 KILBRANDON KIRK, BALVICAR, ISLE OF SEIL

NM 758 155

On the B8003, 1 mile south of the
Balvicar turn-off

Kilbrandon Kirk was built in 1866 and
contains a beautiful set of five stained glass
windows – the work of Douglas Strachan.
The windows were commissioned by Miss
Mackinnon of Ardmaddy Castle in 1937 in
memory of her friend the Marchioness of
Breadalbane. Sunday Service: 10.00am,
except last Sunday 11.00am
Open all year
CHURCH OF SCOTLAND ♿ (two steps) wc ◔ **C**

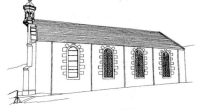

KILBRANDON KIRK, BALVICAR,
ISLE OF SEIL

150 SOUTH KNAPDALE PARISH CHURCH

NR 781 775

Achahoish, by Lochgilphead

Parish of South Knapdale was formed in 1734 and
churches were built at Achahoish and Inverneill
(now a ruin). Achahoish was completed 1775,
rectangular in plan with a square castellated tower
added in the 19th century. Ancient font basin from
St Columba's Cave. Sunday Services: May to
September 9.45am, October to March 12.30pm
Open by arrangement with Mr Brown, Inn Cottage,
Achahoish, telephone 01880 770269
CHURCH OF SCOTLAND ♿ wc 🚻 **C**

SOUTH KNAPDALE PARISH CHURCH

151 STRONE (ST COLUMBA'S)

NS 193 806

Shore Road, Strone

The square, battlemented tower and spire survive of the original 1858 church and
are used as a navigation aid for shipping. The rest of the building 1907-8 by Peter
MacGregor Chalmers using material from the old church. Stained glass by Stephen
Adam and Gordon Webster. United with Ardentinny in 1932.

Sunday Service: 10.30am

Open daily

CHURCH OF SCOTLAND ♿ wc 🚻 🍵 (after Service) **B**

152 TARBERT PARISH CHURCH

NR 863 686

Campbeltown Road, Tarbert

Built in 1886 on the site of an earlier
mission church dating from 1775 and
granted *quoad sacra* status in 1864.
Architects J McKissack and W G Rowan of
Glasgow. The building features an
imposing square tower rising over 100ft,
surmounted by a crown and lantern.
Stained glass windows and unusual roof
decoration. Eighteenth-century graveyard
within walking distance.

Sunday Service: 11.30am

Open April to September, 10.00am-5.30pm

CHURCH OF SCOTLAND 🍵 🚻 **B**

TARBERT PARISH CHURCH

153 MUCKAIRN PARISH CHURCH, TAYNUILT

NN 005 310

Built in 1829 the church stands adjacent to the ruins (1228) of Killespickerill, once the seat of the Bishop of Argyll. Two stones of antiquity are built into the walls of the present church. Tombstones from the 14th century can be seen in the graveyard. Linked with Kilchrenan and Dalavich.

Sunday Service: 11.30am

Open during daylight hours

CHURCH OF SCOTLAND ⓦⓒ ⓐ 📖

MUCKAIRN PARISH CHURCH, TAYNUILT

154 HEYLIPOL CHURCH, TIREE

NM 964 432

Barrapol, Tiree

The distinctiveness of Heylipol church or Eaglais na Mointeach – the Church of the Moss – is enhanced by its location at a crossroads in a stretch of open country. Built 1902 by architect William MacKenzie of Oban, in cruciform Gothic with a bell-tower over the porch. Sunday Services: 11.30pm and 6.00pm (alternating with Kirkapol Church)

Open at all times. Information on a Tiree pilgrimage route linking ancient and modern ecclesiastical sites can be obtained from the Tiree Heritage Society, c/o Miss Fiona MacKinnon, Lodge Farm, Kirkapol, Tiree PA77 6TW

CHURCH OF SCOTLAND ⓦⓒ

HEYLIPOL CHURCH, TIREE

155 KIRKAPOL CHURCH, TIRE

NM 041 468

Kirkapol, Gott Bay, Tiree

The current church of Kirkapol (Norse for 'Church Town') is a continuing witness to the Christian faith that stretches back to Columban times. Built in 1842 by architect-contractor Peter MacNab as a simple square box with galleries on three sides focused on a central pulpit. Some of the granite came from the same quarry as that for the Skerryvore lighthouse. Inside, the focus is the box pulpit of 1893 at the centre of the north wall. Sunday Services: 11.30pm and 6.00pm (alternating with Heylipol Church)

Open at all times

CHURCH OF SCOTLAND wc **B**

KIRKAPOL CHURCH, TIREE

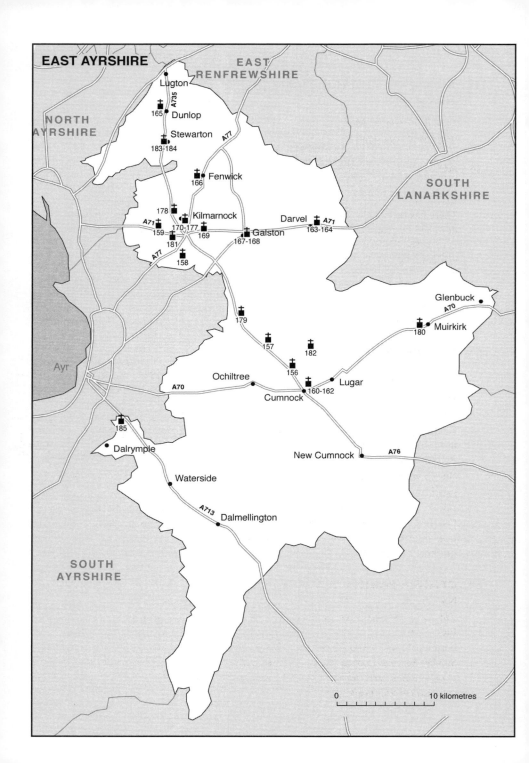

EAST AYRSHIRE

Local Representative: Miss Joan Fish, 31 Oaklands Avenue, Irvine
(*telephone* 01294 272654)

156 AUCHINLECK PARISH CHURCH

NS 552 216
Church Hill
There has been a church on this site since the 12th century. The present building, designed by James Ingram, was begun in 1833 and was funded by the Boswell family. The bell tower, designed by Robert Ingram, was added 1897. The interior was completely rebuilt after a fire in 1938. Organ by Hill, Norman & Beard. James Chrystal, a Moderator of the Church of Scotland, served as Minister for over 60 years. In the churchyard is the Boswell Aisle of 1754. Sunday Service: 11.15am
Open by arrangement, telephone 01290 422946
CHURCH OF SCOTLAND ♿ WC ⊘ **C**

157 CATRINE PARISH CHURCH

NS 528 260
Chapel Brae, Catrine; B713, off A76
Dumfries–Kilmarnock, between Mauchline and
Auchinleck
Charming church, built as a chapel of ease
in 1792, financed by Sir Claud Alexander of
Ballochmyle. It was established as a parish
church when Catrine was made a *quoad sacra*
parish in 1871. Major renovations in 1874,

CATRINE PARISH CHURCH

1960, 1992 and 2003. Stained glass. Harrison & Harrison pipe organ 1883. Overlooking Catrine in the river Ayr valley. Sunday Service: 10.00am
Open by arrangement, telephone Mr McIlvean 01290 551521
CHURCH OF SCOTLAND ♿ WC ⊘ **A**

158 CRAIGIE PARISH CHURCH

NS 427 323
Three miles from Prestwick Airport, off A77 (2 miles along Tarbolton Road)
Pleasant traditional country kirk built 1776. Remains of previous church c.1580, but the site was occupied by a church from medieval times.
Sunday Service: 12.00 noon first and third Sundays
Open by arrangement, telephone Mrs J Morris 01563 860283
CHURCH OF SCOTLAND ♿

CRAIGIE PARISH CHURCH

CROSSHOUSE PARISH CHURCH

159 CROSSHOUSE PARISH CHURCH

NS 395 384

25 Kilmarnock Road

Designed by Bruce and Sturrock, the church was built 1882 in red sandstone with a 60-ft steeple over the front door. Stained glass windows on all sides with a rose window on the rear elevation. Traditional layout to seat 500. Manual pipe organ with pedal board in the chancel has a beautiful sound. The church is the focal point of the parish. Sunday Service: 11.00am

Open weekends and by arrangement with Session Clerk, telephone 01563 535975

CHURCH OF SCOTLAND ♿ wc ✆ ⛪ ⛪

160 OLD CUMNOCK OLD CHURCH

NS 568 202

The Square, Cumnock

Church website: www.e-ayrshire.co.uk/local/oldcumnock

Commanding a prominent position in the square of this old market town, the church was built in 1866 through the patronage of the Marquess of Bute and the Bute family seats remain in the Memorial Chapel. Organ 1966. Mosaic of Jesus walking on the water by James Harrigan. Bell in vestibule was cast in 1697 by Quinus de Vesscher of Rotterdam, and was used in the two churches which preceded the present building. Services: Sunday 11.30am; on days of opening 12.30pm; plus Friday 12.30pm

Open July and August, Tuesday and Fridays 12.00 noon-4.00pm, Thursdays 11.00am-2.00pm

CHURCH OF SCOTLAND ♿ wc ✆ ☕ (at Words of Wisdom opposite church, closed on Wednesday) **B**

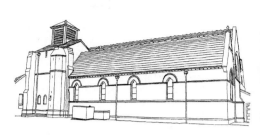

OLD CUMNOCK OLD CHURCH

ST JOHN THE EVANGELIST, CUMNOCK

161 ST JOHN THE EVANGELIST, CUMNOCK

NS 572 196

92 Glaisnock Road, Cumnock

Rare Scottish example of the work of William Burges, 1882, for the Marquess of Bute, and the first ecclesiastical building in Scotland to be lit by electricity. Lush feast of painted surfaces, rich furniture, glorious stained glass and an altarpiece by J F Bentley and N J Westlake. Services: Saturday 6.00pm, Sunday 11.45am

Open by arrangement with Parish Priest, telephone 01290 421031

ROMAN CATHOLIC wc ⏾ **B**

162 CUMNOCK CONGREGATIONAL CHURCH

NS 566 203

4 Auchinleck Road, Cumnock

Church website: www.cumnockcongregational.co.uk

The Church began with twelve members in 1838. The present building is situated beside the River Lugar at the entrance to Woodroad Park. This friendly, compact sandstone church was dedicated in 1883. The first ever Labour Member of Parliament, Keir Hardie, served on the Diaconate. Impressive 2-manual organ with eleven ranks of pipes. Sunday Services: 11.00am and 6.30pm

Open by arrangement with Mr Mitchell, telephone 01290 421982

CONGREGATIONAL wc ⏾ **C**

163 DARVEL PARISH CHURCH

NS 563 375

Hastings Square

The church is prominently set in the centre of the village
square, adjacent to the memorial to Sir Alexander
Fleming, the discoverer of penicillin. Designed by Robert
S Ingram and built 1887-8 in Early English style with a
tower and spire 130 feet high. The Sanctuary has a nave,
transept, aisles and a back gallery with woodwork of
pitch pine. The pulpit of carved oak is particularly
handsome and incorporates a Forster and Andrews pipe
organ and backed by a triple lancet stained glass window.
In the east wall is the Morton of Gowanbank memorial
stained glass window of 1958. Sunday Service 11.00am

Open by arrangement, telephone 01560 322924

CHURCH OF SCOTLAND ♿ w ☞ **B**

DARVEL PARISH CHURCH

164 OUR LADY OF THE VALLEY, DARVEL

NS 563 374

4 West Donington Street, Darvel

Church website: www.saintsophias.fsnet.co.uk

Church built by seceders in 1874 and closed in 1927.
Various users of the building, *eg* Girl Guides, until early
1950s when it again lay empty. Purchased in mid 1960s
by Darvel Parish Church and used as a church hall before
being sold to the Catholic community and opened by
Bishop Maurice Taylor on 25 November 1984.

Services: Wednesday 10.00am; Saturday 10.00am

Open by arrangement, telephone Mr A Dougherty
01560 320346

ROMAN CATHOLIC w

OUR LADY OF THE
VALLEY, DARVEL

165 DUNLOP PARISH CHURCH

NS 405 494

Main Street, Dunlop

A Christian site since the 13th century, the present church dates from 1835, though
the sculptured stonework of the Dunlop Aisle, 1641, was preserved. Magnificent
collection of stained glass by Gordon Webster. Beside the church is Clandeboyes
Hall, 1641, built as a school. Built onto the back of Clandeboyes is the early 17th-
century monumental tomb of Hans Hamilton, first Protestant minister of Dunlop.
Sunday Service: 11.00am

Open Sunday 2.00-4.00pm, June to September

CHURCH OF SCOTLAND w ♔ ▣ ☕ **B** (church) **A** (tomb and hall)

DUNLOP PARISH CHURCH

FENWICK PARISH CHURCH

166 FENWICK PARISH CHURCH

NS 465 435

Kirkton Road, Fenwick

Built 1643 in the shape of a Greek cross, with four arms of equal length. Features of note include outside stairs to Rowallan loft with the coat of arms of the Mures of Rowallan above the door, crowstepped gables and 'the jougs' on the south wall. Several Covenanting artefacts, including the battleflag of the Fenwick Covenanters. Walled graveyard contains several notable graves and monuments.

Sunday Service: 11.00am

Open for half an hour after morning worship, or by arrangement
with the Minster, telephone 01560 600217

CHURCH OF SCOTLAND   ♿ wc (in Hall) wc ② 📖 **A**

167 GALSTON PARISH CHURCH

NS 500 367

Cross Street, Galston

Church website: www. galstonparish.org.uk

Present church, designed by John Brash of Glasgow, erected 1809 on site of Christian worship since 1252. Third church since Reformation. Spire 120feet. Chancel added 1912 and 3-manual pipe organ by J J Binns 1913. Stained glass windows the work of Oscar Paterson, a contemporary of Charles Rennie Macintosh. Full restoration of church building completed in 1999. Floodlit since 2000. Ministers include Dr George Smith, great-grandfather of Robert Louis Stevenson and mentioned by Robert Burns in 'The Holy Fair' (grave on north side of church). Also Rev Robert Stirling, inventor of the Stirling Engine. Gravestone of Andrew Richmond, killed by Graham of Claverhouse, on south porch door along with a memorial to five Covenanters. Sunday Service: 11.00am

Open by arrangement, telephone Mrs Ian Thomson 01563 820623

CHURCH OF SCOTLAND   ♿ ② 🍴 ☕ **B**

168 ST SOPHIA, GALSTON

NS 504 365
Bentinck Street, Galston
Church website: www.saintsophias.fsnet.co.uk
Constructed 1885-6, architect Sir R Rowand Anderson, the church is a distinctive
building freely based on Hagia Sophia in Istanbul. At the behest of Lord Bute,
who commissioned the church, Anderson, and possibly Weir Schultz, brought to
Galston this dark brick echo of the Byzantine Empire.
Services: Sunday 11.30am, Monday 10.00am
Open by arrangement, telephone Mr T Heggan 01563 821587
ROMAN CATHOLIC ♿ (disabled access available on request) wc

169 ST PAUL'S ROMAN CATHOLIC, HURLFORD

NS 458 370
Galston Road, Hurlford
The church is a yellow brick building
dating from the 1850s. Gothic arches
feature in the light and bright
interior. Services: Sunday 10.30am,
Friday 10.00am
Open by arrangement, telephone 01563 525963
ROMAN CATHOLIC ⓘ wc 🍷 A

ST PAUL'S ROMAN CATHOLIC, HURLFORD

170 OLD HIGH KIRK, KILMARNOCK

NS 430 382
Soulis Street, Kilmarnock
Church website: www.old-high-kirk.org.uk
Kilmarnock's oldest church building built 1732
of local stone by the Hunter Brothers to a
design adapted from St Martin's-in-the-Fields,
London. Austere exterior contrasts with
pleasing interior enhanced by unique set of
23 stained glass windows by W & J J Keir,
glaziers to Glasgow Cathedral. Graveyard with
tombs including John Wilson, publisher of
Robert Burns' first book of poems.
Sunday Service: 11.00am
Open July and August 2.00-4.00pm, or by
arrangement, telephone Mr G Thomson
01563 526064
CHURCH OF SCOTLAND ⓘ 📖 wc A

OLD HIGH KIRK, KILMARNOCK

171 LAIGH WEST HIGH KIRK, KILMARNOCK

NS 428 379

John Dickie Street, Kilmarnock

Body of the church by Robert Johnstone 1802.
Enlarged 1831 with later 19th-century session room.
Major refurbishment 1996 by W I Munro Architects,
winning 1997 Civic Trust Award for part of town
centre regeneration. Interesting monuments and stained
glass. Covenanters' graves in adjacent kirkyard.
Close to bus and rail stations. Sunday Services:
11.00am, also 9.30am June to August
Open Monday, Wednesday, Friday and Saturday 12.00 noon-
2.00pm. Other times, telephone 01563 528051
CHURCH OF SCOTLAND ♿ ② 📖 wc **A**

LAIGH WEST HIGH KIRK,
KILMARNOCK

172 HOLY TRINITY CHURCH, KILMARNOCK

NS 426 377

Portland Road, Kilmarnock, junction with Dundonald Road
Church website: www.copinger.org.uk/htk/

The nave to a design by James Wallace 1857, with
chancel and sanctuary by Sir George Gilbert Scott
1876. Wall and ceiling murals in the chancel; stained
glass. Sunday Services: 9.15am Holy Communion,
11.00am Sung Eucharist, 6.00pm Evensong; Matins
11.00am, first Sunday if not a festival
Open daily (except when Rector is on holiday)
SCOTTISH EPISCOPAL ② 📖 **B**

HOLY TRINITY CHURCH, KILMARNOCK

173 HENDERSON PARISH CHURCH, KILMARNOCK

NS 431 380

London Road, Kilmarnock

Brilliantly individual Arts & Crafts treatment of Gothic motifs
by Thomas Smellie, Kilmarnock, completed in 1907. Very tall
tower above church built on rising ground, with halls below.
Carillon of bells 1950. Fine Norman & Beard 3-manual organ
restored in 1987. Stained glass windows by Gordon Webster,
and, in side chapel, by Wendy Robertson 1987. On Burns
Heritage Trail, leading to Dean Castle Country Park (open all
year). Church in town centre, adjacent to Grand Hall, Palace
Theatre and bus station. Sunday Services: 9.45am and 11.00am
Open by arrangement, telephone Mr J Neil 01563 528212
CHURCH OF SCOTLAND ♿ ② 🍴 📖 ☕ wc **B**

HENDERSON PARISH
CHURCH, KILMARNOCK

174 OUR LADY OF MOUNT CARMEL, KILMARNOCK

NS 428 401

Kirkton Road, Onthank, Kilmarnock

Opened in 1963, Our Lady of Mount Carmel
serves the areas of Onthank, Altonhill and
Wardneuk in Kilmarnock as well as the
villages of Kilmaurs and Fenwick. A large
church, possibly its most distinctive features
are its stained glass windows and the figure
of Christ Crucified.

OUR LADY OF MOUNT CARMEL, KILMARNOCK

Services: Saturday 6.30pm; Sunday 10.00am
Open by arrangement with the Parish Priest, telephone 01563 523822
ROMAN CATHOLIC ⊘ wc

175 ST MARNOCK'S PARISH CHURCH, KILMARNOCK

NS 427 377

St Marnock Street, Kilmarnock

Perpendicular Gothic, rectangular plan 6-bay church
with centrally placed tower on north gable end, by
John Ingram 1836. Fine carillon of bells. Three-
manual pipe organ 1872, painted organ screen.
Extensive restoration programme completed in 1997.
In centre of town with easy access from bus and
railway station. Sunday Service: 11.00am
(and 9.30am June to mid August)
*Open by arrangement, telephone the Session Clerk
01563 520210. E-mail: jwrca@globalnet.co.uk*
CHURCH OF SCOTLAND ⊘ ⍭ ⬚ ⬤ (free) wc **B**

ST MARNOCK'S PARISH
CHURCH, KILMARNOCK

176 ST MATTHEW'S, KILMARNOCK

NS 442 388

Grassyards Road, Kilmarnock

Modern building built in 1977 to have a dual
purpose of both hall and church combined.
Services: Saturday 6.30pm; Sunday 9.30am
and 11.00am; Monday, Tuesday, Friday and
Saturday 10.00am; Wednesday 8.15am
Open for services
ROMAN CATHOLIC ♿ wc

ST MATTHEW'S, KILMARNOCK

177 WINTON PLACE E U CONGREGATIONAL CHURCH, KILMARNOCK

NS 426 377

Dundonald Road

Founder church of the Evangelical Union, started in 1843 by the Rev James Morrison. The present grey sandstone building, designed by James Ingram, was built in 1860. Three stained glass windows behind the pulpit by Keir of Irvine, 1890, restored 1995. Three-manual pipe organ by James Conacher. Sunday Service: 11.00am

Open by arrangement, telephone Dr Barclay 01292 313139

CONGREGATIONAL wc B

WINTON PLACE E U
CONGREGATIONAL CHURCH, KILMARNOCK

178 ST MAUR'S GLENCAIRN PARISH CHURCH, KILMAURS

NS 415 408

On A735

The church at Kilmaurs was in the possession of Kelso Abbey as early as 1170. In 1413 the present foundation was endowed by Sir William Cunninghame as a collegiate church. Rebuilt by Robert S Ingram 1888 in a cruciform shape. Stained glass, 20th-century, including a window by Roland Mitton of Livingston, and three rose windows. The clock tower holds the original bell inscribed 'Michael Burgerhuys Me Fecit 1618'. Glencairn Aisle adjacent to the church with sculptured mural 1600 commissioned by James 7th Earl of Glencairn, in memory of the Earl and Countess of Glencairn, and worked by David Scougal, mason and burgess.

Sunday Service: 11.00am

Open by arrangement, telephone Rev John Urquhart 01563 538289

CHURCH OF SCOTLAND B

ST MAUR'S GLENCAIRN PARISH CHURCH, KILMAURS

179 MAUCHLINE PARISH CHURCH

NS 498 272

Loudoun Street, Mauchline; junction of B743 with A76
Church website: www.mauchlineparish.org.uk
Present church by William Alexander 1829 stands on site of
St Michael's Church founded in 13th century. Single bell cast
in 1742. Willis pipe organ 1888 rebuilt in 1980. Associations
with Covenanters and Robert Burns, many contemporaries
of whom are buried here. Sunday Service: 11.00am
Open July and August, Tuesday and Wednesday 2.00-4.00pm;
or by arrangement with Session Clerk 01290 550356.
Mauchline Holy Fair held in late May
CHURCH OF SCOTLAND 🦽 ⓘ 📖 ⓟ wc B

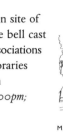

MAUCHLINE PARISH CHURCH

180 ST THOMAS THE APOSTLE, MUIRKIRK

NS 699 278

Wellwood Street, Muirkirk
The material for this church, built in 1906, was
transported from Belgium. Sunday Service: 10.00am
Open by arrangement with Parish Priest,
telephone 01290 421031
ROMAN CATHOLIC ⓟ

ST THOMAS THE APOSTLE, MUIRKIRK

181 RICCARTON PARISH CHURCH

NS 428 364

Old Street, Riccarton, Kilmarnock
Classical square-plan church of 1825 by John Richmond with the chancel added in
1910. Beautiful War Memorial window of 1919 in memory of those of the
congregation and parish who gave their lives in the Great War. A former Minister,
the Rev Alexander Moodie, mentioned by Burns in 'The Twa Herds' and 'The
Holy Fair', is buried in the churchyard. Sunday Service: 11.00am
Open by arrangement with John Henderson, telephone 01563 537982
CHURCH OF SCOTLAND wc ⓟ B

182 SORN PARISH CHURCH

NS 550 268

Main Street, Sorn
A rather splendid edifice, quietly assured, built in 1656 and
much reconstructed in 1826. Outside stairs to three galleries.
Jougs on the west wall. East wall memorial to George Wood,
last Covenanter to die 1688. Sunday Service: 10.00am
Open by arrangement, telephone Miss McKerrow 01290 551256
CHURCH OF SCOTLAND ⓘ wc B

SORN PARISH CHURCH

183 OUR LADY AND ST JOHN'S, STEWARTON

NS 417 457

69 Lainshaw Street, Stewarton

Church website: www.e-ayrshire.co.uk/churchofourlady

Our Lady and St John's was built in 1974 and functions as church and hall. Modern stations of the Cross by a local arts teacher. Services: Tuesday, Wednesday, Friday 11.00am; Monday, Thursday 10.00am; Saturday Vigil 5.00pm; Sunday 11.45am

Open by arrangement with the Sisters, telephone 01560 483322

ROMAN CATHOLIC ⏺ wc

OUR LADY AND ST JOHN'S, STEWARTON

184 ST COLUMBA'S PARISH CHURCH, STEWARTON

NS 419 457

1 Kirk Glebe, Stewarton

Built in 1696, renovated in 1775, and widened in 1825 with later additions. Bell-tower. Lainshaw Loft used for smaller services. New and restored windows installed for tercentenary in 1996. Beside the mini-roundabout at the south end of Stewarton. Sunday Service: 11.00am

Open by arrangement, telephone the Minister 01560 482453

CHURCH OF SCOTLAND ♿ ⏺ 📖 📗 wc **B**

ST COLUMBA'S PARISH CHURCH, STEWARTON

185 ST FRANCIS XAVIER, WATERSIDE

NS 445 080

On A713, 10 miles south-east of Ayr

Brick-built church with red sandstone dressings. The church was opened 1895 to cater for the workers of Waterside ironworks. At its peak, the ironworks was one of the largest in Ayrshire and is now being developed as an interpretative centre for the industrial heritage of Ayrshire. Saturday: Vigil Mass 6.00pm

Open only for Services

ROMAN CATHOLIC ♿ wc

ST FRANCIS XAVIER, WATERSIDE

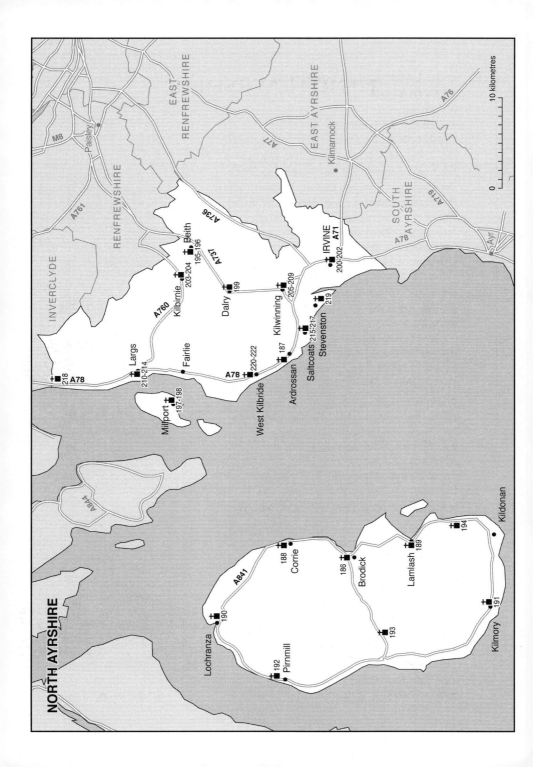

NORTH AYRSHIRE

Local Representative: Mr Norman MacGilvray, 20 Well Street, West Kilbride (*telephone* 01294 829221)

186 BRODICK CHURCH, ISLE OF ARRAN
NS 012 359
Knowe Road, Brodick (1 mile north of pier, turn left at sports park)
The present church was built in 1910 from local red sandstone. The pulpit, built by local craftsmen, is an exact replica of John Knox's pulpit. Two stained glass windows are in memory of church member Bethia Torrance who died in 1958. Originally the church hall was Bennecarrigan Free Church on the west side of the island. Since it was no longer in use it was transported in March 1950 alongside Brodick Church as a hall. Sunday Service: 10.45am
Open by arrangement, telephone
Mr Hannah 01770 302248
CHURCH OF SCOTLAND ♿ wc ✆ **B**

BRODICK CHURCH, ISLE OF ARRAN

187 ST PETER IN CHAINS, ARDROSSAN
NS 233 421
1 South Crescent, Ardrossan
Designed by Jack Coia and opened in 1938, St Peter in Chains is probably the most academic of this period. The church, in reddish facing brick, has a high west gable as at St Columba, Hopehill Road, Glasgow and a tower to the right reminiscent of Stockholm Town Hall. Striking brick main doorway with stone keystone; the door feature continues to the gable roof and ends in a small well-detailed cross. Services: Monday to Saturday Mass 9.30am, 7.00pm; Saturday Vigil Mass 6.30pm; Sunday 10.00am, 12.00 noon and 6.30pm
Open daily 9.00am-7.30pm
ROMAN CATHOLIC ✆ **A**

ST PETER IN CHAINS, ARDROSSAN

188 CORRIE CHURCH, ISLE OF ARRAN

NS 024 437

Six miles north of Brodick

Designed by J J Burnet 1887 as 'one of a family of long, low friendly churches'.
Constructed in red sandstone in an early Gothic style with a simple stone belfry
and wooden porch. An unusual baptismal font
is set into the arch and church wall and rush-
bottomed chairs take the place of pews. Lit
by circular candelabra. Two tapestries by Mrs
Sandeman and two recently installed stained
glass windows by Richard Leclerc. Sunday
Service: 12.00 noon

Open by arrangement, telephone the Session Clerk,
E Stevenson 01770 810268, Mr McConnachie
01770 810246 or Mrs Pringle 01770 810210

CHURCH OF SCOTLAND [WC] **B**

CORRIE CHURCH, ISLE OF ARRAN

189 LAMLASH PARISH CHURCH, ISLE OF ARRAN

NS 026 309

Shore Road, Lamlash, Isle of Arran

Church website: http://homepage.ntlworld.com/morritek/lamlashchurch/index.htm

A massive campanile tower over 90ft high sits above this Gothic-style, red
sandstone building by H & D Barclay 1886. The church was built by 12th Duke
of Hamilton to replace an earlier building of 1773. Boarded, barrel-vaulted ceiling
and carved, wooden tripartite Gothic sedilia. The tower hosts a peal of nine bells
played every Sunday before service, the largest
peal still existing, cast for a Scottish church in a
Scottish foundry. Seven stained glass windows
by Anning Bell, Meiklejohn, Gordon Webster
and Christian Shaw; all other windows are hand
painted, German cathedral glass. Pipe organ,
William Hill, Norman and Beard 1934. In the
front grounds are an ancient cross and baptismal
font from the old monastery on Holy Isle in
Lamlash Bay. Major restoration programme
begun 1997. Sunday Service: from start to end
of BST, 10.00am, otherwise 11.45am

Open by arrangement. See church notice board for
information, or contact Captain J L Davidson, Rock
Cottage, Cordon, Lamlash, telephone 01770 600787

CHURCH OF SCOTLAND [&] [?] [📁] [WC] [🍴] **A**

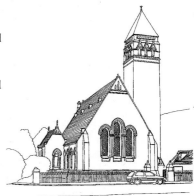

LAMLASH PARISH CHURCH, ISLE OF ARRAN

ST BRIDE'S, LOCHRANZA,
ISLE OF ARRAN

190 ST BRIDE'S, LOCHRANZA, ISLE OF ARRAN

NR 937 503

At T-junction in centre of Lochranza

Church website: http://homepage.ntlworld.com/morritek/lamlashchurch/lochranza.htm

The present church was rebuilt in 1712 on the site of the previous church of 1654. A beautiful, simple and attractive church featuring a circular stained glass window in the east gable depicting the Ship of the Gospel sailing through the troubled Sea of Life. This window and the unusual lych gate were given by Miss Edith Kerr in memory of the Rev John Colville, minister here 1922-31. Sunday Service: 10.30am

Key available from Lochranza Field Centre 01770 830637 or May Fenton 01770 830222

CHURCH OF SCOTLAND ♿ wc ☕ **A**

191 KILMORY PARISH CHURCH, ISLE OF ARRAN

NR 700 449

Present church built 1880 over previous building 1765. Small, delightful church with plain windows surrounded by red-coloured stained glass, providing a warm ambience. Situated in village of Kilmory, turn right after Creamery on road from Whiting Bay. Sunday Service: 10.00am

Open by arrangement, telephone Mrs Mairi Duff 01770 870305

CHURCH OF SCOTLAND **B**

192 PIRNMILL CHURCH, ISLE OF ARRAN

NR 873 443

On main street, at the north end of the village

Church website: http://homepage.ntlworld.com/morritek/lamlashchurch/pirnmill.htm

Known locally as 'the tin kirk', the building previously belonged to the Free Church of Scotland. A small and friendly congregation which warmly invites visitors to join them for worship. Access is by a footpath through a field – it looks worse than it is! Sunday Service: 12.00 noon

Open for services

CHURCH OF SCOTLAND **B**

193 ST MOLIOS, SHISKINE

NR 910 295

On B880, 1 mile north of junction with A841
Church website: http://homepage.ntlworld.com/
morritek/lamlashchurch/shiskine.htm

Known locally as 'The Red Kirk' because the
local Machrie sandstone of its construction is
of a warm, red hue, this church was built in
1889 to a design by J J Burnet. The tower
contains a single bell. Set into the west wall
of the tower is a carved stone graveslab,

ST MOLIOS, SHISKINE

possibly of a 13th-century abbot taken from Clauchen graveyard. The north gable
has a double window in Norman style with Celtic motifs. A small wooden carving
of St Molios, who lived as a hermit on Holy Island, is set into a bench end on the
south side of the sanctuary. Sunday Service: 11.45am in summer, 10.00am in winter
Open during daylight hours
CHURCH OF SCOTLAND   ♿ wc ② ☕ **B**

194 ST MARGARET OF SCOTLAND, ISLE OF ARRAN

NS 047 273

On main road just inside northern boundary of Whiting Bay
Church website: www.scotland-anglican.org/argyll

Built *c*.1960 for the Free Church; acquired (after a period as a holiday home) with
a legacy from Elsie Wood, widow of Canon Charles Wood; dedicated 1995.
Friendly ambience. Stained glass window by Eilidh Keith of Glasgow. Eagle
lectern from St Andrew's-on-the-Green, Glasgow, and a Slavonic (possibly Serbian)
icon. Sunday Service: 11.00am Holy Communion (1970 Liturgy on 2nd Sunday);
Evensong 4th Sunday 6.00pm March to September, 3.00pm October to February
Open by arrangement with the Minister, telephone 01770 700225
SCOTTISH EPISCOPAL ♿ wc ☕ (after Sunday service) 📖 **B**

195 BEITH HIGH CHURCH

NS 350 539

Kirk Road, Beith

Built in 1807 and extended in 1885. Gothic T-plan
kirk dominated by the tall 5-stage tower. Stained
glass by Gordon Webster. Harrison & Harrison pipe
organ 1885. From Beith bypass along Barrmill Road
to Kirk Road. Sunday Service: 10.30am. Joint service
with Beith Trinity during the month of August
Open by arrangement, telephone 01505 502686
CHURCH OF SCOTLAND ♿ ② ⛪ 📖 ⛩ wc **B**

BEITH HIGH CHURCH

196 BEITH TRINITY CHURCH

NS 351 544

Wilson Street, Beith

Built 1883, architect Robert Baldie. The chief
external feature is a graceful octagonal tower.
Interior destroyed by fire 1917, rebuilt 1926. Gothic
style, with rectangular nave, Gothic arched chancel
and one transept on the east side. Stained glass by
John C Hall & Co. Organ 1937 by Hill, Norman &
Beard. Sunday Service: 11.00am. Joint service with
Beith High during the month of July
Open by arrangement, telephone 01505 502131
CHURCH OF SCOTLAND [wc] ⊘

BEITH TRINITY CHURCH

197 THE CATHEDRAL OF THE ISLES, CUMBRAE

NS 165 561

College Street, Millport, Isle of Cumbrae
Church website: www.scotland.anglican.org/argyll
Cathedral, college and cloister by William
Butterfield 1851. A Tractarian church built by 6th
Earl of Glasgow. Peal of bells, organ, stained glass
by William Wailes and Hardman. Visitors welcome
to picnic in the grounds. Ferry from Largs and bus
to Millport. Sunday Service: 11.00am Sung
Eucharist; other times see notice board in porch
Open daily
SCOTTISH EPISCOPAL 🏠 [wc] **A**

THE CATHEDRAL OF THE ISLES, CUMBRAE

198 CUMBRAE PARISH CHURCH

NS 160 550

Bute Terrace, Millport
The church, with battlemented tower, pinnacles and
clock, was erected in 1837. There are two very
interesting grotesques, from the old Kirkton Church,
in the chancel also a lintel with inscribed Hebrew
lettering. Flower Festival summer 2007. Services:
Sunday 11.00am, Thursday 9.30am
Open by arrangement, Mr McCubbin,
telephone 01475 530393
CHURCH OF SCOTLAND [wc] ⊘ **B**

CUMBRAE PARISH CHURCH

199 ST MARGARET'S PARISH CHURCH, DALRY

NS 291 496

The Cross, Dalry

Church website: www.btinternet.com/ ~stmargarets_church

Landmark Victorian Gothic building (David Thomson 1871-73). Inventive 159ft broach spire 'worthy of the many tasks thrust upon it'; the whole building is a 'powerful, carefully handled composition'. The restored interior (with good acoustics) of the early 1950s presents 'a space of deep solemnity enhanced' by Beith-made pulpit, table, lectern and stained glass by Guthrie & Wells, Charles Payne and C L Davidson, plus the only decent amount of

ST MARGARET'S PARISH CHURCH, DALRY

Munich glass and only Francis Hemony bell (1661) in a UK church. Three-manual Blackett & Howden organ (1899) moved here in 1953. Communion silver of 1618. Bronze sundial and some interesting stones in Kirkyard. Kirk bears the name of the original medieval dedication: St Margaret of Antioch (see modern Rona Moody window), the only such in Scotland. In the vicinity – Blair House (may be viewed from outside); Cleeves Cove (interesting limestone cave system). Sunday Services: 10.30am all year round

Open by arrangement, telephone 01294 833135. Also Ayrshire Doors Open Day

CHURCH OF SCOTLAND 📖 wc **B**

200 IRVINE OLD PARISH CHURCH

NS 322 387

Kirkgate

The church, 1774 by David Muir, is the third to occupy the site. A large classical building with round-headed windows lighting the gallery. The clock in the 6-stage octagonal steeple was presented by Irvine Volunteers in 1803. The stained glass windows are a fine example of Keir brothers work. The graveyard contains fine classical monuments. Sunday Service: 11.00am

Open by arrangement with the Minister, telephone 01294 279265

CHURCH OF SCOTLAND ♿ wc 🔊 **A**

IRVINE OLD PARISH CHURCH

ST ANDREW'S PARISH CHURCH
(FERGUSON MEMORIAL), IRVINE

201 ST ANDREW'S PARISH CHURCH (FERGUSON MEMORIAL), IRVINE

NS 325 399

Caldon Road junction with Oaklands Avenue, Irvine

St Andrew's was gifted in 1957 to commemorate the centenary of the death of John Ferguson, founder of the Ferguson bequest. Architect Rennie & Bramble of Saltcoats. Stained glass windows by Mary Wood 1957, Ann Marie Docherty 1998 and Stained Glass Design Partnership of Milngavie 2000. The congregation shares the church with the local Scottish Episcopalian congregation who built on a chapel/meeting room, containing tapestry by Vampboulles, and coffee lounge in 1981. Architect R L Dunlop of Troon. Sunday Services: Scottish Episcopal 9.30am; Church of Scotland 11.15am

Open Tuesdays 9.45-11.00am October to May

CHURCH OF SCOTLAND 🦽 ② wc ☕

202 FULLARTON PARISH CHURCH, IRVINE

NS 316 389

Church Street, Marress Roundabout

Church website: www.fullartonchurch.co.uk

Built 1838 and designed by Ingram of Kilmarnock. School of 1640 now forms part of the halls. Vestry of 1907. Two stained glass windows of 1958 by G Maille & Son of London depicting 'The Good Shepherd' and 'Christ Blessing Little Children' in memory of the Rev John Paterson, much-loved Minister from 1903-37. Memorial to James Montgomery, Christian poet and hymn writer. Digital organ by the Bradford Computing Organ Co. 1994. Sunday Services: 11.00am and 6.30pm

Nearby Fullarton Centre Café open Monday, Tuesday, Thursday and Friday 10.00am-12.00 noon and 2.00-4.00pm. Closed July and August. Church open by arrangement with the Minister 01294 279909 or the Session Clerk 01299 216942

CHURCH OF SCOTLAND 🦽 wc ② ☕ **B**

203   THE AULD KIRK OF KILBIRNIE

NS 315 536
Dalry Road, Kilbirnie
Church website: www.//members.tripod.co.uk/auldkirk
A pre-Reformation church on the site of 6th-century cell dedicated to St Brendan
of Clonfert. The nave dates from 1470 and the bell-tower from 1490. Glengarnock

aisle added 1597. Crawfurd aisle added
1642 with unique Renaissance-style
carving. Pulpit *c*.1620. At junction of
B780 and B777. Bus to Kilbirnie, rail to
Glengarnock. Sunday Service: 11.00am
Open July to August, weekdays 2.00–4.00pm
except Mondays. Other times, telephone
Mr J Lauchland 01505 683459
CHURCH OF SCOTLAND ♿ ⚲ 📘 wc A

THE AULD KIRK OF KILBIRNIE

204   ST COLUMBA'S, KILBIRNIE

NS 314 546
Glasgow Street
Church website: www.broster.org
The old church was built in 1843 and reconstructed
and enlarged 1903. The design of a sloping floor
and balcony is unusual. The balcony front is
French Fibre plasterwork. Table runner by Malcolm
Lochhead. Three-light window by Stephen Adam
in the hall which is the former Kilbirnie West
Church. Sunday Service: 11.15am
Open by arrangement, telephone the
Minister 01505 683342
CHURCH OF SCOTLAND ♿ wc ⚲

ST COLUMBA'S, KILBIRNIE

205   THE ABBEY CHURCH, KILWINNING

NS 303 433
Main Street, Kilwinning
Built in 1774 by John Garland and John Wright. The church is on the site of the
ruined abbey, founded in 1188, and replaced the first Reformation church built in
1590. The organ built by Foster & Anderson of Hull was first played in 1897 and
is highly regarded. The church has strong links with the Earls of Eglinton. Sunday
Services: 9.15am and 11.00am September to May; 10.00am June, July and August
Open by arrangement, telephone Mr J Muir, 30 Underwood, Kilwinning 01294 552929
CHURCH OF SCOTLAND ♿ 📘 ⚲

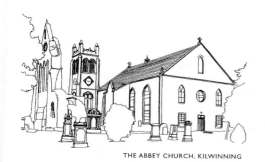

THE ABBEY CHURCH, KILWINNING

ERSKINE CHURCH, KILWINNING

206 ERSKINE CHURCH, KILWINNING

NS 303 434

Main Street, Kilwinning

Simple United Presbyterian style building, 1838, down a lane from Main Street. Pedimented open bellcote flanked by ancones. Gable finials. Pleasant restored interior with gallery. Sunday Service: 11.30am

Open by arrangement, telephone Mr Welsh 01294 554376

CHURCH OF SCOTLAND [♿] [wc] [?] **c**

207 FERGUSHILL CHURCH, KILWINNING

NS 337 430

Benslie Village, Kilwinning

Church extension for the mining community from Kilwinning Parish Church in 1879 to a plan prepared by William Railton of Kilmarnock. Attractive church with bell-tower. Fine views to Arran. Sunday Service: 10.00am

Open by arrangement, telephone

Mrs Borland 01294 850257

CHURCH OF SCOTLAND [wc]

FERGUSHILL CHURCH, KILWINNING

208 ST WININ'S, KILWINNING

NS 300 432

St Winning's Lane, Kilwinning

Church website: www.st-winins.com

Modern, functional building with basic decoration. Seats 400 and is well-used by the 700 or 800 congregation who attend weekend masses. Services: Saturday 6.30pm, Sunday 10.00am and 12.00 noon

Open by arrangement with Parish House, telephone 01294 552276

ROMAN CATHOLIC [♿] (side entrance) [?] [wc] (in Hall) [wc]

ST WININ'S, KILWINNING

MANSEFIELD TRINITY CHURCH, KILWINNING

209 MANSEFIELD TRINITY CHURCH, KILWINNING

NS 290 432

West Doura Way, Stevenston Road

The first church opened by the Church of Scotland in the new millennium.
Designed by architects James F Stephens, the building is multi-purpose and reflects
current thinking, being open, accessible, full of light and atmosphere.

Sunday Service: 11.00am October to June, 10.30am July to September

Open 10.00am-2.00pm Tuesday and Thursday, otherwise by arrangement
telephone 01294 550746

CHURCH OF SCOTLAND ♿ 🚻 ⓘ ☕

210 CLARK MEMORIAL CHURCH, LARGS

NS 202 593

Bath Street, Largs

Gifted by John Clark of the Anchor
Thread Mills, Paisley, and designed by
William Kerr of T G Abercrombie, Paisley
1892. Red sandstone from Locharbriggs
and Corsehill in Early English Gothic
style. Superb stained glass, all manufac-
tured in Glasgow at height of Arts &
Crafts movement. Hammer-beam roof.
Organ by 'Father' Willis 1892. Views of
the Clyde and Cumbraes. Services: Sunday
10.00am, Thursday 10.30am

Open daily 10.00am-4.00pm (except
Tuesdays). Viking Festival one week each
September

CHURCH OF SCOTLAND 🍵 📖 ⓘ 🚻 A

CLARK MEMORIAL CHURCH, LARGS

211 ST COLUMBA'S PARISH CHURCH, LARGS

NS 203 596

Gallowgate, Largs

Church website: www.largscolumba.com

The old parish church was replaced by the present building in 1892. It is a handsome structure by architects Henry Steele and Andrew Balfour, of red stone with a three-stage tower with spire and clock. Interesting carved octagonal oak pulpit and notable windows. 'Father' Willis organ 1892, generally regarded as one of the finest church instruments in Scotland. Memorial to General Sir Thomas MacDougall Brisbane, astronomer, soldier and Governor of New South Wales. Sunday Service: 11.00am

Open 10.00am–12.00 noon, Monday to Friday

CHURCH OF SCOTLAND   ♿   (by arrangement)   🔊   📖

🍽 (Saturdays June to September)   [wc]   **B**

ST COLUMBA'S PARISH CHURCH, LARGS

212 ST MARY'S STAR OF THE SEA, LARGS

NS 203 599

28 Greenock Road, Largs

A bright modern building opened in 1962. The architect was Mr A R Conlon of Reginald Fairlie & Sons. Features include a tapestry at the High Altar depicting Jesus and two disciples at Emmaus, eight stained glass panels above the main door, and a statue outside the main door of Our Lady, Star of the Sea, by eminent Scottish sculptor, Hew Lorimer. Services: Saturday Vigil 6.30pm, Sunday 9.00am and 11.30am

Open 8.30am–8.00pm in summer,

8.30am–3.30pm in winter

ROMAN CATHOLIC   ♿   🔊   [wc]   [wc]

ST MARY'S STAR OF THE SEA, LARGS

213   ST COLUMBA'S, LARGS

NS 201 603
Aubery Crescent
Church website: www.geocities.com/largschurch
Built in 1876 on land gifted by the
Brisbane family and the construction
funded by the Earl of Glasgow. Charming
and delicate exercise in the Early English
style by Ross and McBeth of Inverness.
Victorian stained glass, including a rose
window depicting a dove, symbol of the

ST COLUMBA'S, LARGS

Holy Spirit and St Columba. Memorials to the Brisbane and Boyle (Earls of
Glasgow) families and to the scientist Lord Kelvin. Embroidered kneelers made for
the centenary. Services: Sunday 8.00am, 11.00am, 6.30pm and Wednesday 10.00am
Open 9.00am-5.00pm daily except Friday
SCOTTISH EPISCOPAL [&] [wc] ② ☯ ♻ ☷ **B**

214   ST JOHN'S, LARGS

NS 201 593
Bath Street
Built as a Free Church in 1843 and named St
John's in 1900 after union of the Free and
United Presbyterian Churches. Designed by A J
Graham, the building is in the Romanesque style
with the tall tower at the north-west corner and
vestry to the south-west linked by an arcaded
narthex. Sunday Services: 11.00am and 6.30pm
Open by arrangement, telephone the Session Clerk,
Mr McGregor, 01475 686729
CHURCH OF SCOTLAND [&] ② **B**

ST JOHN'S, LARGS

215   ST BRENDAN'S, SALTCOATS

NS 247 430
63 Corrie Crescent
St Brendan's has a magnificent contemporary stained glass window depicting the
life of St Brendan and a unique crucifix,
designed locally and fabricated in steel.
Services: Saturday 6.30pm, Sunday
11.00am
Open by arrangement, telephone 01294 463483
ROMAN CATHOLIC [&] [wc] ②

ST BRENDAN'S, SALTCOATS

216 ST CUTHBERT'S PARISH CHURCH, SALTCOATS

NS 244 418

Caledonia Road, Saltcoats

Designed by Peter MacGregor Chalmers and
dedicated in 1908, the fourth building of the
congregation of Ardrossan Parish. The chancel
displays a marble reredos of the Last Supper. Sixteen
stained glass windows on the Life of Christ by
William Wilson 1947; two windows by Gordon
Webster 1976. Model of a French frigate of 1804,
by sailor William Dunlop, hangs in the church. He
made it as a thanksgiving for his surviving the
Napoleonic Wars when a cannonball narrowly
missed his hammock. Sunday Service: 11.15am
*Open by arrangement, telephone Mrs Hanlon
01294 466636*
CHURCH OF SCOTLAND ♿ wc ◔ **B**

ST CUTHBERT'S PARISH
CHURCH, SALTCOATS

217 NEW TRINITY PARISH CHURCH, SALTCOATS

NS 246 414

Chapelwell Street

Church website: www.newtrinity.co.uk

Congregation formed by the union of Erskine and
Landsborough Trinity Churches in 1993. The former
Erskine Church buildings of 1866 are used. The
building, designed by William Stewart, has a spire
and pinnacles above a polychrome Venetian Gothic
façade. Additional halls built 1970. Organ, Forster &
Andrews 1899. Four stained glass windows
depicting 'Music', 'The Good Shepherd', 'Dorcas'
and 'The Sower of the Seed'. Services: Sunday
11.15am, Thursday 10.30am
Open by arrangement, telephone 01294 602410
CHURCH OF SCOTLAND ♿ wc ◔ **C**

NEW TRINITY PARISH CHURCH,
SALTCOATS

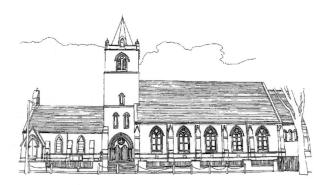

SKELMORLIE &
WEMYSS BAY

218   SKELMORLIE & WEMYSS BAY

NS 192 681

Shore Road, Skelmorlie

Gothic church with nave and chancel and a square tower, built 1895 and designed
by John Honeyman to replace a 'chapel of ease' of 1856. Free-standing wrought-
iron lamp by Charles Rennie Mackintosh, 1895, at the entrance. Stained glass by
Douglas Strachan ('Stilling the Storm'), Stephen Adam, Edward Burne Jones and
Charles E Kempe. Organ by Binns 1910. Sunday Services: 11.00am

Open Saturdays July and August 2.00-4.00pm, otherwise by arrangement with Minister
telephone 01475 520703

CHURCH OF SCOTLAND   🚹 wc wc ⓐ ⓘ **B** (Lamp **A**)

219   ST JOHN, STEVENSTON

NS 271 421

Hayocks Road, Stevenston

Church website: www.stjohnsrc.force9.co.uk

Built 1963 to designs by Mr Houston Jr. Features laminated trusses supporting the
roof and beautiful stained glass by M Gabriel Loire of Chartres representing
biblical scenes and St John the Evangelist. Brass baptismal font depicting a half
tree trunk sheltering a fawn: 'As the
deer longs for streams of water, so
my soul yearns for you, my God.'
Services: Saturday Vigil 6.30pm,
Sunday 11.00am, weekdays 10am
(subject to change)

Open by arrangement with the Parish
Priest, telephone 01294 463225

ROMAN CATHOLIC 🚹 wc ⓐ

ST JOHN, STEVENSTON

220 OVERTON CHURCH, WEST KILBRIDE

NS 203 481

Ritchie Street, West Kilbride

Just over 100 years old, designed by Mr Le Blanc (of Glasgow Baths fame). Very good stained glass with two recent modern additions. Two-manual Binns Organ – tubular pneumatic. Unusual hipped wooden ceiling to nave. Sunday Service: 11.00am all year, 6.30pm during autumn and winter

Open Thursday 10.00am-12.00 noon

CHURCH OF SCOTLAND

 (by arrangement) (Thursday mornings)

OVERTON CHURCH, WEST KILBRIDE

221 ST ANDREW'S, WEST KILBRIDE

NS 207 484

Main Street (200m from railway station)

Built as St Bride's United Presbyterian Church in 1882, in typical U P red sandstone with a fine spire and rose window. In 1972 it united with the Barony Parish, changing its name to St Andrew's. Allen Digital organ 1983.

Sunday Service: 10.30am contemporary in upper room, traditional in sanctuary, 3.00pm, traditional 1st Sunday

Open Monday to Friday 9.30am-12.30pm (enter from the lane at the side of the church), Tuesdays 'Meeting point' coffee, etc, 10.00am-12.00 noon; Wednesdays 'Community Café' 10.30am-2.00pm

CHURCH OF SCOTLAND 🦽 wc ℗ ☕ B

222 ST BRIDE'S, WEST KILBRIDE

NS 206 484

9 Hunterston Road

The church was built and opened in 1908. The Marian shrine in the grounds was erected in 1958 for the Golden Jubilee. Services: Saturday Vigil 6.30pm, Sunday 10.30am, weekdays (including Saturdays) 9.30am

Open daily 9.00am-6.00pm

ROMAN CATHOLIC ℗ wc

ST BRIDE'S, WEST KILBRIDE

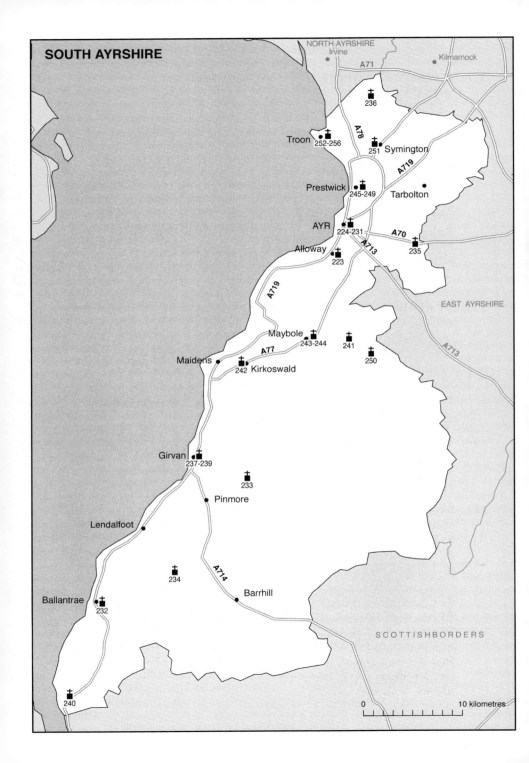

SOUTH AYRSHIRE

Local Representative: Miss Joan Fish, 31 Oaklands Avenue, Irvine
(*telephone* 01294 272654)

223 ALLOWAY PARISH CHURCH

NS 332 181
B7024 south of Burns' cottage
Built in 1858, architect Campbell Douglas.
South transept added in 1877, chancel built
and nave extended in 1890. Excellent stained
glass including Stephen Adam, Clayton & Bell,
Gordon Webster, W & J J Keir. James Crombie
memorial window to D F McIntyre, pilot on
first flight over Mount Everest in 1933. Two
windows by Susan Bradbury were installed in

ALLOWAY PARISH CHURCH

1996, one depicting the four seasons, the other in memory of Robert Burns. Three
further Bradbury windows were added in 2001, enhancing the porch and sanctuary
area throughout with stained glass. Sunday Services 9.45am and 11.15am
Open June to September, Monday to Friday 10.00am-4.00pm.
Conducted tours, contact local tourist office
CHURCH OF SCOTLAND 👤 🎗 🏺 📖 **B**

224 THE AULD KIRK OF AYR (ST JOHN THE BAPTIST)

NS 339 219
Off High Street, Ayr
Church website: www.auldkirk.org
The approach to the Auld Kirk is through Kirkport and the 1656 Lychgate into the
kirkyard. The Commonwealth Government paid for the 1654 T-plan kirk after
Cromwell's troops had occupied the old Church of St John on the sands.
Respectful alterations by David Bryce of
1836. High-quality interior with three
lofts on Corinthian columns and a
splendid double-decker pulpit. One of
the few remaining 'Obit' boards records
money donated to the poor. This church
is not a museum, but living and active.
Sunday Service: 11.00am
Open Saturday mornings by arrangement,
telephone the church office 01292 262938
CHURCH OF SCOTLAND 👤 🚻 ☺ 📖 **A**

THE AULD KIRK OF AYR
(ST JOHN THE BAPTIST)

225   ST QUIVOX, AUCHINCRUIVE, AYR

NS 375 241

St Quivox, B7035 off B743

Christian presence on the site dates back to the
13th century. The medieval building was restored
1595 and extended 1767 to create a T-plan church.
Interior fittings date largely from the late 18th
century, including a good pulpit. In the kirkyard,
mausoleum of the Campbells of Craigie, by W H
Playfair 1822. Sunday Service: 11.30am

Open by arrangement, contact Mrs A C Taylor,
telephone 01292 269746

CHURCH OF SCOTLAND   ♿ wc **A**

ST QUIVOX, AUCHINCRUIVE, AYR

226   HOLY TRINITY CHURCH, AYR

NS 336 218

Fullarton Street, Ayr

Church website: www.episcopalsouthayrshire.org.uk

Dedicated in 1888. Scotland's major example of
the work of J L Pearson, designer of Truro
Cathedral. Pulpit of Caen stone and very fine
stained glass windows by, among others, Clayton &
Bell. Next to Ayr bus station, walking distance from
railway station. Sunday Services: 8.00am, 10.30am
and 6.30pm; Wednesday Eucharist 11.00am

Open mornings in summer. Concert series

SCOTTISH EPISCOPAL

♿ wc ⊙ ⌷ ⬠ ⌷ (for visiting groups by arrangement) **A**

HOLY TRINITY CHURCH, AYR

227   ST ANDREW'S, AYR

NS 338 212

39 Park Circus, Ayr

Church website: wwwstandrewsayr.cwc.net

St Andrew's, identified by its tall red sandstone spire, was opened in November
1893. The worshipping congregation came from the Wallacetown Free Church
disruption. The design, by John B Wilson, is Perpendicular Gothic. The beautiful
stained glass includes work by John Blyth, Marcus McLundie and G Maile Studios,
Canterbury. The church hall (1897) is by William McClelland, major extensions to
provide additional accomodation 1963 and 1983. The church is on the south side
of the town between the railway and the sea front. Sunday Service: 11.00am

Open last Wednesday of the month, May to September 2.00-4.00pm

CHURCH OF SCOTLAND ♿ wc ⊙ ⌷ ⬠ **B**

228   ST COLUMBA, AYR

NS 337 208
Midton Road/Carrick Park, Ayr
Church website: www.ayrstcolumba.co.uk
Originally known as Trinity Church, Ayr, St Columba was dedicated in 1902. Built
of red sandstone to designs by John B Wilson of Glasgow. Fine pipe organ 1904
by J J Binns, restored by Harrison & Harrison 1985,
Festival Trumpet added 2005. Stained glass by Sidney
Holmes, C C Baillie, Susan Bradbury, Rowland Mitton
and Moira Parker. Resurrection window unveiled by
HRH the Princess Royal 2002. Cultured octagonal
pencil tower with carillon of bells. Sunday Services:
9.30 and 11.15am, 1st Sunday of month 6.30pm
Open 9.00am-12.00 noon, Monday, Tuesday, Thursday, Friday
CHURCH OF SCOTLAND   [&] [wc] ⊘ **B**

ST COLUMBA, AYR

229   ST JAMES'S PARISH CHURCH, AYR

NS 342 232
Prestwick Road/Falkland Park Road, Ayr
St James's Church was built as a chapel of ease in 1885 to
designs by John Murdoch. Murdoch, an engineer before
he became an architect, was the most ambitious of the
architects of Ayr in the late 19th century and received
many important commissions. There is a rose window
above the pulpit. Sunday Service: 11.00am
Open by arrangement with the Minister, telephone 01292 262420
CHURCH OF SCOTLAND [wc] **B**

ST JAMES'S PARISH CHURCH, AYR

230   ST LEONARD'S, AYR

NS 338 204
St Leonard's Road/Monument Road, Ayr
Built in 1886, several hundred yards from the site of the
ancient chapel of St Leonard, the patron saint of prisoners.
The architect was John Murdoch and the style belongs
to the geometric period of decorated Gothic. The building
comprises a nave with aisles, transepts and chancel (added
1911). 2-manual pipe organ by Harrison & Harrison, rebuilt
1992. Many beautiful stained glass windows.
Sunday Service: 10.00am
Open by arrangement, telephone Mr William Bruce 01292 263694
CHURCH OF SCOTLAND [&] [wc] ⊘ **B**

ST LEONARD'S, AYR

231 ST PAUL'S ROMAN CATHOLIC, AYR

NS 348 200

Peggieshill Road, Ayr

The dedication stone was laid in 1966 and the
church was opened 1967. Wall hanging by
members of the parish depicts St Paul's meeting
on the road to Damascus. Altar, lectern and
baptismal font in Creetown granite.
Services: Sunday 10.00am and 12.00 noon,
daily usually at 10.00am
Open by arrangement with the Parish Priest,
telephone 01292 260197
ROMAN CATHOLIC [wc] (?)

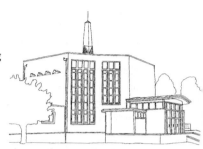

ST PAUL'S ROMAN CATHOLIC, AYR

232 BALLANTRAE PARISH CHURCH

NX 084 825

Main Street, Ballantrae

Church website: www.ballantraeparishchurch.org.uk
Built in 1819. Memorial to Lord Ballantrae.
Regency pulpit. Nephew of Robert Burns was
minister 1826-30. Kennedy tomb beside church.
Ruins of Ardstinchar Castle. A77. Railway station
at Girvan, 13 miles. Buses from Glasgow. United
with Glenapp. Sunday Service: 11.00am
Open daily, May to September 10.00am to sunset
CHURCH OF SCOTLAND [wc] (in village) (?) [] **B**

BALLANTRAE PARISH CHURCH

233 BARR PARISH CHURCH

NX 275 941

Main Street, Barr, by Girvan on B734

Dating from 1878, built to a design by A
Stevenson. Early Gothic gabled chapel. Slate
roof, skew gables, rubble walls, freestone
dressings. Picturesque south-east bellcote.
Fine wooden ceiling. Restored 1978
P J Lorimer, London. Occasional buses
from Girvan. Sunday Service: 12.00 noon
Open all year, 9.00am-7.00pm.
Teas in July and August: Monday, Friday
and Saturday 2.30-5.00pm
CHURCH OF SCOTLAND [wc] [] ▱ **c**

BARR PARISH CHURCH

234 COLMONELL CHURCH

NX 145 858

On A765

Built 1849 and renovated when the organ was installed. Organ screen and chancel by Robert Lorimer. Exceptional stained glass, including windows by Louis Davis and Douglas Strachan. Martyr's stone in graveyard from the time of the Covenanters, and Kennedy vault dating from 1620. Local lore gives a Christian presence here from AD *c.*600 when St Colman of Ella built his cell. Sunday Service: 10.30am

List of keyholders in side porch

CHURCH OF SCOTLAND 📖 **B**

235 ST CLARE'S, DRONGAN

NS 441 185

Watson Terrace, Drongan (1 mile south of A70, 7 miles east of Ayr)

Unassuming church building opened in 1967. Sunday Service: 9.45am

Open only for Sunday Service

ROMAN CATHOLIC 🚻

ST CLARE'S, DRONGAN

236 DUNDONALD PARISH CHURCH

NS 366 343

Main Street, Dundonald

Tranquil setting for this traditional stone church of 1804, built on the site of an earlier building. The clock tower was added 1841, and the chancel 1906. Some fine stained glass, particularly Henry Dearle's unique 'Last Supper'. Pipe organ, Norman & Beard 1906. Interesting grave stones in the tidy graveyard. Sunday Service: 11.00am

Church open by arrangement, telephone Rev Robert Mayes 01563 850703

CHURCH OF SCOTLAND ♿ 🚻 🔊 **B**

DUNDONALD PARISH CHURCH

237 ST JOHN THE EVANGELIST, GIRVAN

NS 186 972

Piedmont Road, Girvan

Church website: www.episcopalsouthayrshire.org.uk

A simple rectangular nave church, designed by A G Thomson 1859. Chancel and the base of a tower added 1900, as first part of scheme for tower and transepts (see drawing in church). 16th-century screen, lectern, altar rails and other carvings, including bishop's throne from Holyrood in Edinburgh. Italian reredos. Painted shields represent various local county families. Sunday Service: Eucharist 9.45am

Open by arrangement, telephone 01465 715763

SCOTTISH EPISCOPALIAN wc **B**

238 SACRED HEARTS OF JESUS AND MARY, GIRVAN

NS 183 979

Harbour Lane, Girvan

A plain Gothic structure of 1860 with a huge prow-like porch added in 1959 by Stevenson & Ferguson. Stained glass windows of 1860. Services: Saturday 7.00pm, Sunday 9.00am and 11.00am

Open during daylight hours

ROMAN CATHOLIC

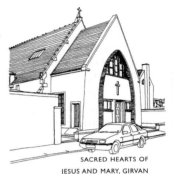

SACRED HEARTS OF
JESUS AND MARY, GIRVAN

239 GIRVAN METHODIST CHURCH

NX 185 977

Dalrymple Street, junction with Wesley Road, Girvan

Red sandstone Arts & Crafts style church with green slate steeply pitched and swept roof. Built in 1902 to replace Methodist chapel in Ailsa Street West. Two stained glass east windows and decorated wooden panels below bodly braced timber roof. Girvan was visited twice by John Wesley *en route* to Glasgow and Portpatrick resulting in local Methodist worship. Sunday Service: 11.00am

Open by arrangement, telephone Mr J Auld, 01465 713234

METHODIST ♿ wc **B**

240 GLENAPP CHURCH

NX 075 746

on A77, 7 miles south of Ballantrae

Church website: www.ballantraeparishchurch.org.uk

This church has a memorial window to Elsie Mackay, 3rd daughter of Earl of Inchcape. She was killed in 1928 attempting to fly the Atlantic.

GLENAPP CHURCH

Modern stained glass window above door, 'The Stilling of the Tempest', in memory of 1st Earl. Graveyard contains tombs of the three Earls of Inchcape. United with Ballantrae. Sunday Service: occasional

Open by arrangement, telephone 01465 831252 or 01465 831393

CHURCH OF SCOTLAND

241 KIRKMICHAEL PARISH CHURCH

NY 345 090

80 Patna Road, Kirkmichael, near Maybole

Believed to stand on the site of a 13th-century church under the care of the monks of Whithorn, the present church was built 1787 by Hugh Cairncross, and the belfry rebuilt 1887. Stone pulpit of 1919 depicting St Michael, St George, St Andrew and St Patrick incorporates the war memorial. Two large stained glass windows either side of the pulpit, one by Christopher Whitworth Whall. The

oldest building is the lychgate; the bell inside is dated 1702 and is still rung when a bride leaves the church after her wedding. Interesting stones in surrounding graveyard, including Covenanter's memorial, open every day. Two miles east of Maybole. Sunday Service: 10.30am

Open by arrangement, telephone the Minister 01655 750286

CHURCH OF SCOTLAND   🦽 wc ☕ (in village) **B**

KIRKMICHAEL PARISH CHURCH

242 KIRKOSWALD PARISH CHURCH

NS 240 074

Off A77, 5 miles south of Maybole and 7 miles north of Girvan

Robert Adam 1777, contemporary with Culzean Castle. It is suggested that while working with Lord Cassillis, his client at Culzean, Robert Adam came across the church during construction and recommended some changes, giving the building fine Palladian details. The church was visited by Robert Burns and more recently by President Eisenhower. Following a fire, the church was fully restored in 1997

and the opportunity was taken to research the original Adam colour scheme. Burns' characters, Tam o' Shanter, Souter Johnnie and Kirkton Jean, are buried in the old graveyard, where also can be seen the baptismal font used to baptise Robert the Bruce. Sunday Service: 11.00am

Open by arrangement, telephone 01655 760210 or 01655 760238

CHURCH OF SCOTLAND   🦽 ⊘ ⛲ 📖 **A**

KIRKOSWALD PARISH CHURCH

243 ST OSWALD'S, MAYBOLE

NS 299 101
Cargill Road / Garden Path, Maybole
Church website: www.episcopalsouthayrshire.org.uk
Built 1883 on land gifted to the church and
seating about 90 people. Organ by Alfred
Kirkland 1892. Hall and toilets added 1970s.
Convenient for Maybole railway station.
Services: Sunday 11.30am, Wednesdays 10.00am
Open by arrangement with keyholders,
Mr and Mrs Pope, telephone 01655 882452
SCOTTISH EPISCOPAL [♿] [wc]

ST OSWALD'S, MAYBOLE

244 OUR LADY & ST CUTHBERT, MAYBOLE

NS 299 094
Dailly Road, Maybole
Church website: www.maybole.org / community / churches
Gothic church with presbytery to west and hall to east,
linked to form a T-plan complex. Built of yellow
sandstone with white ashlar dressings with an
octagonal spire on the north-west corner and a gabled
porch at the north-east corner. Opened in 1878, the
church has unusual bosses depicting the saints looking
out into the church. Services: Saturday 6.30pm, Sunday
10.00am – please telephone 01655 882145 to confirm
Open by arrangement, telephone 01655 882145
ROMAN CATHOLIC [wc] (🎧) 🍵 (after Sunday service) **B**

OUR LADY &
ST CUTHBERT, MAYBOLE

245 MONKTON & PRESTWICK NORTH

NS 353 263
10 Monkton Road, Prestwick
Church website: www.mpnchurch.org.uk
The church was built as a Free Church in 1874, architect
James Salmon & Son, and the bell-tower was added 1890,
architect John Keppie. The congregation, united with the
Church of Scotland in 1900, now uses a computerised
communication system for hymn singing and visual aids. The
pulpit, from St Cuthbert's, Monkton, is mobile. The original
St Cuthbert's Communion Table has been fixed as a panel
between two stained glass windows. Sunday Service: 11.00am
Open by arrangement, telephone the Rev A Christie 01292 477499
CHURCH OF SCOTLAND [♿] [wc] (🎧)

MONKTON & PRESTWICK NORTH

246 MONKTON COMMUNITY CHURCH

NS 357 277
Main Street, Monkton
Church website: www.mpnchurch.org.uk
Meeting place central to the local community, completed 2004 and designed by
Fleming Muir Architects incorporating the old church hall. Three stained glass
windows by Moira Parker on subjects representing the local and world-wide
communities and including references to William Wallace, farming and fishing.
Services: 6.30pm on 2nd and 4th Sundays and non-denominational service
Wednesday evenings
Café open Monday to Friday 10.00am-4.00pm
CHURCH OF SCOTLAND ♿ wc 🔊

247 KINGCASE PARISH CHURCH, PRESTWICK

NS 348 244
Waterloo Road, Prestwick (behind Somerfield store)
Church website: www.kingcase.freeserve.co.uk
The church was built in 1912, extended 1956,
in attractive red sandstone with three small but
beautiful stained glass windows. Fairly small
building in excellent state of repair. Sunday
Services: 9.45am and 11.15am, 7.00pm. Large-
print hymn books available
Open by arrangement with Church Office,
telephone 01292 470755
CHURCH OF SCOTLAND wc 🔊 🕯

KINGCASE PARISH CHURCH, PRESTWICK

248 PRESTWICK SOUTH PARISH CHURCH

NS 352 260
Main Street, Prestwick
Church website: www.south-church.org.uk
First church commission 1879 for James A Morris,
contemporary of Charles Rennie Mackintosh.
Adept, light handling of Gothic forms, enlivened
by Glasgow-style carving. Carefully chosen
interior fittings include glass by Oscar Paterson.
Sunday Service: 11.00am
Open by arrangement with the Minister,
telephone 01292 478788
CHURCH OF SCOTLAND ♿ wc 🔊 📖

PRESTWICK SOUTH PARISH CHURCH

249 ST QUIVOX, PRESTWICK

NS 352 257

St Quivox Road, Prestwick

The building was completed in 1933 and is built of Accrington brick in Romanesque style. Extended in 1969, incorporating the old building to form a rectangular-shaped church. Inside are a sanctuary mosaic panel and the Stations of the Cross. Jubilee 2000 window. Sunday Services: 10.00am, 11.30am and 6.00pm

Open daily 10.00am–5.00pm

ROMAN CATHOLIC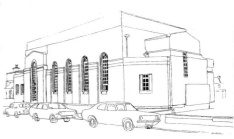

ST QUIVOX, PRESTWICK

250 STRAITON PARISH CHURCH (ST CUTHBERT'S)

NS 380 049

Four miles east of Kirkmichael

The main part of the church dates from 1758. The piscina of the original church is still visible on the east wall. Chantry chapel of late 15th century containing various memorial plaques to members of the Hunter Blair family. In 1901 the church was renovated by John Kinross and the bell-tower was added to the design of John Murdoch. Beautiful carvings on the ceiling and pulpit. Striking 'Millennium Banner' mounted on a pedestal made from a former pew. Tapestry cushions, 1993, depict themes from the life and work of the community and artwork by the local Sewing Guild commemorate 1997 as 'The Year of Faith'; 1998 as 'The Year of Hope'; and 1999 as 'The Year of Love'. The stone font is the gift of the Fergusson family. Splendid stained glass. Covenanter's memorial in graveyard, open every day. Sunday Service: 12.00 noon

Open by arrangement with the Minister, telephone 01655 750286

CHURCH OF SCOTLAND 🚻 WC (nearby) **A**

STRAITON PARISH CHURCH (ST CUTHBERT'S)

251 SYMINGTON CHURCH

NS 384 314

Off A77, 2 miles from Prestwick Airport
Church website: www.symingtonchurch.com
Known as Ayrshire's Norman church,
the rectangular building with 3-feet
thick walls was founded *c.*1160 by
Symon de Loccard whose own story
in itself makes a visit worthwhile.
Restored 1919 by P MacGregor
Chalmers. Norman arched windows,
piscina and ancient oak-beamed ceiling.
The stained glass, much of it by
Douglas Strachan, is glorious in creation

SYMINGTON CHURCH

and colour. Though small in size, its stones breathe the atmosphere of prayer and
praise of all the saints over 800 years. Sunday Service: 10.30am
Open by arrangement, telephone Mrs Margaret Kerr 01563 830289,
or Jim Knox 01563 830043
CHURCH OF SCOTLAND ♿ 🚻 📖 **A**

252 TROON OLD CHURCH

NS 321 309

Ayr Street, Troon
Church website: www.troonold.org.uk
Neo-Gothic building in red sandstone by Hippolyte Blanc and dedicated in 1895.
The stained glass of the Ascension window is by the Morris Studio; other
windows by Gordon Webster. Alabaster reredos depicting Moses, St Paul and the
Last Supper has a finely carved canopy and stands above a mosaic pavement of the
Paschal Lamb. Richly carved pulpit, communion table and font. Various memorials.
Services: Sunday 10.30am; Wednesday 11.15am
Open Tuesday to Sunday 10.00am-12.00 noon
CHURCH OF SCOTLAND 🚻 ♿ 🕯 (by arrangement) 📖 ☕ (Saturday and Sunday) **B**

TROON OLD CHURCH

253 OUR LADY AND ST MEDDAN CHURCH, TROON

NS 327 311

4 Cessnock Road, Troon

Built to a design by Reginald Fairlie
1910, this church is a mixture of
architectural styles and also copies the
rear view of Holy Rude Church in
Stirling. The church has undergone
major restoration funded by Historic
Scotland. Two minutes from railway
station, Glasgow–Ayr, half-hourly train
service. Sunday Mass 9.00am and
11.15am; Saturday Vigil Mass 6.00pm
*Open daily until 4.00pm, and Ayrshire Doors
Open Day, September*
ROMAN CATHOLIC **A**

OUR LADY AND ST MEDDAN CHURCH, TROON

254 PORTLAND PARISH CHURCH, TROON

NS 323 308

South Beach / St Meddan's Street, Troon

Opened in 1914 as a United Free Church by H E Clifford & Lunan. Perpendicular
Gothic in white sandstone with fine tracery in the great north window which is
repeated in the nave windows. Interior has exposed stone with blonde Austrian oak
pews and fittings. The stained glass chancel window was donated in 1920 as a war
memorial by Mr A F Steven. Harrison & Harrison 2-manual organ, rebuilt 1970.
Halls extension added 1964. Two minutes' walk from railway station.

Sunday Service: 10.30am

*Open July and August, Sunday and
Thursday 2.00-4.30pm, and Ayrshire
Doors Open Day, September*
CHURCH OF SCOTLAND
B

PORTLAND PARISH CHURCH, TROON

255 ST MEDDAN'S, TROON

NS 323 309

*Corner of Church Street and St Meddan's
Street, Troon*

Church website: www.troonstmeddanschurch.org

Built 1888-9 for the United Presbyterian
Church, architect J B Wilson, St Meddan's
has many noteworthy features. The tall
and stately spire houses a clock which
was originally part of the University of
Glasgow's Old College in High Street,
Glasgow. Many beautiful stained glass
windows; the largest, opposite the pulpit,
depicts the healing of Jairus's daughter.
Sunday Services: 9.30am and 11.15am
*Open Monday, Tuesday and Thursday
9.00am-2.00pm*
CHURCH OF SCOTLAND   🦽 wc 🔊 **B**

ST MEDDAN'S, TROON

256 ST NINIAN'S, TROON

NS 327 304

Bentinck Drive, Troon

Designed in Arts & Crafts Gothic by James A Morris, nave dedicated 1913, chancel
built and dedicated 1921. Twenty years of planning culminated when the church
was consecrated in 1931. The church contains many examples of fine woodwork by
Yorkshire carver Robert Thomson of Kilburn, whose signature is the carved mouse
(look closely at the main door). Organ by J J Binns, rebuilt 1987. Services: Sunday:
8.00am Holy Communion, 10.30am; Sung Eucharist; 1st and 3rd Sunday 5.00pm
Evening Prayers; Wednesday 10.00am Holy Communion
Open daily 9.00am-4.00pm
SCOTTISH EPISCOPAL   🦽 wc 🔊 **B**

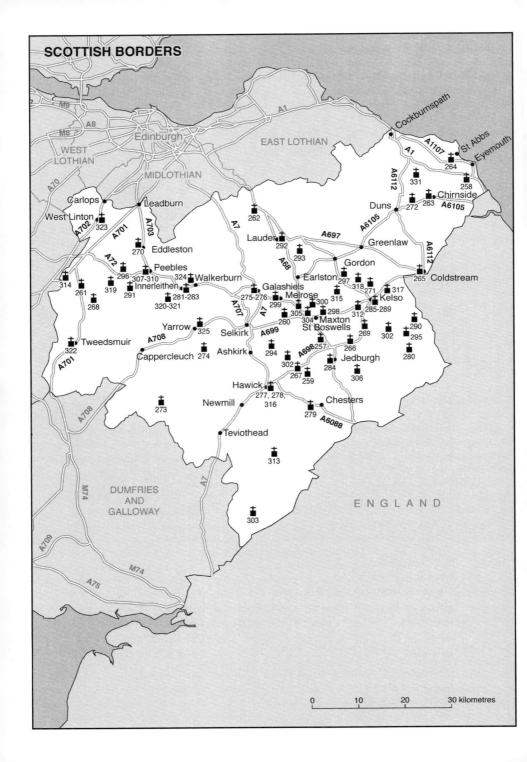

BORDERS

Local Representatives: Mrs Mary Reid, 2 Crookhaugh, by Biggar (*telephone* 01899 880258) and Mr Sandy Gilchrist, 11 Mercat Loan, Biggar (*telephone* 01899 221350) – Tweedale

257 ANCRUM KIRK

NT 627 246

The present church, built of red sandstone, was opened in 1890 to replace an 18th-century building, the remains of which may be seen in the kirkyard, approximately one mile west of the present church. Four stained glass memorial windows. Sunday Service: 10.00am

Open by arrangement with keyholder Mr Rogerson, telephone 01835 830321

CHURCH OF SCOTLAND wc 📖

ANCRUM KIRK

258 AYTON PARISH CHURCH

NT 927 609

South side of village, opposite road to Chirnside

First-pointed Gothic style building with 36-metre spire designed by James Maitland Wardrop 1864-6. High quality stained glass by Ballantine & Sons. Fine organ by Forster & Andrews of Hull 1894, restored by James Lightoller of Berwick 1997. Occasional organ recitals. In the burial ground are the ivy-clad ruins of the 12th-century St Dionysius's church. Sunday Service: 1st and 3rd Sunday 11.00am

Open by arrangement with the Minister, telephone 01890 781333

CHURCH OF SCOTLAND wc 👤 (by arrangement) **A**

259 BEDRULE CHURCH

NT 599 179

Bedrule, by Jedburgh

Beautifully rebuilt in 1914 by T Greenshields Leadbetter, the church has a plaque commemorating Bishop Turnbull, founder of Glasgow University in 1451. Stained glass, including Guild centenary window 1992 and windows by Douglas Strachan 1922. Memorial with interesting link to wartime 'Enigma' decoding project. Fine views over Rule Valley to Ruberslaw. Linked with Denholm and Minto. Time of service normally every three weeks, changes every four months: see notice board for details. 9.45am or 11.30am

Open during daylight hours.

CHURCH OF SCOTLAND 📖 (free) **B**

BEDRULE CHURCH

BOWDEN KIRK

260 BOWDEN KIRK

NT 554 301

Sitting by St Cuthbert's Way, the pilgrim route from Melrose to Lindisfarne, the church has a wealth of architectural history. It was founded in 1128; part of the north wall is possibly 15th century, east end from 1644, cross aisle from 1661, west gable and doorway at west end of north wall 17th century. Repaired in 1794. Major alterations in 1909 by P MacGregor Chalmers. Carved wooden 17th-century laird's loft for Riddell-Carre family. Burial vaults of Riddell-Carre of Cavers-Carre and Dukes of Roxburghe. Memorials, including one to Lady Grizell Baillie, first Deaconess of the Church of Scotland. Many notable tombstones in graveyard.

Sunday Service: 11.00am

Open during daylight hours

CHURCH OF SCOTLAND 🦽 ⓦ ⓒ 📖 (from Post Office) ☕ Ⓡ **A**

261 BROUGHTON, GLENHOLM AND KILBUCHO PARISH CHURCH

NT 111 368

Broughton, Biggar

Built in 1804 and extended by Robert Bryden of Broughton and Glasgow 1886 to whom there is a memorial stained glass window in the north wall. Roof lights above the communion table are based on originals in Copenhagen Museum. Linked with Tweedsmuir, Skirling and Stobo with Drumelzier. Sunday Service: 10.00am

Open by arrangement, telephone

Mr Ian Brown 01899 830365

CHURCH OF SCOTLAND ⓦ ⓒ

BROUGHTON, GLENHOLM AND
KILBUCHO PARISH CHURCH

262 CHANNELKIRK PARISH CHURCH

NT 481 545

Two miles west of Oxton

Commanding a fine view down the valley, this is
a historic site dating back to St Cuthbert; the
Mother Kirk of Lauderdale, established by
Dryburgh Abbey. Present building erected 1817
by James Gillespie Graham in Perpendicular
Gothic. Original pulpit and fittings. Bell of 1702
still rung each Sunday. Sunday Service: 10.00am
Open at all times
CHURCH OF SCOTLAND   **A**

CHANNELKIRK PARISH CHURCH

263 CHIRNSIDE PARISH CHURCH

NT 869 561

South side of village at junction of A6105 and B6237

The chevron-patterned Norman doorway at the south-west corner of the church
dates from the 12th century. The church was largely rebuilt in 1878 with the
church hall, vestry and tower added in 1905-7. Buried in the kirkyard are the
famous 17th-century Reforming minister, Henry Erskine, and the 1960s World
Champion racing driver, Jim Clark. Sunday Service: 11.30am; 10.30am on 5th
Sunday of month
Open Thursday 2.30-5.00pm or by arrangement, telephone 01890 818034
CHURCH OF SCOTLAND   **B**

264 THE PRIORY CHURCH, COLDINGHAM

NT 904 659

Coldingham, Berwickshire

Church website: www.stebba-coldinghampriory.org.uk

Influential centre of Christian witness in Scottish Borders since 7th century.
Successor to nearby St Aebbe's Monastry, attached to Durham Cathedral for 300
years. Present church formed from the choir and sanctuary area which comprised
the eastern arm of the early 13th-century cruciform-plan Priory Church of St
Mary. Splendid free-standing restored arch of original church to the west of the
main building. South and west walls rebuilt 1662 and extensive renovation in
1850s. Interior renovation 1950 providing present chancel and its furnishings. Nine
modern stained glass windows. Detailed scale model of the Priory on exhibition.
Sunday Service: 12.00 noon
*Open Wednesdays, May to September 2.00-4.00pm, and by arrangement, telephone Mr G
Johnston 018907 71880. Annual Pilgrimage to St Abb's Head, usually 3rd Sunday in June*
CHURCH OF SCOTLAND   **A**

THE PRIORY CHURCH, COLDINGHAM

COLDSTREAM PARISH CHURCH

265 COLDSTREAM PARISH CHURCH

NT 844 400

High Street, Coldstream

The square church tower is a distinctive feature of Coldstream. The Tower and the west entrance are part of the original church built in 1718. The rest of the church was rebuilt in 1905 to a design by J M Dick Peddie. A classical nave and aisles church with barrel-vaulted roof supported by eight Tuscan columns. A fine stone pulpit in front of the semi-circular chancel arch. The church contains many reminders of its close association, along with the town, with the Coldstream Guards. The King's and Regimental Colours hang in the chancel. Plaque to the Rev Adam Thomson who formed the Coldstream Free Bible Press in 1845, thus breaking the monopoly held by Oxford and Cambridge Universities and the King's printers in Scotland. Sunday Service: 11.15am

Open June to August, Thursday 2.00-4.30pm. Other times by arrangement, telephone Dr B J Sproule 01890 882271

CHURCH OF SCOTLAND [wc] ⊘ 📖 ☕ **B**

266 CRAILING KIRK

NT 682 250

On A698 Jedburgh–Kelso

Built *c.*1775 on an ancient site of worship; the bell is dated 1702. Aisle added in the early 19th century with further alterations and additions 1892. Restoration by P Macgregor Chalmers 1907. Services: 2nd and 4th Sunday 10.30am, 1st Sunday of winter months 6.30pm. See local press for more details

Open by arrangement, telephone Mrs Rose, The Braeheids, Crailing 01835 850268

CHURCH OF SCOTLAND ♿ ⊘ **B**

CRAILING KIRK

DENHOLM CHURCH

267 DENHOLM CHURCH

NT 569 186

Denholm, by Hawick on A698

Dates from 1845. Interior much altered 1957. Wall hangings for 150th anniversary. Situated in a beautiful conservation village. Time of Sunday service changes every four months: see notice boards for details

Key from the Manse in Leyden's Road, or telephone 01450 870362

CHURCH OF SCOTLAND 🚹 wc ⟲ 📖 (free) **C**

268 DRUMELZIER KIRK

NT 135 343

Drumelzier, by Broughton off B712

A simple rectangular building of pre-Reformation origins. The original date is uncertain, but it owes its present appearance largely to major alterations carried out in 1872. Bellcote, 17th-century, on the west gable. Burial vault 1617 for the Tweedies of Drumelzier. United with Stobo and linked with Broughton, Tweedsmuir, Skirling. Sunday Service: 1st and 3rd Sunday of each month 6.30pm (not January, February, July and August)

For information on access, telephone the Rev Rachel Dobie 01899 830331, or Mr and Mrs Julian Birchall 01899 830319

CHURCH OF SCOTLAND **B**

DRUMELZIER KIRK

269 ECKFORD KIRK

NT 706 270

Eckford, by Kelso on A698

Built 1771 on an ancient site of worship,
incorporating fragments of the 1668 building
and the north aisle of 1724. Very sweet interior
with rich turn-of-the-century furnishings in the
sanctuary. Jougs 1718, mort bell and 19th-
century watch-tower. Many fine 17th-century
gravestones. Service: first Sunday of summer
months at 6.30pm, see local press for details
Open by arrangement, telephone
Mrs Jean Dyet 01573 850308
CHURCH OF SCOTLAND **B**

ECKFORD KIRK

270 EDDLESTON PARISH CHURCH

NT 244 472

Bellfield Road, Eddleston

The site has been in continuous occupation
since the 12th century, the present building
being erected in 1829 incorporating a number
of carved stones of the 17th and 18th
centuries. The church was rebuilt after a fire in
1897 and the vestry and chancel added. The
restoration was paid for by the then Lord
Elibank, and Mr Somerville of Portmore. The
church bell, one of the oldest in the country,

EDDLESTON PARISH CHURCH

was cast in 1507. The 2-manual pedal organ of 1907 from St Blane's in Dunblane
was rebuilt here in 1980. Sunday Service: 11.45am except last Sunday 6.00pm
Open by arrangement with Mrs Margaret Love, 11 Old Manse Road, 01721 730263
CHURCH OF SCOTLAND 🦽 wc ⊘ ⬠ **B**

271 EDNAM PARISH CHURCH

NT 737 372

Ednam, by Kelso

Church built 1800 and recast 1902. Situated
in the village of Ednam where hymnwriter
Henry Francis Lyte was born. In union with
Kelso North. Sunday Service: 10.00am
Open daily 10.00am-4.00pm, July and August
CHURCH OF SCOTLAND 🦽 wc ⊘ ⬠

EDNAM PARISH CHURCH

272 EDROM PARISH CHURCH

NT 826 558

In Edrom village, signposted from A6105

The 15th-century Blackadder Aisle, under the care of Historic Scotland, was built by Robert Blackadder, Archbishop of Glasgow, in 1499. The T-plan kirk had major alterations in 1886 including the open-timber scissor roof. The Edrom Arch (also Historic Scotland) was the entrance to the 12th-century kirk and is now a burial vault. Information plaques on site.

Sunday Service: 10.00am 2nd and 4th Sundays

Open by arrangement telephone 01890 818189

CHURCH OF SCOTLAND &. wc ② ⓘ ⓘ **A**

273 ETTRICK KIRK

NT 259 145

Ettrickhill, 1 mile west of Ettrick village

The present church, built 1824, replaced the post-Reformation Kirk of Ettrick and Rankilburn in which Thomas Boston preached in the early 17th century. Of three lofts, two have separations between the pews to stop the herd's dogs from fighting. The third loft, of the Napier family, has more comfortable seating. Notable features are the pulpit with dove and original ladles for offerings. In the churchyard are the burial plot of the Napier family and the graves of James Hogg, 'The Ettrick Shepherd', and Tibbie Shiell. Sunday service: 2.30pm 3rd Sunday; for 5th Sunday service, see local press

Open at all times

CHURCH OF SCOTLAND **B**

274 KIRKHOPE KIRK, ETTRICKBRIDGE

NT 390 244

B7009, 7 miles south-west of Selkirk

That it shares the same name as Kirkhope in Upper Ettrick shows its ancient association with Melrose Abbey, yet in the Middle Ages, any church here belonged to the Parish of Yarrow. Of simple rectangular plan, the church features a good stained glass window and the Buccleuch Aisle of its original patron. Set in a wooded garden beside the steep bank of the Ettrick Linns, there is a lychgate memorial to two World Wars. Sunday service: 10.00am; for 5th Sunday service, see local press

Open at all times

CHURCH OF SCOTLAND &. wc **C**

275 GALASHIELS OLD PARISH CHURCH & ST PAUL'S

NT 490 362

Scott Crescent, Galashiels

Built in 1881 to plans in the Gothic Revival style by George Henderson, the main feature is the 190ft spire. Front porch added 1922. Good glass, including some by Douglas Strachan. Stone carvings by John Rhind and wood carving by Francis Lynn. 'Father' Willis organ.

Sunday Services: 11.00am and 6.30pm

Open by arrangement, telephone

Mrs N Noble 01896 752724

CHURCH OF SCOTLAND [♿] (via hall) [wc] ⊘ **B**

GALASHIELS OLD PARISH CHURCH & ST PAUL'S

276 ST PETER'S CHURCH, GALASHIELS

NT 496 356

Abbotsford Road, Galashiels

Gothic Revival style Hay & Henderson 1853. Reredos Sir Robert Lorimer 1914. Stained glass, memorial brasses. Setting of church with lawns, graveyard, hall and rectory encapsulates the Tractarian ideal. Quarter-mile south of town centre on A7. Fine 2-manual tracker organ by Brindley and Foster 1881. Sunday Services: Holy Communion 8.30am, Sung Eucharist 10.30am

ST PETER'S CHURCH, GALASHIELS

Open by arrangement. Key from the Rectory, Parsonage Road, Galashiels, telephone 01896 753118, or contact Mr R Brown, 54 Croft Street, Galashiels, telephone 01896 754657

SCOTTISH EPISCOPAL [♿] [wc] 📖 **C**

277 ST CUTHBERT'S CHURCH, HAWICK

NT 501 141

Slitrig Crescent, Hawick

A Sir George Gilbert Scott building of 1858. Reredos J Oldrid Scott 1905. Chancel screen Robert Lorimer. Some fine stained glass including contemporary windows of 1995 and 2002. Sunday Services: 9.30am Holy Communion, 10.30am Family Eucharist; Wednesday 10.30am Holy Eucharist. Festival Service 6.00pm on the Sunday of the Hawick Reivers' Festival

Open Sunday 9.15-11.45am, alternate Mondays 2.00-4.00pm, Wednesday 10.15-11.45am

SCOTTISH EPISCOPAL [♿] [wc] ⊘ ⌷ 📖 **B**

ST CUTHBERT'S CHURCH, HAWICK   HOBKIRK PARISH CHURCH

278 ST MARY'S & ST DAVID'S, HAWICK

NT 499 145

15 Buccleuch Street (A7 to Langholm)

The foundation stone was laid in 1843 and the church opened in 1844 with seating for 400. The side chapel was built 1879, increasing the seating to 500. New Sacristy late 1960s. Stained glass window for Father Taggart, 1895. The organ was updated in 1914. Masses: Sunday 11.30am, Monday, Wednesday, Friday 10.00am, Thursday 7.00pm, Saturday 9.30am

Open Saturday 9.00am to 11.00am. Choral and Flower Festivals

ROMAN CATHOLIC   🚹 🚻 ⊘ ⎀ (by arrangement) 📙 ☕

279 HOBKIRK PARISH CHURCH

NT 587 109

One mile west of Bonchester Bridge on the A6088 Hawick–Newcastle (off A68)

A Christian site for over 900 years. The present church was built in 1862. Stones from the earlier churches are incorporated in the font. The bell is inscribed 'I was made for Hobkirk in 1745'. United with Southdean.

Sunday Service: 9.45am for 4 months, then 11.30am for 4 months, see notice board for details

Open daily all year

CHURCH OF SCOTLAND 📙

280 HOWNAM PARISH CHURCH

NT 778 193

Hownam, Morebattle, Kelso

In an idyllic situation on the haugh by the Kale
Water. The original building appears to have been
cruciform, but was remodelled in 1752 as a
rectangle, and substantially modernised in 1844.
The interior was refurbished in 1986. From the
original church there remains a round-headed
doorway in the south wall, dating from the turn

HOWNAM PARISH CHURCH

of the 15th and 16th centuries. Linked with Linton, Morebattle and Yetholm.
Sunday Service: 12.30pm, 2nd and 4th Sunday of every month
Open all year during daylight hours
CHURCH OF SCOTLAND ♿ **B**

281 INNERLEITHEN CHURCH

NT 332 369

Leithen Road, Innerleithen

Built between 1864 and 1867, the church is
the work of Frederick Thomas Pilkington. Its
most striking features are the beautiful east
elevation, the minaret windows and the
elaborate carving. The chancel was added by
J McIntyre Henry in 1889. Stained glass

INNERLEITHEN CHURCH

windows by Ballantine and son, 2-manual pipe-organ by Brook & Co, 1892. On a
plinth in front of the church stands part of the shaft of a 9th-century decorated
cross, discovered in the foundations of the earlier church. Sunday Service: 11.30am
Open by arrangement with Mr Lunn, telephone 01896 830598
CHURCH OF SCOTLAND wc ⊘ **B**

282 ST JAMES CHURCH, INNERLEITHEN

NT 329 366

High Street, Innerleithen

Built in 1881 to a design by John Biggar, a church
with some interesting works of art including a large
icon of Our Lady of Czestochowa, Poland. This is
by K Kryska 1944, the captain of Polish Forces
based in Peebleshire. Other monuments include
ones dating from 1861 and a copy of the bust of
John Ogilvie. The sanctuary has been brought back
into use, and a narthex has been built inside the

ST JAMES CHURCH, INNERLEITHEN

church to provide toilet and kitchen facilities. A rood screen division within the church provides a gathering and social space towards the rear of the nave.

Sunday Service: 11.30am; Holy Days 7.00pm

Open summer 10.00am-4.00pm and by arrangement, telephone

Mrs Helen Garrett 01896 830025 or Mrs Anne Tait 01896 831184

ROMAN CATHOLIC 📖 **B**

283 ST ANDREW, INNERLEITHEN

NT 333 371

Church Street, Innerleithen

A small yet beautiful church, dedicated in 1904. The altar screen attractively separates the nave and sanctuary. A mural behind the altar depicts the 'Visitation of the Shepherds', painted in the style of Phoebe Traquair by William Blacklock of Edinburgh. Two stained glass windows either side of the

ST ANDREW, INNERLEITHEN

sanctuary, in memory of Capt R M B Welsh, depict St George and the Dragon. A window in the nave, in memory of Mrs F Ballantyne, illustrates the hymn 'All things bright and beautiful', with local scenery, flora, animals and birds.

Sunday Service: 9.30am except 1st Sunday of each month 11.00am

Open Thursdays by arrangement, telephone Julia Sharpe 01896 830637

or Frank Neville 01896 830084

SCOTTISH EPISCOPAL ♿ 🚹

284 ST MARY'S, THE IMMACULATE CONCEPTION, JEDBURGH

NT 653 210

2 Old Bongate, Jedburgh

A good example of architect Reginald Fairlie's simple Catholic churches with attached priest's house. Built in 1937, on the site of a previous building, with an aisleless nave and a semi-octagonal apse; traditional and with good use of materials. Services: Saturday Vigil Mass 5.30pm; details of other services on notice board

Open by arrangement,

telephone 01835 862426

ROMAN CATHOLIC 🚹 ☕ (Sunday) **B**

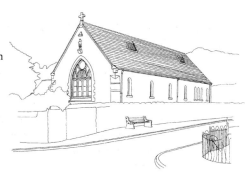

ST MARY'S, THE IMMACULATE CONCEPTION, JEDBURGH

285　KELSO NORTH PARISH CHURCH

NT 727 341

Roxburgh Street, Kelso

Erected 1866 for the congregation of Kelso
North Free Church, architect Frederick T
Pilkington. The front of the church is very
ornate, being designed in the Gothic style, with
the tower and spire rising to some 180ft.
Extensively renovated in 1934 and 1984-9.
Although the exterior is quite massive, in contrast
the interior is fairly neat and compact. Sunday
Services: 11.30am; Evening Worship 6.30pm 1st
Sunday October to June

*Open July and August, Monday to Friday 10.00am-
4.00pm. Also Saturdays all year for coffee mornings*

CHURCH OF SCOTLAND 🦽 wc ② 🕯 📖 ☕ **A**

KELSO NORTH PARISH CHURCH

286　KELSO OLD PARISH CHURCH

NT 729 339

The Butts, Kelso (off Market Square)

Octagonal plan church, James Nisbet,
dating from 1773, and altered by William
Elliot in 1823. Built to continue worship
begun in Kelso Abbey in 1128. Recently
extensively restored. Banners of Blues &
Royals, presented to the church by the
Duke of Roxburghe 1927. By Knowes car
park and adjacent to Kelso Abbey.

Sunday Service: 11.30am

*Open Easter to September, Monday to Friday
10.00am-4.00pm*

CHURCH OF SCOTLAND 🦽 wc ② 🕯 📖 **A**

KELSO OLD PARISH CHURCH

287　THE IMMACULATE CONCEPTION (ST MARY'S), KELSO

NT 724 344

Bowmont Street, Kelso

Dated 1858, designed by W W Wardell of London as a simple 4-bay Gothic
church, with chancel added 1935. Stained glass by Hardman. Altar, reredos and
baldacchino of mahogany, designed by Archibald MacPherson 1916, and depicting
the Annunciation. Services: Sunday 9.30am, Wednesday 10.00am

Open by arrangement, telephone 01573 224725

CHURCH OF SCOTLAND 🦽 wc ② 📖 **C**

288 KELSO QUAKER MEETING HOUSE

NT 729 339
Abbey Row, Kelso
A former coach house adjoining the Old Priory, the
Meeting House is a traditional two-story building of
stone and slate, probably dating from before 1800.
Collection of eight lino-cut prints of Border views
by Earlston artist Tom Davidson. Ministry is welcome
in any language, but is most often in English! Sunday
Meeting for Worship: 10.30am
Open after Sunday Meeting for Worship 11.30am-12.30pm
QUAKER ⟨♿⟩ ⟨wc⟩ ⟨?⟩ ⟨☕⟩ (after Meeting for Worship) **B**

KELSO QUAKER MEETING HOUSE

289 ST ANDREW'S CHURCH, KELSO

NT 728 337
Belmont Place, opposite Kelso Abbey on B6089
Situated close to the banks of the River Tweed,
built 1868 by Sir Robert Rowand Anderson. Altar,
reredos, font and Robertson memorial sculpted in
marble and Caen stone. Decorative wooden chancel
roof and decorated pulpit. Stained glass. Small
garden to rear (including Garden Room for
meetings and Junior Church). Services: Sunday
8.30am and 10.30am; Wednesday Eucharist
10.30am; Thursday Eucharist 7.00pm
Open daily 8.30am-5.00pm
SCOTTISH EPISCOPAL ⟨wc⟩ ⟨?⟩ ⟨♿⟩ **B**

ST ANDREW'S CHURCH, KELSO

290 THE KIRK OF YETHOLM, KIRK YETHOLM

NT 826 281
The church for the delightful twin villages and parish of Yetholm stands on a site
in use since David I's apportionment of parishes. Built by Robert Brown 1837 to
replace a small dank thatched affair, it is a rectangular-plan Gothic church of local
whinstone with cream sandstone dressings, and a tower to the south. A
remodelling in 1935, and the creation of an upper room out of the gallery in the
1970s, gives the interior a lightness belied by the sombre imposing exterior.
Stained glass by Ballantine & Son, Edinburgh. The medieval bell is still in use. As
the nearest burial ground to Flodden, the graveyard is believed to have interred
officers fallen in that battle (1513). Gravestones 17th century. Linked with Linton,
Morebattle and Hownam. Sunday Service: 10.00am
Open daily during daylight hours
CHURCH OF SCOTLAND ⟨♿⟩ **B**

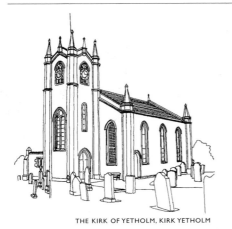

THE KIRK OF YETHOLM, KIRK YETHOLM

MANOR KIRK

291 MANOR KIRK

NT 220 380

Kirkton Manor, by Peebles

First referred to in 1186 as 'the chapel of Maineure'. Tradition speaks of an earlier chapel of the 4th century dedicated to St Gordian, a martyred Roman soldier. The present building was completed in 1874. The bell, rung before every service, is inscribed '*In honore Santi Gordiani MCCCCLXXVIII*' and is one of the oldest bells in use in Scotland. Pewter baptismal basin, inscribed '*Manner Kirk 1703*'. The pipe organ, originally built by Peter Conacher in 1889, came from Pencaitland Church and was re-built in Manor Kirk in October 2002. Sunday Services: 11.00am 2nd, 3rd and 4th Sundays of each month, 6.30pm 5th Sunday

Open daily

CHURCH OF SCOTLAND 🔣 (ramp) 📖

292 LAUDER OLD CHURCH

NT 531 475

Market Place, Lauder

Built 1673 by Sir William Bruce, in the shape of a Greek cross with four equal arms and a central octagonal bell tower. Various alterations were made through the 18th and 19th centuries. The porches were added later. Walled graveyard with watchtower of 1830. Pulpit of 1820. Sunday Service: 11.30am

Open most days 9.00am-5.00pm

CHURCH OF SCOTLAND 🔣 wc 🔊 📖 **A**

LAUDER OLD CHURCH

293 LEGERWOOD PARISH CHURCH

NT 594 434
Legerwood, Berwickshire
The church dates from 1127. Repaired in
1717 and 1804. Its chancel has a fine
Norman arch. Sunday Service: 11.45am,
1st Sunday of each month
Open daily
CHURCH OF SCOTLAND ♿ **B**

LEGERWOOD PARISH CHURCH

294 LILLIESLEAF KIRK

NT 539 253
East of Lilliesleaf village
The church of 1771 was extended in 1883
and transformed by the addition of west
part of nave and belltower in 1910. Good
stained glass by William Wilson, 1966.
Medieval font and ancient child's stone
coffin. Sunday Service: 11.30am
Open during daylight hours
CHURCH OF SCOTLAND ♿ wc 📖

LILLIESLEAF KIRK

295 LINTON KIRK & HOSELAW CHAPEL

NT 773 262 and NT 802 318
Near Morebattle, Kelso
On a sandy knoll, a 12th-century church much altered in 1616, 1774, 1813 and
finally restored to an approximation of its Romanesque appearance in 1912 by P
MacGregor Chalmers. It retains its Norman feel and today the visitor enters under
a unique stone tympanum to discover an attractive nave and substantial chancel, the
arch richly carved (1912). A Norman font and chancel stalls are of particular
interest. Linton Kirk is most noted for the stone above the porch said to depict a
knight on horseback lancing two creatures – the stone is Norman and unique in
Scotland, and legend suggests that this is the first known Somerville killing a
worm. The Leishman father and son ministries completed most of the present
improvements; the son Thomas also had a small chapel built in the district of
Hoselaw (seven miles away) to serve the cottagers; architect P MacGregor
Chalmers. Linked with Morebattle, Hownam and Yetholm. Sunday Service: 1st, 3rd
and 5th of each month; and 5th Sunday at Hoselaw Chapel (except December and
January) 12.15pm
Open daily during daylight hours
CHURCH OF SCOTLAND 👥 **B**

LINTON KIRK

LYNE KIRK

296   LYNE KIRK

NT 192 405

On A72 from Peebles

Located on the site of a 12th-century church, the present church was built between 1640 and 1645 by John Hay of Yester (later 1st Earl of Tweeddale). The porch was added in the 19th century. The church retains its 17th-century interior and of particular interest are the Dutch pulpit and canopied pews dated 1644. Pre-Reformation font. The earliest stone in the graveyard is dated 1707; the Adam and Eve stone, dated 1712, is uncommon. Roman fort of Lyne immediately to the west.

Service: 11.00am, 1st Sunday of each month

Open daily

CHURCH OF SCOTLAND **B**

297   MAKERSTOUN CHURCH

NT 669 331

⅓ mile north of Makerstoun village, 4 miles north-west of Kelso

Built 1808, the bell tower on the south wall, recently repaired, has 1808 inscribed on it. The church is light, with plain windows and original pine pews, pulpit and precentor's desk. Gallery and Sunday School upstairs. The setting of the church and churchyard is beautiful and peaceful. Sunday Service: 10.00am, 2nd and 4th Sunday

Open at all times

CHURCH OF SCOTLAND 👤 **B**

MAKERSTOUN CHURCH

298 MAXTON KIRK

NT 610 303

On the north-west edge of Maxton village
Church website: www.maxton.bordernet.co.uk/church.html
On St Cuthbert's Way and dedicated to St Cuthbert.
Reputed to have been a place of worship on this site
for almost 1000 years. Originally oblong, thatched
until 1790. North aisle added 1866, vestry 1962.

MAXTON KIRK

Wyvern organ. Stained glass by J H Corham gifted
1914, Hebrew and Latin inscriptions, Maxton War Memorial within church.
Burgerhuys bell 1609. Burial vault of Kers of Littledean. Sunday Service: 11.30am,
2nd and 4th Sunday
Open by arrangement, telephone 01835 823745
CHURCH OF SCOTLAND   ♿ wc ⑦ 🏛 📖 **B**

299 HOLY TRINITY, MELROSE

NT 540 342

High Cross Avenue, Melrose
Built in the Early English style by Benjamin Ferrey
1846-50. Decorated chancel and transepts by Hay
& Henderson 1900. The chancel floor is mosaic.
Open timber roof carried on mask corbels. Stained

HOLY TRINITY, MELROSE

glass windows in transept 1900 by Kempe, other
commemorative glass by Mayer & Co and W Wilson 1963. Quarter mile from
Melrose centre, on road to Darnick. Services: Sunday 8.30 and 11.00am;
Wednesday 10.30am; Evensong 1st Sunday of month 6.30pm
Open by arrangement, telephone the Rector 01896 822626. Occasional concerts
SCOTTISH EPISCOPAL   ♿ wc ⑦ wc **B**

300 MERTOUN KIRK

NT 615 318

The original church of 1241, not on this site, was
dedicated to St Ninian. The present church was built
1652, renovated 1820 and enlarged 1898 with the
addition of the north aisle and vestry. On the outside
of the south wall, the remains of a set of jougs can
be seen. Bird-cage belfry, bell dated 1707, sundial on
south-east corner. Rose window in west gable.
Sunday Service: 11.30am, 1st, 3rd and 5th Sunday
Open by arrangement, key available from
Mertoun Estate Office
CHURCH OF SCOTLAND   ♿ ⑦ **B**

MERTOUN KIRK

301 MINTO CHURCH

NT 557 201
Minto, by Hawick
Designed by William Playfair, the church dates from 1830,
the interior recast in 1934. Fine external war memorial.
Panoramic views of Teviotdale and Minto Hill. Union
with Bedrule and Denholm. Sunday Service: usually every
three weeks, changes every four months; 9.45am or
11.30am, see notice board for details
Key from Mrs Marjorie Walton, Kirk View, Minto,
Hawick 01450 870351
CHURCH OF SCOTLAND 🈯 **C**

MINTO CHURCH

302 MOREBATTLE PARISH CHURCH

NT 772 250
Morebattle, Kelso
The church of 'Mereboda' is recorded as
belonging to the Diocese of Glasgow from
about 1116. The building was burnt down in
1544 and rebuilt; the present structure dates
substantially from 1757, extensions having been
made in 1899 and 1903. It is oblong in plan,
with chancel, porch and vestry which seem to
be additions. Look for the plan in the porch

MOREBATTLE PARISH CHURCH

which shows the archaeological work carried out in the early 1900s, and inscrip-
tions painted on fabric on the west wall. Linked with Hownam, Yetholm and
Linton. Sunday Service: 11.15am
Open all year during daylight hours
CHURCH OF SCOTLAND ♿ 🈯 **B**

303 NEWCASTLETON CHURCH

NY 482 877
Montague Street, Newcastleton
A bright and welcoming building dating from
1888 but with a more modern feel. Memorial
to George Armstrong, founder of the world's
first children's hospital. Millennium stained
glass window by Alex Haynes of Brampton.

NEWCASTLETON CHURCH

Sunday Services: 10.00am and 6.00pm
Open Wednesdays 10.00am-11.30am (coffee stop), or by arrangement with Mrs M Henry,
telephone 01387 375353 or Mrs A Forster 01387 375767
CHURCH OF SCOTLAND ♿ 🚾 🈯 📖 ☕

304 ST BOSWELLS PARISH CHURCH

NT 594 310

South side of St Boswells Main Street near village hall

Built 1844 as Free Church, originally square with earth floor.
Wooden floor and seating added later in 19th century.
Became United Free Church in 1900 and St Modans
Church of Scotland in 1929 and St Boswells Parish Church
in 1952 when old church at Benrig was abandoned.
Substantially renovated 1957-59 and chancel added. Pipe
organ. Stained glass in chancel by McLundie and in
east gable by Liz Rowley. Sunday Service: 10.00am
Open April to September 9.00am-9.00pm,
October to March 9.00am-5.00pm

CHURCH OF SCOTLAND ♿ 🚾 (service times only) ♪

ST BOSWELLS PARISH CHURCH

305 NEWTOWN CHURCH

NT 315 693

St Boswells Road, Newtown St Boswells

Church opened in 1868. Contains memorials
to past ministers. On bus routes between
Jedburgh to Edinburgh and Galashiels.
Sunday Service: 9.45am
Open by arrangement, telephone the Minister
01835 822106

CHURCH OF SCOTLAND 🚾

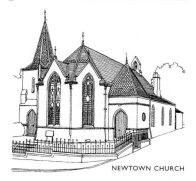

NEWTOWN CHURCH

306 OXNAM KIRK

NT 701 190

Oxnam, by Jedburgh

On the site of a medieval church dating from before 1153. The present church was
built in 1738 and enlarged to form a T-plan in 1874. A characteristic Scottish 18th-
century church with plain glass and white-washed walls. Many fine 17th- and 18th-
century gravestones. Continuo pipe
organ by Lammermuir Pipe Organs
1990. Signposted from A68 at
Jedburgh. Services: 1st and 3rd Sundays,
Christmas and Easter 10.30am
Open by arrangement, telephone Hugh
Fraser 01835 863020. Pennymuir Fair,
ancient Border hill sheep fair, 1st Saturday
in September

CHURCH OF SCOTLAND ♪ **B**

OXNAM KIRK

307 LECKIE MEMORIAL CHURCH

NT 253 404

Eastgate, Peebles

Church website: www.standrewsleckie.co.uk

Handsome Gothic-style church with a fine terraced situation, built 1875-7 to designs by Peddie & Kinnear, in memory of Thomas Leckie, the first pastor of the Associate Burgher Congregation from 1794-1821. Gifted in trust, by the surviving members of his family. Following union in 1976 with St Andrews Church, now home of the St Andrews Leckie congregation. The pews have been removed and replaced with removable seating so the building is now multi-functional. Sunday Services: 10.30am and 6.00pm

Open by arrangement, contact church office Monday to Friday 9.30am-12.30pm, telephone 01721 723121

CHURCH OF SCOTLAND   ♿ wc ⊚

LECKIE MEMORIAL CHURCH

308 PEEBLES OLD PARISH CHURCH

NT 246 406

High Street, Peebles

Built 1887 by William Young of London in Gothic style containing features from earlier church. Fine crown spire dominates the High Street. An inviting flight of steps leads up to the entrance. The chancel was reconstructed by J D Cairns 1937. Entrance screen of 1965, woodwork by Messrs Scott Morton, metalwork by Charles Henshaw & Son, glass by Helen Turner. Pulpit 1913 by P MacGregor Chalmers. Part of pre-Reformation font incorporated in table in crossing, by Mitchall Design 1998. Pipe organ by August Gern 1887, extensively rebuilt. Stained glass by Cottier of London and McCartney of Wiston. Sunday Service: 10.00am; Holy Communion 10.00am on last Sunday of month, January, April and October

Open 10.00am-4.00pm, mid-April to mid-October

CHURCH OF SCOTLAND wc 📖 B

PEEBLES OLD PARISH CHURCH

309 ST JOSEPH'S CHURCH, PEEBLES

NT 248 407

Rosetta Road, Peebles

The present building was opened in 1858. The couthy interior was reordered in 1971. The church includes various stained glass windows and statues. The most significant is the recently restored '14 Stations of the Cross' by the Alinari Brothers of Florence.

Services: Saturday Vigil 6.00pm; Sunday 9.30am

Open daily 9.00am-6.00pm

ROMAN CATHOLIC 🕭 📖 **B**

ST JOSEPH'S CHURCH, PEEBLES

310 ST PETER'S EPISCOPAL, PEEBLES

NT 253 405

Eastgate, Peebles

Built 1836-7 in finely hewn ashlar with an open timber roof. The floor is paved with mosaic tiles as is the reredos, beautifully executed with devices in gold and colour. Choir seats and altar of oak. Piscina on the south side with stone shelf and foliated basin. Fine stained glass. The organ, 1909 by Harrison, is one of the smallest 3-manual instruments ever built and has been praised for its compactness and excellence of tone. Services: Sunday Holy Communion 8.30am, Eucharist 10.30am; Thursday Holy Communion 10.00am

Open 9.00am-5.00pm, or daylight hours

SCOTTISH EPISCOPAL

ST PETER'S EPISCOPAL, PEEBLES

311 BONKYL PARISH CHURCH, PRESTON

NT 808 596

Three miles north of Preston, signposted from B6438

Bonkyl (also spelled Bunkle or Bonkle) is a rectangular building with Romanesque Gothic features. It was built in 1820 with some later insertions. The Old Kirk, of which a semi-circular domed stone-slab apse survives (to south east of the church) was one of the earliest examples of medieval ecclesiastical architecture in Scotland (late 11th century). In nearby Preston is another ruin, Preston Old Kirk, 12th century, its walls having survived because of their conversion to family burial vaults. Sunday Service: 10.00am, 1st and 3rd Sunday

Open at all times

CHURCH OF SCOTLAND ♿ 🚽 (in cottage) 🕭 📖 **B**

312 ROXBURGH PARISH CHURCH

NT 700 307

Two and a half miles west of Kelso on A699

Built in 1752, repaired 1828, with additions 1865. Fine
painted heraldic panels. Stained glass 1947 by W
Wilson. The exterior has a pair of cubical sundials. In
the graveyard the (roofless) burial-vault of the Kers of
Chatto. Fine modern continuo pipe organ,
Lammermuir Pipe Organs 1990.
Services: 11.30am 2nd and 4th Sunday
*Open by arrangement, telephone Mrs Palmer, North Cliff
Cottages, Roxburgh 01573 450263*
CHURCH OF SCOTLAND  **B**

ROXBURGH PARISH CHURCH

313 SAUGHTREE KIRK

NY 562 968

Nine miles north of Newcastleton on B6357

A simple country kirk dating from 1872 enjoying views to the English Border. Fine
patterned coloured glass window. Interesting embroidered pulpit fall depicting the
Trinity. Sunday Services: 9.30am on 2nd Sunday and occasional evening services
Open by arrangement with Mr A Douglas, telephone 01387 376224
CHURCH OF SCOTLAND

314 SKIRLING PARISH CHURCH

NT 075 390

By Biggar

Two miles east of Biggar on A72

The earliest reference to a church in Skirling is in 1275. It was probably situated
near to the present war memorial. It is not known when a church was built on the
present site. However, records show that the church was virtually rebuilt in 1720.
Further significant alterations were made in 1891. The
bellcote is of particular interest, as is the sundial on the
tower. The floral design of the stained glass east
window forms a backdrop to the communion table and
matching chairs presented by the artist, Sir D Y
Cameron, in 1948. Round churchyard enclosed by a
ha-ha and entered through fine wrought-iron gates.
Approached from opposite village green by a steep
metalled access road. Sunday Service: 11.30am
Open by arrangement, telephone A S Goodere 01899 860251
CHURCH OF SCOTLAND

SKIRLING PARISH CHURCH

315 SMAILHOLM CHURCH

NT 649 364
Smailholm village
Built 1630s on 12th-century foundations, altered 1820s and the interior re-ordered during the 20th century. The east window, depicting St Cuthbert & St Giles, was erected in memory of Sir Walter Scott, whose family farmed at Sandyknowes by Smailholm Tower. Birdcage belfry with external bell-rope and outside stairs to the laird's loft. Sunday Service: 10.00am, 1st and 3rd Sunday
Open at all times
CHURCH OF SCOTLAND ♿ **B**

316 SOUTHDEAN PARISH CHURCH

NT 631 092
Southdean, by Hawick
Built in 1876 to a design by George Grant of Glasgow on a site near to the ruins of two previous churches of 12th and 17th centuries. Font, 12th-century. Super-altar set into the communion table, one of only two known in Scotland. Good stained glass. Memorial to James Thomson (1700-48), author of 'Rule Britannia' and 'The Seasons', whose father was parish Minister. Prior to the Battle of Otterburn 1388, the Earl of Douglas and his army met at the 12th-century church, whence the survivors returned to bury their dead. United with Hobkirk. Special Services only and used by children in winter
Open by arrangement, telephone 01450 860692
CHURCH OF SCOTLAND 📖

SOUTHDEAN PARISH CHURCH

317 SPROUSTON KIRK

NT 757 353
There has been a church in Sprouston since the 17th century. The present building was built in 1781, though the bellcote bears the date 1703 and a 12th-century piscina is built into the chancel. The Minister in 1911 won first and third prize out of 36,000 entries in the *Daily Mail* National Sweet Pea Competition, enabling the new chancel to be built with the £1500 prize money. Douglas Strachan window of 'The Fall of Lucifer'. Pulpit falls of sweet peas embroidered by Mrs Doreen West. Sunday Service: 10.00am
Key available from Mr Tom Walker, telephone 01573 228172
CHURCH OF SCOTLAND 📖 **B**

SPROUSTON KIRK   STICHILL, HUME & NEWTHORN PARISH CHURCH

318 STICHILL, HUME & NEWTHORN PARISH CHURCH

NT 711 383

West end of Stichill village, 3 miles north of Kelso

This is the second (or third) church on the site, built around 1780s. It has an outside stairway to the laird's loft, and a burial aisle to the Pringle family on the east gable. The interior is light, with stained glass only in the chancel. Adjoining the church is a stable, altered in 2003 to a small church hall, kitchen and toilet.

Sunday Service: 11.00am

Open at all times

CHURCH OF SCOTLAND   ♿ ᴡᴄ **B**

319 STOBO KIRK

NT 183 377

Stobo, by Peebles

100 yards from B712, off A72, four miles west of Peebles or off A701, one and a half miles south of Broughton

One of the oldest churches in the Borders, and standing on the site of a 6th-century church reputedly founded by St Kentigern (St Mungo). Comprising nave, sanctuary and tower, the latter rebuilt from first-floor level, probably 16th century. Major restoration in 1863, John Lessels. North aisle chapel restored in 1929, James Grieve. A new stone floor laid and a meeting room formed at first-floor level of the tower in 1991. Linked with Broughton, Tweedsmuir and Skirling and united with Drumelzier. Sunday Service: 11.30am

For information on access, telephone Mrs Loudon Hamilton 01721 740393, or Rev Rachel Dobie 01899 830331

CHURCH OF SCOTLAND   **B**

STOBO KIRK

TRAQUAIR KIRK

320 TRAQUAIR KIRK

NT 320 335

There has been a church at Traquair since the early 12th century. The present simple, elegant country church is dated 1778 and has a traditional plan with a central pulpit. Comprehensive restoration completed 2001. A monument on the outside wall commemorates Alexander Brodie (d. 1811), 'Iron Master ... a native of Traquaire (*sic*), First Inventor of the Register Stoves and Fore Hearths for Ships'. Many notable gravestones, the earliest from the late 17th century. Sunday Services: 10.00am, 2nd and 4th Sundays; as announced for 5th Sunday

Open by arrangement, telephone Mr Donald 01896 830781

CHURCH OF SCOTLAND ⏺ **B**

321 TRAQUAIR HOUSE CHAPEL

NT 331 355

Traquair House, near Innerleithen

Church website: www.traquair.co.uk

The chapel, formerly the billiard room above the brewhouse, replaced the 'secret chapel' in the main house used in penal times. Related memorabilia on view in house, which also contains a priest's hole and secret stairway. Chapel has carved oak panels said to have come from the chapel of Mary of Guise in Leith, and to be of Flemish origin. Service: Mass 7.00pm, last Thursday April to October

Easter Egg Extravaganza (April). Traquair Fair first weekend in August. Christmas opening last weekend in November. Open April 12.00 noon-5.00pm; June, July and August 10.30am-5.00pm; October 11.00-4.00pm. Access to chapel is included in admission to grounds

ROMAN CATHOLIC ♿ 🚾 ⏺ ☕ **A**

322   TWEEDSMUIR KIRK

NT 101 245

Eight miles south of Broughton on A701

The present building was erected in 1874 by
John Lessels, to replace a much earlier
church of 1643. Bell of 1773 still in use.
Major restoration in 2002. Two high
circular windows in the north and south
transepts and some interesting stained glass.
Oak for the panelling in the porch is from
a tree planted at Abbotsford by Sir Walter
Scott. First and Second World War
memorials. The churchyard dates back to
the first church and contains table-stone
graves of the 18th century and several other
stones of interest, including a Covenanter's
grave and one, near the gate, to the many
men who died in the construction of the
Talla reservoir. Linked with Broughton,
Skirling and Stobo with Drumelzier.
Sunday Service: 10.00am
Open daily all year
CHURCH OF SCOTLAND  **B**

TWEEDSMUIR KIRK

323   ST MUNGO'S CHURCH, WEST LINTON

NT 148 519

Chapel Brae, West Linton

A 'Gladstone Church' built in
1851 when it served as both
church and school. Unusually, the
church runs from north to south
instead of east to west. Fine
stained glass by C E Kempe.
Services: Sunday 11.00am; 2nd
Sunday Choral Evensong 5.30pm
*Open by arrangement, telephone
the Rector 01968 672862*
SCOTTISH EPISCOPAL [wc]

ST MUNGO'S CHURCH, WEST LINTON

WALKERBURN CHURCH

324 WALKERBURN CHURCH

NT 364 373

Walkerburn came into being as a tweed manufacturing village following the establishment of the first mill by Henry Ballantyne in 1855. After first using the school for worship, the present building was consecrated in 1875 and enlarged 1896. Pipe organ by Ingram. Gallery and space below remodelled in 1979 to create halls separate from the nave. Stained glass windows celebrate the Ballantyne family. Sunday Services: 10.00am, 1st and 3rd Sundays, 5th Sunday as announced

Open by arrangement with the Minister, telephone 01896 870535

CHURCH OF SCOTLAND [wc] (2)

325 YARROW KIRK

NT 358 278

On A708, 8 miles west of Selkirk

The present church, built in 1640, replaced the historic 'St Mary's of the Lowes' or 'The Forest Kirk', dating from the 12th century, on the hillside above St Mary's Loch. Sir Walter Scott and James Hogg, 'The Ettrick Shepherd', were regular worshippers. With a traditional T-plan, it was considerably adapted and improved over the years. It was gutted by fire in 1922 but restored. Memorial windows by Douglas Strachan. Sundial on corner of building. Sunday service: 11.30am, for 5th Sunday, see local press

Open at all times

CHURCH OF SCOTLAND [&] [wc] (2) B

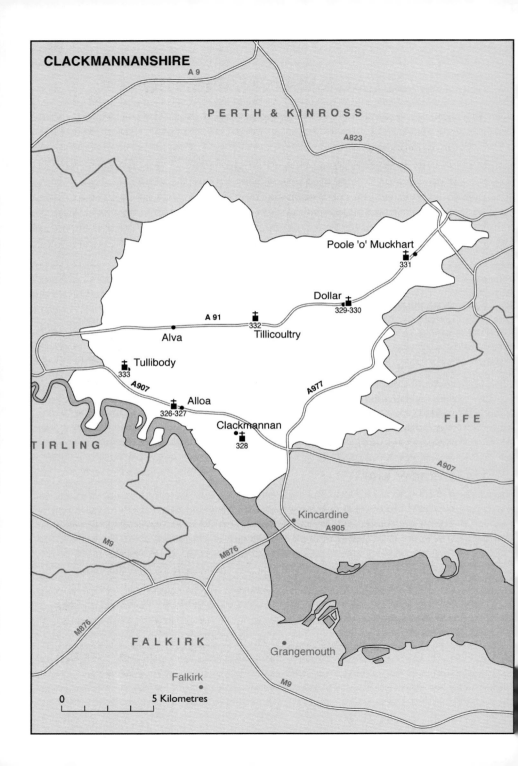

CLACKMANNANSHIRE

326 ALLOA PARISH CHURCH (ST MUNGO'S)
NS 886 929
Bedford Place, Alloa
Delicate and picturesque Gothic Revival church by James Gillespie Graham 1819.
Usual symmetry in plan, but greater felicity than normal in lacy Perpendicular. The
207 ft spire with flying buttresses is visible from most parts of the town. Interior is
by Leslie Grahame MacDougall in Lorimer-derived Gothic.
Sunday Service: 11.15am
Open by arrangement, telephone 01259 214494. Close to Alloa Tower
CHURCH OF SCOTLAND ♿ wc ② 📖 **B**

327 ST JOHN'S CHURCH, ALLOA
NS 886 923
Broad Street, Alloa
Sir Robert Rowand Anderson designed St John's which was opened in 1869 and
enlarged in 1873. Described by Thomas Bradshaw then as the 'most elegant place
of worship in the County'. Early Geometric Gothic with a notable broach spire.
The rich interior includes glass by Kempe, and a reredos with a mosaic of the Last
Supper by the Italian Salviatti. The chancel was refurbished in 1913, its roof
bearing 106 carved bosses. These, together with the woodwork of the choirstalls
1902, organ screen and war
memorial, are all by Lorimer. The
tower contains a ring of eight
bells, six hung in 1871 and a
further two in 1925. Sunday
Service: Family Eucharist 11.00am
*Open usually Wednesday and Friday
10.00am-12.30pm; other times,
telephone 01259 212836*
SCOTTISH EPISCOPAL ♿ wc ② **B**

ST JOHN'S CHURCH, ALLOA

328 CLACKMANNAN PARISH CHURCH

NS 910 918

High Street, Clackmannan

Church website: clackmannamkirk.fsnet.co.uk

There has been a church at Clackmannan since St Serf
visited from Culross in the 8th century. The present
church was built in 1815 by James Gillespie Graham to
replace a 13th-century church. Perpendicular Gothic
with buttressed tower at the west end. Stained glass by
Herbert Hendrie, Gordon Webster, Sadie Pritchard and
Douglas Hamilton. Modern Makin Toccata digital

CLACKMANNAN PARISH CHURCH

computerised organ. Graveyard has stones dating from
the 17th century with several Bruce family memorials. Views over Carse of Forth.
Close to Tower and Tolbooth. Sunday Services: 11.00am, 10.30am July and August
Open weekdays 2.00-4.00pm, 2nd Monday in June to 2nd Friday in September.
Other times, telephone 01259 214238 or 01259 211255
CHURCH OF SCOTLAND ♿ wc ⑦ ⌷ ☐ **B**

329 DOLLAR PARISH CHURCH

NS 964 980

East Burnside, Dollar

Church website: www.dollarparishchurch.org.uk

Built 1842/3 to replace 18th-century church (ruin to
north), designed by Tite of London. Chancel added 1926,
porch added 1963. Triple stained glass window in memory
of Rev Angus Gunn 1910. Three stained glass windows
by Adam Robson and Jennifer Campbell, Union window
1979 by Douglas Hogg. Millennium glass screens designed
by Angus Maclean 2003. Rushworth and Dreaper organ
1926. Reredos tapestry based on Ardchattan Cross
designed by Adam Robson 1963. Sunday Service: 11.15am

DOLLAR PARISH CHURCH

Open by arrangement, telephone the Minister 01259 743432
CHURCH OF SCOTLAND ♿ wc ⑦ ☐ **B**

330 ST JAMES THE GREAT, DOLLAR

NS 958 980

Harviestoun Road, Dollar

A small country church with a prayerful atmosphere, set in a well-kept garden.
Consecrated in 1882, the building was designed by Thomas Frame & Son, Alloa.
The font is a memorial to Archbishop Archibald Campbell Tait of Canterbury
(1868-83). Sunday Services: 8.30am and 10.30am, Thursday 9.45am
Open daily all year
SCOTTISH EPISCOPAL ♿ ⑦ **C**

ST JAMES THE GREAT, DOLLAR

MUCKHART PARISH CHURCH

331 MUCKHART PARISH CHURCH

NO 001 010

North side of A91 at west end of Pool of Muckhart

Church 18th century. Stained Glass windows removed to Fossoway Church, Crook of Devon. Various plaques. Large grave stone on east wall of the church for the Christie family, Cowden. Nearby stone to Matsui, Japanese gardener to Miss Ella Christie. Sunday Service: 9.45am

Open at all times

CHURCH OF SCOTLAND wc **B**

332 TILLICOULTRY PARISH CHURCH

NS 923 968

Dollar Road

Neo-Perpendicular, rectangular church by William Stirling of Dunblane 1829. The original horseshoe gallery was replaced with a single gallery in 1920. Stained glass window of 1924 in memory of the Rev Joseph Conn. Three-light window by Douglas Strachan featuring the Crucifixion, Joseph, and David instructing Solomon. Sunday Services: 9.00am and 10.30am, evening Service 6.30pm (last Sunday of month)

Open June to August 2.00pm-4.00pm, or by arrangement with Session Clerk 01259 750772

CHURCH OF SCOTLAND ♿ wc ? 🕯 **B**

333 ST SERF'S PARISH CHURCH, TULLIBODY

NS 860 954

Menstrie Road

Charmingly simple Norman-style church of 1904 by Peter McGregor Chalmers, with a nave and side aisles separated by five pillared arches, apse and transepts and an open dressed-timber roof. Stained glass by Stephen Adam, Norman M McDougall. Nearby ruins of the former church. Sunday Services: 11.00am and 6.30pm

Open Tuesdays 9.30am-2.00pm

CHURCH OF SCOTLAND ♿ wc ? 🕯 **B**

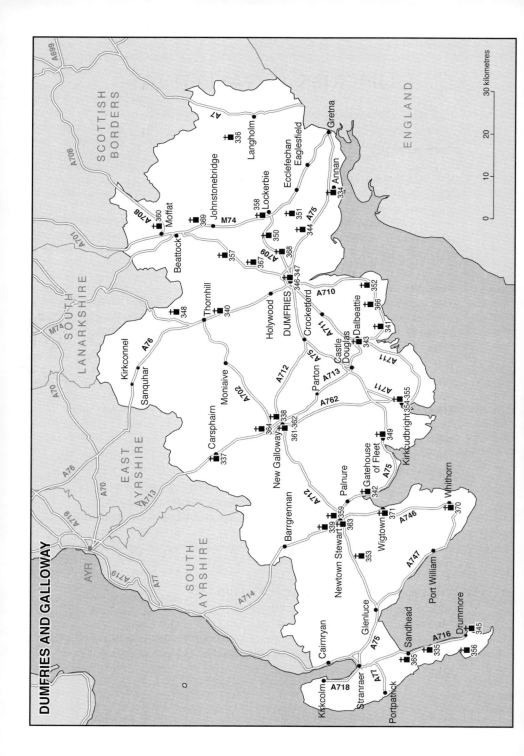

DUMFRIES & GALLOWAY

Local Representatives: The Rev J W Scott, The Manse of Durisdeer, Thornhill (*telephone* 01848 500231); Mr Michael Dunlop, High Baltersan, Newton Stewart (*telephone* 01671 402543)

334 ST COLUMBA'S CHURCH, ANNAN

NY 199 665

Scott's Street, Annan

Built as a Congregational Church in 1794 on the site of a Secession Meeting House and re-opened as a Catholic Church in 1839. Extended at both ends in 1904 by Charles Walker of Newcastle as the gift of the parish priest the Rev Lord Archibald Douglas. Stations of the Cross by Brendan Ellis 1984. Painted panels by Joe Burns 1997. The parish priest also serves St Francis' Church, Drove Road, Langholm (1960) Services: Saturday Vigil Mass 6.00pm, Sunday Mass 11.00am

Open daily 9.00am-6.00pm. When closed, key from adjacent presbytery or at 32 Scott's Street

ROMAN CATHOLIC ⬛wc ⬤ 📖 **B**

ST COLUMBA'S CHURCH, ANNAN

335 ARDWELL

NX 100 457

One kilometre west of Ardwell village

Church website: www.ardwell-church.org.uk

Surrounded by trees and shrubs and fronted with grass and flowerbeds, Gothic cruciform church by P MacGregor Chalmers 1901. Tower with octagonal spire and corner pinnacles. Notable inside are the inscriptions in the masonry. Pulpit, reredos, screen and communion table in oak, elaborately carved. Stained glass window of 'The Calming of the Storm'. Sunday Service: every two weeks (normally) 10.00am

Open by arrangement, telephone 01776 830215

CHURCH OF SCOTLAND ♿ ⬛wc **B**

ARDWELL

336 WESTERKIRK, BENTPATH

NY 312 903

On B709, 7 miles north-west of Langholm

Pleasing Victorian church of 1881 by James Burnet, now fully restored from its former uninhabitable condition; restoration supervised by Richard Jaques of York. A fine organ of like period is currently being installed. Twelve new stained glass windows showing natural life in the Westerkirk valley, including a window commemorating the Golden Jubilee of 2002 donated by the community. In the graveyard is the Johnson Mausoleum, a classical Greek cross by Robert Adam 1790. Church of Scotland service 2.30pm on first Sunday (except July and August); Episcopal services approximately four times a year (see local press)

Open by arrangement, telephone 01387 370201 or 381240 or 370215

CHURCH OF SCOTLAND ⟦wc⟧ **B** (Mausoleum **A**)

337 CARSPHAIRN PARISH CHURCH

NX 563 932

Carsphairn, Castle Douglas on A713

Built in 1815 to replace church of 1636 destroyed by fire. Central communion table. Memorials including John Semple, Covenanting minister, and John Loudon MacAdam, roads pioneer. Covenanter's grave. Linked with Balmaclellan, Kells and Dalry. Sunday Service: 10.30am
Open by arrangement, telephone Mrs Campbell 01644 460208. Carsphairn Pastoral and Horticultural Show, first Saturday in June

CHURCH OF SCOTLAND ⟦wc⟧ ⟦🔊⟧ **B**

CARSPHAIRN PARISH CHURCH

338 BALMACLELLAN CHURCH, CASTLE DOUGLAS

NX 651 791

A harled, T-plan kirk, the body was built in 1753, with the north aisle added in 1833 by William McCandlish. The stained glass west window is dated 1928 and is by Gordon Webster. The graveyard has an early 18th-century table-stone commemorating the Covenanting martyr Robert Grierson. Statue and plaque in churchyard commemorate Sir Walter Scott's 'Old Mortality', who came from Balmaclellan. Sunday Service: first Sunday of every month at 12.00 noon
Open by arrangement, telephone the Minister 01644 430380

CHURCH OF SCOTLAND

BALMACLELLAN CHURCH, CASTLE DOUGLAS

ALL SAINTS CHURCH, CHALLOCH

CLOSEBURN PARISH CHURCH

339 ALL SAINTS CHURCH, CHALLOCH

NX 385 675

Challoch, 2 miles north of Newton Stewart on A714

Built as private chapel of Edward James Stopford-Blair of Penninghame House
and consecrated 1872. Designed by W G Habershon & Pite of London and an
excellent example of a small Victorian church. Ten stained glass windows, 17
memorial plaques, pine altar and wrought iron and brass rood screen. Fine Harston
two-tracker organ 1881, restored 1993. Sunday Services: 9.00am Holy Eucharist,
10.30am Mattins (1st Sunday), Sung Eucharist (2nd, 4th and 5th), Children's Family
Communion (3rd), Litergies for the blind (Braille); daily 8.00am Morning Prayer,
5.30pm Evening Prayer. Thursdays 10.00am Holy Eucharist

Open daily, or telephone 01671 402101

SCOTTISH EPISCOPAL & wc ⊘ ⛾ **A**

340 CLOSEBURN PARISH CHURCH

NX 904 923

Closeburn, by Thornhill

Built by James Barbour 1878 alongside former (1741) church. In Gothic style with a
three-stage tower. Spacious interior with an elaborate hammerbeam roof supported
on foliaged corbels. Pipe organ by Henry Willis & Sons 1887. Window in the
north transept by the St Enoch Glass Studios 1948. Font originally from
Dalgarnock. In the graveyard is the smart mausoleum built by Thomas Kirkpatrick
of Closeburn in 1742. Sunday Service: 10.30am

Keys from either Mrs Lorimer, Lakehead Farm Cottages or
Mr Williamson, Closeburn Village

CHURCH OF SCOTLAND & wc 📖 **B**

341   COLVEND PARISH CHURCH

NX 862 541

Rockcliffe, by Dalbeattie, ¼ mile from A710

A chaste Early Christian church by P MacGregor
Chalmers 1911, of granite with red sandstone
dressings and set on a rise overlooking the Solway
Firth. Its bell-tower is topped by a steep pyramid
roof. A pretty interior with nave, aisle and transept
and a timbered roof. Plain plastered walls are a foil
for the sandstone columns which support round-
headed arches springing from cushion capitals to
form arcades into the aisle and transept. In the

COLVEND PARISH CHURCH

chancel, the deep colour of the stained glass window, the Ascension by Stephen
Adam & Co 1918, forms a lovely backdrop to the High Presbyterian arrangement of
furnishings. Other windows by Adam & Co and by Margaret Chilton and Marjorie
Kemp 1926. Linked with Southwick and Kirkbean. Sunday Service: 11.30am

Open daily 10.00am-6.00pm

CHURCH OF SCOTLAND [wc] Ⓓ 📖

342   KIRKMABRECK PARISH CHURCH, CREETOWN

NX 493 565

On A75, 6 miles from Newton Stewart

Large and tall with a tower above the front
gable, built in 1834 by John Henderson.
Panelling 1645 with Muir family coat of arms.
In spring, churchyard and graveyard carpeted
with crocuses. Sunday Service: 11.30am

*Open by arrangement, telephone Mr J Cutland,
5 Chain Road, Creetown 01671 820228*

CHURCH OF SCOTLAND [♿] [wc] Ⓓ

KIRKMABRECK PARISH CHURCH, CREETOWN

343   ST PETER'S CHURCH, DALBEATTIE

NX 831 613

Craignair Street, Dalbeattie

Hall church 1814 of pinky granite with
red sandstone dressings. Grey granite
tower added *c.*1850.

Sunday Mass 9.00am and 11.00am

Open daily 9.00am-5.00pm

ROMAN CATHOLIC [♿] **B**

ST PETER'S CHURCH, DALBEATTIE

344 DALTON KIRK

NY 114 740

Dalton, by Lockerbie on B725

Close by the roofless shell of the 1704 parish church
stands J M Dick Peddie's 1895 sturdy Romanesque
church. Unusually colourful kingpost-truss roof over the
nave and scissors roof in the chancel. Three-light stained
glass window of the Ascension by A Ballantine and
Gardiner 1896. The graveyard contains a late Georgian
burial enclosure and the suave classical monument to the
Carruthers of Whitecroft. Sunday Services: 9.45am,
11.15am by rotation with Hightae and St Mungo
Open by arrangement, telephone the Manse,
Hightae, Lockerbie 01387 811499
CHURCH OF SCOTLAND ⓦ ⓒ 🍼 📖 **B**

DALTON KIRK

345 ST MEDAN'S, DRUMMORE

NX 135 367

Stair Street, Drummore

Built 1903 in red Dumfries sandstone with an
attractive roof of red and yellow pine. Hymnus IV
electronic organ. Morrison memorial window behind
choir 1951. John McGuffog memorial window above
pulpit, designed and made by Arthur C Speirs DA of
Greenock 1996. Sunday Services: 11.30am, except last
Sunday of month from May to September, when
service is in Kirkmaiden Old Church
Open by arrangement, telephone Mrs Beck 01776 840210
CHURCH OF SCOTLAND ♿ ⓦ ⓒ **B**

ST MEDAN'S, DRUMMORE

346 CRICHTON MEMORIAL CHURCH, THE CRICHTON, DUMFRIES

NY 983 742

The Crichton, Bankend Road, The Crichton, Dumfries

Church website: www.crichton.co.uk

Cathedral-style church designed by architect Sydney Mitchell. Crichton Memorial
Church completed in 1897. Square tower 123 feet high. The richly detailed exterior
is of red sandstone from Locharbriggs, Dumfries. The elegant interior features pink
sandstone from nearby Thornhill. Ornate oak roof. Stone carving by William
Vickers of Glasgow. The boldly designed floor is of Irish and Sicilian marble.
Impressive stained glass by Oscar Paterson of Glasgow 1896 throughout. Pulpit
and choir stalls date from 1897. The magnificent organ by Lewis 1902 has richly

CRICHTON MEMORIAL CHURCH, THE CRICHTON, DUMFRIES   ST GEORGE'S, DUMFRIES

carved screens. Brass angel lectern 1910. Inter-denominational. Regular services
take place. Popular venue for weddings, concerts and other special events
Open by arrangement, telephone Crichton Development Company 01387 247544
NON-DENOMINATIONAL 🦽 wc **A**

347 ST GEORGE'S, DUMFRIES
NX 971 764
George Street, Dumfries
Church website: www.saint-georges.org.uk
Built as a Free Church in 1844 by William McGowan, and remodelled in 1893 by
James Halliday who added the Italianate front of red sandstone. Almost square
interior with north and south aisles marked off by superimposed Corinthian
columns. Compartmented and coved main ceiling. Sunday Service: 11.00am,
additionally July and August 9.30am (Family Service)
Open by arrangement, telephone Dr Balfour 01387 253696
CHURCH OF SCOTLAND 🦽 wc **B**

348 DURISDEER PARISH CHURCH
NS 894 038
One mile east of A702
Unspoilt, peaceful, Georgian country parish church, rebuilt 1716, topped by a belfry
tower. X-plan, one arm of the cross is taller and more sophisticated, built for the
Duke of Queensberry and remaining from the earlier church. Inside is the most
amazing monument over the Queensberry burial vault, a baroque baldacchino carved
in 1695 by John van Nost to the design of James Smith who was also architect of
the later church. 'There are few buildings in which baroque magnificence and
presbyterian decency are so happily combined' (George Hay, *Architecture of Scottish
Post-Reformation Churches*). Martyr's Grave 1685. Sunday Service: 11.45am
Open during daylight hours. Drumlanrig Castle nearby
CHURCH OF SCOTLAND 🦽 wc 📖 ☕ (afternoon teas, Sundays, July, August, September) **A**

DURISDEER PARISH CHURCH

ST MARY'S CHURCH, GATEHOUSE OF FLEET

349 ST MARY'S CHURCH, GATEHOUSE OF FLEET

NX 597 562

Dromore Road

Episcopalians in the area worshipped in the private chapel of Cally house until the present building of 1840 was purchased from the United Presbyterian Church and dedicated to St Mary in 1909. It is probably unique among Scottish Episcopal Churches in having a stained glass window commemorating John Knox! Sunday Service: Holy Communion 9.45am; Wednesday, Holy Communion 9.30am

Open by arrangement, telephone P Taylor 01557 330146

SCOTTISH EPISCOPAL   ♿   ⚫   **B**

350 HIGHTAE KIRK

NY 090 793

On the B7020, 2½ miles south of Lochmaben
Built as a Relief meeting house in 1796 and remodelled for the Reformed Presbyterians in 1865, when the windows were enlarged and the gabled west bellcote and small porch were added. Sunday Services: 9.45am, 11.15am by rotation with Dalton and St Mungo
Open by arrangement, telephone the Manse, Hightae, Lockerbie 01387 811499
CHURCH OF SCOTLAND
♿ wc (adjoining Manse) ⚱

HIGHTAE KIRK

351 ST MUNGO PARISH CHURCH, KETTLEHOLM

NY 143 771
On the B723, 3 miles south of Lockerbie
Built under the patronage of the Rt Hon
Robert Jardine MP of Castlemilk. Late Scots
Gothic by David Bryce 1877 with a pinnacled-
buttressed porch decorated with grotesque
carved heads. Inside, a magnificently elaborate
open roof. Organ 1905 by Abbot & Smith.
Stained glass by James Ballantine & Son 1876.
First World War memorial by F M Taubman.
Sunday Services: 9.45am, 11.15am by rotation
with Dalton and Hightae
Open by arrangement, telephone the Manse,
Hightae, Lockerbie 01387 811499
CHURCH OF SCOTLAND ♿ wc ⛨ **B**

ST MUNGO PARISH CHURCH, KETTLEHOLM

352 KIRKBEAN PARISH CHURCH

NX 980 592
Harled T-plan kirk said to have been designed
by William Craik, sometime Laird of Arbigland.
The tower on the west wall is of two lower
stages, 1776, with a Diocletian window in its
second stage, and two upper stages added in
1836 are by Walter Newall, the first with a clock
and the top with a big octagonal belfry cupola
of polished ashlar under a lantern. Venetian
window in the east gable of the tail of the
church. Inside, plain furnishings of 1883. A
memorial font, presented by the United States
Navy in memory of John Paul Jones, a
gardener's son from Arbigland, who founded it;
designed and sculpted by George Henry Paulin
1946. In the village, turn left at the road
junction to Carsethorn. Adjacent to the school
on left. Linked with Colvend and Southwick.
Sunday Service: 10.00am
Open by arrangement, telephone Mr George
Fazakerley 01387 880662
CHURCH OF SCOTLAND wc **B**

KIRKBEAN PARISH CHURCH

353 KIRKCOWAN PARISH CHURCH

NX 327 610

Main Street, Kirkcowan

At the west end of the village, built in 1834 to
replace a former church, of which only an ivy-
clad east gable remains in its kirkyard (east end of
village). The present church is a harled T-plan
building with external stairs at the east and west
gables leading to two galleries. A tower at the
north side. Inside, three galleries in all, supported
by marbled cast-iron columns. Tall pulpit of 1834
and a late 19th-century chamber organ by J & A
Mirrlees, brought here in 1966. Linked with
Wigtown. Sunday Service: 10.00am

Open by arrangement, telephone Mr J Adair 01671 830214

CHURCH OF SCOTLAND 🚿 wc ② **A**

KIRKCOWAN PARISH CHURCH

354 KIRKCUDBRIGHT PARISH CHURCH

NX 683 509

St Mary Street

The present neo-Gothic building dates from
1838 and was designed by William Burn.
Cruciform in shape, the nave and gallery
together comprise the 'Country End', with
the south transept referred to as the 'Town
End' and the north transept as the 'Trades
End'. A substantial pulpit, also designed by
Burn, incorporates a sounding board and a
precentor's box. Stained glass window of
1913 in south transept by William Meikle in
memory of the Rev A C Campbell. Services:
(May to August) Sunday 9.30am and 11.00am
(only 11.00am on 4th Sunday), 6.30pm
Christian Healing Service (2nd Sunday);
(September to May) 11.00am; 9.30am and
6.30pm Christian Healing (2nd Sunday)

Open June to August, 9.00am-5.00pm.
At other times open by arrangement,
telephone Neil Cavers 01557 331217

CHURCH OF SCOTLAND 🚿 wc ② 🚹 **B**

KIRKCUDBRIGHT PARISH CHURCH

355 GREYFRIARS (ST FRANCIS OF ASSISI), KIRKCUDBRIGHT

NX 682 511

Mote Brae, Kirkcudbright

The sanctuary of Greyfriars Church is the last remaining fragment of a Franciscan friary. Dating from either the 13th or 15th centuries, it has undergone many changes in both design and use over the years. The MacClellan Monument, erected in 1597, is one of the most interesting features of the church. On the left of the High Altar is an ancient piscina. There are

GREYFRIARS (ST FRANCIS OF ASSISI), KIRKCUDBRIGHT

also three fine modern stained glass windows including work by Gordon Webster. The cross and candlesticks are the work of Mabel Brunton, a distinguished member of the artists' colony which flourished in the town in the 1920s. Other interesting furnishings are the 17-century dower chest and the medieval holy water stoup.

Sunday Services: Holy Communion 11.30am all year, and 8.15am end May to August; Friday: Holy Communion 10.00am

Open Easter week, July to August, and by arrangement, telephone the Rector 01557 330146

SCOTTISH EPISCOPAL **A**

356 KIRKMAIDEN OLD KIRK

NX 139 324

Kirkmaiden, Drummore

Built 1638 to replace St Catherine's at Mull of Galloway in the most southerly parish in Scotland. T-shaped church with vaults of the McDouall family of Logan underneath balcony. 'Treacle' Bible on display. Bell from Clanyard Castle, a gift from the Earl of Dalhousie 1532.

Sunday Service: 11.30am last Sunday May to September

Open daily Easter to October, or by arrangement with Mrs Symonds, telephone 01776 840601

CHURCH OF SCOTLAND

KIRKMAIDEN OLD KIRK

357 KIRKMICHAEL KIRK

NY 005 884

Parkgate, off A701

Church website: www.kirkinthor.co.uk

Built in 1815 in the location of churches
thought to date from 9th and 10th
centuries. Classic T-plan of rough
dressed whinstone with sandstone
facings with large round-headed
windows and a birdcage bellcote. Three
stained glass memorial windows ('Our
Lord stilling the storm', 'Our Lord the
Good Shepherd' and 'Our Lady with

KIRKMICHAEL KIRK

Faith and Hope'), three memorial plaques and a laird's loft. Good collection of
18th-century stones in the graveyard. Sunday Services: 9.45am or 11.15am
Open by arrangement, telephone Mrs Copeland 01687 860235
or Mr Findlay 01387 860642
CHURCH OF SCOTLAND   ♿ wc ⊘ **B**

358 HOLY TRINITY, LOCKERBIE

NY 136 815

Arthurs Place, Lockerbie

Church website:

www.lockerbie-and-moffat-rc-churches.freeola.com

Built as Trinity Church 1874 for the United
Presbyterian Church, became Church of
Scotland 1929 and acquired in 1973 by the
Catholic Church and renamed Holy Trinity.
Designed by Ford Mackenzie, built in
Corncockle sandstone in Gothic style with a
large rose window and steeple. The organ,
Ingram of Edinburgh, is a prominent feature.
Plaque in vestibule commemorates 1000 years
of Christianity in the Ukraine. Copy of
Lockerbie Book of Remembrance and
Memorial Plaque. Services: Sunday Mass
11.15am; other days as announced
Open daily 9.00am-5.00pm
ROMAN CATHOLIC **B**

HOLY TRINITY, LOCKERBIE

359 MONIGAFF PARISH CHURCH, MINNIGAFF

NX 410 666

Minnigaff, Newton Stewart

Church completed in 1836 to a design by William
Burn. Stained glass by William Wailes of Newcastle
1868 and Ballantine, Edinburgh 1910. Font from Earl
of Galloway's private chapel. Organ built in 1873,
Bryceson Brothers, London. Ruins of pre-Reformation
church on medieval foundations. East gable 12th- or
early 13th-century. Motte and ditch. Eighth-century
stone slab of Irish missionary influence. Grave stones
including B-listed Heron monument. Yew tree 900
years old. Sunday Service: 10.00am, first Sunday of
month Holy Communion 9.25am

MONIGAFF PARISH
CHURCH, MINNIGAFF

*Open July and August, Monday and Friday 2.00-4.30pm. Or by arrangement,
telephone Mrs Shankland 01671 402164. Historical display June to September*

CHURCH OF SCOTLAND [wc] ⊘ ⫐ ⎕ ⎕ (free) **B**

360 ST ANDREW'S, MOFFAT

NT 075 051

Churchgate, Moffat

Church website: www.standrewsmoffat.org.uk

Impressive church in Early English style by
John Starforth 1884, with a central tower
flanked by bowed stair towers. Richly carved
entrance leads to a wide interior with galleries
on slender iron columns. Profusion of stained
glass including rose window above the pulpit
by Starforth. Other windows by James
Ballantine & Son, Ballantine & Gardiner, and
William Meikle & Sons. Pipe organ by Eustace
Ingram 1894. Sunday Service: 11.15am

*Open June to September, 10.30am-12.30pm
and 2.00-4.00pm*

CHURCH OF SCOTLAND [♿] (rear door) [wc] ⊘ **B**

ST ANDREW'S, MOFFAT

361 KELLS PARISH CHURCH, NEW GALLOWAY

NX 632 784

Kirk Road, New Galloway

Built in 1822 to a design by William McCandlish. A granite T-plan church with three-stage square tower at the centre of south wall. Interior mainly reconstructed in 1911 following original layout. Galleries on three sides with pulpit on long south wall. Notable churchyard with three 'Adam and Eve' stones of 1706-7, and a delightful upright for Captain Gordon's gamekeeper, John Murray. Linked with Carsphairn, Balmaclellan and Dalry.

Sunday Service: 10.30am, not first Sunday

Open by arrangement, telephone 01644 430380

CHURCH OF SCOTLAND ⟨⟩ **B**

KELLS PARISH CHURCH,
NEW GALLOWAY

362 ST MARGARET'S NEW GALLOWAY

NX 636 778

On edge of New Galloway on Ken Bridge road

Built 1904, chancel added 1908. The walls of the church are harled and the roofs are red tiled. The wooden panelling and furnishings are a mixture of Oregon pine and oak and the windows are variously by Kempe, Clayton & Bell, and James Powell & Sons. Services: 10.30am every Sunday and Wednesday

Key at Rectory next door, telephone Rev John Repath 01644 420235

SCOTTISH EPISCOPAL ♿ ▯

ST MARGARET'S NEW GALLOWAY

363 PENNINGHAME ST JOHN'S CHURCH, NEWTON STEWART

NX 410 654

Church Street, Newton Stewart

Church website: www.penninghameparish.org.uk

Church completed in 1840 to a design by William Burn. Groome's *Gazetteer* describes it as 'a handsome Gothic edifice'. Organ by J F Harston of Newark in 1878, believed to be the largest and most intact of all organs built by him; renovated by Hill, Norman and Beard 1962. Spire 151 feet. Tower clock with 32 foot pendulum, 1880, by James Ritchie of Edinburgh, restored 2004. All glass replaced 1996. Interesting display of Communion silver including two chalices dated 1711. Church Street is parallel to town's main street. Sunday Service: 10.30am

Open Tuesday 12.30-2.00pm for lunchtime prayer meeting, or by arrangement, telephone Mr M C Dunlop 01671 402543

CHURCH OF SCOTLAND |wc| ⟨⟩ **A**

PENNINGHAME ST JOHN'S CHURCH, NEWTON STEWART   DALRY PARISH CHURCH, ST JOHN'S TOWN OF DALRY

364   DALRY PARISH CHURCH, ST JOHN'S TOWN OF DALRY

NX 618 813

Main Street, St John's Town of Dalry on A713

Completed in 1831 to a design by William McCandlish to replace a ruinous
building of 1771; probably the third church to occupy the site. Early records are
scarce, but a dilapidated church, existed in 1427. Traditional T-shaped interior,
plainly furnished. Pulpit with carved wooden canopy. Galleries on three sides.
Stands near the Water of Ken with wide views of the Rhinns of Kells. Avenue of
lime trees. Interesting old kirkyard with Covenanters' stone and Gordon Aisle,
burial place of the Gordons of Lochinvar. Robert Burns fashioned his poem 'Tam
o' Shanter' on a local tale. Linked with Balmaclellan and Kells and Carsphairn.
Sunday Service: 12.00 noon

Open by arrangement, telephone Mr D M Bell 01644 430273

CHURCH OF SCOTLAND   [wc] (?) **B**

365   SANDHEAD

NX 097 500

Main Street, Sandhead

Church website: www.ardwell-church.org.uk

Substantial timber construction with steeply pitched tiled roof and cedar-board clad
walls by architects Goudie & Hill 1962. The unusual structure uses laminated timber
portal frames with obscured glass between the frames in both side walls. Flat-roofed
porch with masonry bell-tower. Internally, much varnished wood. Inverted-pyramid
shaped pulpit. Sunday Services: every two weeks, normally 10.00am

Open by arrangement, contact Mrs C McKay, 25 Main Street or
Mr Cowan, Dorlin, Main Street

CHURCH OF SCOTLAND   [♿] [wc] ⌣ (Wednesdays and Sundays, 2.00-4.00pm in summer)

SANDHEAD

SOUTHWICK PARISH CHURCH

366 SOUTHWICK PARISH CHURCH

NX 906 569

Caulkerbush, by Dumfries

Standing by woodland just outside the policies of Southwick House, a stone church of local grey granite with dressings of red sandstone. By Peddie & Kinnear 1891, a mixture of Early Christian and Norman. Its crossing tower was derived from the 14th-century tower of St Monans Parish Church. Neo-Norman font by Cox & Buckley 1898 and a neo-Jacobean pulpit. Wrought iron Arts & Crafts light fittings, once for oil lamps. Late 19th-century stained glass. Organ replaced in May 1999 with Ahlborn SL100. A710 from Dumfries, turn right immediately over Southwick Bridge onto B793 Dalbeattie. Linked with Colvend and Kirkbean. Sunday Service: 10.00am

Open by arrangement, telephone Geo Fazakerley 01387 880662

CHURCH OF SCOTLAND [wc] (?)

367 TINWALD CHURCH

NY 003 816

Off A701, 3 miles north of Dumfries

Church website: www.kirkinthor.co.uk

A plain rectangle with bell-finialled birdcage bellcote built in 1769 on the foundations of an earlier medieval church. Four stained glass windows by Gordon Webster. Interior, with fine hammerbeam roof, has the matching pews arranged to form a central aisle. Chancel area furnished in oak with octagonal pulpit, pedestal font, communion table and Minister's and Elders' chairs. Session Room added 2000. Covenanters' Monument in graveyard. Striking views over Nithsdale.

Sunday Services: 9.45am or 11.15am

Open by arrangement, telephone Mrs Carroll 01387 710551 or Mrs F Little 01387 711196

CHURCH OF SCOTLAND [♿] [wc] (?) **B**

TINWALD CHURCH

TORTHORWALD CHURCH

368 TORTHORWALD CHURCH

NY 035 783
Off A709, 4 miles east of Dumfries
Church website: www.kirkinthor.co.uk
A church was founded in Torthorwald in the mid 13th century by Trinitarian or
Red Friars from Fail Monastery near Tarbolton, Ayrshire. A white T-plan kirk built
in 1872 to replace an earlier church on an adjacent site stones dated 1450 and 1644
are set into the walls of the vestry. Pipe organ 1904. The entrance gates are a
memorial to Dr John G Paton, a pioneer missionary to the islands of the South
Pacific. Sunday Services: 9.45am or 11.25am
Open by arrangement, telephone Mr Cowan 01387 750245 or Mrs Mitchell 01387 750673
CHURCH OF SCOTLAND   [WC] ⏱ 📖 **B**

369 WAMPHRAY PARISH CHURCH

NY 131 965
Neat rectangle by William
McGowan 1834, with a slender
tower and bellcote. Notable 18th-
century headstones in the graveyard
and a monument to the Rt Rev A H
Charteris, Founder of The Woman's
Guild and Moderator of the General
Assembly in 1892.
Sunday Service: 10.00am
Open by arrangement, telephone
Mrs Braid 01576 470275
CHURCH OF SCOTLAND

WAMPHRAY PARISH CHURCH

ST NINIAN'S PRIORY CHURCH, WHITHORN

WIGTOWN PARISH CHURCH

370 ST NINIAN'S PRIORY CHURCH, WHITHORN

NX 444 403

Bruce Street, Whithorn

Built 1822 with later 19th-century tower. Simple rectangular hall church. Carved
oak pulpit. Stained glass east windows gifted by the daughter of Gemmell
Hutcheson RSA in memory of her father. Located on the site of Whithorn 'dig' in
the former precincts of Whithorn Priory. First Scottish Christian community
founded here by St Ninian, pre-dates Iona. Sunday Services: 10.30am and 7.00pm
Open Easter to end of October, 10.00am-5.00pm
CHURCH OF SCOTLAND & & & **A**

371 WIGTOWN PARISH CHURCH

NX 436 555

Bank Street, Wigtown

The parish church on an ancient ecclesiastical site, largely rebuilt in 1730, was by
the middle of the next century thought to be 'an old mean-looking edifice'. A new
church, by the London architect Henry Roberts, was built nearby in 1851, still
using the Georgian T-plan with a French pavilion roof on the tower. Built of
granite, it encloses a broad nave and east transept. P MacGregor Chalmers added a
communion table and font, an organ chamber, and rearranged the seating in 1914.
In the transept are three carved stones, one a Celtic cross shaft decorated on both
faces with interlaced rings, similar to those of the same period at Whithorn.
Stained glass in the east transept window by James Ballantine & Son 1867. Linked
with Kirkcowan. Sunday Services: 11.30am and 6.30pm (in church hall)
Open Easter to September, Monday to Friday 2.00-4.00pm
CHURCH OF SCOTLAND & wc & & & & **B**

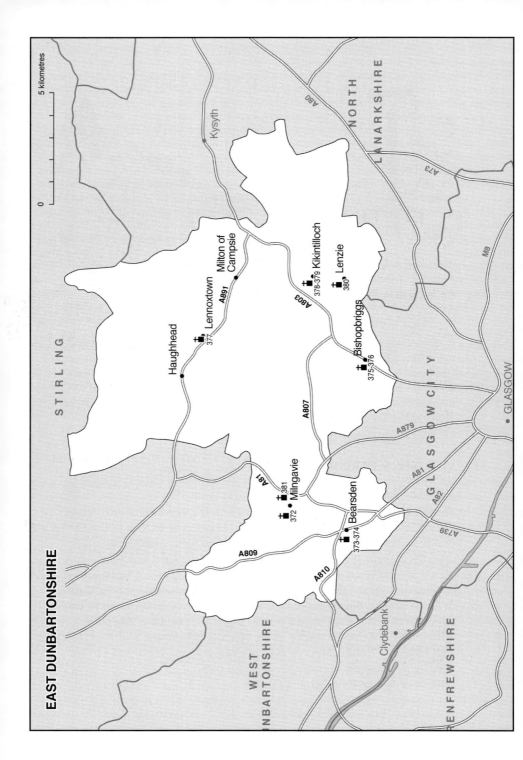

EAST DUNBARTONSHIRE

5 kilometres

0

STIRLING

NORTH LANARKSHIRE

WEST DUNBARTONSHIRE

GLASGOW CITY

RENFREWSHIRE

Kysyth

A80

A73

M8

Milton of Campsie

Kilsintilloch

Lenzie

378-379

380

Lennoxtown

A891

A803

377

Haughead

Bishopbriggs

375-376

A807

A81

381

Milngavie

372

Bearsden

373-374

A809

A810

A879

A81

A82

A739

GLASGOW

Clydebank

EAST DUNBARTONSHIRE

372 BALDERNOCK PARISH CHURCH

NS 577 751

Near Milngavie

The religious history of the site goes back to
the 13th century. The present church was
built in 1795 on the site of an earlier church.
The bell-tower contains a curious panel
which may have come from the nearby
Roman wall. The octagonal gatehouse and
stone stile feature in Moffat's play 'Bunty
Pulls the Strings'. Interesting gravestones,
including Archibald Bulloch from whom
President Theodore Roosevelt and Eleanor
Roosevelt descended. The church stands at
the end of a lovely one-mile walk from
Milngavie. Sunday Service: 11.00am

Open Sunday 2.00-4.00pm, May to September

CHURCH OF SCOTLAND 🚹 🚾 ⊙ 🍴 📖 **B**

BALDERNOCK PARISH CHURCH

373 BLESSED JOHN DUNS SCOTUS CHAPEL, BEARSDEN

NS 535 720

2 Chesters Road, Bearsden, Glasgow

The Chapel of Scotus College was designed by J F Stephen and dedicated in 1997.
The main internal features are its barrel-vaulted ceiling and glass walls. The 14
stained glass panels representing the
Stations of the Cross are by Shona
McInnes and are full of rich
symbolism. A number of other items
were specially commissioned for the
chapel, including processional cross,
presidential chair, candlesticks and a
Christ-figure. A pamphlet is available
giving excellent details

Open during term time 7.00am-9.00pm.

Also telephone 0141 942 8384

ROMAN CATHOLIC 🚹 🚾

BLESSED JOHN DUNS SCOTUS CHAPEL, BEARSDEN

NEW KILPATRICK PARISH CHURCH, BEARSDEN

ST JAMES THE LESS, BISHOPBRIGGS

374   NEW KILPATRICK PARISH CHURCH, BEARSDEN

NS 543 723

Manse Road, Bearsden

Church website: www.nkchurch.org.uk

Building began in 1807 on the site of an earlier church 1649, and within the original settlement established by Paisley Abbey in 1232. Very fine collection of stained glass including windows by Stephen Adam, Alfred and Gordon Webster, Norman M Macdougall, C E Stewart, James Ballantine and Eilidh Keith.

By rail to Bearsden, by bus 59 and 17 to Bearsden Cross.

Services: Sunday 10.30am and 6.30pm; Wednesday 12.00 noon

Open Wednesday 2.00-3.30pm, July and August.

Close to Roman Bath House east of Bearsden Cross

CHURCH OF SCOTLAND ♿ wc ② 🕯 📖 ⚱ **A**

375   ST JAMES THE LESS, BISHOPBRIGGS

NS 612 712

Hilton Road, Bishopbriggs

Church website: www.stjamesbishopbriggs.org.uk

Built 1980 when the congregation moved from Springburn, this church by Glasgow architects Weddell and Thomson preserves the most striking features of the 1881 Springburn building and contains many items from other Glasgow churches: stained glass by Edward Burne-Jones and Stephen Adam and part of the old High Altar of Iona Abbey. Pipe organ by J W Walker & Sons 1964.

Sunday Services: 9.00am Eucharist, 10.30am Sung Eucharist; Thursday 10.30am Morning Prayer and Eucharist

Open Sundays and Thursdays 10.00am-12.00 noon,

or by arrangement with the Rector, telephone 0141 772 4514

SCOTTISH EPISCOPAL ♿ wc ② 📖

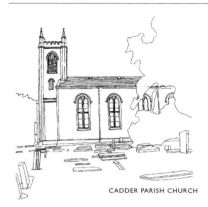

CADDER PARISH CHURCH

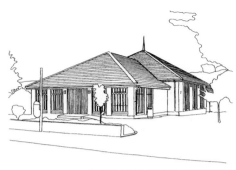

CAMPSIE PARISH CHURCH, LENNOXTOWN

376 CADDER PARISH CHURCH

NS 616 723

Cadder Road, Bishopbriggs

Church website: www.greyfriars@webartz.com

A simple country church in a delightful and peaceful setting, built 1825 to designs by David Hamilton. The chancel was added in 1908 and the gallery altered 1914. Finely carved screen at the front of the gallery of Austrian oak. Very fine stained glass windows by Steven Adam, Alfred Webster, Sadie McLellan and Crear McCartney. Pipe organ by Norman & Beard. Watch-house and cast-iron mort safe in the graveyard. Sunday Service: 11.15am (plus 9.30am in summer)

Open by arrangement with the Minister, telephone 0141 772 1363

CHURCH OF SCOTLAND wc ⓓ **A**

377 CAMPSIE PARISH CHURCH, LENNOXTOWN

NS 629 777

Main Street, Lennoxtown

Modern church with interesting wood carving and stained glass. Craft centre and old church with fascinating graveyard at Campsie Glen, two miles. Bus 175 Campsie Glen via Kirkintilloch. Sunday Service: 11.00am

Open by arrangement, telephone Mrs M Tindall 01360 310 911

CHURCH OF SCOTLAND ♿ wc ⓓ ☕ 📖 **A**

378　ST DAVID'S MEMORIAL PARK CHURCH, KIRKINTILLOCH

NS 654 737

Alexandra Street, Kirkintilloch

The present church by P MacGregor Chalmers 1926, adjacent to site of the original building 1843, was dedicated as a gift of Mrs Paton Thomson in memory of her parents. Two-manual pipe organ, a significant Anneessens 1899 rebuilt and enlarged. Off A803. Sunday Services: 11.00am and (most Sundays) 6.30pm

Open by arrangement,
telephone 0141 777 6485
CHURCH OF SCOTLAND 👤 wc ② 🕯

ST DAVID'S MEMORIAL PARK CHURCH, KIRKINTILLOCH

379　ST FLANNAN'S, KIRKINTILLOCH

NS 663 743

91 Hillhead Road

Parish founded 1948. The present building, close to the Antonine Wall, was designed by William Gilmour and opened in 1970. The form of the building represents praying hands. Services: Saturday 7.00pm, Sunday 10.00am, 12.00 noon, 6.30pm, Monday 7.00pm

Open for services
ROMAN CATHOLIC 👤 wc ② 🕯

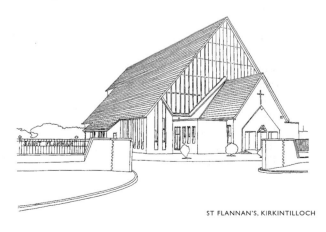

ST FLANNAN'S, KIRKINTILLOCH

380 ST CYPRIAN'S CHURCH, LENZIE

NS 653 727

Beech Road, Lenzie

Built in 1873 by Alexander Ross of Inverness in Gothic style with a three-stage tower at the east end and a gabled porch at the west end. The use of contrasting materials gives a colourful interior. Painting of the Last Supper on the reredos. Memorial choir screen made in local iron foundry. Half-mile north from Lenzie Cross. Sunday Services: 8.30am, 11.00am and 6.30pm (not July and August)

Open by arrangement, telephone the Rector 0141 776 4149

SCOTTISH EPISCOPALIAN [wc] ② **B**

381 CAIRNS CHURCH, MILNGAVIE

NS 556 748

Buchanan Street, Milngavie

The longest serving congregation in Milngavie, services were first held on Barloch Moor before the first building was erected in 1799. The present church was built to the design of J B Wilson in a late decorated Gothic style, and was opened in 1903. The red tiled spire rises above the surrounding roofs. New halls and rooms by Page & Park, 2000, and chancel and sanctuary remodelled 2004 with the whole church enhanced by new lighting and sound systems. The church – intimate, welcoming and friendly – a partnership with history. Interior features a range of banners. A light lunch is available every Tuesday (except during holiday periods). Sunday Services: 10.45am and 6.30pm (summer 10.00am only)

Access by arrangement with church office, telephone 0141 956 4868 Monday to Friday 9.30am-2.30pm

CHURCH OF SCOTLAND

[♿] [wc] ② ☕ **B**

CAIRNS CHURCH, MILNGAVIE

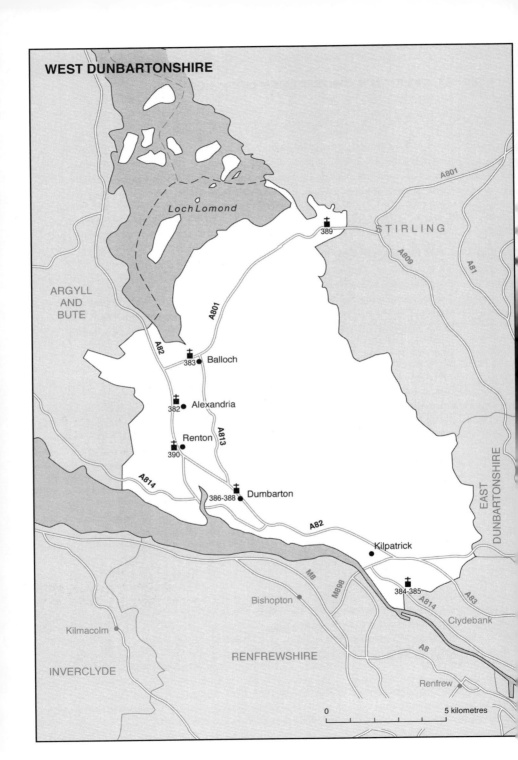

WEST DUNBARTONSHIRE

382 ST MUNGO'S CHURCH, ALEXANDRIA

NS 389 796

Main Street, Alexandria

Church website: //dspace.dial.pipex.com/town/plaza/aaj50/

Dedicated 1894, J M Crawford, architect, in pointed Gothic style. Early 20th-century addition of side aisle. Simple interior with plain altar furniture. Open timber roof with curved brace supported on stone corbels. Three-light stained glass window in memory of Agnes J Burham of New York featuring Christ in Majesty, St Michael the Archangel, St Agnes and St Agatha. Sunday Services: Eucharist 9am, Sung Eucharist 11.00am; Wednesday: Eucharist 10.00am

Open by arrangement, telephone the Priest-in-charge, St Mungo's Rectory 01389 752633

SCOTTISH EPISCOPAL [wc] **B**

383 ALEXANDRIA PARISH CHURCH, BALLOCH

NS 389 798

Lomond Road, Balloch

Church website: www.alexandriaparishchurch.co.uk

Building refurbished and upgraded 1995-6. Digital organ by Allen. The congregational Sewing Group produced the Heritage Tapestry 30 by 27 inches, finely embroidered pulpit falls, communion table cords, and the hand-sewn banners (two on local themes). Several noteworthy items of stained glass. Noah's Ark mural in main hall. In the grounds, a war memorial commemorating members of the congregation killed in action 1914-18 and 1939-45. Off A82. Five to ten minutes' walk from Balloch railway station. Sunday Service: 11.00am also during summer (mid June to last in August) at 9.30am; and regular Jazz Praise services at 7.00pm on Sunday evenings

Festival of Flowers 25-27 August 2006.

Open by arrangement lunches/ afternoon teas for groups, telephone Mrs M Thomson 01389 756553

CHURCH OF SCOTLAND

ALEXANDRIA PARISH CHURCH, BALLOCH

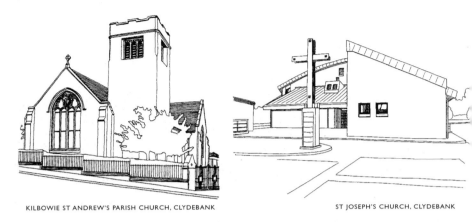

KILBOWIE ST ANDREW'S PARISH CHURCH, CLYDEBANK   ST JOSEPH'S CHURCH, CLYDEBANK

384   KILBOWIE ST ANDREW'S PARISH CHURCH, CLYDEBANK

NS 497 702

Kilbowie Road, Clydebank

For the congregation founded as St John's on the Hill 1897, the present church was
built in 1904 on land gifted by William Black of Auchentoshen. In simple
Perpendicular style, a low cruciform church of red sandstone. Battlemented belfry
added 1933. Recent refurbishment. Memorial side chapel with tapestry and stained
glass window by Eilidh Keith 1997, dedicated to the victims of the Clydebank
Blitz. The bell 1933 is one of few remaining in this former industrial community of
Scotland. Five minutes' walk from railway station. Sunday Service: 11.00am, except
July and August

*Open 13 March each year 10.00am-4.00pm (Blitz Memorial Day), Commemorative Service
12.00 noon. Other times by arrangement, and Doors Open Day, telephone Rev R Grahame
0141 951 2455*

CHURCH OF SCOTLAND ♿ wc ② ⌀ ◻ ☕

385   ST JOSEPH'S CHURCH, CLYDEBANK

NS 510 733

Faifley Road, Clydebank

Replacing a Coia church which was burned down, the building is one of the
newest in the country, being opened in 1997. The award-winning design by
Jacobsen & French utilises tall windows to provide light while natural wood is
featured extensively. Sunday Services: 9.00 and 11.30am; Saturday Vigil 6.00pm;
Daily Mass 9.30am

Open Wednesday 9.00-11.00am, Saturday 5.00-7.00pm, Sunday 9.00am-12.30pm

ROMAN CATHOLIC ♿ ②

RIVERSIDE PARISH CHURCH, DUMBARTON

ST AUGUSTINE'S CHURCH, DUMBARTON

386 RIVERSIDE PARISH CHURCH, DUMBARTON

NS 398 752

High Street, Dumbarton

Church website: www.dumbartonriverside.org.uk

Built in 1811 to a design by John Brash on the site of earlier 13/14th-century and 17th-century churches. The steeple and pedimented gable command the westward curve of the High Street. Urns perch on the belfry and adorn the gatepiers. The interior was refurbished 1886. Stained glass includes the Queen Margaret window by the Abbey Studio of Glasgow and Ascension window by C E Stewart. Spectacular new millennium window by John Clark 2002. Crusader stone of 11th/12th century now housed in gallery. Sunday Service: 11.15am

Open weekdays 9.30am-12.30pm

CHURCH OF SCOTLAND ♿ wc ⦿ 📖 **A**

387 ST AUGUSTINE'S CHURCH, DUMBARTON

NS 397 752

High Street, Dumbarton

Church website: www.staugustinesdumbarton.co.uk

Built in 1873, the architect Sir Robert Rowand Anderson designed the building in the Gothic Revival Style. Stained glass at baptismal font by Stephen Adam with others to a design by Carl Alnquist. The organ was designed and built for the church by Smith and Brock. Total restoration of building 2003. Sunday Services: 9.00am and 11.00am

Open Saturday mornings, and by arrangement, telephone church office 01389 734514

SCOTTISH EPISCOPAL ♿ **A**

388 ST PATRICK'S, DUMBARTON

NS 339 754

Strathleven Place

Church website: www.stpatricksdumbarton.com

An elegant red sandstone building by Dunn and Hansom completed in 1903. It was
enhanced in 1926-7 with a fine tower by Pugin & Pugin and carillon of bells. The
Sanctuary was extended in 1935 and the marble work started in 1926 was
completed. In 1997 the sanctuary was re-ordered to make it compatible with the
renewed liturgy of the Eucharist. Services: Saturday Vigil 6.30pm; Sunday
10.00am, 12.00 noon and 5.30pm

Open daily from 8.00am until evening (4.00pm in winter)

ROMAN CATHOLIC   🔲 🔲 ⊘ **B**

389 THE CHURCH OF KILMARONOCK

NS 452 875

By Drymen

North side of A811, 3 miles west of Drymen

The present church building dates from 1813 and has a stout classical dignity.
Parish long-established when documented records began; the screen at the entrance
to the nave lists incumbents since 1325. Memorial wall plaques. Ancient stones in
graveyard. Sunday Service: 11.00am, May to September

Open by arrangement. Occasional events by the Friends of Kilmaronock

CHURCH OF SCOTLAND 🔲 🔲 🔲 **B**

THE CHURCH OF KILMARONOCK

390 RENTON TRINITY PARISH CHURCH

NS 390 780

Building originally constructed as Renton Old Parish Church 1892, architects H & D Bradlay. United with Renton Union Church and Renton Millburn Church 1969. Has since been refurbished and upgraded. Five stained glass windows by Oscar Paterson, Glasgow 1912-22. Sunday Services: 11.00am, and at 6.30pm second Sunday of March, June, September, December

Open Thursdays 10.30am-1.30pm, or by arrangement, telephone Rev Cameron Langlands 01389 752017

CHURCH OF SCOTLAND 🦽 ⓐ 📖 🕯 ☕ **A**

RENTON TRINITY PARISH CHURCH

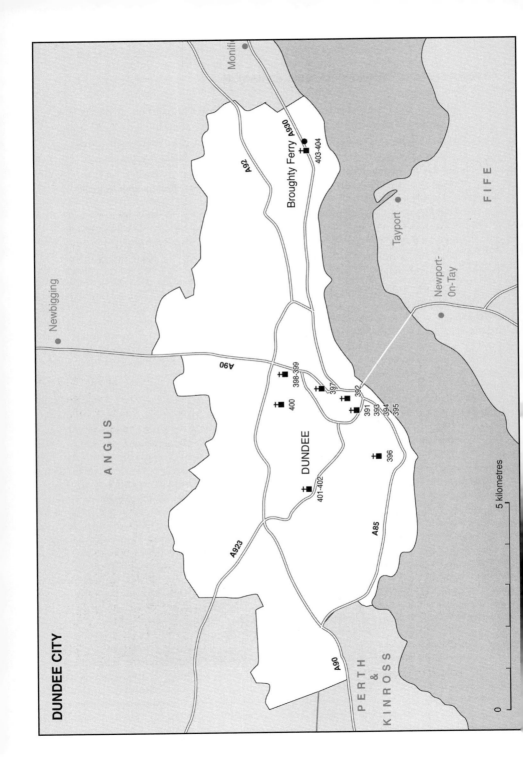

DUNDEE CITY

DUNDEE

Local Representative: Dr Anne Weatherhead, Newton Park, 59 Brechin Road, Kirriemuir (*telephone* 01575 572237)

391 DUNDEE PARISH CHURCH (ST MARY'S)

NO 401 301
Nethergate, Dundee
Founded in 1190 by Earl of Huntingdon. Rebuilt 1844 by William Burn. Beautiful 19th and 20th-century stained glass windows. War memorial 1914-18. Impressive organ installed 1865. Reading desk with interesting history. North of Discovery Point and railway station. Sunday Service: 11.00am; Holy Communion last Sunday of month
Open May to September, Tuesday, Thursday, Friday 10.00am-12.00 noon
CHURCH OF SCOTLAND ♿ wc ② 🕯 🚪 ⚲ **B**

392 ST PAUL'S CATHEDRAL

NO 404 303
Castlehill, 1 High Street, Dundee
Designed by Sir George Gilbert Scott, the cathedral stands on the site of Dundee's ancient castle. Gothic in style, but Gothic with a difference. Tall, graceful columns give an impression of lightness and airiness. Organ by Hill 1865, rebuilt by Hill, Norman & Beard 1976. East end of High Street at junction with Commercial Street. Walking distance from rail and bus stations. Sunday Services: 8.00am, 9.40am, 11.00am and 6.30pm
Open Monday to Saturday 11.00am-5.00pm
SCOTTISH EPISCOPAL wc ② 🕯 🚪 ☕ **A**

393 ST ANDREW'S CATHEDRAL

NO 400 299
150 Nethergate, Dundee
Designed by George Mathewson in 1835; impressive arcaded interior. Outstanding 19th- and 20th-century stained glass by Mayer of Munich. Sunday Mass: 11.30am and 7pm; weekday Mass: 10.00am
Open Monday to Saturday 9.00am-3.00pm
ROMAN CATHOLIC 🕯 🚪

ST ANDREW'S CATHEDRAL

394 THE STEEPLE CHURCH

NO 402 301

Nethergate, Dundee

Church building dates from 1788, Samuel Bell.
Entry through 15th-century St Mary's Tower.
A landmark, known as 'Old Steeple'. City
centre. Sunday Services: 11.00am and 7.00pm
Open July to August, Tuesday and Saturday 12.00
noon-3.00pm. Also Doors Open Day and other
summer activities. Mary Slessor Exhibition, July
to August (details in church)
CHURCH OF SCOTLAND   🧑‍🦽 wc ✋ 📖 **B**

THE STEEPLE CHURCH

395 MEADOWSIDE ST PAUL'S CHURCH

NO 401 300

114-116 Nethergate, Dundee

Church website: www.mspdundee.com

Built in 1852, replacing the Mariners' Church, to a design by Charles Wilson. It
'boasts a fine spire terminating the elevation of Nethergate'. Hammerbeam roof.
Organ by Walker & Co 1902, overhauled by Rushworth & Dreaper 1971. Stained
glass, some by Jones & Willis, and by Alexander Russell. Sets of tapestried pulpit
falls, tapestry kneelers. Doorway mosaics by Elizabeth McFall. A hall complex,
M J Rodgers 1988, the location of regular meetings of Presbytery of Dundee, as
well as providing storage for the Presbytery Resources Centre. A feature of the
garden is an artistic stone wall by David Wilson. Sunday Service: 11.00am
Open Wednesday 12.00 noon-1.30pm for prayer and meditation; key from Cornerstone on
weekdays
CHURCH OF SCOTLAND   🧑‍🦽 wc ✋ 📖 ☕ (Cornerstone Coffee House adjoining) **B**

396 ST PETER'S FREE CHURCH

NO 390 298

St Peter Street, Dundee

Built by Hean Brothers, 1836. Remarkably douce
for a revivalist kirk; yet this was the seat of the
Rev Robert McCheyne (1813-43), a major player in
the Evangelical revival, who made these sober
rafters ring. An elegant, classical church with a
gallery carried on cast-iron columns. Original
pulpit. The plain simplicity of the building is
ennobled by the tower and stone spire against its
east gable. The church has served different
denominations since its opening: Free, United Free,

ST PETER'S FREE CHURCH

and Church of Scotland. It became a Free Church again in 1987. From city centre, west for one mile along High Street, Nethergate and Perth Road. Turn right into St Peter Street. Sunday Services: 11.00am and 6.30pm; Wednesday: Prayer Meeting 7.30pm

Open by arrangement, telephone Rev D Robertson 01382 861401
FREE CHURCH OF SCOTLAND ♿ wc 📖 **B**

397 ST ANDREW'S PARISH CHURCH

NO 404 307

King Street, Dundee

Church website: www.standrewschurch.co.uk

Trades kirk with interesting history, dating from 1774; Samuel Bell with plans by James Craig, Edinburgh. Beautiful stained glass. Includes Glasite Kirk 1777, now part of church hall complex. Handsome spire with peal of fine musical bells. Lovely gardens. Teas on Saturdays. Next to Wellgate Shopping Centre. Sunday Service: 11.00am all year; also 9.30am June, July and August

Open Tuesday, Thursday, Saturday
10.00am-12.00 noon all year.

Also Doors Open Day

CHURCH OF SCOTLAND
♿ wc 🎧 🚻 📖 🚻 ☕ (Saturdays) **A**

ST ANDREW'S PARISH CHURCH

398 ST JOHN THE BAPTIST CHURCH

NO 411 314

116 Albert Street, Dundee

Church website: www.stjohns.ik.com

The present building was consecrated in 1886. Designed with a French-style roof by the Rev Edward Sugden 1885. The sanctuary and chancel are panelled in late Gothic style, the details suggested by the woodwork in King's College Chapel, Aberdeen. Open wood roof and pillars give this interior a Scandinavian feel. Reredos by William Hole. The font cover is a splendid carved wooden spire. Services: Sunday 10.15am; Thursday 10.00am

Open Thursday 9.00-11.00am, other times by arrangement,
telephone the church office 01382 455656

SCOTTISH EPISCOPAL ♿ wc 📖 **B**

399 STOBSWELL PARISH CHURCH

NO 411 315
Albert Street, Dundee
On a prominent site, by Charles Edward and
Thomas S Robertson 1874. The buildings have
recently undergone extensive refurbishment.
L-shaped church. Fine stained glass windows
by William Wilson. From city centre buses 15,
17, 32, 33, 35 and 36. Sunday Service: 11.00am
(July and August 10.30am)
Dundee Doors Open Day, September
CHURCH OF SCOTLAND ♿ 🚻 ⊘ **B**

STOBSWELL PARISH CHURCH

400 ST SALVADOR'S CHURCH

NO 403 313
Church Street, Dundee
Glorious painted interior with stencilled wall decoration and open roof, built in
1868 in early Arts & Crafts Gothic by G F Bodley. Organ by Wadsworth &
Maskell 1882, recently restored. Carnegie Street end of Church Street, off
Hilltown. Buses 20 and 22. Daily Services: Tuesday 9.30am, Wednesday 10.00am,
Thursday 12.30pm, Friday and Saturday 8.00am; Evensong daily 5.30pm except
Sunday 5.00pm; Sunday Services: 9.00am, 11.00am, 5.00pm
Open most mornings. Also Doors Open Day, September
SCOTTISH EPISCOPAL ♿ 🚻 ⊘ 📖 **B**

401 ST MARGARET'S, LOCHEE

NO 382 312
17/19 Ancrum Road, Dundee
The roof of this church, 1888, designed by the Rev E Sugden, has attracted the
attention of the Architecture Department of Duncan of Jordanstone College. The
font, in the form of an angel holding a
large shell, is thought to be a copy of
a font by Danish artist Bertel
Thorvaldsen in Copenhagen Cathedral.
Sunday Services: Holy Communion
8.00am, Sung Eucharist 11.00am;
Thursday: Holy Communion 10.00am
Open by arrangement, telephone the Rector,
Fr James Milne 01382 667227
SCOTTISH EPISCOPAL
♿ 🚻 🕯 ☕ (after Sunday Sung Eucharist)

ST MARGARET'S, LOCHEE

402 IMMACULATE CONCEPTION (ST MARY'S), LOCHEE

NO 380 314

41 High Street, Lochee

Remarkable Gothic revival church of 1866 by Joseph A
Hansom ennobled by a polygonal chancel which soars
up into the spire and gives a contrast between the dark
nave and well-lit chancel. Notable stonework and superb
detail and craftsmanship. Flamboyant altarpiece by A B
Wall of Cheltenham, 1897. Stained glass by Mayer of
Munich. Floodlit well Twelve metres deep. Services:
Saturday 6.00pm Vigil, Sunday 10.00am and 11.30am,
Monday to Saturday 10.00am

Open by arrangement, telephone Mr McLean 01382 611662

ROMAN CATHOLIC ♿ wc ⊘ 📖 **A**

IMMACULATE CONCEPTION
(ST MARY'S), LOCHEE

403 ST MARY'S CHURCH, BROUGHTY FERRY

NO 461 310

Queen Street, Broughty Ferry

Designed by Sir George Gilbert Scott 1858 and added
to 1870. Sir Robert Lorimer extended the chancel
1911. The pulpit, screen, choir stalls and reredos are all
by Lorimer. Garden of Remembrance. On the main
road from Carnoustie and Monifieth to Dundee.
Frequent bus service. Sunday Services: 8.30am,
11.00am, 6.30pm; weekdays: Matins 7.00am, Evensong
6.00pm; Holy Communion Wednesday 10.00am

Open daily all year

SCOTTISH EPISCOPAL ♿ ⊘ **A**

ST MARY'S CHURCH,
BROUGHTY FERRY

404 OUR LADY OF GOOD COUNSEL, BROUGHTY FERRY

NO 458 309

Westfield Road, Broughty Ferry

Designed by T M Cappon in a Gothic style, 1904.
The tower at the west end has a statue of the
Madonna and Child. Services: Sunday Mass 9.00am
and 11.00am; Monday, Wednesday, Friday 9.00am;
Tuesday, Thursday, Saturday 10.00am

Open by arrangement with the Parish Priest,
telephone 01382 778750

ROMAN CATHOLIC ♿ wc ⛪ ☕ **C**

OUR LADY OF GOOD COUNSEL,
BROUGHTY FERRY

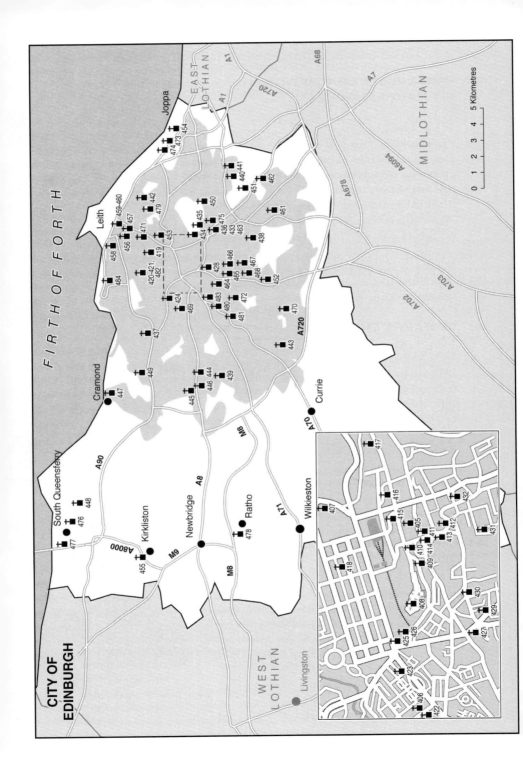

EDINBURGH

Local Representatives: Mr Andrew Thackrey, 3 Strathearn Place, Edinburgh
(*telephone* 0131 447 3232). Mrs Deirdre Howie, 41a Fountainhall Road, Edinburgh
(*telephone* 0131 667 8836)

405 ST GILES' CATHEDRAL

NT 257 736
High Street, Edinburgh
Church website: www.stgilescathedral.org.uk
The Cathedral was founded in the 1100s and mostly rebuilt during the 15th and 16th
centuries. It was the church of John Knox during the Reformation and played an
important part in the history of that time. The church contains fine examples of late
medieval architecture and a wide range of traditional and modern stained glass and
memorials. The magnificent Rieger organ was installed in 1992. The Thistle Chapel,
designed by Robert Lorimer for the Order of the Thistle, was added in 1911.
Sunday Services: 8.00am, 10.00am, 11.30am and 8.00pm
Open May to September, Monday to Friday 9.00am-7.00pm, Saturday 9.00am-5.00pm,
Sunday 1.00-5.00pm. October to April, Monday to Saturday 9.00am-5.00pm,
Sunday 1.00-5.00pm. Regular weekday recitals during summer months.
For details of events telephone 0131 225 9442 or check website
CHURCH OF SCOTLAND ⓦ ⓒ ⓘ ⓓ ⓤ **A**

406 ST MARY'S EPISCOPAL CATHEDRAL

NT 242 735
Palmerston Place, Edinburgh
Church website: www.cathedral.net
Built in 1879 to the award-winning design of Sir George Gilbert Scott, this neo-
Gothic building reflects the spirit of that age and rejoices in a wealth of ornate and
symbolic detail. Of particular note are the pelican lectern, Lorimer's rood and the
J Oldrid Scott's reredos of the high altar, featuring the Scottish saints Columba and
Margaret. Organ by 'Father' Willis 1879, rebuilt by Harrison & Harrison of Durham.
In the grounds stand the 17-century Old Coates House (now the Theological
Institute of the Scottish Episcopal Church) and the Song School, famous for its
murals painted by Phoebe Anna Traquair 1888-92 on the theme of '*Benedicite omnia*
opera'. The Cathedral maintains an internationally renowned choir, which sings on
Sundays and for Evensong on weekdays. During holiday periods the Cathedral
welcomes visiting choirs. Services: for full details contact the Cathedral answering
machine on 0131 225 6293
Open daily 7.30am-6.00pm (5.00pm Saturday). The Song School may be visited by appointment
SCOTTISH EPISCOPAL ⓦ ⓒ ⓘ ⓓ ⓠ **A**

407 ST MARY'S R C CATHEDRAL

NT 259 743

Broughton Street, Edinburgh

Church website: www.stmaryscathedral.co.uk

St Mary's Cathedral occupies the site of
the much smaller chapel of St Mary's,
1814. The church was created a pro-
Cathedral on the restoration of the
Scottish Hierarchy in 1878 and when
'Edinburgh' was added to the ancient title
of the see of St Andrews, that had been
vacant for 307 years. In 1886, at the
request of Bishop Smith, the church was
raised in status to that of Metropolitan
Cathedral of the new Archdiocese of St
Andrews & Edinburgh, with all the rights
and privileges thereof. On the Gothic

ST MARY'S R C CATHEDRAL

central section, at the front of St Mary's, are remains of the 1814 chapel.
Organ by Ernest Lawton 1932. Cathedral Hall complex added 2005.
Sunday Masses: 9.30am, 11.30am and 7.30pm; Holy days of Obligation: 6.00pm
previous evening, 9.30pm, 12.45pm and 7.30pm; Daily Mass: Monday to Friday
12.45pm; Saturday: Vigil Mass 6.00pm

Open daily 8.00am-6.00pm (later on Saturday and Sunday)

ROMAN CATHOLIC   🦽 ⌾ ☕ **A**

408 ST MARGARET'S CHAPEL

NT 253 735

Edinburgh Castle, Edinburgh

The oldest surviving structure in the castle built by King David I (1124-53). Interior
divided into two by a fine arch decorated with chevron ornament. Semi-circular
east chancel. Copy of the Gospel Book owned by St Margaret to whom the chapel
was dedicated by her son, David I. Stained glass windows depicting St Andrew,
St Ninian, St Columba and St Margaret by Douglas Strachan *c.*1930. Magnificent
views from castle ramparts. Other attractions within the castle (Historic Scotland)
include 'Honours of the Kingdom' exhibition, now with the Stone of Destiny.

Open summer 9.30am-6.00pm, winter 9.30am-5.00pm

(last ticket sold 45 minutes before closing)

NON-DENOMINATIONAL 🦽 wc ⍾ 📖 ☕ **A**

409 ST COLUMBA'S BY THE CASTLE

NT 254 735

14 Johnston Terrace, Edinburgh

By John Henderson, 1847, a single-nave building with a battlemented tower. Triple arcading at the west wall, originally supporting a gallery, now subsumed into a suite of rooms served by a new staircase. Stone altar, font and pulpit. Gifted oak panelling on lower east wall *c.*1914. The blocked east window has been filled with a mural of 'Christ Enthroned' by John Busby 1959. Pipe organ, James Conacher & Sons 1880, rebuilt in 1965 by N P Mander and relocated in 1998 by Lightoller. Church hall, originally a school, below the church. Redevelopment and refurbishment, Simpson & Brown 1998. Sunday Service: Eucharist 10.00am, and other times as announced

Open by arrangement, telephone the Rector 0131 228 6470

SCOTTISH EPISCOPAL   🚻 ⊘ 📄 ⚲ **B**

410 QUAKER MEETING HOUSE

NT 256 736

7 Victoria Terrace, Edinburgh

Church website: www.quakerscotland.gn.apc.org/edinburgh

Built originally as a chapel for the United Original Secession Church (Paterson & Shiells 1865) as part of the City's Victoria Street redevelopment. Following the return of the 'Auld Seceders' to the Kirk, it became 'Kirk House', headquarters of the Edinburgh Battalion of the Boys' Brigade (conversion by Basil Spence & Partners 1960). Converted as Quaker Meeting House by Religious Society of Friends in 1987 (Architects Walmesley & Savage). Venue café during the Edinburgh Festival Fringe in August. Services: Sunday 11.00am; Wednesday 12.30pm

Open by arrangement, telephone the Wardens 0131 225 4825

QUAKER   🚻 🚾 ⊘ ⚲ **B**

QUAKER MEETING HOUSE

411 AUGUSTINE UNITED CHURCH

NT 257 734
41 George IV Bridge, Edinburgh
Church website: www.augustine.org.uk
Built 1857-61 by J J & W H Hay with Romanesque, Renaissance and Classical
elements. The projecting centre is carried up as the 'bride's-cake' tower, restored
2005. The Bradford computer organ of 1994 uses the pipes and case of the 1929
Ingram organ. Alterations by Stewart Tod & Partners 1995. Two stained glass
windows by Robert Burns, formerly in the gallery, now the main floor. The church
has an ecumenical outlook and is in covenant with Greyfriars Tolbooth and
Highland Kirk and with St Columba's by the Castle. The home of Christian Aid in
Scotland. Used by a variety of organisations and during the Edinburgh Festival.
Sunday Service: 11.00am
Open by arrangement, telephone 0131 220 1677
UNITED REFORMED wc ② 👤 **B**

412 EDINBURGH SEVENTH-DAY ADVENTIST CHURCH

NT 235 767
61 Boswall Parkway, Granton
Church website: www.adventist-scotland.co.uk
Simple Gothic building with side aisles and clerestory windows. The church is
blessed with visitors from all over the world. Services: Saturday 10.00am (Bible
Study) and 11.15am (Worship Service)
Open by arrangement, telephone Pastor Llewellyn Edwards 01764 653257
SEVENTH-DAY ADVENTIST

413 GREYFRIARS TOLBOOTH & HIGHLAND KIRK

NT 256 734
Greyfriars Place, Edinburgh
Church website: www.greyfriarskirk.com
The first post-Reformation church built in Edinburgh 1620, altered 1722, 1858, 1938,
1990 and 2004. The National Covenant signed here in 1638. Fine 19th-century
coloured glass by Ballantine, and Peter Collins organ 1990. Historic kirkyard, has
fine examples of 17th-century monuments, the Martyrs' Monument, Covenanters'
Prison and memorial to Greyfriars Bobby. South end of George IV Bridge. Sunday
Services: 11.00am and 12.30pm (Gaelic), first Sunday of month Holy Communion
9.30am; Thursdays all year Lunchtime Service with organ music 1.10-1.30pm
Open April to October, Monday to Friday 10.30am-4.30pm, Saturday 10.30am-2.30pm,
November to March, Thursday 1.30-3.30pm. Churchyard open all year. Special events: year
round programme of concerts and lectures (programme available). Tours for groups, telephone
Visitors Officer 0131 226 5429
CHURCH OF SCOTLAND ♿ wc ② 👤 📖 ⚲ 🖥 (by arrangement) 🅡 **A**

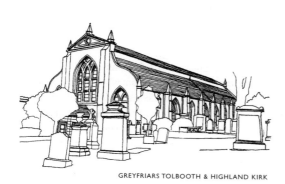

GREYFRIARS TOLBOOTH & HIGHLAND KIRK

MAGDALEN CHAPEL

414 MAGDALEN CHAPEL

NT 256 734

41 Cowgate, Edinburgh

Church website: www.scottishreformation.com.uk

The chapel was built in 1541 by Michael McQuhane and his wife Janet Rhynd and contains in site medieval stained glass roundels. The panelling records gifts from members of the Incorporation of Hammermen who were patrons of the chapel until 1862. The chapel is now owned by the Scottish Reformation Society and serves as its headquarters

Open Monday to Friday 9.30am-4.00pm. Other times by arrangement. Parties welcome, telephone Rev A S Horne 0131 220 1450

INTER-DENOMINATIONAL 📖 ♟ **A**

415 OLD ST PAUL'S

NT 260 737

Jeffrey Street, Edinburgh

Church website: www.osp.org.uk

The hidden gem of the Old Town. Dating from 1884, Hay & Henderson. Entrances in Carrubber's Close and Jeffrey Street give little clue to the splendour within. This historic Episcopal church with Jacobite past has magnificent furnishings. A living church with daily worship and a prayerful atmosphere. Off Royal Mile. Sunday Services: Holy Eucharist 8.00am, 10.30am and 5.00pm; Evensong 6.30pm; Daily Worship 12.20pm, except Wednesday 9.00am

Open daily, 9.00am-6.00pm

SCOTTISH EPISCOPAL [wc] 🔊 📖 **B**

OLD ST PAUL'S

416   ST PATRICK'S

NT 262 736

5 South Gray's Close, between High Street and Cowgate
Church website: www.stpatricksparish.co.uk

Today St Patrick's is a vibrant worshipping Catholic parish. Built 1772-4 as an Episcopalian Church, architect John Baxter. Alexander Runciman painted four panels depicting 'The Prodigal Son', 'Christ and the Samaritan Woman', 'Moses and Elijah' and 'The Ascension of Christ' in the apse. In 1856 the Roman Catholics took possession and a north-facing sanctuary was added, architect J Graham Fairley. Other additions were made in 1929, including a triumphal entrance arch on the south façade, architect Reginald Fairlie. Sunday Masses 9.00am, 11.00am, 4.30pm; Weekdays; 8.00am and 12.30pm; Saturday Vigil 5.00pm
Open Monday to Friday 7.30am-4.30pm, Saturday and Sunday 8.00am-6.00pm
ROMAN CATHOLIC 🚾 📶 ⊘ **B**

417   CANONGATE KIRK

NT 265 738

Canongate, Royal Mile, Edinburgh

This interesting and recently restored 17th-century church was opened in 1691, its plan by James Smith being unique among 17th-century Scottish churches. Restored in 1991, Stewart Tod Partnership. The churchyard contains the remains of many famous Scots, including economist Adam Smith. 'Open Kirk' information sheets in several languages. Frobenius organ 1999. On the Royal Mile, opposite Huntly House Museum. Sunday Services: Family Service 10.00am, Parish Worship 11.15am
Open mid June to mid September, Monday to Saturday, 10.30am-4.30pm. Churchyard open all year
CHURCH OF SCOTLAND 🚾 ⊘ 🍴 📖 📶 **A**

CANONGATE KIRK

418   ST ANDREW'S AND ST GEORGE'S PARISH CHURCH

NT 255 741

George Street, Edinburgh
Church website: www.standrewsandstgeorges.org.uk

This beautiful elliptical church with its delicate spire and Adam-style plaster ceiling has been described as the architectural gem of the New Town. Built in 1784, designed by Major Andrew Frazer. Two fine 20th-century stained glass windows, one by Douglas Strachan (1875-1950), the other by Alfred Webster (1884-1915). Organ by Wells-Kennedy 1984. Light lunches in undercroft. At the east end of George Street and one block north of Princes Street. Sunday Services: 9.00am (Communion),

ST ANDREW'S AND ST GEORGE'S PARISH CHURCH

BROUGHTON ST MARY'S PARISH CHURCH

9.45am, 11.00am; Weekday Prayers: 1.00pm (Communion Service: Tuesday) *Open all year, Monday to Friday 10.00am-3.00pm. Undercroft open 12.00-2.00pm, telephone 0131 225 3847 or fax 0131 225 5921. Special Edinburgh Festival programme of events. Week-long Christian Aid book sale in May*

CHURCH OF SCOTLAND wc ⊙ 🍴 📖 ☕ A

419 BROUGHTON ST MARY'S PARISH CHURCH

NT 256 748

12 Bellevue Crescent, Edinburgh

Church website: www.broughtonstmarys.org.uk

A burgh church, built to serve Edinburgh's spreading New Town. Designed in 1824 by Thomas Brown as centrepiece of Bellevue Crescent. Neo-classical style, graceful interior with fluted Corinthian columns supporting gallery. Unaltered organ by Lewis, 1882, recently restored. Original pulpit. Nathaniel Bryson's stained glass 'Annunciation' is of particular note. Robert Stevenson, lighthouse builder and grandfather of Robert Louis Stevenson, elder 1828-43. Ten to fifteen minutes' walk from east end of Princes Street. City buses 8, 17 to Bellevue Crescent.

Sunday Service: 10.30am

Open May to September, Wednesday 10.00am-12.00 noon, and Monday to Saturday during the first week of the Edinburgh Festival in August 10.00am-4.00pm

CHURCH OF SCOTLAND wc ⊙ 🍴 📖 ☕ A

420 ST STEPHEN'S CENTRE

NT 250 746
St Vincent Street, Edinburgh
Built 1828 as St Stephen's Church, this is the ecclesiastical masterpiece of W H
Playfair. Severe Greek detail but Baroque in spirit, with a large tower dominating
the vista from Queen Street downhill through the northern New Town. Interior
recast in 1956 when a floor was inserted at the level of the former gallery whose
cast-iron Egyptian columns were retained. Outstanding original example of an
organ by 'Father' Willis. Built 1880. No Services
Open Monday to Friday 9.00am-9.00pm, telephone Development Officer, David Nicholson
0131 556 2661
CHURCH OF SCOTLAND 🏛 ☕

421 ST VINCENT'S EPISCOPAL CHAPEL

NT 259 746
13 St Vincent Street
Small Gothic gem by J W H & J M Hay of Liverpool, 1856. It ceased parish
functions in the 1960s and was bought by Lt. Col. Gayre of Nigg for continued
use by the congregation and the Order of St Lazarus. Since 1992 the chapel has
reverted completely to parish use. Though the Order no longer has a connection
with the chapel, its armorial features remain. There are fine sets of parish
vestments. Sunday Services: Sung Eucharist 10.30am (Scottish Liturgy 1929),
Evensong 6.00pm; Wednesday: Eucharist 7.00pm; Thursday: Eucharist 10.00am
Open by arrangement with Priest-in-charge 0131 229 1857
SCOTTISH EPISCOPALIAN 🚻 ② ⚲ 🏛 ☕ **A**

422 PALMERSTON PLACE CHURCH

NT 241 734
Palmerston Place, Edinburgh
Church website: www.palmerstonplacechurch.com
Inspiration for Peddie & Kinnear's design of 1875
came from the 17th-century St Sulpice in Paris. A
notable feature is the central ceiling motif of a dove
within a sunburst. Wells Kennedy organ 1991
incorporates the oak case of the earlier 1902 organ.
Meeting place for the Presbytery of Edinburgh and
the Synod of the Scottish Episcopal Church. Sunday
Services: 11.00am, 6.30pm (except July and August)
Open by arrangement, telephone 0131 220 1690
CHURCH OF SCOTLAND 🚻 ② **B**

PALMERSTON PLACE CHURCH

423 ST GEORGE'S WEST CHURCH

NT 245 736

Shandwick Place, Edinburgh

Church website: www.stgeorgeswest.com

Designed by David Bryce 1869 with campanile by
Sir R Rowand Anderson 1881. Special features are the
rose window and the pulpit. Woodwork excellent,
mainly original. The organ by Thomas Lewis 1897.
The first organist was Alfred Hollins, famous blind
organist and composer (1897-1942). City Centre West
End. Sunday Services: 11.00am and 7.00pm;
Prayers: Monday to Friday 1.00pm

*Busy Church Centre, Fairtrade shop and café open Monday to
Friday 10.00am-3.30pm; Saturday 10.30am-12.30pm, all year*

CHURCH OF SCOTLAND ♿ wc ② 📖 ☕ **B**

ST GEORGE'S WEST CHURCH

424 ST ANDREWS RC

NT 235 740

77 Belford Road

Built as a temporary church in 1902, this wooden building in Early English style
reflects a warmth of tradition. Some fine statuary in wood and plaster.
Sunday Service: 9.15 am

Open by arrangement with Parish Priest 0131 334 1693

ROMAN CATHOLIC ♿ ②

425 ST JOHN THE EVANGELIST

NT 247 736

Princes Street, Edinburgh

Church website: www.stjohns-edinburgh.org.uk

St John's Edinburgh is one of architect William Burn's finest
early 19th-century buildings and is known for having perhaps
the finest collection of stained glass in the country. Organ
originally by 'Father' Willis 1901. In addition to daily worship
in the church, it also houses a vibrant community including
One World Shop, Cornerstone Bookshop, Peace and Justice
Centre and Cornerstone Café. Sunday Services: Holy
Communion 8.00am, 10.30am (1st Sunday), Sung Eucharist
9.45am, and Choral Matins 11.15am (all other Sundays),
Choral Evensong 6.00pm; Weekday Service 1.00pm;
Communion Service Wednesday 11.00am

Open 8.00am-4.15pm each weekday, 9.00am-12.00 noon on Saturday

SCOTTISH EPISCOPAL ♿ wc ② 🍴 📖 ☕ (Cornerstone Café) **A**

ST JOHN THE EVANGELIST

THE PARISH CHURCH OF ST CUTHBERT

EDINBURGH METHODIST MISSION

426   THE PARISH CHURCH OF ST CUTHBERT

NT 248 736

Lothian Road, Edinburgh

Church website: www.st-cuthberts.net

The present church, the seventh on the site, was built in 1894, and designed by Hippolyte Blanc, retaining the 1790 spire. Altered in 1990, Stewart Tod. Tradition has it that St Cuthbert had a cell church here. If so, Christian worship has taken place here for 1300 years. Furnishings include marble communion table, murals and stained glass window by Tiffany. Fine organ originally by Hope-Jones 1899, rebuilt 1928, 1957 and 1997. Display of life of St Cuthbert in vestibule. Interesting graveyard, with many famous names. An oasis in the centre of the city. Gift shop and refreshments. Buses to Princes Street and Lothian Road. Sunday Services: 9.30am, 11.00am and 6.30pm (Service of Healing)

Open end April to mid September, Monday to Saturday 10.00am-4.00pm,

CHURCH OF SCOTLAND 🧑‍🦽 wc ② 🕯 🕯 🏠 ☕ **A**

427   EDINBURGH METHODIST MISSION

NT 248 730

Central Hall, 2 West Tollcross, Edinburgh

1901 by Dunn & Findlay, Edinburgh. Main hall has a curved and ribbed ceiling on arches rising from Ionic columns. Leaded windows of clear 'cathedral' glass embellished in the style of Glasgow Art Nouveau. Lower landings are decorated with mosaic tiles. A well-known venue for concerts, conferences and meetings. Half-mile south of Princes Street west end, via Lothian Road. Sunday Services: 11.00am

Open Monday to Friday 9.00am-10.00pm. Venue for the National Association of Youth Orchestras during Edinburgh Festival; daily performances

METHODIST 🧑‍🦽 (lift access via Dunbar Street) wc ② **B**

BARCLAY CHURCH   ST MICHAEL'S AND ALL SAINTS' CHURCH

428 BARCLAY CHURCH

NT 249 726

Bruntsfield Place, Tollcross, Edinburgh

1864 in powerful Ruskinian Gothic, this is Frederick T Pilkington's greatest
achievement. Spire 230 feet is well-known landmark. Spectacular theatrical space
within with double gallery. Painted ceiling. Organ originally by Hope-Jones,
reconstructed by Lewis. Removal of centre and other pews in sanctuary with other
minor alterations and the installation of spiral staircases to the first gallery 1999,
by Gray, Marshall Associates of Edinburgh. One hundred metres south of King's
Theatre. Sunday Services: 11.00am and 6.30pm

Open by arrangement, telephone church office 0131 229 6810 (afternoons)

CHURCH OF SCOTLAND **A**

429 ST MICHAEL'S AND ALL SAINTS' CHURCH

NT 251 729

Brougham Street, Edinburgh

Church website: www.stmichaelandallsaints.org.uk

A shrine of the Anglo-Catholic movement in Scotland. The church was mostly built
in 1867 but the west end not completed until 1876 and the Lady Chapel added in
1897, all to designs by R Rowand Anderson. Austere Gothic externally but the
interior is a magnificently spacious setting for a sumptuous display of furnishings,
including an elaborate Spanish pulpit of *c*.1600, carved and painted altarpieces by
William Burges 1867, Hamilton More-Nisbet 1901, and by C E Kempe 1889.
Extensive collection of stained glass with windows by Wailes, Clayton & Bell,
Kempe, and Sir Ninian Comper. Organ originally by Forster & Andrews, installed in
1992. Sunday Services: Low Mass 8.00am, High Mass 11.00am, Choral Evensong
and Benediction 6.30pm; Tuesday: Low Mass 8.00am; Wednesday: Low Mass

12.30pm; Thursday: Low Mass 6.00pm; Friday: Low Mass 10.30am; Saturday: Low
Mass 12.30pm (1st Saturday in month)

*Open all year, Wednesday 12.00 noon-2.30pm, Friday 10.00am-2.00pm, Saturdays during
Edinburgh Festival; and by arrangement, telephone the Rector 0131 229 6368*

SCOTTISH EPISCOPAL 🔣 wc 📖 ☕ (Saturdays during Edinburgh Festival) **A**

430　SACRED HEART CHURCH

NT 252 730

28 Lauriston Place, Edinburgh

Church website: www.rc.net/standed/sacredheart

Stone-fronted building designed by Father Richard
Vaughan SJ 1860, altered by Archibald Macpherson
1884. Holyrood Madonna of carved wood,
probably late 16th century. Stations of the Cross by
Peter Rauth 1874. Organ originally constructed by
Hamilton of Edinburgh 1874, rebuilt 1907 by
Scovell (who also designed the pulpit). A gift of
fine oak panelling from St Margaret's Convent
(now Gillis Centre) has enabled the Choir Loft to
be greatly enhanced. Restoration and conservation
2002. Buses to Tollcross. Masses: Saturday Vigil
6.30pm; Sunday 7.45am, 10.45am, and 8.00pm

Open every day

ROMAN CATHOLIC 🔣 wc ⊘ 📖 🕯 **B**

SACRED HEART CHURCH

431　ST ANDREW'S ORTHODOX CHAPEL

NT 262 728

2 Meadow Lane

Church website: www.edinburgh-orthodox.org.uk

Originally Buccleuch Parish School (built 1830s). Edinburgh Parish was founded as
a chaplaincy for Polish servicemen. Greek and Slavonic are used as well as English.
Orthodox furnishings and icons. Services: daily 6.30pm; Sunday and Feasts 9.00am
Matins; and Liturgy 10.30am

*Open by arrangement, telephone Archimandrite John Maitland-Moir 0131 667 0372 or
Raphael Pavouris 0131 662 1846*

ORTHODOX wc 📖 ☕ **A**

432 NICOLSON SQUARE METHODIST CHURCH

NT 261 732

Nicolson Square, Edinburgh
Church website: www.nicsquare.org.uk
By Thomas Brown 1815, set diagonally
across the corner of the square behind a
forecourt. Classical two-storey front based
on Adam's design for the west block of the
university. Inside, fluted cast-iron columns
support the U-plan gallery. Substantial
modernisation 1972. Organ by Forster &
Andrews of Hull dating from 1864.

NICOLSON SQUARE METHODIST CHURCH

Interesting modern chapel in basement created in 1989 by Nira Ponniah.
Small public garden at rear. Sunday Services: 11.00am and 6.30pm
Open Monday to Friday 8.30am-3.30pm. Fringe performances during Edinburgh Festival,
and concerts at other times
METHODIST 🔶 wc ⏺ ▯ ☕ (café in basement) **A**

433 BUCCLEUCH & GREYFRIARS FREE CHURCH

NT 261 728

West Crosscauseway (off Nicolson Street)
Church website: www.buccleuchfreechurch.co.uk
Built 1857 by Hays of Liverpool in Gothic style for the
Free Buccleuch congregation established at the 1843
Disruption. The congregation has sought to remain true to
the original Free Church vision of reformed theology and
evangelical outreach. One of the largest hammerbeam roofs
in the country and an impressive spire. Services: Sunday
11.00am and 6.30pm; Wednesday 7.30pm
Open by arrangement with the Minister, telephone 0131 664 6306
FREE CHURCH OF SCOTLAND 🔶 wc ⏺ **A**

BUCCLEUCH & GREYFRIARS
FREE CHURCH

434 KIRK O' FIELD PARISH CHURCH

NT 264 732

140 Pleasance, Edinburgh
Built as Charteris Memorial Church in 1912. Late Scots Gothic by James B Dunn.
Lorimerian vine enrichment on the vestibule ceiling. Wagon-roofed nave with west
gallery. Memorial to the Rev A H Charteris 1908. Mission Hall 1891 dedicated to
St Ninian. City buses 2, 21. Sunday Service: 11.00am
Open the first Saturday in September, 10.00am-1.00pm
CHURCH OF SCOTLAND wc ⏺ ▯ ▯ ☕

435   ST PETER'S, LUTTON PLACE

NT 265 725

16 Lutton Place (off South Clerk Street)
Church website: www.stpetersedinburgh.org

Early Geometric church by William Slater, its 56 metre spire diapered with bands
of ornament and cinquefoils. Octagonal baptistery (now the Miller Chapel). Nave
arcade supported on polished granite piers. Stencilled decoration on roofs by G H
Potts. Panels on chancel walls of Evangelists and the Agnus Dei by George Dobie
1890. Round Caen stone pulpit by Poole, stained glass by Clayton & Bell and
Isobel Goudie. Organ by Federick Holt 1856, rebuilt Scovell 1913, and Rushworth
& Dreaper 1959. Sunday Services: 8.30am, 10.45am, 6.30pm; Tuesday, Wednesday,
Thursday, Friday 9.00am and 5.00pm; Thursday 11.00am

Open by arrangement, telephone 0131 667 1107

SCOTTISH EPISCOPALIAN [&] [wc] (?) **A**

436   ST COLUMBA'S CHURCH, NEWINGTON

NT 265 721

9 Upper Gray Street, Edinburgh

A free treatment of the classic Renaissance style by R
M Cameron 1888. West façade has a large semi-circular
window and pedimented gable finished with a plain
Latin cross. Oblong interior with open timber roof and
semi-circular end forming a chancel and apse. The
chancel arch is a later addition. Notable features
include a collection of statues in the window niches.
Extensive natural lighting from roof lights and west
window. Two-manual pipe organ by Matthew Copley,
1997. Masses: Monday-Friday 9.30am; Saturday
11.00am; Sunday 11.00am and 6.30pm

Open after Masses, or by arrangement with the
Parish Priest, telephone 0131 667 1605

ROMAN CATHOLIC [wc] [wc] (toilet adapted in church hall) (?) **B**

ST COLUMBA'S CHURCH,
NEWINGTON

437   BLACKHALL UNITED FREE CHURCH

NT 216 750

1 House o' Hill Road, Edinburgh

Modern church completed in 1968. A90 at
the junction between Telford Road and
Queensferry Road. LRT buses 32, 52 and
41. Sunday Service: 11.00am

UNITED FREE CHURCH OF SCOTLAND [wc]

BLACKHALL UNITED FREE CHURCH

438 REID MEMORIAL CHURCH

NT 261 710

182 West Savile Terrace, Edinburgh

Church, hall and church officer's house by Leslie
G Thomson 1933 form an architectural oasis.
A lofty, cruciform church with meticulous neo-
Perpendicular detail. Stained glass windows by
James Ballantine, pipe organ Rushworth &
Dreaper, painting on reredos of 'Last Supper' by
William R Lawson. Cloister court to rear with
carved panel of 'Christ at the well of Samaria'
by Alexander Carrick. On local bus routes
24, 38, 38a and 41. Sunday Services: 10.30am
and first Sunday of month 6.30pm
Open 12.30-3.00pm on Fridays during
Edinburgh Festival; also open by arrangement,
telephone Henry Philip 0131 662 1494.
Organ recitals at 1.10pm during Festival
CHURCH OF SCOTLAND ♿ wc ⊘ 🏠 ⛪ **A**

REID MEMORIAL CHURCH

439 CARRICK KNOWE PARISH CHURCH

NT 203 721

Saughton Road North, Edinburgh

Built in 1953, of Norman design with a strong Scottish character. The last post-war
church to be built of stone – the external walls of Blaxter dressed stone, and
Darney rubble, both from Northumberland quarries. Furnishings in Scottish Border
oak, commissioned by the Church of Scotland as part of their exhibit for the
Empire Exhibition in Glasgow of 1938 – beautiful examples of ecclesiastical crafts-
manship. Baptismal bowl gifted
by Her Majesty Queen Elizabeth
The Queen Mother. Tapestry,
Dovecot Studios, Edinburgh.
Organ installed by Ronald Smith
1973. Opposite Union Park.
Buses 1 and 6. Sunday Service:
11.00am
Open every morning 9.30am-
12.00 noon, except Wednesday
CHURCH OF SCOTLAND
♿ ⊘ ⛪ 🏠 ☕ **A**

CARRICK KNOWE PARISH CHURCH

440   ST TERESA OF LISIEUX

NT 295 716

120 Niddrie Mains Road

Octagonal church with pebble-dashed walls,
green copper roof topped by a cross. Designed
by architect Charles W Gray, it was opened in
1962. Stone statue of St Teresa above the main
entrance. Pipe organ. Redecorated 2002. In the
weekday chapel is a copy of the San Damiano
crucifix, a reminder that the church has been

ST TERESA OF LISIEUX

staffed since its opening by Franciscan Friars. Services: Monday to Friday 6.55am,
9.30am; Saturday 10.00am, Vigil 6.00pm; Sunday 10.30am

Open for services and by arrangement, telephone 0131 661 2185

ROMAN CATHOLIC 🔵 wc

441   THE ROBIN CHAPEL

NT 295 715

Thistle Foundation, Niddrie Mains Road

Memorial to Robin Tudsbery, killed in the last days of the
Second World War, built by Architect John F Matthew 1950, at
the centre of a housing complex for physically disabled people
and their families. Peaceful and secluded interior enhanced by
stone capitals carved by Maxwell Adam, wood carvings by
Thomas Good, wrought-iron work by James Finnegan and
stained glass by Sadie McLellan. Sunday Service: 4.30pm

Open by arrangement with the Chaplain, telephone 0131 661 3366

NON-DENOMINATIONAL 🔵 wc ⓘ **A**

THE ROBIN CHAPEL

442   ST CHRISTOPHER'S

NT 292 748

Craigentinny Road, Edinburgh

Built by James McLachlan in 1934-8, the foundation stone was laid by John
Buchan, author of *The Thirty Nine Steps*. The exterior is of variegated red brick
with round arched windows and tiled roof. The interior is a darker plum-coloured
brick with a low wagon roof and segmental arches. The organ, Ingram 1900, came
from St Catherine's Argyll and was installed here in 1969. There are two stained
glass windows by Sax Shaw and one by George Reid. Sunday Service: 10.30am;
Communion on last Sunday in January, March, June and October; short
Communion after Family Services on the first Sunday of the month

Open 10.00am-12.00 noon Tuesdays and Saturdays, and by arrangement,
telephone Mr Ian Ramsay 0131 669 2129

CHURCH OF SCOTLAND wc ⓘ

ST CHRISTOPHER'S

COLINTON PARISH CHURCH (ST CUTHBERT'S)

443 COLINTON PARISH CHURCH (ST CUTHBERT'S)

NT 216 692

Dell Road, Edinburgh, at foot of Colinton village, beside Water of Leith

Church website: www.colinton-parish.com

The church of 1650 was rebuilt in 1771 and enlarged by David Bryce in 1837. Sydney Mitchell transformed the building in a neo-Byzantine style between 1907 and 1908. Mitchell adorned the semi-circular apse with murals and fine woodwork including the pulpit, communion table and rood-screen. To the south of the church, Page and Park have built new rooms which, through their contemporary design, embrace the wonderful woodland setting. The Offertory House of 1807 heralds this most interesting of buildings with its ancient graveyard set within a bend of the Water of Leith. Sunday Services: 9.30 and 11.00am

Open Monday to Friday 9.00am-4.00pm. Swing Café open for morning coffee and light lunches, Monday to Friday 10.00am-2.00pm. Contact the church office, telephone 0131 441 2232

CHURCH OF SCOTLAND ♿ wc ② ☕ **B**

444 CORSTORPHINE OLD PARISH CHURCH

NT 201 728

Kirk Loan, Corstorphine, Edinburgh

Interesting 15th-century church with tower, pre-Reformation relics, Scottish heraldic panels and fine medieval tombs, including those of the founders Sir Adam Forrester, Lord Provost of Edinburgh (died 1405) and Sir John Forrester, Lord Chamberlain of Scotland in the reign of James I. Fine Victorian stained glass. Interesting gravestones in churchyard. Sunday Service: 10.30am

Open Wednesdays 10.30am-12.00 noon, except December and January. Coincides with opening of nearby 17th-century Dower House (Corstorphine Trust) serving refreshments

CHURCH OF SCOTLAND ♿ (partial) ② 🕯 ⚱ 📖 **A**

CORSTORPHINE OLD PARISH CHURCH

CORSTORPHINE UNITED FREE CHURCH

445   ST JOHN THE BAPTIST RC

NT 197 731

37 St Ninan's Road, Corstorphine

Built in 1964, a modern, spacious and light building, and home to a congregation of about 400 each week. Stained glass by Felix McCulloch is one of its notable features. Services: Saturday 6.00pm; Sunday 10.45am

Open by arrangement, telephone Parish Priest 0131 334 1693

ROMAN CATHOLIC ♿ wc 🎧

446   CORSTORPHINE UNITED FREE CHURCH

NT 199 727

Glebe Terrace, Corstorphine (off St John's Road, opposite Harp Hotel)

Intimate, secluded, friendly little church. Various ante-rooms and large hall, with new modern kitchen. Good grassed area for barbecues. Sunday Service: 10.30am

Open by appointment, telephone Pastor George Banks 0131 552 3666

UNITED FREE CHURCH OF SCOTLAND wc 🎧

447   CRAMOND KIRK

NT 190 768

Cramond Glebe Road, Edinburgh

Church website: www.cramondkirk.org.uk

A cruciform kirk of 1656 with 15th-century tower. Interior altered 1701, 1811, large reconstruction 1911 by Donald McArthy and James Mather. Pitch pine hammerbeam roof, oak furnishings, white marble font. Burgerhuys bell 1619. Jock Howieson mosaic. Plan of kirkyard available. Roman settlement remains. Off Whitehouse Road. City buses 24 and 41. Sunday Services: 8.45 and 10.00am, 6.00pm (1st Sunday)

Open daily during Edinburgh Festival 2.00-5.00pm.

Cramond Village exhibition at the Maltings

CHURCH OF SCOTLAND ♿ wc 🎧 ⛲ **B**

CRAMOND KIRK   DALMENY PARISH CHURCH (ST CUTHBERT'S)

448 DALMENY PARISH CHURCH (ST CUTHBERT'S)

NT 144 775

Main Street, Dalmeny, near South Queensferry

The most complete example of Romanesque architecture in Scotland. Dates from
*c.*1130. Superb medieval south doorway, arch stones elaborately carved with
animals, figures and grotesque heads. Historic graveyard. Pipe organ by
Lammermuir 1984. Sunday Service: 11.30am

*Open April to September, Sunday 2.00-4.30pm. Other times, key from the Post Office, or 5
Main Street. Parties please telephone Mr W Ross in advance 0131 331 1479*

CHURCH OF SCOTLAND ♿ wc 🚾 📖 A

449 DAVIDSON'S MAINS PARISH CHURCH

NT 207 752

1 Quality Street, off Queensferry Road

Church website: www.davidsonsmainsparishchurch.org.uk

Originally Cramond Free Church. A small T-plan kirk with flat Gothic windows
by David Cousin 1843. The timber bellcote with a prickly slated hat was added to
the centre gable in 1866. Interior enlarged
to the north in 1970. Major refurbishment
to the chancel area in 1999. To the east the
little school and house by Robert R
Raeburn 1846 were extended with a hall by
Auldjo Jamieson & Arnott 1933 maintaining
the domestic scale by means of a dormered
roof. Essentially a village church.

Sunday Services: 10.30am and 6.30pm

Open Tuesday to Thursday 10.00am-2.00pm

CHURCH OF SCOTLAND wc 🎭 ☕ ⌨

DAVIDSON'S MAINS PARISH CHURCH

450 DUDDINGSTON KIRK

NT 284 726

Old Church Lane, Duddingston Village, Edinburgh

Church website: http://duddingston-kirk.org.uk

12th-century Duddingston Kirk is one of the oldest churches used for regular worship in Scotland. Sir Walter Scott was an Elder. The painter Turner was a visitor and Minister John Thomson was himself a notable landscape painter. The founding family of the Pinkerton Detective Agency is commemorated in a stained glass window and Duddingston Loch is the birthplace of the rules of curling. Sunday Services: 10.00am and 11.30am

Open July and August, Wednesday, Thursday and

Sunday 2.00-4.00pm. Fringe venue during Edinburgh Festival

CHURCH OF SCOTLAND ♿ wc ② 🍴 🏠 ☕ A

DUDDINGSTON KIRK

451 ST BARNABAS EPISCOPAL CHURCH

NT 290 693

4 Moredun Park View, Edinburgh

Small modern church in housing scheme 1950. Altered in 1969. St Barnabas tapestry. Moredun Scheme is between A7 and A772 on south side of city. Sunday Service: Eucharist 10.30am; Tuesday, Prayer Group 6.30pm

Open Wednesday mornings

SCOTTISH EPISCOPAL ♿ 🏠 ☕ A

452 GREENBANK PARISH CHURCH

NT 243 702

Braidburn Terrace/Comiston Road

Church website: www.greenbankchurch.org

Founded in 1900 as the last United Presbyterian congregation in Edinburgh. Original building now used as halls. The present Gothic-style church (A Lorne Campbell 1927 is an early example of reinforced concrete construction, with stone cladding. Furnishings to Campbell's designs by Scott Morton & Co. Current scheme of decoration by Sir William Kininmonth. Organ by A E Ingram 1927, rebuilt R L Smith 1972. Stained glass by James Ballantine, Alexander Strachan (2), William Wilson (3). Pulpit falls by Archibald Brennan, Penelope Beaton and Malcolm Lochhead. New suite of halls by Lee Boyd Partnership 2001. Sunday Services: 10.30am all year, plus 9.30am 1st Sunday of September to December and February to May, every Sunday June to August

Open by arrangement, telephone the Minister 0131 447 4032

CHURCH OF SCOTLAND ♿ wc ② ☕ (after service)

GREENBANK PARISH CHURCH   GREENSIDE PARISH CHURCH

453 GREENSIDE PARISH CHURCH

NT 263 745

Royal Terrace, Edinburgh

T-plan design by Gillespie Graham 1839 with tower added in 1851, set amidst Playfair's great terraces. Connections with Robert Louis Stevenson who knew it as 'the church on the hill'. Pipe organ, rebuilt here by Ingram 1933. Off London Road. Sunday Services: 11.00am and 6.30pm (no evening service July and August)

Open by arrangement, telephone the Session Clerk 0131 669 5324

CHURCH OF SCOTLAND ② wc **B**

454 ST PHILIP'S, JOPPA

NT 313 736

Abercorn Terrace, Joppa, Edinburgh

A really striking edifice in the Early Decorated style by J Honeyman 1877. Ravaged by fire 1998 and fully restored. Broach spire 170 feet over a lofty belfry. Aisled nave with entry in the south gable. Inside, a remarkably complete interior. Clustered piers with leafy capitals support the nave arcade; foliated corbels on the clerestorey support the wood-lined tunnel-roof. Fine stained glass windows to aisles. Sunday Service: 11.00am

Open by arrangement, telephone Mr Lockhart 0131 669 3641

CHURCH OF SCOTLAND ♿ wc ② **B**

455 KIRKLISTON PARISH CHURCH

NT 125 744
The Square, Kirkliston
Mainly 12th-century church. Two Norman
archways, the largest of which was blocked
up in the 19th century. Two beautiful modern
stained glass windows. Organ by Ingram of
Edinburgh 1925. In the 19th century a small
watchtower was built in the graveyard where
the earliest identifiable stone is dated 1529.
Sunday Service: 11.00am
*Open by arrangement, telephone Mrs Keating
0131 333 3298, or Mrs Brechin 0131 333 3252*
CHURCH OF SCOTLAND 🔾 wc ⊘ 🛈 📖 A

KIRKLISTON PARISH CHURCH

456 EBENEZER UNITED FREE CHURCH, LEITH

NT 266 764
31 Bangor Road, Leith
The Ebenezer congregation was founded
in 1891. The original church building in
Great Junction Street was demolished in
1979 to make way for new housing. The
present building, by Sir Frank Mears &
Partners, was opened in 1984. Bangor
Road runs south from Great Junction
Street in Leith.
Sunday Services: 11.00am and 6.30pm
*Open first Saturday of each month
10.00am–12.00 noon*
UNITED FREE CHURCH OF SCOTLAND 🔾 wc

EBENEZER UNITED FREE CHURCH, LEITH

457 LEITH METHODIST CHURCH

NT 268 761
1 Junction Place, Leith
Built 1932 by Maclennan & Cunningham as 600-seater Central Hall in artificial
stone and harl on site of former Secession Church. In Methodist use from 1868.
Horizontally subdivided in 1987 with flexible worship area upstairs and
community centre downstairs. Off Great Junction Street, behind McKenzie-Millar.
Sunday Service: 11.00am
Open weekdays except Wednesday 10.00am–2.00pm, Saturday 10.00am–12.00 noon
METHODIST 🔾 ⊘ 📖 ☕ A

458 NORTH LEITH PARISH CHURCH

NT 263 765
Madeira Street, Leith
Church website: www.northleith.freeserve.co.uk
Classical building with portico and spire by William
Burn 1816. Renovated Ian G Lindsay & Partners
1950, and Stewart Tod & Partners 1993. Impressive
two-storey 'country house' front. Light interior with
galleries supported by Ionic columns. Stained glass
James Ballantine. Three-manual pipe organ, built by
Wadsworth of Manchester 1880. Small graveyard
and garden. Off Ferry Road, close to Leith Library.
Sunday Services: 11.00am all year, 6.30pm
(excluding July and August)
Open by arrangement, telephone the
church office 0131 553 7378
CHURCH OF SCOTLAND 🚿 wc ② **A**

NORTH LEITH PARISH CHURCH

459 SOUTH LEITH PARISH CHURCH

NT 271 761
Kirkgate or Constitution Street, Leith
Church website: www.slpc.co.uk
A church was erected in 1483 as a chapel attached to the collegiate Church of
Restalrig. The present building dates from 1847, built to a design by Thomas
Hamilton. Tower and porch incorporate
coats of arms of four successive Scottish
monarchs. Fine hammerbeam roof. Italian
marble pulpit. Stained glass and emblems of
the Trade Guilds. Organ by Brindley &
Foster 1887. Set in ancient graveyard with
interesting monuments. At the foot of
Leith Walk. Sunday Services: 11.00am,
also 6.30pm October to May, and
9.30am June to July
Open Thursdays 12.30-1.30pm; other times
by arrangement, telephone 0131 554 2578
CHURCH OF SCOTLAND 🚿 wc ② 🍴 📖 🚹 **A**

SOUTH LEITH PARISH CHURCH

460 ST MARY, STAR OF THE SEA, LEITH

NT 272 762

106 Constitution Street, Edinburgh

E W Pugin and Joseph A Hansom's church of
1854 had no chancel, no north aisle and was
orientated to the west. The north aisle was
added in 1900 and the chancel in 1912 when
the church was turned round and the present
west entrance made. Inside, the church has
simple pointed arcades and a high braced collar
roof. Organ originally by Brindley & Foster

ST MARY, STAR OF THE SEA, LEITH

1897. Access from Constitution Street or New Kirkgate. Services: Monday to
Friday 10am; Saturday 10am and Vigil Mass 6.00pm; Sunday 10.00am and 11.30am
Open Monday to Friday 9.00-11.00am, Saturday 9.00-11.30am, Sunday 9.00am-12.30pm
ROMAN CATHOLIC 🚹 wc ② **B**

461 LIBERTON KIRK

NT 275 700

Kirkgate, Liberton, Edinburgh

Church website: www.libertonkirk.freeserve.co.uk

Sitting in a commanding position overlooking the city, a church was founded here
in 1143 by David I, although there is evidence of an earlier church dating from AD
800. The present building was erected in 1815. Designed by James Gillespie
Graham, it is a rectangular semi-Gothic building with corbelled parapet tower. A
memorial stained glass window depicting Cornelius, by Ballantine 1905. Three
striking contemporary pulpit falls and four outstanding wall hangings by D
Morrison. The kirkyard contains many stones of special interest, including a table-
top tomb to a local farmer, its ends carved in relief with agricultural scenes.
Sunday Services: 9.30am and 11.00am (10.30am, July and August)
Open Monday to Friday 9am-5pm by arrangement, telephone Mrs W Munro 0131 664 3795
CHURCH OF SCOTLAND 🚹 wc ② 📖 **A**

462 LIBERTON NORTHFIELD PARISH CHURCH

NT 280 699

280 Gilmerton Road, Edinburgh

Built 1869 as a Free Church to designs by J W Smith. North-east tower and
broach spire added by Peddie & Kinnear 1873. Interior with raked floor and an
ornate arch-braced timber roof springing from short ashlar colonnettes with a
variety of leafy capitals. Transepts entered by triple arches expressed on the
exterior by triple gables. Virtually unaltered organ by E F Walcker 1903.
Sunday Services: 11.00am and 6.30pm
Open by arrangement, telephone Rev John McPake 0131 658 1754
CHURCH OF SCOTLAND wc **B**

463 MAYFIELD SALISBURY CHURCH

NT 266 717

West Mayfield

Originally built as Mayfield Free Kirk 1897, this is a fine example of the French Gothic style of Hippolyte Blanc. Spire 48 feet added 1894. Magnificent collection of stained glass by Ballantine & Gardiner, Charles L Davidson, Henry Dearl of Morris & Co, Guthrie & Wells and William Meikle. Church House, orginally the manse, now houses the Mayfield Radio Unit which broadcasts to hospitals in the Edinburgh area. Sunday Services: 10.30am and 6.30pm September to June; 9.30am, 10.30am and 8.00pm July to August

Open weekdays 9.00am-4.00pm, except Wednesdays, Saturday 9.00am-12.00 noon (coffee)

CHURCH OF SCOTLAND ♿ wc ② **B**

MAYFIELD SALISBURY CHURCH

464 CHRIST CHURCH, MORNINGSIDE

NT 245 719

Holy Corner, Bruntsfield, Edinburgh

Church website: www.christchurchmorningside.co.uk

French Gothic by Hippolyte Blanc, a member of the congregation, 1876. Gables and flying buttresses face onto the road; the main entrance is beneath the tower. Original murals in chancel and nave roof. Extensive stained glass by Ballantine. Sunday Services: Holy Communion 8.00am, Sung Eucharist 10.00am, Evensong 6.30pm; Monday to Friday Morning Prayer and Eucharist 8.00am; Thursday Holy Communion 11.00am

Open 11.00am-3.00pm Wednesday and Friday

SCOTTISH EPISCOPAL wc ② 🍴 **B**

465 ERIC LIDDELL CENTRE

NT 246 719

15 Morningside Road, Holy Corner

Church website: www.eric-liddell.org

Former North Morningside Church of Scotland in neo-Norman by David Robertson 1879-81. Dramatic intervention by Nicholas Groves-Raines 1992 and 1999 for conversion to Eric Liddell Centre which provides community services and accommodation for organisations of Christian witness. Galleries provide viewing of impressive collection of stained glass, including windows by William Wilson and John Duncan. Chinese Evangelical Church Services in Mandarin and Cantonese 1.00pm every Sunday

Open daily 10.00am-5.00pm, or in evenings by arrangement, telephone 0131 447 4520

CHINESE EVANGELICAL CHURCH ♿ wc ② 🍴 (on request) ☐ ☕ (The 1924 café and cards) **B**

ERIC LIDDELL CENTRE   ST BENNET'S

466 ST BENNET'S

NT 248 717

42 Greenhill Gardens, Church Hill, Edinburgh

The chapel attached to the home of the Archbishops of St Andrews and
Edinburgh. A charming Byzantine church built by R Weir Schultz 1907, under the
will of the 3rd Marquess of Bute, to take the outstanding Italianate classical
interior designed by William Frame in 1889 for the chapel at House of Falkland.
Porch by Reginald Fairlie 1934. There are examples of stained glass windows by
Gabriel Loire of Chartres dating from the 1970s; other windows were installed in
1999 commemorating the 1600th anniversary of St Ninian and the 1400th
anniversary of St Columba, as well as a millennium window. The chapel contains
memorabilia of the Archbishops since the restoration of the hierarchy.
Church Service times as announced
Open weekdays 9.00am-5.00pm
ROMAN CATHOLIC ♿ wc **A**

467 ST PETER'S CHURCH

NT 248 715

77 Falcon Avenue

Regarded as Robert Lorimer's most innovative design, St Peter's was built in two
stages: 1906-27 and the nave completed 1928-9. A tall square Italianate campanile
watches over a welcoming courtyard. Sculpture on the apse of 'The Crucifixion' by
Joseph Hayes. The towering nave in white-washed brick is lit by six tall windows.
Stained glass by Morris and Gertrude A Meredith Williams, Nina Millar Davidson,
and Pierre Fourmaintraux. Lead font with fish motif by G P Bankart. Masses:
Sunday 9.00am, 11.00am and 5.30pm; Saturday 12.00 noon; Weekdays 9.00am
Open 20 minutes before services and during confessions on
Saturdays 11.15-11.45am and 6.30-7.00pm
ROMAN CATHOLIC ♿ ◐ **A**

MORNINGSIDE PARISH CHURCH   CHURCH OF THE GOOD SHEPHERD

468 MORNINGSIDE PARISH CHURCH

NT 246 707

Cluny Gardens, Morningside, Edinburgh

Church website: www.morningsideparishchurch.net

Built as St Matthew's 1890 by Hippolyte Blanc, inspired by late 13th-century Gothic. Fourteen stained glass windows on side aisles of nave, including the new St Cuthbert window to mark the 2003 union, and the St Andrew Window in North Transept. East window: 'Four Apostles', Sir Edward Burne-Jones 1900; west window: four scenes from the ministry of Jesus, Percy Bacon & Co 1905. Last 'Father' Willis organ in Scotland, installed 1901. Morningside Parish Church is a union of five former churches – the former St Matthew's and then Cluny Parish Church, now the new Morningside Parish Church; Morningside Parish Church (Newbattle Terrace); Morningside High Church, now the Churchill Theatre; South Morningside Church now the Cluny Centre; Braid Church, now the Braid Centre. Sunday Services: autumn, winter, spring 11.00am and 6.30pm; summer 9.30am and 11.00am

A regular venue for concerts, open also during Edinburgh Festival with organ recitals at 1.00pm as advertised. The church, the Cluny Centre and the Braid Centre can be opened for viewing by arrangement, telephone church office 0131 447 6745

CHURCH OF SCOTLAND 🔛 ⊘ ⱷ 📄

469 CHURCH OF THE GOOD SHEPHERD

NT 228 734

Murrayfield Avenue, Edinburgh

Designed by Sir Robert Lorimer and dedicated in 1899, the building contains some fine examples of stained glass, including a modern window depicting 'The Good Shepherd'. There is a fine Brindley and Foster organ which was rebuilt by Willis in 1967. Sunday Services: Holy Communion 8.30am, Sung Communion 10.00am; Wednesday Holy Communion 11.00am

Open by arrangement, telephone James Young 0131 337 7615

SCOTTISH EPISCOPAL ⬚ ⊘ 📄 ℝ **B**

470 ST MARK'S CHURCH

NT 237 691

29 Oxgangs Avenue

Opened by Archbishop Gordon Gray in 1962.
Designed by Peter Whiston with a slated roof
above walls made of cobbles and a rich interior.
Stained glass by Dom Basil Robinson, OSB.
Stations of the Cross by Vincent Butler (Saltire
Award 1971). Statues of Our Lady and St Mark
by Norman Forrest. Services: Saturday Vigil
6.00pm; Sunday Mass 10.00am

Open Wednesday and Saturday 11.00am-1.00pm

ROMAN CATHOLIC [λ] [wc] ⎆

ST MARK'S CHURCH

471 PILRIG ST PAUL'S CHURCH

NT 266 752

Junction of Pilrig Street and Leith Walk

Splendidly bold French Gothic by Peddie & Kinnear
1861-3. A spectacular interior with leafy stone capitals
carrying a diagonal arch-braced roof of laminated timber.
Gothic spire with chiming clock at the south corner.
Windows by Ballantine and Field & Allen. The chancel
furnishings make an impressive pitch-pine Gothic display
beneath the organ by Forster & Andrews 1903. Sunday
Service: 11.00am

*Open Tuesday, Wednesday, Thursday 11.00am-1.00pm; or by
arrangement with Dr Sime 0131 552 9652*

CHURCH OF SCOTLAND [λ] [wc] ⎆ ☕ [] **B**

PILRIG ST PAUL'S CHURCH

472 POLWARTH PARISH CHURCH

NT 750 495

36-38 Polwarth Terrace, Edinburgh

Church website: www.polwarth.org.uk

Splendid example of late 19th- and early 20th-century architecture by Sydney
Mitchell and Wilson 1901, with the tower by James Jerdan & Sons 1913. The
architecture shows pre-Reformation influences, including stone carvings of the
face of Mary, the mother of Christ, and several 'Green men'. Marble chancel
augmented by one of the finest pulpits in the country, sculpted by William
Beveridge in 1903. Ascension window at the east end of the chancel by Clayton
& Bell. Pipe organ by Forster & Andrews 1903.

Sunday Service: 11.00am; and other Services as advertised

Open by arrangement with Church office, telephone 0131 346 2711

CHURCH OF SCOTLAND [λ] [wc] ⎆ [] **B**

473 PORTOBELLO OLD PARISH CHURCH

NT 309 738

Bellfield Street, off Portobello High Street

The oldest church in Portobello, built 1809 by
William Sibbald, in classical style with a pediment.
The clock tower was added in 1839. Organ by
Peter Conacher 1873, rebuilt by Henry Willis 1984.
Furniture of Austrian oak. Mort safe and
interesting memorials in graveyard. Public
swimming baths and safe, sandy beach at end of
the street. Good bus service from city centre.
Sunday Service: 11.00am; meditation (5 minutes)
weekdays at noon

Open 10.00am-2.00pm Monday to Friday all year

CHURCH OF SCOTLAND ♿ wc ⊘ 🛏 ☕ **B**

PORTOBELLO OLD PARISH CHURCH

474 ST MARK'S PORTOBELLO

NT 309 738

287 Portobello High Street

Church website: www.saintmarks-edinburgh.org.uk

One of the first Episcopal churches to be built in the Edinburgh area, St Mark's is
a villa-like Neo-Classical church, square in plan, of 1824, most notable for its
dome and semi-circular Doric porch. The Venetian windows and chancel were
added by Hay & Henderson in 1892. Stained glass by Ballantine & Sons of the
'Good Samaritan' and 'The soul of Jonathan knit with the soul of David'. Organ,
1828 by D & T Hamilton, relocated by Ingram 1899. Eucharist: Sunday: 8.30am
and 10.30am; Thursday: 10.00am

Open first Saturday of each month (except January) 9.00am-2.00pm

SCOTTISH EPISCOPALIAN ♿ wc ⊘ 🛏 **B**

475 PRIESTFIELD PARISH CHURCH

NT 271 721

Dalkeith Road, corner of Marchhall Place

Church website: www.priestfield.org.uk

Built in 1879, Sutherland & Walker, in the Italian Lombardic style. Beautiful stained
glass windows designed as a War Memorial by Alexander Strachan, Douglas
Hamilton and Mary Wood in 1921. Other features of note are the handsome pulpit
and organ gallery and a most unusual baptismal font after Danish original. Sunday
Service: 11.00am; Evening Services, September to June, 2nd and 4th Sunday

Open by arrangement, contact the Minister 0131 668 1620. Concerts during Festival

CHURCH OF SCOTLAND ♿ wc wc ⊘ 🚻 🛏 **A**

476 QUEENSFERRY PARISH CHURCH, SOUTH QUEENSFERRY

NT 130 782

The Loan, South Queensferry, Edinburgh
Church website: www.qpc.freeuk.com

Well-used and well-loved Burgh Church, built in 1894 and extended in 1993. Of special interest is the display of banners and the wrought iron railings which incorporate a burning bush motif. Centre of village. Sunday Services: 10.00am and 11.30am

QUEENSFERRY PARISH CHURCH, SOUTH QUEENSFERRY

Open all year, Monday to Friday 10.00-11.30am. Access to historic graveyard (1635-early 1900s) can be arranged in advance, telephone 0131 331 1100

CHURCH OF SCOTLAND   🧑‍🦽 ⓐ 👤 📖 ☕ **c**

477 PRIORY CHURCH OF ST MARY OF MT CARMEL, SOUTH QUEENSFERRY

NT 129 784

Hopetoun Road, South Queensferry, Edinburgh
Church website: www.priorychurch.com

Originally a Carmelite Friary founded in 1330, the church fell into disrepair during the 16th century. It was restored for the use of the Episcopal church in 1890, the work being started by John Kinross. Later work was carried out in the 1960s by Ian Lindsay. Church extensively refurbished in 2000, new floor (with underfloor heating), and a glass engraved screen to side chapel. Font cover designed by Lorimer. Fourteenth-century aumbry. Mass dial on outside south wall.

Sunday Services: 9.00am Scottish Liturgy Communion, 10.00am All-ages Service (1st Sunday), 10.00am Communion (all other Sundays); Thursday 10.00am

Open by arrangement, telephone the church office 0131 331 1958. Also open during Ferry Fair Week in August

SCOTTISH EPISCOPAL

🧑‍🦽 wc 📖 **A**

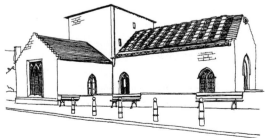

PRIORY CHURCH OF ST MARY OF MT CARMEL, SOUTH QUEENSFERRY

478   RATHO PARISH CHURCH

NT 138 710

Baird Road, Ratho, Edinburgh
Church website: www.rathoparishchurch.org.uk
An interesting medieval cruciform church,
with later aisles. The east aisle dated 1683,
the south 1830. To the west of the south
aisle is a 12th-century doorway, partially
visible, with scalloped capitals and decorated
hoodmould. Twentieth-century
refurbishment revealed a Celtic cross stone
which might suggest early worship on this

RATHO PARISH CHURCH

site. In the south porch a 13th-century tomb slab belonging to one of the Knights
Templar who owned Ratho in the Middle Ages. In the graveyard are several
interesting headstones and a panelled coffin formed of a single stone.
Organ by Smethurst of Manchester 1964. Sunday Service: 11.00am
Open by arrangement, telephone Mrs Watson 0131 333 1732
CHURCH OF SCOTLAND ♿ wc ⏍ 📖 **A**

479   ST MARGARET'S PARISH CHURCH

NT 284 745

27 Restalrig Road South, Edinburgh
Church website: www.st-margarets-church.com
Rebuilt by William Burn 1836 on the foundations of the previous 15th-century
church. The flowing window tracery follows the original design, stained glass by
William Wilson 1966. Attached to the
south-west corner is the hexagonal St
Triduana's Chapel, once the lower storey of
a two-tier chapel built for James III about
1477. The vault springs from a central pier,
its six shafts topped by foliate capitals.
Notable 17th- and 18th-century monuments
in the graveyard. Sunday Service: 10.30am;
Wednesday, short act of worship 1.00pm
Open Wednesday 12.00 noon-2.00pm, or by
arrangement, contact Mr Skakle 0131 661 2510,
or the church office 0131 554 7400
CHURCH OF SCOTLAND ♿ wc ⏍ 📕 **A**

ST MARGARET'S PARISH CHURCH

480 ST MICHAEL'S CHURCH

NT 234 722

1 Slateford Road, Edinburgh

Church website: www.stmichaels-kirk.co.uk

One of architect John Honeyman's most notable buildings,
completed 1883. Square 135-ft tower and longest aisle in
the city. Sanctuary illuminated by clerestoried nave
beneath dark-timbered roof. Unusual reredos bearing Ten
Commandments, Beatitudes and the Creed. Pulpit and
lectern decorated with biblical fruits by Gertrude Hope.
Communion table, fall and Bible markers by Hannah Frew
Paterson, dedicated in April 2001. Organ by Brindley and
Foster 1895. Stained glass, including work by Douglas

ST MICHAEL'S CHURCH

Strachan (1895-1925). The building has been extensively restored inside and out
and provides for a variety of worship, cultural and outreach activities. Bus routes 4,
34 and 44. Sunday Service: 11.00am; July and August 10.30am

Open by arrangement, telephone 0131 478 9675

CHURCH OF SCOTLAND & wc ?

481 ST CUTHBERT'S CHURCH

NT 227 715

104 Slateford Road

Built to a design by J B Bennett and opened in 1896. Major renovation 1969.
Significant works of art including original stained glass windows and several
tapestries by the Edinburgh Tapestry Company at the Dovecot Studios, the most
recent being of 1996 to mark the centenary. Services: Weekdays 9.00am,
Saturday 10.00am, Vigil Mass 6.00pm; Sunday Mass 10.00am

Open during and after services every day, or by arrangement with the

Parish Priest, telephone 0131 443 1317

ROMAN CATHOLIC & wc (in hall) ? ☕ (after Sunday Mass)

482 STOCKBRIDGE PARISH CHURCH

NT 247 748

Saxe Coburg Street, Edinburgh

Classical church by James Milne 1823 with an Ionic pilastered and pedimented
front and a small domed steeple. The interior contains the original U-plan gallery.
In 1888 Hardy & Wight added the apse which was decorated in 1987 with war
memorial murals by the German artist Reinhardt Behrens depicting the Lothian
coastline 'at the going down of the sun and in the morning ...'. Historic 2-manual
organ by August Gern 1883, installed 1995. Services: Sunday 11.00am

Telephone the Administrator 0131 332 0122

CHURCH OF SCOTLAND & wc ? **A/B**

STOCKBRIDGE PARISH CHURCH

WARDIE PARISH CHURCH

483 VIEWFORTH ST DAVID AND ST OSWALD

NT 244 725

104 Gilmour Place, Edinburgh

Church website: www.viewforth.org

Originally a Free Church. Built by Pilkington and Bell 1871 to an orthodox four-square plan with restrained detail. The massive upward growth contrasts with the fragile shafted geometric window in the central gable. Octagonal belfry, truncated in 1976. Powerful interior, rebuilt after a fire in 1898, with very thin cast-iron columns supporting huge transverse beams over the side galleries. Organ reconstructed 1976 from two instruments by Blackett & Howden 1899 and Forster & Andrews 1904. Sunday Service: 10.30am.

Modern and contemporary service 12.00 noon

Telephone the Church Administrator 0131 229 1917

CHURCH OF SCOTLAND [wc] (?) **B**

484 WARDIE PARISH CHURCH

NT 246 768

Primrose Bank Road, Trinity

A jolly Gothic church with Francophile detail, by John McLachlan 1892. Distinctive silhouette with central lantern and conical pinnacles. Inside, a clear-span tunnel roof. A complete and perfect set of Gothic oak furnishings by Scott Morton & Co 1935 including the organ case (organ by Rushworth & Dreaper). Sunday Services: 11.00am, 10.30am, July and August

Open Tuesday, Thursday and Friday 9.00am-12.00 noon,

telephone the church office 0131 551 3847

CHURCH OF SCOTLAND [♿] [wc] (?)

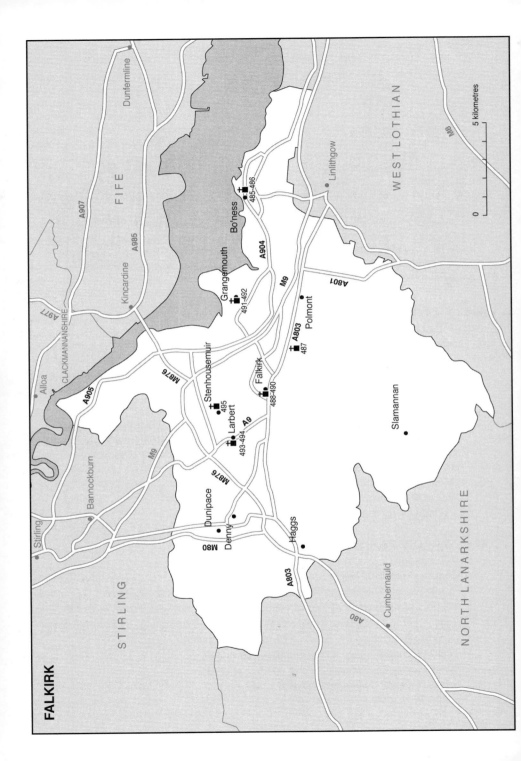

FALKIRK

FALKIRK

Local Representative: Mr Robert Tait, 18 Polmont Park, Polmont
(*telephone* 01324 713746)

485 ST CATHERINE'S CHURCH, BO'NESS

NS 999 812

Cadzow Crescent, Bo'ness

The congregation was formed in 1888 and
moved to the present building in 1921. The hall
was added in 1928. The sanctuary windows
depict the children of the Bible. Organ by
Miller of Dundee. Off Dean Road, adjacent to
Douglas Park. Services: Sunday 11.30am (Sung
Eucharist); Wednesday 10.15 (Said Eucharist)
*Open by arrangement, telephone the
Rector 01324 482438*
SCOTTISH EPISCOPAL & wc

ST CATHERINE'S CHURCH, BO'NESS

486 CARRIDEN PARISH CHURCH, BO'NESS

NT 019 812

Carriden Brae, Carriden, Bo'ness

The first church of Carriden was consecrated in 1243 by Bishop David de Bernam,
although it is believed that the parish goes back to the time of St Ninian, AD
*c.*396. The present church is the third.
Designed by P MacGregor Chalmers 1909,
in simple Romanesque style with a west
tower and stone spire. The bell was cast in
Rotterdam, Peter Oostens 1674. Inside, a
wooden sailing ship 'The Ranger' hangs from
the barrel-shaped pitch pine roof. Six-bay
nave. Baptistry chapel with a wall painting
thought to be of the Scottish School.
Sounding board on north wall 1655. A fine
stone arcaded baptismal font, 2-manual pipe
organ moved from the John Knox Church,
Gorbals after the Blitz of 1941.
Sunday Service: 11.15am
Open by arrangement, telephone 01506 822141
CHURCH OF SCOTLAND & wc ⊘ B

CARRIDEN PARISH CHURCH, BO'NESS

487 BRIGHTONS PARISH CHURCH

NS 928 778

Main Street, Brightons, 4 miles south of Falkirk
Church website: www.brightonsparishchurch.org.uk
Built in 1847. Local quarry owner Alexander
Lawrie gifted the stone to build the church
to a design by Brown & Carrick of Glasgow.
T-plan church with small steeple with bell.
Side galleries added in 1893. Chancel area
modernised 1935. Windows 1993 by Ruth
Golliwaws of New Orleans, USA. Sunday
Services: 11.00am and first Sunday;
September to May 6.00pm

BRIGHTONS PARISH CHURCH

Open for prayer, September to June, Thursday 10.00am-12.00 noon
CHURCH OF SCOTLAND [♿] [wc] ⊘

488 FALKIRK FREE CHURCH

NS 884 826

Beaumont Drive, Newcarron, Falkirk
Church website: www.falkirkfreechurch.com
The present congregation began in 1991 and moved into its new building in 1998.
The building, extended in 2004, reflects modern architecture but maintains a
spiritual and practical ambience. Sunday Services: 11.00am and 6.30pm; Prayers:
Wednesday and Saturday 7.30pm, Saturday 7.00pm. Other activities, contact the
Minister
Open by arrangement, telephone the Rev R MacLeod 01324 631008
FREE CHURCH OF SCOTLAND [♿] [wc] ⊘ ⌂ ☕

489 FALKIRK OLD AND ST MODAN'S PARISH CHURCH

NS 887 800

Manse Place, off High Street, Falkirk
Church website: http://fkoldstm.webspace.fish.co.uk
Dating from 1811, although 12th-century pillars remain in the vestibule. There has
been a Christian church on this site for 1200 years; local legend links the earliest
foundation with the Celtic St Modan in the 6th century. The square tower dates
from the 16th century, and the gable marks of the earlier nave and chancel are
visible. Above the tower an 18th-century bell-tower with 13 bells. Pipe organ 1892
Foster and Andrews. Twelfth-century sanctuary cross. Two stained glass windows
by Christopher Whall. Major refurbishment in the 1960s. Sunday Service: 11.15am
Open Monday to Friday 12.00 noon-2.00pm. Lunches served
CHURCH OF SCOTLAND [♿] [wc] ⊘ ⚲ ☕ **B**

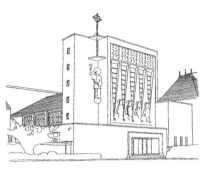

FALKIRK OLD AND ST MODAN'S PARISH CHURCH

ST FRANCIS XAVIER, FALKIRK

490 ST FRANCIS XAVIER, FALKIRK

NS 886 812

Hope Street

Church website: www.stfx.info

Opened in 1961 replacing 1843 building destroyed by fire 1955. Architect A R
Conlin. Twelve-foot statue of St Francis by Maxwell Allan and of the Four
Evangelists by Miss E Dempster. Stations of the Cross on laminated glass panels by
Felix McCullough, mosaics by Casa Group, painting of St John the Baptist by
Peter Brady. Services: Sunday 10.00am, 12.00 noon, 1.15pm Polish Mass, 7.00pm;
Monday-Friday 10.00am; Saturday 10.00am; and Vigil Mass 7.00pm

Open 8.00am-6.00pm

ROMAN CATHOLIC 🦽 wc ♿ ☕ (after 10.00 am Mass)

491 ST MARY'S CHURCH, GRANGEMOUTH

NS 932 818

Ronaldshay Crescent, Grangemouth

The present church was built in 1938 to replace
a 'tin kirk' of 1901; the architect was Maxton
Craig of Edinburgh. A small hall was added in
1978. The west window, 1962, depicts the
industries of Grangemouth. Altar cross, candlesticks and vases by Edward Spencer, the
Artificers' Guild, his last work. Services:
Sunday: 8.45am Said Eucharist, 9.45am Sung
Eucharist; Tuesday: 10.00am Said Eucharist

Open by arrangement, telephone the

Rector 01324 482438

SCOTTISH EPISCOPAL 🦽 wc

ST MARY'S CHURCH, GRANGEMOUTH

GRANGEMOUTH: ZETLAND CHURCH, GRANGEMOUTH   LARBERT OLD CHURCH

492 GRANGEMOUTH: ZETLAND CHURCH, GRANGEMOUTH

NS 931 818

Ronaldshay Crescent, Grangemouth

Building by Wilson & Tait completed 1911. Cruciform in plan with a south aisle and north and south transepts. Four arches support a timber barrel roof and there is a small gallery at the end of the nave. Second World War memorial stained glass window by Douglas Hamilton, Glasgow, with four lights depicting Peace, Victory, Willingness to Lay Down Life and The Glory of the King of Heaven. Willis organ of 1890 installed 1983. Memorial Chapel furnished in the south transept 1990 used for private prayer and small services. Award-winning grounds. Sunday Service: 11.15am

Open Wednesday mornings 9.30-11.30am, March to October

CHURCH OF SCOTLAND ♿ wc **B**

493 LARBERT OLD CHURCH

NS 856 822

Denny Road, Larbert

Near site of earlier chapel – 12th-century dependency of Eccles Kirkton of St Ninian's and Cambuskenneth Abbey. The present church was built in 1820, architect David Hamilton, replacing a pre-Reformation church which was located within the adjacent churchyard. The chancel was added in 1911. The fine oak panelling dates from 1887. There are good memorial windows including Gordon Webster and Stephen Adam. The apsidal triptych of the Transfiguration is believed to be the only example of Frank Howard's work (1805-66) in Scotland and was executed by Edmundson of Manchester. There are some interesting memorial plaques. The graveyard includes the burial place of James Bruce, Abyssinian

OUR LADY OF LOURDES AND ST BERNADETTE, LARBERT

explorer, and Master Robert Bruce, the post-Reformation divine, as well as the early partners of the Carron Company. The bell-tower has a carillon of chimes dating from 1985. Sunday Services: 11.00am and 6.30pm

Open by arrangement, telephone 01324 562955

CHURCH OF SCOTLAND

494 OUR LADY OF LOURDES AND ST BERNADETTE, LARBERT

NS 865 829

323 Main Street, Larbert

The present building designed by J N Scott & A Lorne 1934 was intended to be a hall but was used for worship until a permanent church could be built. When this plan was abandoned in the 1950s the building was adapted to become exclusively the place of worship. Entrance porch by Sam Sweeney added 1995. Wall hangings by Maison Bouvrier 2002. Marian Grotto in grounds 1983 to mark the Golden Jubilee, recently embellished and decorated by local talent from within the church community. Sunday Services: 11.30am and 6.30pm Mass

Open 9.00am-dusk, or apply to Presbytery adjacent to Church

ROMAN CATHOLIC

495 STENHOUSE & CARRON PARISH CHURCH, STENHOUSEMUIR

NS 876 831

Church Street, Stenhousemuir

Built 1897-1900 with linked Manse, 1906, architect J J Burnet, the assembly is dominated by the massive square tower and timbered porch. The silvered-bronze font of 1900 is by Albert Hodge and the pipe organ of 1902 by J J Binns. The communion table, 1921, was designed by J J Burnet and carved by Wylie & Lochead with figures by William Vickers. Stained glass by Douglas Strachan from 1914, 1922, 1937 and 1950. Sunday Service: 11.15am

Open by arrangement with Mr Watters 01324 562688

CHURCH OF SCOTLAND A

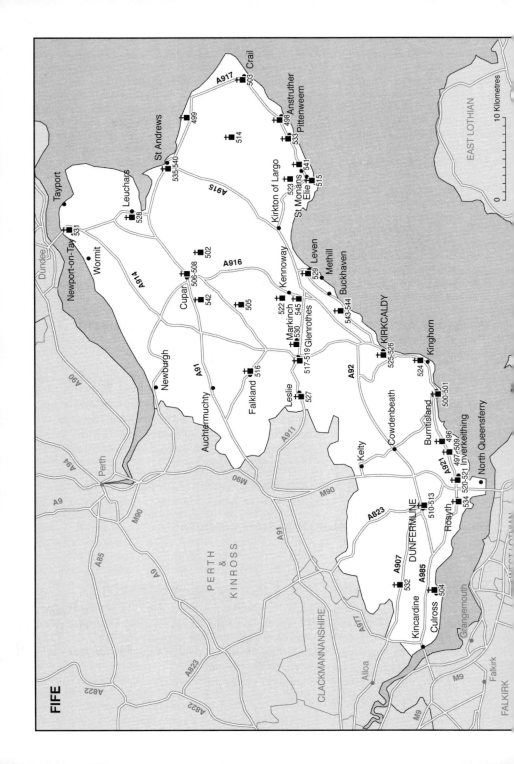

FIFE

Local Representative: The Rev Malcolm Trew, 155 Park Road West, Rosyth (*telephone* 01383 420949)

496 ST COLUMBA'S CHURCH, ABERDOUR

NT 186 851

Inverkeithing Road, Aberdour

Built in 1843 for the Earl of Moray as a private chapel for his employees in Aberdour. It was transferred to the Scottish Episcopal Church in 1918. A cruciform plan, tall and light with lancet windows. The west window blocked off by the addition of a balcony, which has recently been enclosed. A921 from Dalgety Bay, in the village on the right. Linked with St Peter's, Inverkeithing and St Serf's, Burntisland. Sunday Service: 11.00am

Open by arrangement, telephone Mrs Clifford 01383 860521, or Mrs Wallington 01383 860795

SCOTTISH EPISCOPAL wc ⑦ **C**

ST COLUMBA'S CHURCH, ABERDOUR

497 ST FILLAN'S, ABERDOUR

NT 193 855

Hawkcraig Road, Aberdour

Church website: www.stfillans.presbytery.org.uk

One of the finest examples of Norman architecture in Scotland, this 'miniature Cathedral' sits in its own graveyard overlooking Aberdour harbour. The early church, standing in 1123, consisted of the nave and chancel, lit by deep splayed windows which still exist. The church was enlarged in the 15th century by the addition of a side aisle, and in the 17th by the small transeptual aisle, now used by the choir. The church fell into disrepair in the 18th century and was restored in 1925. 'Even to enter St Fillan's is to worship.'

Sunday Service: 10.30am

Open daily during daylight hours.

Flower Festival 1st week of August

CHURCH OF SCOTLAND ⑦

ST FILLAN'S, ABERDOUR

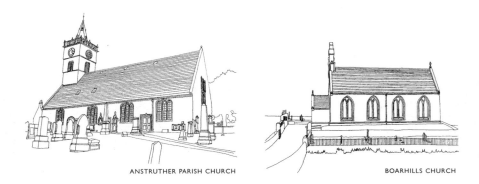

ANSTRUTHER PARISH CHURCH

BOARHILLS CHURCH

498 ANSTRUTHER PARISH CHURCH

NO 567 037

Burial Brae (off Crail Road), Anstruther

James Melville (brother of Andrew, the leading Covenanter) inspired the purchase of land in 1590 for a new church, but he was exiled by James VI and the church was not built until 1634. Described in 1837 as 'one of the most elegant country churches anywhere to be seen'. Tahitian Princess buried outside the south wall. Many interesting features. Anstruther is the birthplace of Thomas Chalmers. A917 Crail, 400 yards east of St Andrews cross road. Bus services: Fife Scottish 95 and 57, Minibus M1 and M611, Stagecoach X23. Sunday Service: 11.00am; healing service 2nd Sunday of month 2.00pm

Open April to September, Tuesday 2.00-3.00pm, Thursday 11.00am-12.00 noon.
All year coffee morning, Tuesday 10.00am-12.00 noon in Hew Scott Hall
(converted 13th-century West Anstruther Church)
CHURCH OF SCOTLAND ♿ **B**

499 BOARHILLS CHURCH

NO 562 137

On A917 west of Boarhills

Church built 1866/7, although there has been a burial ground here considerably longer. The architect was George Rae. Original oil lamps, now converted to electricity. Sunday Service: 10.00am in February, April, June, August, October and December

Open by arrangement with the Session Clerk, telephone 01334 880315
CHURCH OF SCOTLAND ♿ (back door) **C**

BURNTISLAND PARISH CHURCH

ST SERF'S CHURCH, BURNTISLAND

500 BURNTISLAND PARISH CHURCH

NT 234 857

East Leven Street, Burntisland

Built in 1592 to an unusual square plan. One of the first post-Reformation churches built in Scotland, still in use. The General Assembly of the Church of Scotland met in Burntisland in May 1601 in the presence of James VI when a new translation of the Bible was approved. Organ originally by Cousans 1909. Information available on the churchyard. Extensive refurbishment completed in 1999. Sunday Service: 11.00am

Open June to August, 10.00am–12.00 noon and 2.00–4.00pm;
other times key from Curator, telephone 01592 873275

CHURCH OF SCOTLAND ♿ wc ⟳ ⌇ 📖 ⚲ **A**

501 ST SERF'S CHURCH, BURNTISLAND

NT 230 864

Ferguson Place junction with Cromwell Road, Burntisland

Built in 1905 to a design by Truro Cathedral architect J L Pearson, the stone is from the local Grange quarry. The chancel is divided from the nave by a fine Gothic arch. The east end of the chancel is semi-octagonal behind a tri-form arch springing from slender columns, surmounted by a Gothic arch. Linked with St Peter's, Inverkeithing and St Columba's, Aberdour.

Services: Sunday 9.30am; Tuesday 11.00am

Open by arrangement, telephone Mrs M McQuarrie 01592 873117

SCOTTISH EPISCOPAL ♿ wc ⟳ 📖 ☕ **B**

502 CERES CHURCH

NO 399 117

Kirk Brae, Ceres

Built 1806 to a design by Alexander Leslie, with
a battlemented tower, its spire added in 1852, the
building has the original box pews and long
communion tables running the full length of the
church. The 17th-century stone-slated Lindsay
vault in the kirkyard was possibly attached to the
medieval church. Linked with Springfield
Church. Sunday Service: 11.00am

Open on September Doors Open Day, and by
arrangement, telephone the Minister 01334 828233

CHURCH OF SCOTLAND [wc] (2) [] **B**

CERES CHURCH

503 CRAIL PARISH CHURCH

NO 613 080

Marketgate, Crail

Consecrated 1243 with alterations 1526, 1796. Restored 1963. Judith Campbell
windows (1970 and 1975). Pictish cross slab. Seventeenth-century carving. Pipe
organ by Harrison & Harrison 1892, rebuilt and
installed here 1936. Graveyard (with dead
house). Hourly bus service, Leven–St Andrews
(some to Dundee). Sunday Service: 11.15am; also
17 June to 2 September at 9.30am (informal)

Open 2.00-4.00pm, mid June to end August
(Tuesday, Wednesday and Thursday)

CHURCH OF SCOTLAND [&] [wc] (2) [] [] [] **A**

CRAIL PARISH CHURCH

504 CULROSS ABBEY

NS 989 863

Kirk Street, Culross

Church website: www.culrossandtorryburnchurch.org.uk

Built on the site of a Celtic Christian Culdee church. Abbey founded in 1217 by
Malcolm, 7th Earl of Fife; dedicated to St Mary and St Serf. Much of the original
building remains, although a great deal of it is in ruins. The monks' choir forms
the present parish church, in continuous use since 1633. Modernised in 1824 and
restored in 1905 by Sir R Rowand Anderson. Many features of interest. Situated in
16th-century small town of Culross. Seven and a half miles west of Dunfermline.
Sunday Service: 11.30am

Open daily, summer 10.00am-dusk, winter 10.00am-4.00pm

CHURCH OF SCOTLAND [wc] [] **A**

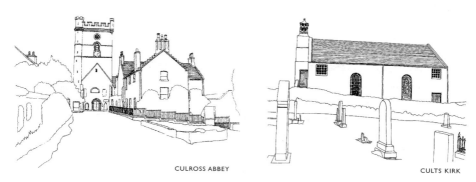

CULROSS ABBEY

CULTS KIRK

505 CULTS KIRK

NO 347 099

Kirkton of Cults, south side of A914, half a mile from Pitlessie,
four miles south west of Cupar

A place of worship since the 12th century, the present kirk built 1793. Bell
inscribed 'John Meikle, Edinburg, fecit for the Kirk of Cults, 1699'. Lepers
window, Laird's Pew, memorials, one by Chantry of Sir David Wilkie RA, the most
famous son of the Manse, one by Samuel Joseph of his father and mother. Wilkie
Hall, Pitlessie village, collection of etchings and engravings by Wilkie, viewing by
appointment 01337 830491. Sunday Service: 11.30am until July 2002, then 10.00am
Open 8.00am-8.00pm

CHURCH OF SCOTLAND   ♿ 🚹 📖 **B**

506 CUPAR OLD AND ST MICHAEL OF TARVIT PARISH CHURCH

NO 380 146

Kirkgate, Cupar

The tower dates from 1415; its spire and belfry
(containing two bells 1485 and 1689) were added in
1620 and the four-face clock in 1910. The church
itself was rebuilt in 1785. Inside are war memorials on
the east and south walls and the guidon of the Fife
and Forfar Yeomanry. A recess in the west wall
contains the 15th-century recumbent figure of a
knight ('Muckle Fernie'). Adjacent graveyard contains
hand of David Hackston, a Covenanter from
Rathillet. Sunday Service: September to May 11.00am,
June to August 10.00am, September to May;
Evening Service 6.30pm

Open by appointment, telephone 01334 655271

CHURCH OF SCOTLAND   🚾 ♿ 🚹 **A**

CUPAR OLD AND ST MICHAEL
OF TARVIT PARISH CHURCH

507   ST JAMES THE GREAT CHURCH, CUPAR

NO 376 146

St Catherine Street, Cupar

Built in 1866 to a design by Sir R Rowand Anderson.
Fine choir screen, reredos and panelling, Lorimer 1920.
Organ originally by D & T Hamilton of Edinburgh
1875. Town centre, A91 Stirling to St Andrews. By rail
from Edinburgh and Dundee. By coach from Kirkcaldy,
Dundee, St Andrews and Stirling. Services: Sunday
8.00am and 11.00am; Wednesday 10.00am

Open weekdays, 10.00am-3.00pm

SCOTTISH EPISCOPAL   wc **B**

ST JAMES THE GREAT CHURCH, CUPAR

508   ST JOHN'S PARISH CHURCH, CUPAR

NO 373 147

Bonnygate, Cupar

Church website: www.churchofscotland/congregations/stjohn's
The 150-ft spire with belfry dominates the view of
Cupar from the many approaches. Built 1878,
Campbell Douglas & Sellars, Glasgow, when first
Cupar Free Church became too small. Galleried
interior. Set on a raised area in stepped gardens.
Sunday Service: 11.00am; Midweek half-hour
service every Wednesday 9.30am

Open all year, Wednesday 9.30am-11.30am.
Other times by arrangement 01334 655851

CHURCH OF SCOTLAND   wc ⌾ ▯ ◡ ◡ **B**

ST JOHN'S PARISH CHURCH, CUPAR

509   DALGETY PARISH CHURCH,
DALGETY BAY

NT 155 836

Regents Way, Dalgety Bay

Church website: www.dalgety-church.org.uk
A hall church designed by Marcus Johnston, built
in 1981 and extended in 1991. Worship area and
suite of halls which are used by congregation and
local community groups. War memorial in grounds.
Sunday Services: 9.30am and 11.00am all year; also
2nd Sunday of the month, September to June

Open by arrangement, telephone church office
01383 824092 or Manse 01383 822316

CHURCH OF SCOTLAND

DALGETY PARISH CHURCH,
DALGETY BAY

510 DUNFERMLINE ABBEY

NT 090 873

St Margaret Street, Dunfermline
Church website: www.dunfermlineabbey.com
Founded in 1072. Consists today of the nave of
medieval monastic church (1150) and the modern
parish church (1821) erected over foundations of
original Choir. Burial place of King Robert the
Bruce and numerous other Scottish royals
including Malcolm III (Canmore) and his Queen,
St Margaret of Scotland. Exquisitely carved
pulpit by William Paterson, Edinburgh 1890. Fine

DUNFERMLINE ABBEY

pipe organ of 1882, rebuilt Walker in 1966. Sunday Services: 9.30am and 11.00am
Open April to October, Monday to Saturday 10.00am-4.30pm, and Sunday 2.00-4.30pm.
Abbey shop also open as above. Groups by arrangement, telephone Mr F Tait 01383 872242
CHURCH OF SCOTLAND wc ⌖ ⌖ ⌖ ⌖ **A**

511 ST LEONARD'S, DUNFERMLINE

NT 096 869

Brucefield Avenue
Church website: www.stleonardsparishchurch.org.uk
The most striking feature of the church, P McGregor Chalmers
1904, is a round Celtic tower. Inside, the semi-circular apse has
a dramatic painting of the Risen Christ surrounded by Gospel
characters, designed by the architect and painted by Mr A
Samuel 1927. Heraldic gallery dedicated to the Scottish Wars of
Independence led by Wallace and Bruce. Sunday Service: June
to August 10.00am; September to May 9.30am and 11.00am
Open Tuesday and Thursday mornings (church office)
CHURCH OF SCOTLAND ♿ wc ⌖ **B**

ST LEONARD'S,
DUNFERMLINE

512 ST MARGARET'S MEMORIAL CHURCH, DUNFERMLINE

NY 096 876

Holyrood Place, Dunfermline
A commanding building forming part of the ancient gateway to the
town at the East Port. Built in 1896 to a design by Sir R Rowand
Anderson in 12th-century Transitional style. Stained glass circular
window by John Blyth, stone reredos by Hew Lorimer, wood
carving by Steven Foster and historical prints by Jurek Pütter.
Three new stained glass windows by Douglas Hogg. Services:
Saturday 6.30pm; Sunday 9.00am and 11.00am; Weekdays 10.00am
Open by arrangement, telephone Father Barr 01383 625611
ROMAN CATHOLIC ♿ wc ⌖ ⌖ **B**

ST MARGARET'S MEMORIAL
CHURCH, DUNFERMLINE

513 VIEWFIELD BAPTIST CHURCH, DUNFERMLINE

NT 095 875

East Port, Dunfermline

Church website: www.viewfield.org.uk

Gothic design by Peter L Henderson, 1882-84.
Front façade skewed giving a vestibule narrower at
one side than the other and making necessary the
cylindrical addition for the east gallery staircase.
Wood vaulted ceiling upheld by laminated wood
arches, supported internally by six cast-iron pillars.
Pipe organ. Sunday Services: 11.00am and 6.30pm
Church office open 9.30am-2.30pm every weekday,
telephone 01383 620465

VIEWFIELD BAPTIST
CHURCH, DUNFERMLINE

BAPTIST [wc] (?) 🍵 (open 10.00am-2.00pm Monday to Friday, in adjacent Viewfield Centre)

514 DUNINO CHURCH

NO 541 109

In woods up farm road off B9131, between St Andrews and Anstruther

There has been a church at Dunino since 1240.
The present building is 1827 by James Gillespie
Graham with the chancel and porch 1928 by
J Jeffrey Waddell & Young. Font by Sir Robert
Lorimer, stained glass by J Jennings of London
and W Wilson. Early Celtic carved stone in the
churchyard. Sunday Service: 10.00am in January,
March, May, July, September and November
Open daily

CHURCH OF SCOTLAND [&] [wc] [] **B**

DUNINO CHURCH

515 ELIE PARISH CHURCH

NO 491 001

High Street

Church website: www.eliekirk.co.uk

Originally erected in 1639, the tower was added in 1726
and the body of the kirk rebuilt 1831. The building is a
typical T-plan post-Reformation kirk with the pulpit on
the south wall. Opposite the pulpit is a laird's loft with
the family vault beneath. 'Russell' stained glass windows
either side of the pulpit and four further windows
designed by Edward Burne-Jones. Sunday Service: 10.00am
Open by arrangement with Session Clerk 01333 330336

CHURCH OF SCOTLAND [&] (?) [] (on sale at Post Office) **B**

ELIE PARISH CHURCH

516 FALKLAND PARISH CHURCH

NO 252 074

The Square, Falkland

On the site of an earlier building, the present church was
completed in 1850 to a design by David Bryce and gifted to the
people of Falkland by Onesiphorus Tyndall Bruce, of the family
of Bruce of Earlshall. The style is Victorian Gothic. Centre pews
convert to long communion tables. Stained glass 1897. Organ by
Hill, Norman & Beard 1923. A912 Perth–Kirkcaldy.
Bus service: 36 from Perth. Sunday Service: 10.00am
Open June to August, Monday to Friday 2.00-4.00pm. Teas/coffee,
bookstall. Contact Robert M Herd, Session Clerk, telephone 01337 857732
CHURCH OF SCOTLAND ♿ wc ② ⌷ ⌂ ⌷ **B**

FALKLAND
PARISH CHURCH

517 ST COLUMBA'S PARISH CHURCH, GLENROTHES

NO 270 009

Rothes Road, Glenrothes

Built in 1960 and designed in conjunction with the
theologians at St Mary's College of St Andrews University
with the emphasis on how the Scottish Reformation could
be best expressed in a church building. The sanctuary
features seating around three sides, with the Lord's table in
the centre. Mural by Alberto Morocco measuring 59 feet by
9 feet of scenes from the last days of Christ. Iron bell-
tower is a landmark in the centre of the town. Sunday
Service: 11.00am September to June, July to August 10.00am
Open by arrangement, telephone Carol Gibson 01592 754320
CHURCH OF SCOTLAND ♿ wc

ST COLUMBA'S PARISH
CHURCH, GLENROTHES

518 ST LUKE THE EVANGELIST, GLENROTHES

NO 273 008

Ninian Quadrant, Glenrothes

By J Cassells 1960, the church is in a Perpendicular style, set alongside a playpark
in the earliest and most central part of the new town of Glenrothes. Furnished
with the warmth of pine, its interior is
light and airy with an unusual layout,
and houses several items of interest.
Sunday Services: 9.30 and 11.00am
Open Monday and Thursday 10.00am-1.00pm,
Tuesday 9.00-10.30am, Sunday 9.15am-1.00pm
SCOTTISH EPISCOPAL ♿ wc ⌷ **A**

ST LUKE THE EVANGELIST, GLENROTHES

519   ST PAUL'S CHURCH, GLENROTHES

NO 281 005

Warout Road, Glenrothes

Church website: www.stpaulsandstmarys.co.uk

Completed 1957 from design by Isi Metzstein
and Andy McMillan of Gillespie, Kidd & Coia.
Described by *The Scotsman* as 'the most
significant piece of architecture north of the
English Channel' and in *The Twentieth Century*
Church as 'a homage to architecture's liberating

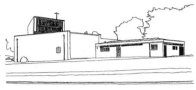

ST PAUL'S CHURCH, GLENROTHES

function'. Interior contains the 'Catalonian' altar crucifix 1957 and 'The Madonna'
or 'Lady Piece' by Benno Schotz 1960. Carved Stations of the Cross and figure of
St Paul by Harry Bain 1983. Follow Woodside Road from town centre, corner of
Woodside Road/Warout Road. Sunday Service: 11.30am

Open 1st Saturday of the month, 11.00am-6.00pm

ROMAN CATHOLIC ♿ ⚲ **B**

520   ST PETER'S PARISH CHURCH, INVERKEITHING

NT 131 830

Church Street, Inverkeithing

A Norman foundation, church dedicated to St Peter 1244.
The present building is a nave and aisles church by
Gillespie Graham 1827 attached to a 14th-century tower.
Refurbished 1900, P MacGregor Chalmers. Fourteenth-
century stone font, one of the finest in Scotland, thought
to have been gifted by Robert III for the baptism of his
son the Duke of Rothesay. Sunday Service: 11.15am

Open July to August, Friday 2.00-4.00pm,

Saturday 10.00am-12.00 noon, 2.00-4.00pm

CHURCH OF SCOTLAND ⚲ ⚲ ⚲ ⚲

ST PETER'S PARISH CHURCH,
INVERKEITHING

521   ST PETER'S EPISCOPAL CHURCH, INVERKEITHING

NT 128 827

Hope Street, Inverkeithing

The church was built to serve the Scottish Episcopal community in Jamestown, at
one time outside the Royal Burgh of Inverkeithing. The nave was built in 1903 to
a design by Henry F Kerr and the chancel added in 1910. The interior was altered
in 1980 to form a worship area and hall. Set in well-kept gardens on the southern
approach to the town from the Forth Road Bridge. Linked with St Columba's,
Aberdour and St Serf's, Burntisland. Sunday Service: Holy Communion 11.00am

Open by arrangement, telephone D Macdonald 01383 414194

SCOTTISH EPISCOPAL wc

ST PETER'S EPISCOPAL CHURCH, INVERKEITHING   ST KENNETH'S PARISH CHURCH, KENNOWAY

522 ST KENNETH'S PARISH CHURCH, KENNOWAY

NO 350 023

Cupar Road, Kennoway

Church website: www.st-kenneths.freeserve.co.uk

The church in Kennoway dates back to St Kenneth, who preached in the 6th century. The present Romanesque church was built in 1850 and was designed by Thomas Hamilton. Six stained glass windows by Marjorie Kemp 1950. Monuments to past ministers. Sunday Services: 11.15am and, during term-time, 7.00pm

Open Monday to Friday 9.30am-12.30pm, plus Tuesday 1.00-3.00pm and
Thursday 5.00-7.00pm

CHURCH OF SCOTLAND ♿ wc ⓘ 🕯 📖 ☕ **B**

523 KILCONQUHAR PARISH CHURCH

NO 485 020

Main Street, Kilconquhar

Church website: www.kilconquharchurch.co.uk

The church, with its prominent tower, stands on an elevated position between the road and Kilconquhar Loch. The ruins of an earlier church, dating from 1243, are to the east of the present building. The church, designed by R & R Dickson, is an exact copy of Cockpen Church in Midlothian, though in larger dimensions, by the same architect. Sunday Service: 11.30am April to September

Open during daylight hours during summer months

CHURCH OF SCOTLAND ♿ wc **B**

524 KINGHORN PARISH CHURCH

NT 272 869

St James Place, Kinghorn

The Kirk by the Sea for over 750 years has an
unrivalled view across the beach to the Firth of
Forth and Edinburgh. It has a historic bell-tower
and a 'Sailors' Aisle' built in 1609 celebrating the
naval connection and a model of the first Unicorn.
Sunday Services: 9.30am and 11.00am (except first
Sunday of month; 10.30am in church hall)

Open every Tuesday 6.00pm-8.00pm

CHURCH OF SCOTLAND

KINGHORN PARISH CHURCH

525 ST BRYCE KIRK
(formerly Kirkcaldy Old Parish Church)

NT 280 917

Kirk Wynd, Kirkcaldy

Church website: www.stbrycekirk.org.uk

Consecrated in 1244 by the Bishop of St Andrews,
the ancient tower offers excellent views of Kirkcaldy.
The body of the church is by James Elliot 1808.
Good stained glass windows, some by Morris & Co
from Burne-Jones designs of 1886. United with St
Brycedale. Historic graveyard. Sunday Service: 11.00am

CHURCH OF SCOTLAND [♿] [wc] ⊘ ⌾ ⌾ **B**

ST BRYCE KIRK

526 ST BRYCE KIRK (formerly St Brycedale)

NT 279 917

St Brycedale Avenue, junction with Kirk Wynd

Church website: www.stbrycekirk.org.uk

Built as a Free Church 1877-81 by James Matthews of
Aberdeen. A 197-ft tower and spire and associated pyramid-
roofed twin towers lift the church out of the ordinary. In
1988 a transformed church at first-floor level was created
above a multi-purpose ground-floor. Organ by Brindley &
Foster 1893. Stained glass includes windows by Adam &
Small 1881, Douglas Strachan 1923, and Edward Burne-
Jones (executed by William Morris & Co) 1889. Now
united with Kirkcaldy Old. Sunday Service: 11.00am

Open Monday to Thursday 9.00am-10.00pm,
Friday 9.00am-3.00pm. Coffee Bar open Monday to
Thursday 10.00am-9.00pm, Friday 10.00am-3.00pm

CHURCH OF SCOTLAND [♿] [wc] ⊘ ⌾ ⌾ ⌴ **B**

ST BRYCE KIRK

527 ST MARY, MOTHER OF GOD, LESLIE

NO 251 018

High Street, Leslie

Church website: www.stpaulsandstmarys.co.uk

Gothic church with 120-ft spire by R Thornton Shiells 1879. Originally Leslie Free Church, it was opened as Roman Catholic in 1959. Closed in 2004 following a devastating fire, the congregation is currently raising funds for its restoration. Services at St Paul's Church, Glenrothes (see entry 519)

Closed for restoration

ROMAN CATHOLIC **B**

ST MARY, MOTHER OF GOD, LESLIE

528 ST ATHERNASE CHURCH, LEUCHARS

NO 455 214

Main Street, Leuchars

Church website: www.leucharstathernase.org.uk

Twelfth-century Norman church in a historic conservation setting. Distinctive octagonal belltower added in 18th century. Chancel and apse of outstanding architectural interest (original masons' marks and carving). Sunday Service: 11.00am

Open April to October daily 9.30am-5.00pm. Further enquiries to the Minister 01334 870038 or email: enilorac@fish.co.uk

CHURCH OF SCOTLAND [wc] (?) [] **A**

ST ATHERNASE CHURCH, LEUCHARS

529 LEVEN PARISH CHURCH (formerly Scoonie Kirk)

NO 383 017

Durie Street, Leven

Church website: www.levenparish.org.uk

Scoonie Kirk is the original Parish Church of Leven with its roots going back over 16 centuries. The church moved to its present site in 1775. In 1904 the building was rebuilt and enlarged to a design by the eminent church architect P MacGregor Chalmers which incorporated some of the earlier building. The unique pipe organ was built by the French organ builder August Gern 1884 and was restored 1992. The building also has some very striking stained glass windows. Sunday Service: 11.00am

Open Easter to September, Tuesdays 11.00am-1.00pm

CHURCH OF SCOTLAND [&] [wc] (?) [] [] [☕] **B**

LEVEN PARISH CHURCH

530   MARKINCH PARISH CHURCH

NO 297 019
Kirk Brae
Church website: www.markinchchurch.org.uk
Originally named St Drostan, after the 6th-century
missionary. Records show the site has been a place
of worship for almost 1500 years. The Norman
tower is 12th century; the body of the church was
built 1768-88 and designed by Thomas and George
Barclay. Session house by E Robert Hutchison 1839.
Organ chamber by Gillespie & Scott 1913. Clock of
1839. Sunday Service: 11.00am
Open June to August, Tuesday and Thursday
1.30pm-4.30pm, Saturday 10.00am-4.30pm
CHURCH OF SCOTLAND 🔲 wc ⊘ ⌷ ⌷ **A**

MARKINCH PARISH CHURCH

531   ST MARY'S EPISCOPAL, NEWPORT ON TAY

NO 420 278
10 High Street, Newport on Tay
Simple but picturesque church by architect T M Cappon, consecrated 1887. A plain
interior, beautified from 1920 onwards with panelling, pulpit and windows – all
donated as memorials. The rood screen of 1940 is by William Lamb. Organ
1903/4 by John Miller of Dundee, refurbished 2000 by Alex Edmonstone of
Perth. Sunday Service: Eucharist 10.45am
Open by arrangement, telephone Frank Smith 01382 542109
SCOTTISH EPISCOPAL ⊘ ⌷ ⌷ (after service) **B**

532   CHURCH OF THE HOLY NAME, OAKLEY

NT 025 885
Station Road, Oakley
Built by the Smith-Sligo family of Inzievar
House to a design by Charles Gray.
Consecrated October 1965. Outstanding
features include stained glass windows by
Gabriel Loire of Chartres. Carved Stations
of the Cross also by Gabriel Loire.
Services: Vigil Mass Saturday 6.30pm;
Sunday Mass 10.15am
Open by arrangement, telephone the Parish Priest
at Priest's House (adjacent via grass path to right of church)
ROMAN CATHOLIC

CHURCH OF THE
HOLY NAME, OAKLEY

533 PITTENWEEM PARISH CHURCH

NO 549 026

Kirkgate, Pittenweem

This ancient monument has developed over a long time.
The earliest work is around 1200. The Church was
extended in 1532 with an entrance from Cove Wynd and
the addition of the Tolbooth Tower with Bailies Loft. The
interior was refurbished in 1883 in Victorian style with
new entrance, galleries and stairs. The bell dates from
1662, while the clock in the tower is a fine example by
John Smith. Stained glass by William Wilson and John
Blyth of the 1950s and 1960s. Sunday Service: 11.30am
Open weekdays 8.00am-6.00pm; keys from the
Post Office (C & A Campbell's) in Market Place
CHURCH OF SCOTLAND ♿ wc ② 📖 **A**

PITTENWEEM PARISH CHURCH

534 ROSYTH METHODIST CHURCH

NT 114 842

Queensferry Road x Woodside Avenue, Rosyth

Founded in 1916, the present building was opened in
1970. A sanctuary of A-frame design with single-storey
hall and ancillary rooms adjoining by Alan Mercer,
architect. Striking 30ft-high mural, painted in Byzantine
style by Derek Seymour. Sunday Services: 9.30am
(Scottish Episcopal), 11.00am (Methodist)
Open by arrangement, telephone Mr Martin Rogers 01383 415458
METHODIST ♿ ②

ROSYTH
METHODIST CHURCH

535 ALL SAINTS', ST ANDREWS

NO 512 168

North Castle Street, St Andrews

Complex of church hall, rectory and club in Scottish vernacular
with an Italian flavour. Orange pantiled roofs and lots of
crowsteps. Slated chancel and bell-tower by John Douglas of
Chester 1906-9; the rest is by Paul Waterhouse 1919-24.
Woodwork of rood, chapel altarpiece and front canopy by
Nathaniel Hitch, stone Madonna and Child by Hew Lorimer
1945, marble font and wrought iron screen by Farmer & Brindley.
Three windows by Herbert Hendrie, Louis Davis and Douglas
Strachan. Sunday Services: 8.00am, 10.00am and 6.00pm
Open daily 10.00am-4.30pm
SCOTTISH EPISCOPAL ♿ wc 📖 ☕ (Ladyhead book and coffee shop) **B**

ALL SAINTS',
ST ANDREWS

536 PARISH CHURCH OF THE HOLY TRINITY, ST ANDREWS

NO 509 167

South Street, St Andrews

Tower and occasional pillars 1412, completely
rebuilt on original ground-plan in 1909, architect
McGregor Chalmers. South porch commemorates
John Knox preaching here. Much fine stained
glass by Strachan, Davis, Hendrie, Wilson and
others: clerestory windows have badges of all
Scottish regiments of First World War. Elaborate
memorial pulpit of Iona marble, alabaster and

PARISH CHURCH OF THE HOLY TRINITY,
ST ANDREWS

onyx. Decorated font of Caen stone. Memorial tomb of Archbishop Sharp. Oak
barrel roof. Hunter and Memorial Aisle has much fine wood-carving. Seventeenth-
century sacramental silver. Harrison and Harrison organ. Twenty-seven-bell Taylor
of Loughborough carillon. Sunday Services: 11.00am and 6.00pm

Open Tuesday and Saturday 10.00am-12.00 noon, as advertised, or by arrangement,
telephone 01334 474494

CHURCH OF SCOTLAND   🚹 🚾 ⊘ 🍴 ☕ **A**

537 HOPE PARK CHURCH, ST ANDREWS

NO 505 167

St Mary's Place, St Andrews

Church website: www.hopeparkchurch.co.uk

Completed in 1865, Peddie & Kinnear. Unusual
canopy pulpit. Stained glass. Pewter communion
ware, pulpit falls. A91 St Andrews, turn right at first
mini roundabout, 300 yards on left opposite bus
station. Rail service to Leuchars. Sunday Services:
9.30am and 11.00am

Open Holy Week and Christmas week, Monday to
Friday 10.00am-4.00pm, July to August,
Wednesday 10.00am-4.00pm

CHURCH OF SCOTLAND   🚹 🚾 ⊘ 🍴 📖 **A**

HOPE PARK CHURCH, ST ANDREWS

538 MARTYRS CHURCH, ST ANDREWS

NO 510 168

North Street (opposite University Chapel)

Originally United Free Church, 1926-8 by Gillespie
& Scott. Woodwork by Andrew Thom & Sons of St
Andrews. Stained glass by Douglas Strachan, Herbert
Hendrie, William Wilson, Sadie McLellan and
Marjorie Kemp. Roll of Honour designed and
painted by J D Macgregor. Sunday Service: 11.15am
Open by arrangement with Session Clerk 01334 474840
CHURCH OF SCOTLAND 🚹 (side door) 🚾 ⊘ 🛈 **B**

MARTYRS CHURCH, ST ANDREWS

539 ST ANDREW'S CHURCH, ST ANDREWS

NO 509 164

Queen's Terrace, St Andrews
Church website: www.st-andrews-church.net

Sir R Rowand Anderson Church 1869. Fine 19th-
century stained glass in the east and west walls. Two
bays of excellent modern stained glass work. An
open church policy and friendly welcome are a stable
mission of this vibrant and enthusiastic congregation.
Sunday Services: Holy Communion 8.00am and
10.00am, Choral Evensong 6.00pm (not Sundays
after Christmas, Easter, nor in July and August);
Monday to Friday Morning Prayer 8.30am,
Friday Holy Communion 11.00am
Open by arrangement, telephone 01334 473344
SCOTTISH EPISCOPAL 🚹 🚾 ⊘ 🛈 **B**

ST ANDREW'S CHURCH, ST ANDREWS

540 ST SALVATOR'S, ST ANDREWS

NO 510 168

North Street
Church website: www.st-andrews.ac.uk/chaplaincy

Consecrated in 1460, the Church of St Salvator was established as an integral part
of St Salvator's College, founded in 1450 by Bishop James Kennedy. Since 1904 it
has been the official University Chapel. Refurnished by Reginald Fairlie from 1931.
Notable features include Kennedy's tomb, a medieval Sacrament House, the 'John
Knox' pulpit, the Communion table and World War I memorial with mosaics by
Strachan. Hradetzky organ. Fine stained glass. Sunday Service (term-time only):
11.00am, Evensong: Wednesday 5.30pm (as advertised)
Open 9.00am-5.00pm Monday to Friday
ECUMENICAL 🚹 ⊘ **A**

541　ST MONANS PARISH CHURCH

NO 523 014

Braehead, St Monans

Occupying a striking position close to the sea, the church was built by Sir William Dishington 1370, with alterations by William Burn 1828 and Ian G Lindsay 1961. Fourteenth-century sedilia, piscina and aumbry. Medieval consecration crosses. Early 19th-century votive model ship of the line, heraldic bosses. Organ from Saughtonhall Congregational Church, Edinburgh, installed here 1995. External angled buttresses and 'buckle' corbels. Sunday Service: 10.00am

Open April to October during daylight hours

CHURCH OF SCOTLAND　ⓐ 🛈 📖 **A**

ST MONANS PARISH CHURCH

542　SPRINGFIELD CHURCH

NO 342 119

Manse Road, Springfield near Cupar, Fife

Built in 1861 to a plain, rectangular design. It contains notable late Victorian stained glass windows. The building was refurbished in 1970. Linked with Ceres Church. Sunday Service: 9.45am

Open by arrangement, telephone the Minister 01334 828233

CHURCH OF SCOTLAND　♿ 🚾 🛈

SPRINGFIELD CHURCH

543　WEMYSS PARISH CHURCH

NT 340 968

Main Road, East Wemyss

Red sandstone church 1937, Peter Sinclair. United with West Wemyss and Lower Wemyss in 1976, now known as Wemyss Parish Church. Light oak furnishings, pipe organ, memorial stained glass. Surrounded by gardens with lovely views. A915 Kirkcaldy–Leven. Sunday Service: 11.00am

Open by arrangement, telephone Mr Barker 01592 714874, or Miss Tod 01592 651495.
Open in conjunction with Wemyss Environmental Centre Open Day. Second Sunday each
summer month until September 2.00-4.30pm. Close to famous caves, some with Pictish and
Viking markings, and Macduff Castle

CHURCH OF SCOTLAND　♿ ⓐ 🛈

WEMYSS PARISH CHURCH

THE CHURCH AT WEST WEMYSS

544   THE CHURCH AT WEST WEMYSS

NT 328 949

Main Street, West Wemyss

Built in 1890, Alexander Tod, simple crow-stepped cruciform church of pink sandstone. Spiral tracery in the gable's big rose window. Repurchased from the Church of Scotland in 1972 by Captain Michael Wemyss, who agreed to maintain the building externally if the church continued to be used for worship. The congregation of Wemyss Parish Church is responsible for the interior and continuing worship. Beautiful mural by William McLaren on the inner wall of the transept which now accommodates halls, vestry and kitchen. New wall hangings 2001, sewn by members on the theme 'Jesus, Light of the World'. Old graveyard. Signed off A915 Kirkcaldy–Leven. Sunday Service: 9.30am

Open by arrangement, telephone A Tod, Corner Cottage, 40 South Row,
Coaltown of Wemyss 01592 651498

CHURCH OF SCOTLAND   A

545   ST KENNETH'S PARISH CHURCH, WINDYGATES

NO 346 006

Church website: www.stkenneths.freeserve.co.uk

Originally the United Free Church built by James McIntosh in 1926.

Sunday Service: 9.45am

Open by arrangement with St Kenneth's,
Kennoway, telephone 01333 351372

CHURCH OF SCOTLAND wc

ST KENNETH'S PARISH CHURCH, WINDYGATES

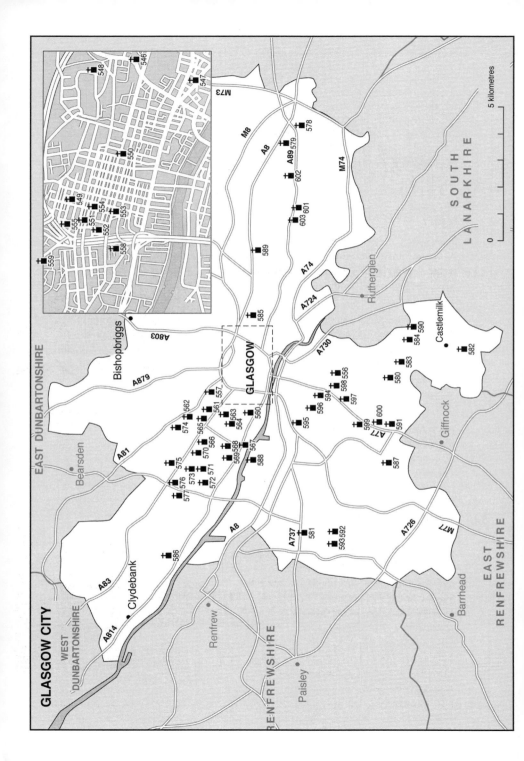

GLASGOW

Local Representatives: Mrs Jane Boyd, Manager, Renfield St Stephen's Church Centre, 260 Bath Street, Glasgow G2 4JP (*telephone:* 0141 332 4293)
Mrs Mary Canavan, Flat 10, 9 Victoria Circus, Glasgow G12 9LB
(*telephone:* 0141 334 5462)

546 CATHEDRAL CHURCH OF ST MUNGO

NS 603 656

Castle Street, Glasgow

Dedicated in 1136, the largest and most complete of Scotland's medieval cathedrals still in use. Medieval stone screen. Crypt with shrine of St Mungo. Outstanding collection of 20th-century glass by Francis Spear, Herbert Hendrie, Robert Armitage and Sadie McLellan, William Wilson, Gordon Webster and Harry Stammes. Modern tapestry. Organ by Willis 1879, last rebuilt by Harrison & Harrison 1996.
Sunday Services: 11.00am and 6.30pm
Open daily, April to September 9.30am-6.00pm, Sunday 1.00-5.00pm; October to March 9.30am-4.00pm, Sunday 1.00pm-4.00pm. Light lunches etc in adjacent St Mungo's Museum
CHURCH OF SCOTLAND ♿ ⊘ ⍭ (May to September) 📖 **A**

CATHEDRAL CHURCH
OF ST MUNGO

547 ST ALPHONSUS CHURCH

NS 600 646

217 London Road, Glasgow

Church website:
www.alphonsus.fsbusiness.co.uk/home.htm

A late work by Peter Paul Pugin 1905. Rock-faced sandstone screen façade. The tracery in the gable window formalised into a saltire cross. Inside, the nave arcades have polished granite piers. One hundred and fiftieth anniversary commemorative window 1996 by Lorraine Lamond. Church is in the middle of the 'Barras', 500 metres east of Glasgow Cross. Services: Saturday 4.30pm (Vigil); Sundays 10.00am, 11.00am, 12.00 noon, 5.00pm
Open Monday to Friday 12.00 noon-2.00pm, Saturday and Sunday 9.00am-6.00pm
ROMAN CATHOLIC 🚾 ⊘ **B**

ST ALPHONSUS CHURCH

548 ST MUNGO'S CHURCH

NS 600 659

Parson Street, Glasgow

Designed by the London architect George
Goldie 1869 in French Gothic style. High
altar by Gillespie, Kidd and Coia 1952.
The church is in the care of the Passionist
congregation. Five apsidal chapels include
St Paul of the Cross – founder of the
Passionists – St Margaret of Scotland, and
Our Lady of Sorrows which has a
Portuguese polychrome wood statue. Late
19th-century stained glass by Mayer of
Munich. Gothic-style timber confessionals.
Opposite Charles Rennie Mackintosh's

ST MUNGO'S CHURCH

Martyrs School, and five minutes walk from Glasgow Cathedral and the
St Mungo Museum. Sunday Services: 10.00am, 12.00 noon and 7.00pm
Open Monday to Friday 9.30am-1.00pm, 5.30-6.30pm; Saturday 9.30am-1.00pm,
4.30-8.00pm; Sunday 9.30am-1.00pm, 6.30-8.00pm
ROMAN CATHOLIC wc ⊘ **B**

549 ST ALOYSIUS CHURCH

NS 586 660

25 Rose Street, Glasgow
website: www.aloyius-glasgow.org

Fine late-Renaissance style church, designed in 1910 by
Belgian-born architect Charles Menart, with a 150-ft
campanile, domed crossing and ornate marble-lined
interior. The church is in the care of the Jesuit Order,
and Jesuit saints figure in the stained glass. The shrine
of St John Ogilvie SJ is in the east transept, with
mosaics depicting his martyrdom in Glasgow in 1615.
Near Glasgow School of Art and Sauchiehall Street.
Sunday Services: 9.00am, 10.30am,
12.00 noon (Sung), and 9.00pm
Open daily 7.30am to 6.30pm, and on Sunday
until 10.00pm. Full details of services on the website
ROMAN CATHOLIC ♿ wc ⊘ ⚲ **A**

ST ALOYSIUS CHURCH

550 ST GEORGE'S – TRON PARISH CHURCH

NS 590 655

165 Buchanan Street, Glasgow

Church website: www.thetron.com

Designed by William Stark and completed 1808. Originally
St George's Parish Church and the eighth burgh church to
be built in Glasgow in what was then the extreme west end
of the city. St George's united with Tron St Anne's in
1940. Baroque-style tower with five stages capped by a
ribbed dome and obelisk. Plain, galleried interior with flat
ceiling. The Christ-centred life and ministry of the Rev
Tom Allan (1955-64) was instrumental in the awakening of
the evangelical Christian church in Glasgow and beyond.
Sunday Services: 11.00am and 6.30pm; The 30 Minute
Service each Wednesday 1.10-1.40pm; Wednesday Prayer
Meeting 1st and 3rd Wednesday of each month; House
Groups 2nd and 4th Wednesday of each month

*The church is open for prayer and meditation Tuesday to Friday 12.00-2.00pm and Saturday
and Sunday 2.00-4.00pm. Other times by arrangement, telephone Mr William Bradford
0141 332 0187*

CHURCH OF SCOTLAND   **A**

ST GEORGE'S –
TRON PARISH CHURCH

551 RENFIELD ST STEPHEN'S PARISH CHURCH AND CENTRE

NS 582 659

260 Bath Street, Glasgow

Designed as an Independent Chapel by London architect
J T Emmett in 1852 in Decorated Gothic style. Built in
beautiful polished Kenmure sandstone with tall
clerestoried nave supported on clustered columns with
finely moulded capitals each with carved musical angels.
Windows by Norman Macdougall 1905, depicting the
four evangelists, and representations of Christian vertues,
flanking Christ in Glory, and John Clark. A Church
Centre with Side Chapel, offices, extensive halls and
restaurant was added in the 1960s. Patio with fountain
from Glasgow garden festival. Following the collapse of
the steeple during a storm on St Stephens Day 1998, the
church and basement have been sensitively restored and
modernised. Sunday Service: 11.00am

Open daily 9.00am-10.00pm.

Oasis Restaurant open 9.00am-4.00pm

CHURCH OF SCOTLAND

RENFIELD ST STEPHEN'S PARISH
CHURCH AND CENTRE

552 GLASGOW QUAKER MEETING HOUSE

NS 581 656

38 Elmbank Crescent

There has been a Quaker Meeting House in Glasgow since 1660. The present
Meeting House was opened in 1993 in this two-storey-and-basement classical
townhouse with balustraded parapet. Services: Sunday 11.00am with children's
class; Wednesdays 12.30pm with simple shared lunch

Open by arrangement with the Warden 0141 248 8493

QUAKER [♿] [wc] (?)

553 ST VINCENT STREET –
MILTON FREE CHURCH

NS 583 656

265 St Vincent Street, Glasgow

Church website: www.greekthomsonchurch.com

Alexander Thomson's masterpiece, distinctive
Victorian Presbyterian church, designed in the
classical style, and embellished by a unique
Thomsonian combination of Egyptian, Indian and
Assyrian influences 1859. Owned by Glasgow City
Council. Sunday Services: 11.00am and 6.30pm

Open by appointment. Also Doors Open Day,
telephone Mr Duncan 0141 842 1823

FREE CHURCH OF SCOTLAND [♿] [wc] **A**

ST VINCENT STREET –
MILTON FREE CHURCH

554 ADELAIDE PLACE BAPTIST CHURCH

NS 584 658

209 Bath Street, Glasgow

(corner of Bath Street and Pitt Street)

Church website: www.adelaides.co.uk

Built 1877, T L Watson. Stunning
redevelopment 1995 of decaying
building creating a multi-functional
centre including sanctuary, guest house
and nursery. Sunday Services: 11.00am;
Monthly Evening Services

Open daily 8.00am-8.00pm. Takes part in
Glasgow Doors Open Day/Churches Open
Day. Also wide variety of concerts and other
events; telephone 0141 248 4970 for details

BAPTIST [♿] [wc] (?) [Ⓘ] [☕] **B**

ADELAIDE PLACE BAPTIST CHURCH

555 GARNETHILL SYNAGOGUE

NS 502 661

129 Hill Street, Glasgow

Opened in 1879, the first purpose-built synagogue
in Scotland. It was designed by John McLeod of
Glasgow in Romanesque-cum-Byzantine style. A
round-arched portal with highly decorated orders
leads to the body of the synagogue. Ladies' gallery
is carried on octagonal piers with ornate Byzantine
capitals. Stained glass by J B Bennet & Sons.
Refurbished in 1996. From Sauchiehall Street walk
up Garnet Street to Hill Street. Services: Saturday
10.00am, Jewish Festivals 9.30am

Open by arrangement. Contact the caretaker, Mr David
Wright, preferably by letter, or telephone 0141 332 4151.
Scottish Jewish Archives open by arrangement,
telephone 0141 332 4911

JEWISH 🚹 (three steps) wc 🕐 ⚲ **B**

GARNETHILL SYNAGOGUE

556 HOLY CROSS

NS 586 624

113 Dixon Avenue / Belleisle Street

Romanesque style church designed by Pugin and Pugin and opened in 1911. Rich
interior with marble carvings. Stained glass windows above the sanctuary by
Hardman, representing St John the Evangelist and St Margaret of Scotland, and
above the gallery depicting the Exaltation of the Holy Cross, St Peter, St Andrew,
St Helen and St Sylvester. Mosaic of 1961 of Christ Triumphant above the altar.
Organ by Forster & Andrews,
built 1895 for Alva Parish Church
and installed 1983. Stations of
the Cross by Beyeart.
Services: Saturday Vigil 6.00pm;
Sunday Masses 9.30am, 11.00am,
12.15pm, 8.00pm
Open Monday to Saturday
7.30am-7.00pm

ROMAN CATHOLIC 🚹 wc 🕐 **B**

HOLY CROSS

ST COLUMBA'S CHURCH

557 ST COLUMBA'S CHURCH

NS 583 671

74 Hopehill Road, Glasgow

By Gillespie, Kidd & Coia, completed in 1941, the year of the Clydebank and
Govan blitz, and the cost met by the families of the area, each of whom paid 6d
per brick. Italian Romanesque style with an imposing west front. Sculpture of the
Paschal Lamb over central door. Painted panels of the Stations of the Cross by
Hugh Adam Crawford, from the Catholic Pavilion at the Glasgow Empire
Exhibition 1938. In the sanctuary a marble reredos with a carved crucifix by Benno
Schotz. North of St George's Cross, via Maryhill Road. Services: Saturday Vigil
Mass 6.00pm; Sunday Mass 11.00am and 5.00pm

Open at any time, by contacting the Priest in the house adjacent

ROMAN CATHOLIC [♿] [🔊] **A**

558 ST PATRICK'S

NS 580 655

137 William Street

Designed by Messrs Pugin of London in early
Decorated style, and opened for worship in 1898.
One of the most striking of the many features
within the church is the High Altar of white
marble, supported on six columns of Connemara
marble with floreated capitals. The throne is
surmounted by a magnificent cupola of Caen
stone. Services: Saturday 6.00pm; Sunday
10.00am and 12.00 noon; various daily services

Open daily, dawn to dusk

ROMAN CATHOLIC [♿] [wc] [🔊] [☕] **B**

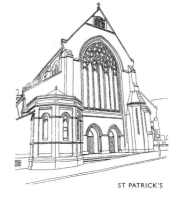

ST PATRICK'S

559 WOODLANDS METHODIST CHURCH

NS 576 665

229 Woodlands Road, Glasgow

Built for Swedenborgians by David Barclay 1909 in use
by Methodists since 1977. A wide stair leads to the
church. Organ 1876 from Cathedral Street Swedenborgian Church, originally built by Foster & Andrews
and augmented with pipes from Willis organ at St John's,
Sauchiehall Street. Windows by Guthrie & Wells and
George Benson, and war memorial window from St
John's. Nearest rail station Charing Cross; nearest
underground Kelvinside. Services: Sunday 11.00am
Open by arrangement, telephone the church office 0141 332 7779
METHODIST 🦽 wc ?

WOODLANDS METHODIST
CHURCH

560 SANDYFORD HENDERSON CHURCH

NS 570 659

13 Kelvinhaugh Street

Church website: www.sandyfordhenderso.co.uk

Early Gothic style 1855 by J T Emmett, completed
by John Honeyman. Fine stained glass aisle
windows in geometric/floral patterns by
Ballantine & Allan, Edinburgh 1857, and three
pictorial west windows by William Wailes,
Newcastle 1859-60. Three-manual 'Father' Willis

SANDYFORD HENDERSON CHURCH

organ 1866, moved into First World War memorial chancel, added in 1922.
Exterior stonework restored in 2000; interior refurbishment 2004. Sunday
Services: 11.00am and 6.30pm; Wednesday 7.30pm Prayer and Bible Study
Open Wednesday 10.00am-12.00 noon or by arrangement, telephone 0141 886 5871
CHURCH OF SCOTLAND **B**

561 ST MARY'S CATHEDRAL

NS 578 668

300 Great Western Road, Glasgow

Fine Gothic revival church by Sir George Gilbert Scott with outstanding contem-
porary murals by Gwyneth Leech and reredos by Phoebe Traquair reredos.
Three-manual pipe organ. Glasgow's only full peal of bells. Major restoration
2001. A82, three-quarters of a mile west of St George's Cross. Two minutes walk
Kelvinbridge Underground. Sunday Services: Eucharist 8.00am,
Sung Eucharist 10.00am, Eucharist 12.00 noon, Choral Evensong 6.30pm
Open daily, 9.30am-5.00pm
SCOTTISH EPISCOPAL 🦽 wc wc ? 📖 **A**

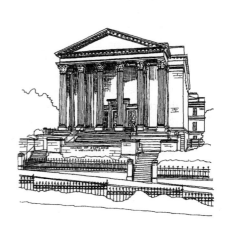

ST MARY'S CATHEDRAL

WELLINGTON CHURCH

562 ST CHARLES BORROMEO

NS 576 676

1 Kelvinside Gardens

Designed by MacMillan and Metstein of Gillespie Kidd & Coia for a tight, steep hillside site and built 1959-60. The most notable internal features are the excellent Benno Schotz sculptures: bronze altar frontal, crucifix and lampholder and twelve terracotta Stations of the Cross based on parishioners and friends of Schotz.

Services: Monday-Saturday 10.00am; Saturday Vigil 6.00pm;

Sunday 11.00am, 6.00pm

Open 9.00-10.30am Monday to Saturday and one hour before all other services

ROMAN CATHOLIC ⓑ ⓓ ⓔ (on Sunday mornings) **B**

563 WELLINGTON CHURCH

NS 570 667

University Avenue, Glasgow

Church website: www.wellingtonchurch.co.uk

T L Watson's Roman Classical church with mighty Corinthian columned portico 1884. Renaissance style interior with fine plaster ceilings. Pipe organ Forster & Andrews. Refectory situated in crypt. City buses 11 and 44. Underground to Hillhead or Kelvinbridge, ten minutes walk. Sunday Services: 11.00am and 7.00pm

Access to church via crypt, open Monday to Friday, during University term

CHURCH OF SCOTLAND ⓑ ⓦⓒ ⓓ ⓔ ⓕ ⓖ (and lunch during term time) **A**

564 UNIVERSITY MEMORIAL CHAPEL

NS 568 666

The Square, Glasgow University, Glasgow

1923-27 by Sir J J Burnet in Scots Gothic and in harmony
with the University buildings of Sir George Gilbert Scott.
The structure is reinforced concrete, faced with stone. Tall
interior with sculpture by Archibald Dawson. Ten of the
stained glass windows are by Douglas Strachan in a cycle
depicting the whole of human life as a spiritual enterprise.
Other windows by Gordon Webster and Lawrence Lee.
The chapel incorporates the Lion and Unicorn Stair
salvaged from the Old College. Sunday Service: 11.00am;
Monday to Friday 8.45am during term time

*Open 9.00am-5.00pm Monday to Friday, 9.00am-12.00 noon
Saturday. Chapel Choir Service December.*

Tours available from visitors' centre

ECUMENICAL ♿ ⊘ 🕯 📖 ☕ (all in visitors' centre) **A**

UNIVERSITY MEMORIAL CHAPEL

565 LANSDOWNE PARISH CHURCH

NS 576 669

416 Great Western Road, Glasgow

Built 1863 to a design by John Honeyman. Spire 218 feet, one of the slimmest in
Europe, a powerful landmark on Great Western Road. Box pews. Beautiful stained
glass by Alfred and Gordon Webster, and war memorial frieze by Evelyn Beale.
Pipe organ 1911, Norman & Beard, said to have the finest tuba rank in Glasgow
with some wonderful flutes. On corner with Park Road, opposite Kelvinbridge
underground. City buses 20, 41, 59, 66, from city centre.
Sunday Service: 11.00am (crèche available)

Open by arrangement, 0141 339 2794, or Mr J Stuart 0141 339 2678

CHURCH OF SCOTLAND 🚻 ⊘ 📖 ☕ **A**

566 KELVINSIDE HILLHEAD PARISH CHURCH

NS 567 673

Saltoun Street Observatory Road, Dowanhill, Glasgow

1876 by James Sellars, the design is said to have been much influenced by William
Leiper. A tall apsed church, the west front is full of carving. The interior was recast
in 1921 by P MacGregor Chalmers. Communion table of Rochette marble. Good
stained glass by Burne-Jones for William Morris & Co 1893 and Sadie McLellan
1958. Organ by H Willis & Son 1876, restored in 1930. City buses and
underground to Hillhead. Sunday Services: 11.00am; also October to May 6.30pm

Open Saturday 10.30am-12.30pm.

Other times by arrangement, telephone the Minister 0141 339 2865

CHURCH OF SCOTLAND ♿ 🚻 ⊘ 🕯 📖 ☕ **A**

KELVINSIDE HILLHEAD PARISH CHURCH   ST SIMON

567   ST SIMON

NS 562 659

33 Partick Bridge Street

Church website: www.stsimonspartick.org.uk

Founded by Daniel Gallagher, famous as 'the priest who taught David Livingstone Latin'. Built 1858 by Charles O'Neill as St Peter's, renovated in 1956 by Gillespie, Kidd & Coia. Marble altar has a panel by Mortimer depicting Christ comforted by His Mother. Used by the Polish Community since World War II. Services: Sunday 10.00am 11.00am (in Polish), 12.15pm and 6.30pm; Monday to Saturday 12.30pm

Open daily 9.00am-5.00pm

ROMAN CATHOLIC ♿ wc ☺ ☕

568   ST PETER'S

NS 561 668

46-50 Hyndland Street

Church website: http://peelcom.com/partickchurches/stpeters

Substantial church by Peter Paul Pugin 1903 in revived Gothic style. Bright interior lit by clerestory windows. Elaborate reredos. Pipe organ 1916, restored 1999. Good stained glass 1903 and 1937. Redecorated for Centenary celebrations 2003. Services: Vigil Saturday 6.00pm; Sunday 10.00am, 12.00 noon and 6.00pm; Weekdays 8.00am and 10.00am

Open daily Monday, Wednesday and Friday 7.00am-11.00am; Tuesday and Thursday 9.00am-11.00am; Saturday 9.00am-11.00am and 5.00pm-7.00pm; Sunday 9.00am-1.00pm and 5.00pm-7.00pm

ROMAN CATHOLIC wc ☺ **B**

ST PETER'S

PARTICK METHODIST CHURCH

569 PARTICK METHODIST CHURCH

NS 553 666

524 Dumbarton Road, G11 6SN

Church and halls by W F McGibbon, opened in 1881, celebrating its 125th anniversary in 2006. Good stained glass by Abbot & Co 1957. Fine organ by Forster & Andrews 1886. Organ recitals most Saturday afternoons (contact church to confirm times). Public transport by bus, underground and train.
Sunday Service: 11.00am; occasional evening services
Open by arrangement, telephone 0141 334 1181
METHODIST 🦽 wc

570 CATHEDRAL CHURCH OF ST LUKE

NS 563 675

27 Dundonald Road, Dowanhill, Glasgow

Formerly Belhaven United Presbyterian Church by James Sellars 1877, powerfully vertical Normandy Gothic. The congregation of St Luke's relocated here in 1960. The main front is inspired by Dunblane Cathedral. Marvellous display of stained glass, Stephen Adam 1877, richly stencilled roof timbers, and original light fittings and furniture. Modern iconostasis featuring icons, some of which were painted on Mount Athos in the traditional Byzantine style. Sunday Service: 10.30am-1.00pm
Open by arrangement, telephone Mr N Pitticas 0141 339 7368
GREEK ORTHODOX **B**

CATHEDRAL CHURCH
OF ST LUKE

571 ST BRIDE'S CHURCH, HYNDLAND

NS 559 676
69 Hyndland Road, Glasgow
Designed by G F Bodley, who built the chancel
1904, the nave 1907 and part of the north aisle. H O
Tarbolton completed the church (1913-16), including
rebuilding part of the nave and adding two north
aisles and the tower. The interior scheme is mainly
Bodley's. Carved woodwork by Scott Morton & Co.
Sculpture of Our Lady and Child by Eric Gill 1915.
Very fine 2-manual organ by Hill 1865, installed here
1972. Sunday Services: Sung Eucharist 10.30am;
Daily Eucharist, times vary
*Open by arrangement, telephone Mr Rae 0141 332 8430 or
Rev R F Jones 0141 334 1401. Occasional Choral Evensong,
usually with visiting choirs and concerts as advertised*
SCOTTISH EPISCOPAL wc **B**

ST BRIDE'S CHURCH, HYNDLAND

572 BROOMHILL CHURCH

NS 549 674
Randolph Road, Marlborough Avenue, Glasgow
Church website: www.broomhillchurch.co.uk
Red sandstone church 1902, and hall 1899,
designed by Stewart & Paterson. Stained glass
by Guthrie & Wells, Glasgow, Abbey Studio,
Edinburgh and Brian Hutchison. Pipe organ
refurbished by Harrison and Harrison 1997.
City buses: 16, 44. Sunday Services: 11.00am
and 6.30pm
*Open by arrangement, telephone
Mr J Boyle 0141 339 2552*
CHURCH OF SCOTLAND ♿ ✆ **B**

BROOMHILL CHURCH

573 HYNDLAND PARISH CHURCH

NS 559 675
79 Hyndland Road, Glasgow
website: www.hyndlandparishchurch.org
William Leiper 1887 in red Ballochmyle sandstone. Floodlit timber vaulted interior
roof, columns with richly carved capitals. Gleaming original terrazzo floor.
Original furnishings, beautiful marble pulpit and common table, Henry Willis pipe
organ, the whole building complemented by a collection of stained glass with

windows by Norman Macdougall 1889, Douglas Strachan 1921, Douglas Hamilton 1930, Gordon Webster 1961, William Wilson 1962, Sax Shaw 1968, Paul Lucky 1984, Rab MacInnes 1999. Additionally three windows by Oscar Paterson 1897 salvaged from St Bride's Church, Partick. Travel by Underground to Hillhead or Partick from the city centre, or by train from Queen Street Low Level to Hyndland. Bus from city centre, 44 to top Clarence Drive, or 11 to Church itself. Sunday Service: 11.00am 1st Sunday in October until Palm Sunday; 10.30am Easter Day until last Sunday in September; 7.00pm 1st Sunday in October to Easter Day

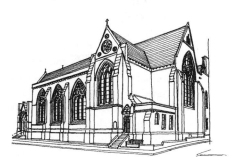

HYNDLAND PARISH CHURCH

Open by arrangement with church officer, telephone 0141 338 6637

CHURCH OF SCOTLAND [♿] [wc] (?) [ ] ⚲ **A**

574 ST GREGORY BARBARIGO

NS 565 686

130 Kelvindale Road

website: www.stgregorybarbarigo.co.uk

The church, dedicated to St Gregory Barbarigo, is strategically placed in the centre of the parish. The parish was founded in 1965 and the church, designed by Borthwick & Watson, was opened in 1971. The Kelvin walkway, which runs along the west side of the church, enhances the complex of buildings. One of the many attractive features of the church is the stained glass Stations of the Cross. Mass times: Saturday Vigil 6.00pm; Sunday 9.30am and 11.00am; Weekdays 9.10am Morning Prayer, 9.30 Morning Mass

Open every day 9.00am until after Mass, or until 6.30pm Tuesday. Library open after Mass every day and 10.00am-2.00pm Saturday

ROMAN CATHOLIC [♿] [wc] (?) ☕

ST GREGORY BARBARIGO

575 ST JOHN'S RENFIELD, KELVINDALE

NS 558 683

Beaconsfield Road, Kelvindale, Glasgow
website: www.stjohns-renfield.org.uk
Bold and striking church in a commanding
position, celebrating its 75th anniversary in 2006.
Topped by an openwork flèche, the stonework
has the understated detail characteristic of its
time, 1931 (architect James Taylor Thomson).
Light and lofty interior, complete with original

ST JOHN'S RENFIELD, KELVINDALE

fitments, and stained glass by Douglas Strachan and Gordon Webster.
Turn off Great Western Road to Kelvindale. Sunday Service: 11.00am
Open Wednesday, Thursday, Friday 9.30am-12.30pm
CHURCH OF SCOTLAND ♿ wc ② **B**

576 TEMPLE-ANNIESLAND CHURCH

NS 547 699

869 Crow Road, Glasgow
Red sandstone Gothic-style church built by
Badenoch & Bruce 1905. Adjoining hall was
original United Presbyterian church built in
1899 by Alexander Petrie. U-plan interior
with red pine panelled gallery and pews. War

TEMPLE-ANNIESLAND CHURCH

memorial, from Temple Parish Church (now demolished) with unique clock
designed and built 1921 by first minister, Rev J Carswell. Sunday Services: 11.00am
and 6.30pm, July to August 11.00am only; Thursday 11.00am
Open Thursdays 10.00am-12.00 noon (not July)
CHURCH OF SCOTLAND ♿ ② 🚻 ☕ **B**

577 JORDANHILL PARISH CHURCH

NS 544 682

28 Woodend Drive, Glasgow
Church 1905 and hall, west aisle and gallery
1923 by James Miller in Perpendicular style.
Battlemented and pinnacled tower. Mock
hammerbeam roof spans the broad interior.
Further extensions to hall 1971 and sanctuary

JORDANHILL PARISH CHURCH

refurbishment 1980 by Wylie Shanks. Organ by Lewis 1923. Woodend Drive is off
Crow Road (A739 Clyde Tunnel to Bearsden). Sunday Services: 10.30am and
6.30pm, 1st Sunday of the month; Wednesday 10.00am, September to June
Open Monday to Friday 8.30am-12.30pm and 1.30pm-5.00pm
CHURCH OF SCOTLAND ♿ wc ② 🚻 📖 **B**

578 BAILLIESTON ST ANDREW'S CHURCH

NS 681 639

Church Street, Baillieston, Glasgow
Present church completed 1974 following the
union of Baillieston Old and Rhinsdale Churches
in 1966. Sexagonal design with slim spire, by
James Houston & Sons of Kilbirnie. Allen organ
installed. Sunday Services: 11.00am and 6.30pm
*Open Monday, Wednesday and
Friday 9.30am-12.00 noon*
CHURCH OF SCOTLAND 👤 ✏️

BAILLIESTON ST ANDREW'S CHURCH

579 ST BRIDGET'S CHURCH, BAILLIESTON

NS 680 642

15 Swinton Road, Baillieston, Glasgow
Built 1893 by Pugin & Pugin in light
sandstone. Notable 'Creation' rose
window above sanctuary area and carved
'Christ Triumphant' below. Mosaic work
'Suffer the Children', 'Nativity', 'Glories
of Mary', 'Annunciation', and stained
glass windows 'Christ with Saints' and
'Sacred Heart' 1945-9 by the John
Hardman Studios. 'St Bridget' and 'St
Colmcille' windows by Shona McInnes

ST BRIDGET'S CHURCH, BAILLIESTON

1999. Located 200 yards west of Edinburgh Road/Coatbridge Road A8/A89.
Sunday Services: 9.00am and 10.30am, 12.00 noon and 6.00pm; Daily Service
9.30am; Saturday 5.30pm
Open for some hours each day; otherwise contact Church House adjacent
ROMAN CATHOLIC ✏️

580 BATTLEFIELD EAST PARISH CHURCH

NS 586 613

1220 Cathcart Road
The first church on this site was by John Honeyman 1865 in Early English style. It
became the hall in 1912 when the adjacent red sandstone church by John Galt was
opened. Spacious interior with galleries supported on cast-iron columns and a fine
timber wagon roof. Stained glass includes windows by Abbey Studios 1937, Sadie
McLellan 1972 and Susan Laidler 1980. Pipe organ by Ingram of Edinburgh.
Near Mount Florida railway station. Sunday Service: 11.00am; and various early-
afternoon events
Open Monday to Friday 9.45am-11.45am. Ring bell on door of glass corridor for the Beadle
CHURCH OF SCOTLAND 👤 wc ✏️ 📖 ☕ **B**

BATTLEFIELD EAST PARISH CHURCH   CARDONALD PARISH CHURCH

581 CARDONALD PARISH CHURCH

NS 526 639

2155 Paisley Road West, Glasgow

website: www.cardonaldparishchurch.org.uk

Opened 1889 as a mission church. This is the first church designed by
P MacGregor Chalmers. Early English Gothic of Ballochmyle red sandstone.
Chancel has alabaster and stone pulpit by Jackson Brown & Co and fine
workmanship in its oak communion table, reading desk and elders' benches. North
wall screen by Ross & Manson. Rich and varied collection of stained glass
windows including three-light chancel window by J & W Guthrie, series of six
windows by Sadie McLellan, Millennium window (2000) by Roland Mitton.
Sunday Services: 11.15am, Communion Sundays 11.15am and 6.30pm
Open Tuesday mornings, September to May, 10.00am-11.00am. Viewing by arrangement
11.00am-12.00 noon 0141 882 6264. Open daily Christmas week 10.00am-12.00 noon
CHURCH OF SCOTLAND ♿ wc ⦿ ☕ 🕯 ⚥ **B**

582 CARMUNNOCK PARISH CHURCH, 'THE KIRK IN THE BRAES'

NS 599 575

Kirk Road, Carmunnock

Rebuilt 1767 on pre-Reformation site and repaired in 1840. External stone
staircases to three galleries. Laird's gallery. Stained glass by Norman Macleod
MacDougall. Ancient graveyard has watch-house with original instructions for
grave watchers 1828, and burial vault of Stirling-Stuart family, Lairds of
Castlemilk. City bus 31. Sunday Service: 11.00am
Open April to September, Saturday 2.00-4.00pm. Other times by arrangement, telephone
0141 644 1578
CHURCH OF SCOTLAND ♿ ⦿ 🕯 📖 ⚥ ☕ (in village) **B**

CARMUNNOCK PARISH CHURCH, 'THE KIRK IN THE BRAES'

CATHCART OLD PARISH CHURCH

583 CATHCART OLD PARISH CHURCH

NS 587 606

119 Carmunnock Road

Church website: www.glasgowthecaringcity.org

Original design 1923 by Clifford & Lunan, but completed 1928 by Watson, Salmon & Gray. The size is enhanced by the low porch and range of vestries. South transept contains a display of the Church's history over 800 years; the north transept was converted in 1962 to the McKellar Memorial Chapel. Tapestry of The Last Supper by Charles Marshall, stained glass by James Crombie. Organ by John R Miller 1890, restored and converted to electro-mechanical action 1994.
Services: Sunday 11.00am

Open Monday to Friday 10.00am-2.00pm

CHURCH OF SCOTLAND ⬚ ⬚ ⬚ **B**

584 CROFTFOOT PARISH CHURCH

NS 603 602

318 Croftpark Avenue, Glasgow

website: www.croftfootparish.co.uk

Keppie & Henderson 1936. A neat Byzantine design in red brick with ashlar facings. Carved patterns, symbolising scriptural themes, decorate the main door portico, nave and chancel columns and chancel furnishings. The bell is the Second World War memorial. Ten minute walk from Croftfoot railway station. Sunday Services: 11.00am and 6.30pm

Open Monday to Friday, 9.00am-12.00 noon, and 1.30pm-4.00pm, except public holidays.

Tours, telephone Mr W Yule 0141 637 7613

CHURCH OF SCOTLAND ⬚ ⬚ ⬚ ⬚ ⬚ ⬚ (Wednesday am) **B**

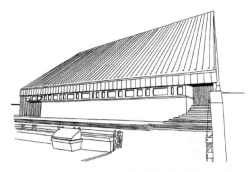

CROFTFOOT PARISH CHURCH

OUR LADY OF GOOD COUNSEL

585 OUR LADY OF GOOD COUNSEL

NS 610 655

73 Craigpark, Dennistoun

Church website: www.olgc.org.uk

Designed by Glasgow Architects, Gillespie, Kidd & Coia, and opened in 1965.
Features a dramatic tapering and sloping copper-clad roof with deep eaves. Inside
there is outstanding brickwork and a high wooden ceiling. Imposing altar. Services:
Daily 10.00am; Saturday Vigil 5.30pm; Sunday 10.00am, 12.00 noon, 5.30pm

Open 9.00am-11.00am weekdays, 9.00am-1.00pm and 5.00pm-6.00pm Sundays

ROMAN CATHOLIC   🚾 📖 **A**

586 DRUMRY ST MARY

NS 515 709

Drumry Road East, Drumchapel

Simple church (Ross, Doak & Whitelaw, 1955-7) with shallow-pitched roof, linked
to hall by a vestibule with a bell turret. Contains a 120-year old marble font from
Old Partick Parish Church. Main feature
is the Garden of Remembrance for
Bereaved Parents as designed by and
featured in BBC's 'Beechgrove Garden'.
Stones in the garden from the 'Peel of
Drumry'. Sunday Service: 11.00am

Church open weeknights evenings; Garden
open at all times (access via rear gate)

CHURCH OF SCOTLAND 🚾 ☕

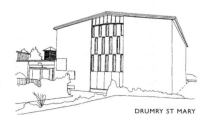

DRUMRY ST MARY

EASTWOOD PARISH CHURCH   GOVAN OLD PARISH CHURCH (ST CONSTANTINE'S)

587 EASTWOOD PARISH CHURCH

NS 558 607

5 Mansewood Road, Glasgow

Built 1863, in transitional Gothic, arranged on a cruciform plan. Designed by
Charles Wilson, who died before its completion, assisted by David Thomson. Its
stained glass windows include examples by the Königliche Glasmalerei-Anstalt,
München (Royal Glass Painting Establishment, Munich) and by Gordon Webster.
The family church of the Maxwells of Pollock. Sunday Service: 11.15am

Open by arrangement, telephone 0141 586 6684 or 0141 883 7923

CHURCH OF SCOTLAND wc 📖 **B**

588 GOVAN OLD PARISH CHURCH (ST CONSTANTINE'S)

NS 554 659

866 Govan Road, Glasgow

Affectionately called 'the people's cathedral'. Set well back in a churchyard dating
back to Celtic times. Completed 1888, the design by Robert Rowand Anderson
proved very influential for the next 50 years. Its style is Early English in the Scottish
manner, with details based on Pluscarden Priory near Elgin. Windows by Charles E
Kempe, Burlison & Grylls, Clayton & Bell and by Shrigley & Hunt. Large collection
of early medieval sculpture including hogback stones, cross shafts, cross slabs and
the richly ornamented and recently conserved Govan Sarcophagus. Fine pipe organ
originally built by Brindley and Foster. City buses and underground to Govan
Station. Sunday Service: 11.00am; Daily Service, Monday to Friday 10.00am

*Open 1st Wednesday in June to 3rd Saturday in September, Wednesdays 10.30am-12.30pm,
and Wednesdays, Thursdays and Saturdays 1.00-4.00pm. Also open by arrangement,
telephone 0141 440 2466*

CHURCH OF SCOTLAND wc ♿ 🍵 📖 ☕ **A**

589 HIGH CARNTYNE PARISH CHURCH

NS 636 653

358 Carntynehall Road, Glasgow

First church extension charge of Church of Scotland. Congregation met in 'the hut' until building was completed by J Taylor Thomson 1932. Original single bell still in use. Extensive suite of halls built alongside the church in 1955. Buses 33, 41, 42, 43, 51. Sunday Service: 11.00am; Wednesday 9.30am

Open after Wednesday morning service

CHURCH OF SCOTLAND 🔗 wc **B** 🔗 ☕

590 KING'S PARK PARISH CHURCH

NS 601 608

242 Castlemilk Road, Glasgow

Church website: www.kingsparkparishchurch.co.uk

Red brick with stone dressings, Romanesque in style by Hutton & Taylor 1932, an innovation in church design specially evolved by the Presbytery of Glasgow. Notable collection of stained glass windows by Sadie McLellan, Gordon Webster, David Hamilton, Eilidh Keith and others. Set in a pleasant

KING'S PARK PARISH CHURCH

small garden. Floodlit as part of 'City of Light' project. Ample parking. By rail to King's Park or Croftfoot, ten minute walk. First Bus number 7 to Castlemilk Road. Sunday Services: 11.00am, 6.30pm; 11.00am only July to August

Open Monday to Friday 9.30am-12.00 noon, all year except public holidays.

Tours, telephone Mr Ian Henderson 0141 589 5603

CHURCH OF SCOTLAND 🔗 wc 🔗 🎺 (on request) 📖 ☕ (Tuesday am) **B**

591 ST MARGARET'S, NEWLANDS

NS 569 610

Kilmarnock Road, Newlands, Glasgow

Church website: www.st-margarets.gn.apc.org

The church, a 'classic of the Romanesque Revival', was designed by Dr Peter MacGregor Chalmers and built in stages between 1910 and 1935. A basilica with double apse, it is splendid in size and simple beauty. The stained glass windows include examples by Morris & Co, the St Enoch Studio and Gordon Webster and three new windows by John Clark.

ST MARGARET'S, NEWLANDS

Sunday Services: Holy Communion 9.00am, Sung Eucharist 10.30am, Evensong 6.30pm 2nd Sunday; Monday to Thursday 8.45am Morning Prayer, 5.00pm Evening Prayer

Open 9.00-12.30pm, Monday to Friday. Other details from church office 0141 636 1131

SCOTTISH EPISCOPAL (Anglican) ♿ ⓘ **B**

592 ST JAMES'S PARISH CHURCH, POLLOK

NS 530 626

183 Meiklerig Crescent, Pollok, Glasgow

Church built 1895 as Pollokshields Titwood Church, and moved stone by stone from its original site four miles away by Thomson, McCrae & Sanders, and rededicated in 1953. Congregation worshipped in a school hall and then in a wooden hut until the building was completed. Good stained glass. Within the Sanctuary there is a storytelling centre – 'The Village' – which provides programmes of events for the community. Bus service 3 from

ST JAMES'S PARISH CHURCH, POLLOK

Glasgow city centre. M8, junction for Paisley Road West. Sunday Service: 11.00am

Open Saturdays 10.00am-12.00 noon. Close to Pollok House, the Burrell Collection, Crookston Castle and Ross Hall

CHURCH OF SCOTLAND ♿ wc ⓘ ☕ ἷ **B**

593 ST JAMES THE GREAT

NS 525 625

20 Beltrees Road (junction with Crosstobs Road)

Parish established in 1949 and the present building by Alexander McAnally was opened in 1968. The external walls are of pink Accrington brick with stone dressings and a stone façade. Inside the walls are of cream brick and the ceiling is of cedarwood. Wrought-iron work by Thomas Bogie and Sons of Edinburgh. The circular nave can seat 544. The high altar is of various marbles. Services: Saturday 10.00am, Vigil 5.30pm; Sunday 10.00am and 12.00 noon, daily Mass 10.00am

Open daily from 8.00am-11.00am, Tuesdays and Wednesdays 8.00am-8.00pm

ROMAN CATHOLIC ♿ wc ⓘ ἷ ☕

ST JAMES THE GREAT

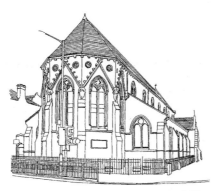

ST NINIAN'S CHURCH, POLLOKSHIELDS

SHERBROOKE ST GILBERT'S CHURCH, POLLOKSHIELDS

594 ST NINIAN'S CHURCH, POLLOKSHIELDS

NS 582 632

1 Albert Drive, Pollokshields, Glasgow

The foundation stone of St Ninian's was laid in 1872, and building commenced to
a design by David Thomson. Completed in 1877, and extended west in 1887. The
apse is decorated with frescoes painted by William Hole 1901, and the charming
little sacristy designed by H D Wilson, a member of the congregation, in 1914.
Good stained glass including windows by Heaton, Butler & Bayne. The windows
in the chancel represent The Gospel Story, by Stephen Adam. Sunday Services:
Holy Communion (Said) 8.30am, Sung Eucharist and Sermon 10.15am,
Evening Prayer (Said) 6.30pm

Open by arrangement, telephone Mrs Y Grieve 0141 638 7254

SCOTTISH EPISCOPAL   🚫 (from rear of church, notification needed) wc ⊘ 📖 ⛷ **B**

595 SHERBROOKE ST GILBERT'S CHURCH, POLLOKSHIELDS

NS 561 636

240 Nithsdale Road, Pollokshields, Glasgow

The original building by William Forsyth McGibbon was ravaged by fire in 1994,
its centenary year. Now the church is restored. The interior features the work of
Scottish craftsmen: stained glass windows, inspired by the themes of creation, the
Cross and rebirth, by Stained Glass Design Partnership, Kilmaurs; 3-manual pipe
organ by Lammermuir Pipe Organs; pulpit, tables and font by Bill Nimmo, East
Lothian. Close to Dumbreck railway station, and on 59 bus route.

Sunday Service: 10.30am

Open by arrangement, telephone the Church Officer 0141 427 1968

CHURCH OF SCOTLAND 🚫 wc ⊘ ⛷ 📖 **B**

596 POLLOKSHIELDS PARISH CHURCH

NS 569 615

Junction of Shields Road and Albert Drive

Church website: www.pollockshieldschurch.org.uk

Large Gothic church with a tall spire by Robert Baldie, 1877-8, the chancel was remodelled 1911-14. White marble pulpit by Peter McGregor Chalmers. Stained glass by Stephen Adam, W & J J Keir and Robert Anning Bell. Organ by Harrison & Harrison 1913. At the rear of the church are four needlework panels by Sally Moodie Harkness representing the Sun, Moon, Earth and Sea.

Services: Sunday 11.00am; Wednesday 9.45am.

Open Wednesday 10.00am-12.00 noon; or by arrangement,

telephone the Church Officer 07855 288801

CHURCH OF SCOTLAND ♿ 🚻 ✍ ☕ (Wednesday) **B**

597 QUEEN'S PARK BAPTIST CHURCH

NS 579 266

180 Queen's Drive and Balvicar Drive, Glasgow

Church website: www.qpbc.org

'QP', an evangelical-charismatic church, is a changing church and recent years have seen significant growth which parallels spiritual renewal in the fellowship, preaching, ministry, outreach and worship. The church occupies two nearby sites: a Romanesque building (Camphill), McKissack & Rowan 1887; and a French Gothic building (Queen's Drive), William Leiper 1876. The interiors of both buildings have been significantly modernised and renovated to make them relevant places for Christian worship and work in the 21st century. Queen's Drive/Pollokshaws Road, two minutes from Queen's Park Station. Sunday Services: 10.30am, 6.30pm and 8.00pm

Open Sundays, and other times by arrangement, telephone Church Office 0141 423 3962

BAPTIST ♿ 🚻 ✍ 🍴 📖 ♀ **A** (Camphill) **B** (Queen's Drive)

QUEEN'S PARK BAPTIST CHURCH

598   QUEEN'S PARK CHURCH

NS 579 625

170 Queen's Drive, on junction with Albert Avenue
Church website: www.qpp.org.uk
Nave and aisles Gothic church with spire on corner site
by James Thomson 1873-5. Halls added 1879. Galleried
interior with two tiers of cast-iron columns and a barrel-
vaulted roof. Stained glass window by Daniel Cottier
and some exposed wall decoration. Organ by Lewis &
Co 1903. War memorial plaques for Queens Park West,
Strathbungo, Queens Park High and Crosshill Queens
Park Church. Sunday Services 11.00am and 6.30pm
Open by arrangement, telephone 0141 637 9605 or
0141 423 2302 or 0141 632 9013
CHURCH OF SCOTLAND   wc **B**

QUEEN'S PARK CHURCH

599   SHAWLANDS UNITED REFORMED
CHURCH, GLASGOW

NS 570 622

111 Moss-side Road, Shawlands, Glasgow
Church website: www.shawlands-urc.co.uk
Formerly a Churches of Christ church, by
Miller & Black 1908, in red sandstone. Open
baptistry. From Shawlands Cross 300 yards.
Sunday Service: 11.00am
Open by arrangement, telephone 0141 638 2442
UNITED REFORMED   ♿ wc ⌂ ⌁

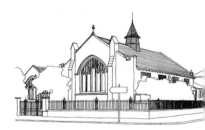

SHAWLANDS UNITED
REFORMED CHURCH, GLASGOW

600   SOUTH SHAWLANDS CHURCH

NS 569 615

Regwood Street / Deanston Drive
Perpendicular Gothic by Miller and Black,
dedicated in 1913. An unusual feature of the
interior is the cantilevered gallery. Beautiful
stained glass including a window in the
chancel by Douglas Hamilton 1959. Sunday
Services: 11.00am (10.00am in school
holidays) and 6.30pm on 2nd Sunday
Open by arrangement, telephone 0141 632 0013
CHURCH OF SCOTLAND
wc ⌁ ⌁ (by arrangement) ⌁ **B**

SOUTH SHAWLANDS CHURCH

601 SHETTLESTON OLD PARISH CHURCH

NS 649 370

111 Killin Street, Shettleston, Glasgow

Church by W F McGibbon, opened in 1903. Fine
collection of stained glass, including windows by
Alfred Webster and Gordon Webster. Fine 2-manual
organ. Train to Shettleston. City buses 40, 46,
62, 162, 262. Sunday Service: 11.00am
Open by arrangement, telephone the
Church Officer 0141 778 2484
CHURCH OF SCOTLAND 🚹 wc ② 📖 **B**

SHETTLESTON OLD PARISH CHURCH

602 ST PAUL THE APOSTLE, SHETTLESTON

NS 653 641

1653 Shettleston Road

Basilican church by Jack Coia 1959. Exterior copper
calvary and stations of the cross by Jack Mortimer.
Spacious interior with much marble and slate, re-ordered
for modern liturgy. Interesting baptistry and a rebuilt
organ from Greenlaw Parish Church, Paisley. Services:
daily 9.30am; Saturday 5.30pm; Sunday 10.00am; Family
Service 11.30am, Youth Mass 6.30pm; Morning Prayer
9.10am weekdays; Evening prayer 5.30pm weekdays
Parish Feast Day Conversion of St Paul, 25 January.
Open 8.00am-7.30pm; access to Blessed Sacrament Chapel
8.00am-7.30pm
ROMAN CATHOLIC 🚹 wc (adapted in Hall) wc **B**

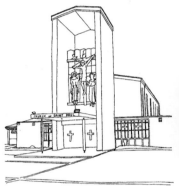

ST PAUL THE APOSTLE,
SHETTLESTON

603 SHETTLESTON METHODIST CHURCH

NS 643 642

1104 Shettleston Road, Glasgow

Church website: www.shettlstonmc.com

Former Primitive Methodist Church of 1902
which replaced a tin tabernacle of 1889. The Church
incorporates windows from the former Parkhead
Methodist Church. Opposite Shettleston Police
Station. Services: Sunday 11.00am; Tuesday 10.30am
Open by arrangement, telephone the
Church Office 0141 778 5063
METHODIST 🚹 wc

SHETTLESTON METHODIST CHURCH

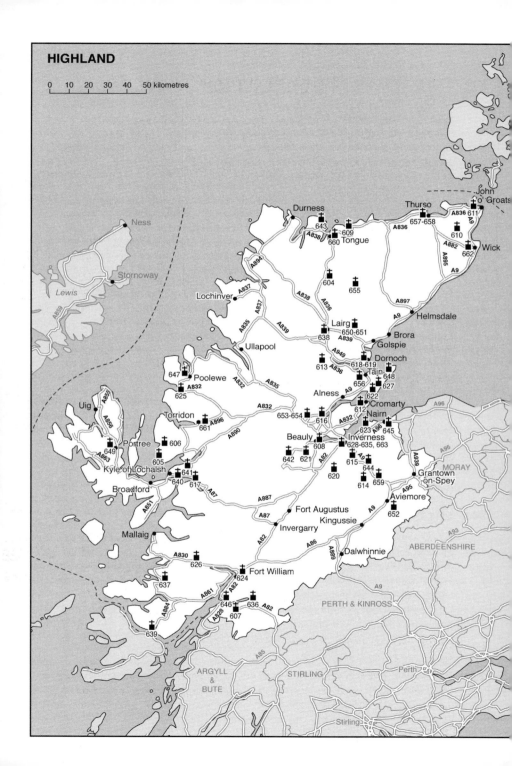

HIGHLAND

0 10 20 30 40 50 kilometres

Ness

Stornoway

Lewis

Durness

Thurso

John 'o' Groats

657-658

A836

611

A9

A838

643

609

660 Tongue

610

A882

Wick

662

A895

604

655

A897

A9

Helmsdale

Lochinver

A837

A838

A836

A837

A835

A839

Lairg

Brora

A9

638

650-651

A839

Golspie

Ullapool

A949

Dornoch

A836

618-619

613

Tain

648

656

627

622

647

Poolewe

A832

A832

A835

Alness

A9

Cromarty

612

Nairn

625

653-654

A832

623

A96

645

Uig

A855

A832

616

Inverness

Torridon

A896

661

A890

Beauly

628-635, 663

A939

MORAY

606

608

615

A95

Portree

A863

642

621

A82

644

659

Grantown-on-Spey

649

605

620

614

Kyle of Lochalsh

641

617

A87

A887

Aviemore

Broadford

640

A87

Fort Augustus

652

A851

Invergarry

Kingussie

A886

ABERDEENSHIRE

Mallaig

A82

A86

Dalwhinnie

A830

626

A889

A9

637

624

Fort William

A861

PERTH & KINROSS

646

636

A82

A884

607

A828

639

A85

ARGYLL & BUTE

STIRLING

Perth

Stirling

HIGHLAND

Local Representative: Mrs Lyndall Leet, 8 Burnside, Thurso, Caithness
(*telephone* 01847 896989)

604 ALTNAHARRA PARISH CHURCH, SUTHERLAND

NC 568 355

Half-way between the school and the Telford
bridge, the church was built 1854-7 by Hugh
Mackay as a Free Church. Fine stonework and
interior woodwork. Oil lamps now converted
to electricity. Long communion tables between
front pews for Communicants to sit at. Stained
glass window in memory of Kathleen Joan
Kimball. Sunday Service: 3.00pm on 1st and
3rd Sundays of each month
Open at all times
CHURCH OF SCOTLAND

ALTNAHARRA PARISH CHURCH, SUTHERLAND

605 APPLECROSS CHURCH, ROSS-SHIRE

NG 711 417

*Camusterrach, Applecross (two miles
towards Toscaig from Post Office)*
Plain harled church built 1855 for the
Free Church. Became United Free
Church in 1900 and Church of
Scotland in 1929. Clachan Church
(see below) at head of Applecross Bay
is also open to visitors. Applecross has
connections with 7th-century St
Maelrubha. Sunday Services: 12.00
noon in hall, 6.00pm in church
*Open by arrangement with the Minister,
telephone 01520 744263*
CHURCH OF SCOTLAND ♿ wc

APPLECROSS CHURCH, ROSS-SHIRE

606 CLACHAN CHURCH, APPLECROSS, ROSS-SHIRE

NG 712 459

Standing on the ancient site of St Maelrubha's church (AD 673), the present church
was built in 1817. The beauty and tranquillity of the surroundings complement the
quiet simplicity of the plain stone building. To the left of the gate stands a tall,

plain slab with an incised Celtic cross, said to
mark the grave of Ruairidh Mor MacAogan,
abbot of Applecross, who died in AD 801. The
remains of carved Celtic crosses, dating from the
8th century, are in glass cases in Heritage Centre
opposite. The church is recommended for its
simplicity and peace, a fitting heritor of the old
Gaelic name of 'A'Chomraich' – the Sanctuary.
SCS St Maelrubha Millenium Pilgrimage to this
church. No regular services, but used for
weddings, funerals and memorial services

Open daily

INTERDENOMINATIONAL **B**

CLACHAN CHURCH, APPLECROSS, ROSS-SHIRE

607   ST MUN'S, BALLACHULISH, ARGYLL

NN 083 579

Built 1837 by Bishop Scott, Vicar-Apostolic for West of Scotland. Simple Highland
church in good condition. Adjacent building was originally the priest's house.

Sunday Service: 11.00am; daily as announced

Open at all times

ROMAN CATHOLIC [wc]

608   ST MARY'S CHURCH, BEAULY, INVERNESS-SHIRE

NH 528 467

High Street, Beauly

Nave, chancel and north aisle, and
adjoining house, built as a unit in red
sandstone 1864, probably by Joseph A
Hansom. Nearby the ruins of Beauly
Priory, founded for Valliscaulian monks
in 1230, maintained by Historic
Scotland. Also serves St Mary's,
Eskadale. Sunday Mass: 11.00am

Open Easter to September; other times,
call at Priest's house adjoining

ROMAN CATHOLIC [♿] [wc] ⊘ **B**

ST MARY'S CHURCH, BEAULY, INVERNESS-SHIRE

609 FARR PARISH CHURCH, BETTYHILL, SUTHERLAND

NC 708 622

Built 1909 to a standard design used for
United Free Churches in the Highlands.
Nearby, at Clachan, stands the old Parish
Church, built 1774, now a museum of the
Clearances and Clan Mackay. Amongst the
gravestones is the Farr Stone, a Christianised

FARR PARISH CHURCH, BETTYHILL, SUTHERLAND

Pictish stone. Strathnaver Trail of 29 sites of archaeological, historical and natural
heritage interest runs from the museum to Altnaharra. Sunday Service: 11.30am
Open at all times
CHURCH OF SCOTLAND [wc]

610 BOWER PARISH CHURCH, CAITHNESS

ND 238 622

Midway between Thurso and Wick on B876
Built 1847, architect William Davidson. Re-
casting and alterations, architect Donald
Leed 1902. Finialled and panelled Gothic
screen flanks pulpit. Unusual in that two

BOWER PARISH CHURCH, CAITHNESS

long windows which formerly flanked the pulpit are in the north, not south, wall.
Stained glass window dedicated to Sir John Sinclair, 7th Baronet of Dunbeath.
Mural memorials to members of Henderson and Sinclair families and plaque in
memory of Zachary Pont, minister 1605-13, and his wife Margaret, daughter of
John Knox. Ongoing restoration work has uncovered bronze bell from pre-
Reformation church. Sunday Service: 12.15pm
Open by arrangement, telephone Mrs McAdie 01955 661252
CHURCH OF SCOTLAND [&] [wc] [wc] ⊘ ⓘ **B**

611 CANISBAY CHURCH

ND 343 728

Most northerly place of worship on the Scottish mainland, the site occupied by
the chapel of St Drostan, who headed a mission to Pictland in the 6th century.
The present cruciform church is largely 17th century, but the nave incorporates
walling from the medieval church and a worn 17th-century monument flanked by
pairs of Corinthian pilasters. John de Groat stone of 1568 stands in the vestibule.
Sunday Service: 12.15pm
Open daily 9.00am-9.00pm, Easter to end October.
In winter, key from Mrs Cormack (next to church)
CHURCH OF SCOTLAND [&] **A**

CANISBAY CHURCH

EAST CHURCH, CROMARTY, ROSS-SHIRE

612 EAST CHURCH, CROMARTY, ROSS-SHIRE

NH 791 673
Church Street, Cromarty
Church website: www.srct.org.uk

Described by John Hume as 'unquestionably one of the finest 18th century parish churches in Scotland'. Starting as a simple east-west rectangle in the late 16th century, the north aisle was added 1739 to create a T-plan church. Further alterations in 1756 and 1798. The interior dates principally from the 18th century with galleries added to accommodate the growing congregation, the most elaborate being the Cromartie loft of 1756. Several fine monuments. Owned and maintained by the Scottish Redundant Churches Trust. Four Sunday services during summer months, telephone the SRCT 01334 472032 for dates and times. Occasional services, including weddings, by arrangement

Open 8.30am-5.00pm (4.00pm in winter)
FORMER CHURCH OF SCOTLAND wc A

613 CROICK CHURCH, ARDGAY, SUTHERLAND

NH 457 915
Ardgay, Strathcarron, 10 miles west of A9/A836

Harled T-plan 'Parliamentary' church built by James Smith 1827 from a Thomas Telford design. One of the few Parliamentary churches still in use in its original form. Furnishings virtually unchanged since first built; old-style long communion table and original pulpit. East window has messages scratched in 1845 by evicted inhabitants of Glencalvie. Pictish broch in church glebe. Sunday Services: 2nd Sunday, May to September, 3.00pm; Communion 2nd Sunday in July, 3.00pm

Open during daylight hours
CHURCH OF SCOTLAND 📖 A

CROICK CHURCH,
ARDGAY, SUTHERLAND

DALAROSSIE CHURCH, INVERNESS-SHIRE

DAVIOT CHURCH, INVERNESS-SHIRE

614 DALAROSSIE CHURCH, INVERNESS-SHIRE

NH 767 242

3 miles from old A9

Church website: www.strathsnairnanddearn.co.uk

Dalarossie Church, on the River Findhorn, is an ancient place of worship dating back to the 8th century at the time of St Fergus. The present building, set within the walled graveyard, dates from 1790 and features an ancient baptismal font as well as a 'covenant stone'. Services: April to October, 1st and 3rd Sundays 10.30am; November to March, 1st Sunday 10.30am

Open by arrangement, telephone 01463 772242 or Mrs Vivian Roden 01808 511355

CHURCH OF SCOTLAND ⏐ (by arrangement) **B**

615 DAVIOT CHURCH, INVERNESS-SHIRE

NH 722 394

On A9, 6 miles south of Inverness

Church website: www.strathsnairnanddearn.co.uk

Built in 1826 and restored 1991. There has been a place of worship on the site since early times, long before its charter was granted in the 13th century. The surrounding graveyard tells of the changing history of this interesting parish. Sunday Service: 12.00 noon

Open by arrangement, telephone 01463 772242

CHURCH OF SCOTLAND ♿ ⊘ ⏐ (guides by arrangement) **B**

616 ST JAMES THE GREAT CHURCH, DINGWALL, ROSS-SHIRE

NH 552 588

Castle Street, Dingwall

The building is on the site of an earlier chapel, 1806, which was demolished in 1851 and the new building erected to a New Gothic design by J L Pearson. It was consecrated in 1854 but gutted by fire in 1871. Restoration, by Alexander Ross, Inverness, began immediately, following the original design. Services: 9.30am or 11.00am on alternate Sundays; Wednesdays Morning Prayer and Eucharist 10.30am. Please check notice board for details

*Open daily during daylight hour*s

SCOTTISH EPISCOPAL ♿ wc

ST JAMES THE GREAT CHURCH,
DINGWALL, ROSS-SHIRE

617 ST DUTHAC'S CHURCH, DORNIE, ROSS-SHIRE

NG 884 268

Dornie, by Kyle of Lochalsh (beside Eilean Donan Castle)

The first Catholic church on the site was built in 1703. The present building dates from 1860, architect Joseph A Hansom. It is in simple Gothic style with nave and chancel. The stone reredos has polished granite shafts, while similar columns support the altar. The simplicity continues with the demi-octagonal stone pulpit and braced rafter roof. Sunday Service: 10.30am; Saturday Vigil 7.30pm

Open daily

ROMAN CATHOLIC 📖 **B**

ST DUTHAC'S CHURCH,
DORNIE, ROSS-SHIRE

618 DORNOCH CATHEDRAL, DORNOCH, SUTHERLAND

NH 797 897

High Street, Dornoch

Cathedral founded by Bishop Gilbert de Moravia in the 13th century; the first service in the building was held in 1239. The medieval masonry of the chancel and the crossing piers remains mostly intact today. The nave was destroyed by fire in 1570, the transepts and choir were reroofed 1616, and the nave rebuilt 1837. In 1924 the interior stonework was exposed. Lavish display of stained glass, including several windows by James Ballantine, others by Percy Bacon, and the St Gilbert window by Crear McCartney 1989.

Sunday Services: all year 11.00am, summer months 8.30pm

Open during daylight hours

CHURCH OF SCOTLAND ♿ 🔊 📖 **A**

DORNOCH CATHEDRAL, DORNOCH, SUTHERLAND

DUNLICHITY CHURCH, DUNLICHITY, INVERNESS-SHIRE

619 ST FINNBARR'S, DORNOCH, SUTHERLAND

NH 799 898

Schoolhill, Dornoch

Simple but picturesque Gothic by Alexander Ross 1912-13. Stained glass triple lancet east window by Percy Bacon. Of special note are the 70 tapestry kneelers with highland themes created by 14 members of the congregation between 1981 and 1993. Sunday Services: Eucharist 1st and 3rd Sunday 9.45am, 2nd and 4th 11.30am, 5th Sunday varies, check with Vestry Secretary

Open April to October 10.00am-4.00pm; at other times by arrangement with Vestry Secretary, telephone 01862 810877

SCOTTISH EPISCOPAL ⏦

620 DUNLICHITY CHURCH, DUNLICHITY, INVERNESS-SHIRE

NH 659 327

near Loch Duntelchaig

Church website: www.strathsnairnanddearn.co.uk

An ancient place of worship, much earlier than the present building which dates back in part to the 16th century. Many interesting features, including a 1702 handbell, and surrounded by a graveyard of much historical interest, with its own 1759 watch-house. Services: April to October 1st Sunday 7.00pm; November to March, 1st Sunday, 10.45am

Open by arrangement, telephone 01463 772242

CHURCH OF SCOTLAND ⏻ (guides by arrangement) **B**

ST MARY'S CHURCH, ESKADALE, INVERNESS-SHIRE

FEARN ABBEY, ROSS-SHIRE

621   ST MARY'S CHURCH, ESKADALE, INVERNESS-SHIRE

NH 453 399

A spacious white harled church in a picturesque woodland setting. Built 1826 by
the 14th Lord Lovat. Alterations and additions by Peter Paul Pugin 1881. Founder's
tomb in the chancel. Lovat family graveyard to the west of the church. The
contemporary stable to accommodate horses ridden by those attending Mass, 50
metres to the west of the church, is an unusual feature. On a minor road on the
south east side of the River Beauly. Served by St Mary's, Beauly. Sunday Mass:
9.00am alternate Sundays

Open by arrangement, telephone Mr James Christie 01463 741536

ROMAN CATHOLIC   **B**

622   FEARN ABBEY, ROSS-SHIRE

NH 837 773

Hill of Fearn

Known as 'The Lamp of the North', it is one of the oldest pre-Reformation
Scottish churches still in use for worship. Rebuilt 1772 by James Rich and restored
by Ian G Lindsay & Partners 1972. Further restoration in summer 2001. Originally
a monastery of Premonstratensian monks of the Order of St Augustine. Patrick
Hamilton, burnt for heresy at St Andrews in 1528, was the Commendatory Abbot
from 1517 to 1528. A9, Hill of Fearn Village. Sunday Service: 11.30am

Open daily Easter to September, 10.00am-4.30pm; or by appointment,
telephone Mr J Maxwell 01862 871247

CHURCH OF SCOTLAND   wc 📖 **A**

623 FORT GEORGE CHAPEL, INVERNESS-SHIRE

NH 761 567

Fort George, Ardersier

(off A96 north-east of Inverness)

The garrison chapel built in 1767, probably to a design by William Skinner. Interior, two-tiered arcade on three sides supported by Roman Doric columns. Eighteenth-century three-decker pulpit. Working garrison. Visitor displays, Historic Scotland

Open April to September, Monday to Saturday 9.30am-6.30pm, Sunday 9.30am-6.30pm; October to March, Monday to Saturday 9.30am-4.30pm, Sunday 2.00-4.30pm

NON-DENOMINATIONAL 🦽 📖 ☕ **A**

FORT GEORGE CHAPEL, INVERNESS-SHIRE

624 ST MARY'S ROMAN CATHOLIC, FORT WILLIAM

NN 107 741

Belford Road, Fort William

Designed by Reginald Fairlie and built 1936-8. the nave is a plain box of grey granite with round-arched windows with a tower of pink and grey granite. Inside, a simple barrel-vaulted nave with oak pews. Lady chapel with oak reredos. The chancel has a huge baldacchino by Thomas Bogie. Lovely wrought-iron work throughout the church. Organ by Sniffen & Stroud. Services: Saturday Vigil: 7.00pm; Sunday 9.00am, 11.00am, 4.00pm; Monday to Saturday 10.15am

Open every day 9.00am-6.30pm

ROMAN CATHOLIC 🦽 wc ⑨ Gaelic spoken **A**

625 GAIRLOCH FREE CHURCH, GAIRLOCH, ROSS-SHIRE

NG 804 761

On a commanding site overlooking Loch Gairloch. Gothic in style, to a design by Matthews & Lawrie 1881. Simple interior with original fittings and Gothic panelled gallery across east end. Spandrels of roof trusses with cusped decoration. A832 to Gairloch. Sunday Services: 11.00am and 5.00pm; Gaelic Service; 12.00 noon alternate Sunday

Open by arrangement, telephone the Minister 01445 712371

FREE CHURCH OF SCOTLAND 🦽 wc 📖 **C**

626   ST MARY AND ST FINNAN CHURCH, GLENFINNAN, INVERNESS-SHIRE

NM 904 808

The church was consecrated in 1873. Designed by E
Welby Pugin in the Gothic style, the church enjoys
an elevated and commanding position overlooking
Loch Shiel with a spectacular view of the loch and
surrounding hills. The church is a memorial chapel
to the MacDonalds of Glenaladale, the family with
whom Bonnie Prince Charlie stayed prior to the
raising of the Jacobite standard at Glenfinnan in
August 1745. The church contains memorial stones
to the Prince and to members of the MacDonald
family. Located in the village, 15 miles west of Fort
William on A830 to Mallaig. Sunday Mass: 1.00pm
Open daily sunrise to sunset
ROMAN CATHOLIC **B**

ST MARY AND ST FINNAN CHURCH,
GLENFINNAN, INVERNESS-SHIRE

627   INVER MEETING HOUSE, INVER, ROSS-SHIRE

NH 863 828

New Street, Inver

A meeting house in the style of cottages. Inver, largely in original form, originates
as a settlement of persons displaced during clearances. Memorial, to north of
village on the shore, marks common grave of cholera victims, a large proportion of
the population. Sunday Service: 10.00am

Open by appointment, telephone Mr Skinner 01862 871522
CHURCH OF SCOTLAND ♿

628   OLD HIGH CHURCH, INVERNESS

NH 665 455

Church Street, Inverness

Present building completed 1772 to a plan by George
Fraser of Edinburgh on site of medieval church; lowest
portion of the west bell-tower is 15th or 16th century.
Traditionally thought to be the site where St Columba
converted Brude, King of the Picts, to Christianity.
Porches, apse and chancel arch date from 1891, to designs
by Ross & Macbeth. The colours of the Queen's Own
Cameron Highlanders are hung and the Regiment's
Books of Remembrance are housed in the church. Two-
manual organ by Henry Willis & Sons 1895, rebuilt by

OLD HIGH CHURCH, INVERNESS

H Hilsdon 1923. Stained glass by, amongst others, Douglas Strachan 1925, Stephen Adam & Co 1893, and A Ballantine & Gardiner 1899. Sunday Service: 11.15am all year; mid June to mid September Fridays 1.00pm-1.15pm

Open June, July and August, Fridays 12.00 noon-2.00pm. Guided tour at 12.30pm
CHURCH OF SCOTLAND 🛉 🛆 **A**

629 CROWN CHURCH, INVERNESS

NH 66 45

Kingsmill Road

Church website: www.crown-church.co.uk

Designed by J R Rhind and completed in 1901, though without intended spire and with subsequent extensions to the halls. Stained glass in rose and west windows. Organ 3-manual by Makin. Centenary wallhanging. Sunday Service: 11.00am, in summer also 9.30am; Wednesday 1.00pm; Evening Worship as advertised

Open daily 9.00am-4.00pm

CHURCH OF SCOTLAND 🚹 wc 🔊

630 ST ANDREW'S CATHEDRAL, INVERNESS

NH 664 450

Ardross Street, Inverness

One of the first new cathedrals completed (1869) in Great Britain after the Reformation 1869, by local architect Alexander Ross. Polished granite pillars, stained glass, fine furnishings. Angel font after Thorvaldsen. Founder's memorial, icons presented by Tsar of Russia. Peal of bells. Fine choir. On west bank of River Ness, just above Ness Bridge, A862, close to town centre. Sunday Services: Eucharist 8.15am, Family Eucharist 9.30am, Sung Eucharist 11.00am, Choral Evensong 6.30pm; Matins, Eucharist and Evensong daily

Open daily 8.30am-6.00pm (later June to September)

SCOTTISH EPISCOPAL wc 🔊 🛉 May to September ☕ **A**

631 ST MARY'S CHURCH, INVERNESS

NH 662 455

30 Huntly Street, Inverness

On the west bank of the River Ness, very close to the city centre. Built 1837 by William Robertson in Gothic Revival manner. Re-decorated and new stained-glass window installed to mark the Millennium and the Great Year of Jubilee. Sunday Services: Mass 10am and 6.30pm; Vigil Mass Saturday 7.00pm, June to September

Open daily, summer 9.00am-6.00pm, winter 9.00am-3.00pm

ROMAN CATHOLIC 🚹 🔊 **A**

ST MARY'S CHURCH, INVERNESS

ST MICHAEL & ALL ANGELS, INVERNESS

ST STEPHEN'S, INVERNESS

632   ST MICHAEL & ALL ANGELS, INVERNESS

NH 659 457
Abban Street/Lochalsh Road, Inverness
Church website: www.angelforce.co.uk/stmichael
In 1877 Canon Edward Medley established a mission in a thatched cottage on the
Maggot Green, close to River Ness. The church was built in 1886, but as the site
proved liable to flooding, it was re-built in Abban Street in 1903-4, Alexander Ross.
Many interior fittings, altar with gilded angels and tester, and font with lofty
steeple cover were designed by Sir Ninian Comper and installed in 1904. A major
reconstruction, 1924-8 by Comper, saw six new tracery windows, including a
magnificent stained glass window of the four archangels, being created. Restored
2002. Situated close to the town centre, by the riverside, to the north-west of
Friar's Bridge. Sunday Services: Sunday Low Mass 8.00am,
Parish Mass 11.00am, Low Mass daily
Open daily 9.00am-4.00pm; other times, telephone Canon Black 01463 233797
SCOTTISH EPISCOPAL 🔲 wc ⊘ 🚹 🚻 📱 **B**

633   ST STEPHEN'S, INVERNESS

NH 672 449
Southside Road, junction with Edinburgh Road, Inverness
By W L Carruthers 1897 in Arts & Crafts Gothic, the hall added later. The church
consists of a nave, single north transept and an apsidal chancel. Square tower with
a delicate needle spire. High open roof, pulpit of locally grown native oak.
Noteworthy stained glass of 1897 and 1906 by A Ballantine & Son. Two-manual
organ by Wadsworth Bros 1902. Substantially renovated in 2000 by Sandy
Edmonstone. Sunday Service: 10.00am; Evening Communion 8.00pm Easter
Sunday, 4th Sunday of June and last Sunday of January and September
Open by arrangement, telephone the Minister 01463 237129
CHURCH OF SCOTLAND 🔲 wc ⊘ 🚹 **B**

634 TWEEDMOUTH MEMORIAL CHAPEL, INVERNESS

NM 663 445
Royal Northern Infirmary,
Ness Walk, Inverness
Earliest example of purpose-built
ecumencial worship space in Scotland,
built in 1898, architect A Ross and R B
MacBeth. Three sanctuary areas for
Reformed, Roman Catholic and
Episcopalian worship. Occasional services,
weddings and baptisms
Keys available from Hospital Porters
INTERDENOMINATIONAL   🚹 🚻 ② **B**

TWEEDMOUTH MEMORIAL CHAPEL, INVERNESS

635 INVERNESS METHODIST CHURCH

NH 663 455
50 Huntly Street
Church website: www.invernessmethodist.org.uk
The present building was built 1964-5 to replace one destroyed by fire: the
architect was Kenneth Finlayson of John R Chisholm & Co. A new entrance and
floodlighting were provided in 2003. The building seats some 420 including the
balcony. Wood pews with ash stringing to provide contrast. Six main windows
have stained glass; one commemorates the visit of John Wesley to Inverness in
1764. Organ by Rushworth & Dreaper 1965. Sunday Service: 11.00am all year,
5.00pm November to March, 6.00pm April to October
Open by arrangement with Minister 01463 231170
METHODIST 🚹 🚻 ② 🕯 ☕ 📖

636 KINLOCHLEVEN PARISH CHURCH, INVERNESS-SHIRE

NS 187 621
Riverside Road, Kinlochleven (off A82)
Built 1930 to a simple but elegant design by J
Jeffrey Waddell with a high arch at the chancel
end. Chancel area is a round bell-shape with
stained glass windows depicting biblical scenes.
Two stained glass windows in the south wall
of the nave depicting St Andrew and St
George. Linked with Nether Lochaber in 1981.
Sunday Services: 10.00am and 6.30pm
Open by arrangement, telephone 01855 831227
CHURCH OF SCOTLAND 🚹 ②

KINLOCHLEVEN PARISH CHURCH,
INVERNESS-SHIRE

ST FINAN'S CHURCH, KINLOCHMOIDART, INVERNESS-SHIRE   LAIRG PARISH CHURCH, SUTHERLAND

637   ST FINAN'S CHURCH, KINLOCHMOIDART, INVERNESS-SHIRE

NM 710 728

Up a track leading off the A861, half-mile north of the bridge over the River Moidart

The church stands on a ledge of level ground in woodland above the mouth of
the River Moidart and below an impressively steep hillside. It was built in 1857 to
a design by Alexander Ross in simple Early English style, with crow stepped
gables, a small belfry and a porch. There are two unusual stained glass windows
by the Victorian artist Jemima Blackburn. Services: Christmas, Easter and Sundays,
May to September 5.30pm

Open daily

SCOTTISH EPISCOPAL **C**

638   LAIRG PARISH CHURCH, SUTHERLAND

NC 583 065

Church Hill Road, Lairg

A simple Gothic church, built of local granite 1847, designed by William Leslie.
Renovated 2001. The graveyard, one and a half miles away, served the original
church and contains some interesting monuments, including a large marble
monument to Sir James Matheson of Achany. Linked with Rogart (St Callan's)
and Pitfure. Sunday Service: 10.45am; also 6.30pm on 1st Sunday of month

Open by arrangement, telephone Rev J Goskirk 01549 402373.

Adjacent church hall (built 1998) has level access and adapted toilets

CHURCH OF SCOTLAND ♿ wc wc ✎

639 KIEL CHURCH, LOCHALINE, INVERNESS-SHIRE

NM 972 538
Lochaline, Morvern
One mile out of Lochaline on the Drimnin road
The present church is the third on this site.
Ruins of a medieval church are on the site
of the original and much earlier building
which, according to legend, was erected at
the command of St Columba. Today's
church was designed by P MacGregor
Chalmers 1898. Interesting stained glass.
Memorial plaque to the MacLeods, father
and son, whose ministry here spanned more

KIEL CHURCH, LOCHALINE, INVERNESS-SHIRE

than a century. Fifteenth-century cross outside the front of the church. The nearby
18th-century Session House contains a collection of carved stones 8th to 16th
centuries. Sunday Service: 11.00am
Open daily all year
CHURCH OF SCOTLAND ② 🗍 **c**

640 ST DONNAN'S, LOCHALSH, ROSS-SHIRE

NG 855 272
Nostie, by Lochalsh
Unassuming, simple church by Stevenson & Dunworth 1962-4. East wall inside is
patterned with panels inset with stones from the Nostie Burn. The angels on the
altar pedestal were carved by F R Stevenson. Sunday Service: 10.30am
If church is locked, key obtainable from Mrs C Dodds, Fernfield, Nostie (opposite the church)
SCOTTISH EPISCOPAL 🚾 🗍

641 LOCHCARRON PARISH CHURCH (WEST CHURCH), ROSS-SHIRE

NG 893 391
Former United Free Church designed by
William Mackenzie 1910, sited in centre
of Lochcarron. Crisply painted; standard
UF layout. Also of interest the burial
ground one mile east of the village.
Services (West church only): every
Sunday 11.00am, and 2nd and 4th
Sunday 6.00pm
Open during daylight hours in summer months
CHURCH OF SCOTLAND
♿ 🚾 🍵 (after services)

LOCHCARRON PARISH CHURCH
(WEST CHURCH), ROSS-SHIRE

642 OUR LADY AND ST BEAN, MARYDALE, CANNICH, INVERNESS-SHIRE

NH 342 317

On the north side of the A831, between
Cannich Bridge and Comar Bridge
Church website: www.sanctiangeli.org
Simple stone church in Gothic style,
with adjoining presbytery, walled
garden, school and schoolhouse, built
as a unit by Joseph A Hansom 1868. St
Bean is said to have been a monk of
Iona, a cousin of St Columba, and the
first to evangelise Strathglass. Sputan
Bhain (NH 334 305) was the spring at

OUR LADY AND ST BEAN, MARYDALE,
CANNICH, INVERNESS-SHIRE

which he baptised. On the other side of the road is Clachan Comair, a walled
graveyard with the ruins of a small 17th-century church, on the site of an early 10th-
century chapel dedicated to St Bean. In 1998 a new altar made from 300-year-old
oak, designed by local artist Alistair MacPherson. The former presbytery is being
developed as a monastic retreat, with an icon painting workshop. Mass 9.00am
Open daily
ROMAN CATHOLIC wc **B**

643 MELNESS CHURCH, SUTHERLAND

NC 586 634

Near Talmine, 4 miles from junction with A838 (Tongue–Durness)
Built at the turn of the 20th century by local craftsmen to replace an earlier
building at an adjacent site.
Interior totally wood lined.
Local feeling was that it should
have been called the 'Kerr
Memorial Church' as it was due
to the Minister at the time, Rev
Cathel Kerr, that the church
was completed. Sunday Service:
12.30pm (Holy Communion
held twice yearly)
Open at all times
CHURCH OF SCOTLAND wc ⟨?⟩

MELNESS CHURCH, SUTHERLAND

644 MOY CHURCH, INVERNESS-SHIRE

NH 772 342

On old A9, 13 miles south of Inverness
Church website: www.strathsnairnanddearn.co.uk
Built in 1765, on a previous site, and surrounded
by an interesting graveyard with its own watch-
house. Memorial stone to Donald Fraser, the
hero of the 'Rout of Moy', just before the
Battle of Culloden in 1746. Services: April to
October, 4th Sunday 10.45am; November to
March, 3rd and 5th Sunday, 10.45am
Open by arrangement, telephone 01463 772242
or Mrs Vivian Roden 01808 511355
CHURCH OF SCOTLAND ⓘ (by arrangement) **B**

MOY CHURCH, INVERNESS-SHIRE

645 NAIRN OLD PARISH CHURCH, NAIRN

NH 879 564

Academy Street/Inverness Road, Nairn
Considered the finest structure in the area, 1897 by John Starforth. Architecture of
Early English Transition period; Gothic reminiscences are abundant. Transeptal in
form but almost circular in shape. Square tower is almost 100 feet high. Lovely
light interior. Glorious stained glass. Sunday Service: 10.30am
Open weekdays 9.30am-12.30pm
CHURCH OF SCOTLAND ♿ wc ② ⓘ 📖 **A**

646 NETHER LOCHABER PARISH CHURCH, ONICH, INVERNESS-SHIRE

NN 031 614

Onich, 11 miles south of Fort William on A82
Built in 1911 to replace original Telford church at
Creag Mhor, using some of the original stone. Known
as one of the finest rural churches in the Highlands.
Most illustrious minister was Dr Alexander Stewart
1851-1901, known as 'Nether Lochaber' and renowned
throughout the Celtic world for his wide-ranging
learning and writing. Celtic cross, 20 feet, erected by
the Stewart Society at Innis-na-Bhirlin cemetery off
A82 five miles north of Onich. Linked with
Kinlochleven 1981. Sunday Service: 12.00 noon
Keys available from Tigh-na-Mara, Onich
CHURCH OF SCOTLAND ♿ ②

NETHER LOCHABER PARISH CHURCH,
ONICH, INVERNESS-SHIRE

647 ST MAELRUBHA'S, POOLEWE, ROSS-SHIRE

NG 857 807

St Maelrubha's Close, Poolewe

The first Episcopal church to be built on the north-west coast of Scotland since
the Jacobite rebellion of 1745, St Maelrubha's (a former cow byre) was dedicated in
1965. Tiny, simple and made of local stone, it houses a fragment of the Celtic
cross erected as a monument to the saint and brought from Applecross. Memorial
to the Highland Fieldcraft Training Centre. Visiting clergy take Sunday Services
during the summer. Close to Inverewe Garden (National Trust for Scotland).
Sunday Service: 11.00am; Wednesday 10.00am

Open during daylight hours

SCOTTISH EPISCOPAL ♿ wc ⓘ 📖 ☕

648 PORTMAHOMACK CHURCH, ROSS-SHIRE

NH 917 846

Off Main Street

Simple rectangular former United Free Church
building, architects Andrew Maitland & Sons
1908. Flower Festival during Gala Week (last in
July). Tarbat Discovery Centre (former Tarbat Old
Parish Church) has displays of church and
archaeology, including Pictish stones, and place for
private prayer in crypt. Adjacent archaeological
dig ongoing. Sunday Service: 10.00am

Please ask for key at Village Shop (50m), shop hours only

CHURCH OF SCOTLAND wc

PORTMAHOMACK CHURCH,
ROSS-SHIRE

649 PORTREE PARISH CHURCH

NG 482 436

Somerled Square

St Columba brought Christianity to Skye and the
ruins of earlier churches are to be seen in and
around Portree. The present building, designed by
John Hay of Liverpool, was built as a Free Church
in 1854, became the United Free Church in 1900
and the Church of Scotland in 1929. St Columba
and St Taraglen are depicted in stained glass
windows. Other windows by Douglas Hamilton
and Thomas Webster. Sunday Services: 11.00am
and 6.30pm

Open throughout the summer 11.00am-4.00pm

CHURCH OF SCOTLAND ♿ wc 🔊 ⓘ Gaelic services **C**

PORTREE PARISH CHURCH

650 PITFURE CHURCH, ROGART, SUTHERLAND

NC 710 038

A simple, pleasant place in which to worship. Built by the United Free congregation in 1910, architect Robert J Macbeth, Inverness. Linked with Lairg. Sunday Service: 1st, 3rd and 5th Sundays of month, October to May 12.15pm; July and August 11.30am (check locally or telephone the number below); 2nd Sunday of month 6.30pm
Open by arrangement, telephone
Rev J Goskirk 01549 402373
CHURCH OF SCOTLAND ♿ ⓦⓒ ⌕ 📖

PITFURE CHURCH, ROGART, SUTHERLAND

651 ST CALLAN'S CHURCH, ROGART, SUTHERLAND

NC 715 038

2 miles from crossroads at Pittentrail, take Rhilochan / Balnacoil road
Rebuilt in 1777 on the site of a medieval church. The austere whitewashed exterior with its plain sash windows gives little hint of the warm, gleaming interior. A high canopied pulpit stands against the east wall. Long communion table and pews. Other pews are tiered from the entrance to the west end. Two small stained glass memorial windows on either side of the pulpit: 'Nativity' and 'Penitence' by Margaret Chilton and Marjorie Kemp 1929. Modern vestry wing built in 1984. Linked with Lairg. Sunday Service: 2nd and 4th Sundays of month, September to June 12.15pm; July and August 11.30pm
Open by arrangement, telephone Rev J Goskirk 01549 402373
CHURCH OF SCOTLAND ⓦⓒ ⌕ 📖 **B**

652 ST JOHN THE BAPTIST CHURCH, ROTHIEMURCHUS, INVERNESS-SHIRE

NH 900 111

Church founded by John Peter Grant, 11th Laird of Rothiemurchus and consecrated in 1931. Architect, Sir Ninian Comper. A plain white interior with a groin vaulted ceiling and a rose damask baldacchino. Simple burial ground surrounds the church. Approximately one mile from the centre of Aviemore, 'the little white church on the ski road'. Sunday Service: Holy Eucharist 10.30am
Open by arrangement, contact the
Parish Administrator 01540 661875
SCOTTISH EPISCOPAL ♿ **B**

ST JOHN THE BAPTIST CHURCH, ROTHIEMURCHUS, INVERNESS-SHIRE

FODDERTY & STRATHPEFFER PARISH CHURCH, ROSS-SHIRE   ST ANNE'S CHURCH, STRATHPEFFER, ROSS-SHIRE

653 FODDERTY & STRATHPEFFER PARISH CHURCH, ROSS-SHIRE

NH 482 480

Strathpeffer

Church website: www.strathpefferchurchofscotland.org

Designed by William C Joass and built 1888-90 as part of the development of
Strathpeffer as Britain's most northerly Spa. A rectangular building with side aisles
and balcony to the rear; the chancel extends from the nave under a low roof.
Services: Sunday 11.00am; also last Sunday in the month, April to October 8.00pm
Open by arrangement, telephone the Minister on 01997 421398
CHURCH OF SCOTLAND [wc] ⊘

654 ST ANNE'S CHURCH, STRATHPEFFER, ROSS-SHIRE

NH 483 580

Designed by John Robertson as a memorial to Anne, Duchess of Sutherland and
Countess of Cromartie, it was constructed between 1890 and 1892 with the
chancel added in 1899. The pulpit is of Caen stone and alabaster, the altar and
reredos of marble and alabaster showing carved reliefs. Stained glass windows are
by J Powell & Sons 1891 and Heaton, Butler & Bayne 1892-c.1910. Sunday
Service: 9.30am or 11.00am. Please check notice board for details
Open daily, Easter to September
SCOTTISH EPISCOPAL [♿] ⊘ [📖] **B**

STRATHNAVER CHURCH, SYRE, SUTHERLAND

ST ANDREW'S CHURCH, TAIN, ROSS-SHIRE

655 STRATHNAVER CHURCH, SYRE, SUTHERLAND

NC 694 439

Junction of Kinbrace and Syre roads

Built 1901 as a mission station from Altnaharra. Pre-fabricated by Speirs and Co, Glasgow and erected on site. Neat and tiny corrugated iron church lined with wood. Plaque in memory of the Rev Robert Sloan, Minister 1969-74. Modern cemetery and car park across the road. Nearby is the Rossal clearance village, maintained by the Forestry Commission, and Patrick Sellar's House. Sunday Service: on the 2nd, 4th and 5th Sundays of each month 3.00pm

Open at all times

CHURCH OF SCOTLAND **C**

656 ST ANDREW'S CHURCH, TAIN, ROSS-SHIRE

NH 777 822

Manse Street, Tain

Church website: www.moray.anglican.org

Designed 1887 by Ross & Macbeth, replacing an earlier corrugated iron structure. The earliest stained glass, by Ballantyne and Gardner, was moved from the earlier church. Other glass by A L Ward 1910, and W Wilson 1955 and 1961. Fine organ by Hamilton & Muller, restored 1986. Forward altar designed and carved from American oak by Peter Bailey of Skye 1995. Services: Sunday Eucharist 11.15am 1st and 3rd Sunday, 9.30am 2nd and 4th Sunday, and 11.15am on 5th Sunday; Thursday Eucharist 6.00pm

Open 9.00am-5.00pm

SCOTTISH EPISCOPAL wc **B**

657 ST PETER'S & ST ANDREW'S CHURCH, THURSO, CAITHNESS

ND 115 684

Princes Street, Thurso

Built in 1832 to a design by William Burn, the church is the centre point of the town, fronted by town square garden and war memorial. U-plan gallery. Pipe organ, Norman & Beard 1914. Stained glass includes 'The Sower' by Oscar Paterson 1922. Sunday Services: 11.00am and 6.30pm

Open July to August daily, 2.00-4.00pm, 7.00-8.00pm

CHURCH OF SCOTLAND [wc] ⟲ 👤 📖 👤 **B**

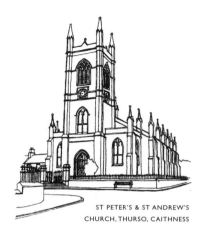

ST PETER'S & ST ANDREW'S
CHURCH, THURSO, CAITHNESS

658 ST PETER & THE HOLY ROOD, THURSO

ND 117 682

Sir George's Street

The church was built in 1885 to the design of Alexander Ross, the chancel being added in 1905 in memory of Mr Norman Sinclair. The stained glass by A L Moore depicting 'The Good Samaritan' is in memory of Sir George Sinclair of Ulbster. The 2-manual organ by George Benson 1894, built for a Lancashire Chapel, was dismantled and moved here in 1973. The carved oak reredos depicts the Ascension and the first Pentecost. Services: Sunday Communion 8.00am and 9.30am, Choral Evensong 6.30pm; Tuesday Communion 10.30am; Friday Compline 7.00pm

Open Wednesday 10.30am-4.00pm, May to September; at other times by arrangement with Mr Southwick 01847 821295. 1-3 September 2006 centenary celebrations

SCOTTISH EPISCOPAL ♿ ⟲ 👤 📖 **C**

ST PETER & THE HOLY ROOD, THURSO

TOMATIN CHURCH, INVERNESS-SHIRE

659 TOMATIN CHURCH, INVERNESS-SHIRE

NH 803 290
On east side of old A9 in village of Tomatin
Church website: www.strathsnairnanddearn.co.uk
A fine example of the 'tin churches' erected *c*.1910 by the United Free Church to
serve as mission churches and halls in areas of new population.
Services: April to October, 2nd and 5th Sundays 10.30am; November to March,
2nd and 4th Sundays 10.30am
Open by arrangement, telephone 01463 772242 or Mrs Vivian Roden 01808 511355
CHURCH OF SCOTLAND 🛡 (by arrangement)

660 ST ANDREW'S PARISH CHURCH, TONGUE, SUTHERLAND

NC 591 570
On A838 Durness road, past Tongue Hotel
Rebuilt by Donald Mackay, Master of
Reay, in 1680 following the Reay
family's conversion to Protestantism
(*c*.1600). The site was that of the
ancient Celtic and latterly Roman
Catholic Church (St Peter's Chapel).
During a renovation in 1729 a vault
was built covering the graves of
earlier members of the MacKay
family. Information leaflets are
available free in the church.
Sunday Service: 11.00am
Open all year, daylight hours
CHURCH OF SCOTLAND 👂 📖 **A**

ST ANDREW'S PARISH CHURCH, TONGUE, SUTHERLAND

661 CORRY CHURCH, TORRIDON, ROSS-SHIRE

NG 864 572

The architect for Corry Church was Alexander Ross. The church was built in 1887, originally as a Free Church. Situated near the head of Loch Torridon, it is constructed with the local red sandstone inside and out. Splendid views all around of the majestic Torridon mountains. Sunday Service: May to September 12.15pm

Open May to September; at other times, contact keyholder 01445 791323

CHURCH OF SCOTLAND

662 ST JOHN THE EVANGELIST, WICK, CAITHNESS

ND 363 505

Francis Street / Moray Street

Built 1870 to a design Alexander Ross of Inverness, St John's is especially attractive with a warm friendly atmosphere. Four-light windows known affectionately as the 'I am' windows ('I am the Good Shepherd, ... the Resurrection and the Life, ... the True Vine, ... the Bread of Life'), by David Gulland, a former member of the vestry of St John's and a recognised expert in glass. Sunday Service: Sung Eucharist 11.30am

Open by arrangement with Peter MacDougall, telephone 01955 602914

SCOTTISH EPISCOPAL

ST JOHN THE EVANGELIST, WICK, CAITHNESS

663   NESS BANK CHURCH, INVERNESS

NH 664 444

Ness Bank/Haugh Road

The church, which seats 700, was built in 1901 on a steeply sloping site with the church hall and other accommodation under the church. Designed by William Mackintosh in early Gothic revival style in red sandstone with freestone dressings. Stained glass by Gordon Webster, St Enoch Studios, Isobel Goudie and William Wilson. Organ James F Binns 1903, altered by Rushworth & Dreaper 1980.

Sunday Service: 11.00am, 10.00am July and August

Open by arrangement, telephone 01463 243165

CHURCH OF SCOTLAND ♿ wc ⊘ c

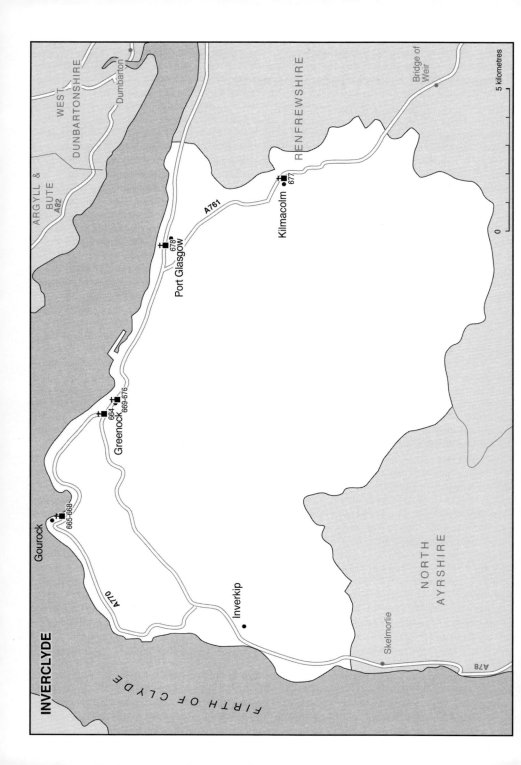

INVERCLYDE

664 ARDGOWAN PARISH CHURCH, GREENOCK

NS 271 768

31 Union Street, Greenock

Built as Trinity United Presbyterian Church, 1871, and designed by John Starforth in Gothic style. Became St Andrews in 1967 when united with St Andrews, and became Ardgowan in 1992 when united with Union Church. Refurbished 2002 after the ceiling collapsed. Sunday Service: 11.00am

Open by arrangement with the Minister, telephone 01475 790849

CHURCH OF SCOTLAND ♿ 🚾 ⟲ **B**

665 ST BARTHOLOMEW'S, GOUROCK

NS 239 777

Barrhill Road, Gourock

This beautiful little church sits on a cliff overlooking the River Clyde. Designed by J C Sharp of Gourock 1867. Chancel extension enhanced by a beautiful window depicting the Ascension designed by George Walton. Mural of the Nativity on the west wall. Memorial lectern and font. Plaque of Dutch tiles in remembrance of the hospitality given to Dutch soldiers, sailors and airmen during the Second World War. Sunday Service: Sung Eucharist 10.30am; Wednesday and Saints' Days Holy Eucharist 10.30am

Open by arrangement, telephone Mrs Boeker 01475 521411

SCOTTISH EPISCOPAL 🚾 ⟲ 📖 **B**

ST BARTHOLOMEW'S, GOUROCK

666 ST JOHN'S, GOUROCK

NS 246 778

Bath Street

Church website: www.gourockweb.com/st_johns/

Gothic style church built 1857 (J J and W H Hay) and tower with open-work
crown added 1878 (Bruce and Sturrock). Interior whitewashed with tall arch-
braced timber roof. The sanctuary underwent major renovations in 1998 when
wooden flooring was laid and the pews replaced by chairs to give greater
flexibility. Makin Organ. Number of stained glass windows. Lively and quiet
worship when we can come together to praise and glorify God. The church is used
daily by many organisations. Sunday Service: 11.00am and 6.30pm

Open by arrangement, telephone 01475 630879

CHURCH OF SCOTLAND & ⊘ ⊑ ⚲ (Sunday Surfers and crèche) ⛨ **C**

667 ST NINIAN'S CHURCH, GOUROCK

NS 242 777

18 Royal Street, Gourock

Church website: www.st-ninians-gourock.org

Gourock formed part of the pre-Reformation parish of Inverkip, mentioned in
Papal registers of 1216-27. In 1878 Archbishop Eyre of Glasgow arranged for the
construction of a chapel-school to be dedicated to St Ninian. The foundation stone
was laid in 1879. Extended 1982 for the visit to Scotland of Pope John Paul II, the
altar contains marble from the papal altar at Bellahouston. Mosaics by Frank
Tritschler, stained glass by Dom Ninian Sloan of Pluscarden Abbey, and a chasuble
fashioned from an original Paisley shawl by Debbie Gonet. Small museum. Sunday
Mass: 9.30am and 11.30am; daily 10.00am and Vigil Mass Saturday 5.30pm

Open daily 9.00am-6.00pm. Information leaflets in French, Spanish, Italian and German –
children's worksheets also available. For access to museum, telephone Parish Priest
01475 632078 or fax 01475 631984

ROMAN CATHOLIC & wc ⊘ ⛨ ⚲

ST NINIAN'S CHURCH, GOUROCK

668 OLD GOUROCK AND ASHTON PARISH CHURCH

NS 243 775

Royal Street (up Church street from Shore Street)

Congregation is the union of Old Gourock Parish and Ashton Parish Church in 1989 in the building of the former, opened 1832 and enlarged 1872 and 1900. Dominant square crenallated tower on entrance façade. Pulpit and choir stall with panels by C R Mackintosh 1900. Centenary screen behind the pulpit lists the names of ministers. Twelve stained glass windows, four by Gordon Webster. Sculpture by George Wyllie. Allen computer organ, 1991.

Sunday Service: 9.30am and 11.00am; July and first two Sundays in August: 10.00am only

Open by arrangement with Minister 01475 631516

CHURCH OF SCOTLAND 🦽 ᵂᶜ ② 𝄐 📖 **B**

669 ST PATRICK'S, GREENOCK

NS 271 761

5 Orangefield Place

Unique and striking example of the work of G Antonio Coia 1935. The soaring gable characterises a church of great strength. A framework of steel is encased in reinforced concrete and enveloped in red Lancashire brick with a backing of Scots clay cement bricks. Exquisite stone sculpture by Archibald Dawson, including bas relief of St Patrick blessing a child, rising from between the two doors.

Services: Saturday Vigil 7.00pm; Sunday Masses 8.00, 10.00, 11.30am and 7.00pm

Open daily 8.00am-7.30pm

ROMAN CATHOLIC 🦽 ② **A**

670 FINNART ST PAUL'S, GREENOCK

NS 265 774

Newark Street

Church website: www.finnart-stpauls-church.org

Finely detailed late-Gothic church designed by Sir Robert Rowand Anderson and opened for public worship in 1893. Stained glass by Burne-Jones, Douglas Strachan and William Wilson. Three-manual and pedal pipe organ by Father Willis 1894.

Sunday Service: 11.00am

Open by arrangement with Minister 01475 639602 or Session Clerk 01475 722232

CHURCH OF SCOTLAND 🦽 ᵂᶜ ② 𝄐 (by arrangement) ☕ (by arrangement) **A**

671 THE OLD WEST KIRK, GREENOCK

NS 279 765

Esplanade, Greenock
Church website:
www.greenockoldwestkirk.freeserve.co.uk
Cruciform church first built 1591 at Westburn,
but rebuilt here 1926-8 with a new tower
designed by James Miller. The masonry, window
tracery and balustraded forestair are all original.
Also brought from the old site are the
surrounding headstones and graveslabs, some
bearing trade emblems or coats of arms. Inside
the church are galleries originally intended to
be occupied by the laird, the sailors and the

THE OLD WEST KIRK, GREENOCK

farmers of the parish. Notable collection of stained glass including windows by
Morris, Marshall & Faulkner and Daniel Cottier. Behind the octagonal pulpit is a
mural panel by the local artist Ian Philips 1991. Sunday Service: 11.00am
Open Wednesdays mid-May to mid-September from 10.30am-12.00 noon; 2nd Saturday,
September 10.00am-4.00pm (Inverclyde Doors Open Day).
Open by arrangement, telephone Rev Ian Johnson, telephone 01475 888277
CHURCH OF SCOTLAND   ♿ wc ⊘ 📖 ☕ **B**

672 ST JOHN'S EPISCOPAL, GREENOCK

NS 274 766

Union Street (opposite Watt Library), Greenock
The present building was consecrated in 1878,
designed by Paley and Austin of Lancaster –
their only Scottish church. The intricately carved
rood screen, based on a medieval screen in
Gloucestershire and designed by H O Tarbolton,
was given by the family of Sir John Kerr, one-
time Governor of Bengal. The font is a copy of
a 15th-century font in Suffolk. Organ by Mirrlees
of Glasgow. Services: Sunday Eucharist 9.00am,
Sung Eucharist 11.00am (1st Sunday Matins
and Eucharist), Evensong 6.30pm (2nd and
last Sundays)
Open by arrangement with Ian Milne,
telephone 01475 796331
SCOTTISH EPISCOPAL wc ⊘ **B**

ST JOHN'S EPISCOPAL, GREENOCK

673 HOLY ROSARY CHAPEL, GREENOCK

NS 274 765

44 Union Street, Greenock

Church website: www.littlesistersgreenock.org

The Chapel lies at the heart of each of the Homes of the Little Sisters of the Poor; a place of sanctuary and tranquility for the Sisters, residents and visitors. The residence opened in August 2004, replacing the original residence dating from 1884, offering care for those in need regardless of creed. Stained glass by Susan Bradbury on the theme of the Holy Rosary and on Baptism and the Water of Life. Mass 8.30am and 10.00am daily

Open by arrangement with Mother Superior, telephone 01475 722465

ROMAN CATHOLIC [♿] [wc] [☉]

674 ST LUKE'S, GREENOCK

NS 273 763

Nelson Street, Greenock

Designed by David Cousin and built in 1840, with the spire being added in 1855. The clock 1856 was the gift of Miss Frances Ann Wood. The interior was completely gutted by fire in 1912 and replaced by a new chancel, designed by John Keppie, with four stained glass windows, a new organ and seating for 1144. Services: Sunday 11.00am; Wednesday Advent and Lenten lunches and service 12.00 noon

Open by arrangement, telephone Mr Mitchell 01475 726916 or Mr Robertson 01475 725451

CHURCH OF SCOTLAND [♿] [wc] [☉] [☕] (after morning service) [🕯] [📖] **A**

675 ST MARY'S, GREENOCK

NS 274 768

14 Patrick Street, Greenock

Church website: www.stmarysgreenock.org

Designed in Early French Gothic style by George Goldie and opened in 1862. The tower was left incomplete. Major alterations 1914, including a new Lady Chapel. The sanctuary was remodelled in 1960s and 1970s. Complete renovation in 2003 included new altar, main entrance porch and side door. Stained glass windows depicting Our Lady and various saints by Wailes of Newcastle. 'Lourdes' window by Patrick Feeny installed 1965. Services: daily 10.00am; Saturday Vigil 6.30pm; Sunday 10.00am and 12.00 noon

Open daily 9.00am-2.00pm; Sunday 9.00am-4.00pm

ROMAN CATHOLIC [♿] [wc] [☉] [☕] [📖] **B**

676 GREENOCK METHODIST CHURCH

NS 274 765

Ardgowan Street, Greenock

The roots of this church go back to two visits by John Wesley in 1772 and 1774.
The first Wesleyan Methodist Chapel was built in 1814 and replaced with the
present building 1883. Simple church with Gothic details.

Sunday Service: 11.00am

Open Wednesdays 10.00am-12.00 noon

METHODIST   ♿ wc ✆ ⚲ ☕

677 KILMACOLM OLD KIRK

NS 359 670

Near centre of Kilmalcolm village, west of junction of B786 with A761

Built in 1830 James Dempster, Greenock, on the site of 13th- and 16th-century
churches. Thirteenth-century chancel is incorporated as the Murray Chapel. South
aisle, J B Wilson, Glasgow, added 1903. Early 20th-century stained glass windows
by C E Moira, Norman Macdougall and Horace Wilkinson. Modern examples by
John K Clark and Lorraine Lamond.

Sunday Service: 11.00am, July and August 10.00am

Open daily 10.00am-4.00pm

CHURCH OF SCOTLAND ♿ wc ✆ 📖 **B**

KILMACOLM OLD KIRK

678 ST JOHN THE BAPTIST, PORT GLASGOW

NS 319 746
Shore Street, Port Glasgow
Church website: www.johnthebaptist.portglasgow@btinternet.com
Built 1854 with pinnacles rising from the buttressed gable front. Refurbished 2000.
Stained glass including 'The Risen Christ' above the main door by Edward
Harkness. Fresco of St Thérèse by George Duffy above Sacristy door. Services:
Sunday 9.30 and 11.00 am; Monday Mass 9.30 am; Tuesday Mass 6.30 pm;
Wednesday to Friday Mass 9.30am; Saturday Mass 10.00am, Vigil Mass 6.00pm
Open by arrangement with the Housekeeper, telephone 01475 741139
ROMAN CATHOLIC   ♿   🚾   ✍

ST JOHN THE BAPTIST, PORT GLASGOW

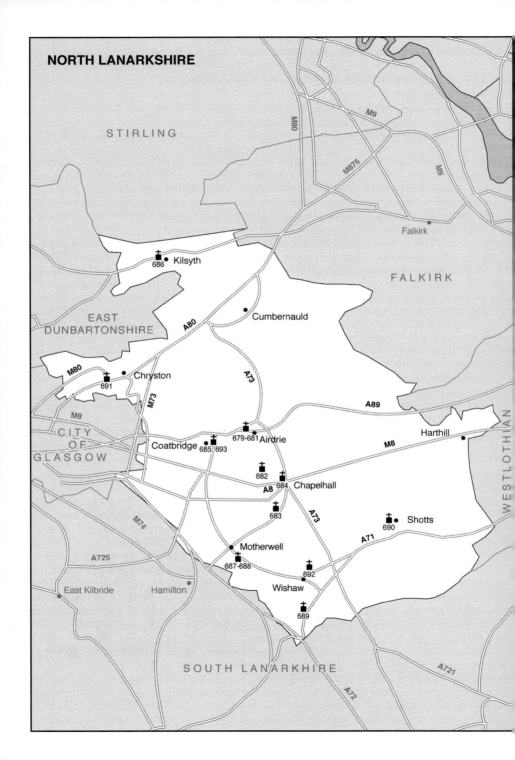

NORTH LANARKSHIRE

Local Representative: Mrs Mary Canavan, Flat 10, 9 Victoria Circus, Glasgow
G12 9LB (*telephone* 0141 334 5462)

679 NEW MONKLAND PARISH CHURCH, AIRDRIE

NS 753 678
Condorrat Road, Glenmavis, Airdrie
A fine old Scots plain kirk which hides an attractive
interior, by Andrew Bell of Airdrie 1776. It holds a
commanding position at the highest point in the
village, and incorporates the bell-tower of an earlier
church (1698) which housed a cell for minor offenders.
The old church was replaced when it 'suffered so badly
from overcrowding that youthful members of the
congregation colonised the exposed joists to roost!'
The apse was added in 1904 by John Arthur.
Extensive restoration 1997. Simple watchhouse
by the cemetery. Sunday Service: 10.30am
Open by arrangement, telephone
Mr John Blades 01236 766511
CHURCH OF SCOTLAND [wc] (?) **B**

NEW MONKLAND PARISH
CHURCH, AIRDRIE

680 FLOWERHILL PARISH CHURCH, AIRDRIE

NS 765 655
Hallcraig Street, Airdrie
Opened in 1875, the architect was
Matthew Forsyth of Airdrie, who
designed the church, campanile, Manse
and hall in Italianate style. Major
refurbishment 2002/03. Six stained
glass windows by Stephen Adam,
James Ballantine, J T Stewart and
J S Melville. Pipe organ 1886, by
Harrison & Harrison.
Sunday Services: 11.00am and 6.00pm
Open by arrangement with the
Minister, telephone 01236 763025
CHURCH OF SCOTLAND [♿] [wc] (?) 🍴 **B**

FLOWERHILL PARISH CHURCH, AIRDRIE

681 ST MARGARET'S, AIRDRIE

NS 765 656

96 Hillcraig Street, Airdrie

Parish founded in 1836, this simple
neo-classical church by Wilkie &
Gray, 1839, has a square tower and
spire rising above the pedimented
front. Before it was built, adherents
had to travel to Glasgow for
services, many on foot. Services:
weekdays 10.00am; Saturday Vigil
5.00pm; Sunday 10.00am, 12.00
noon and 4.00pm

Open during summer 9.00am-6.00pm,
winter 9.00am-4.00pm, or by
arrangement with Parish Priest,
telephone 01236 763370

ROMAN CATHOLIC

ST MARGARET'S, AIRDRIE

682 CORPUS CHRISTI, CALDERBANK

NS 768 630

In the middle of Calderbank village

The parish was founded in 1948 and the church was opened in 1952. It has
undergone several renovations inside to accommodate liturgical changes. Stained
glass window of the Sacraments 1985, designed by Shona McInnis. New church
furnishings by J McNally, made by a local craftsman. Sunday Services: 9.00am,
11.00am; weekdays 10.00am; Saturday 8.45am and Vigil 6.00pm

Open 8.00am-8.00pm (if main door closed, use right-hand side door)

ROMAN CATHOLIC

CORPUS CHRISTI, CALDERBANK

683 ST FRANCIS XAVIER CHURCH, CARFIN

NS 776 588

Carfin Grotto is signposted from A723
Church website: www.carfin.org.uk/church.htm
The Parish was founded 1862; the present
buildings (church and hall) 1973. The
church grounds contain the Carfin Lourdes
grotto, founded in 1920s which is open
throughout the year with public services
from May to mid-October on Sundays at
3.00pm. Glass chapel in memory of
Lockerbie tragedy dedicated to Our Lady,
Maid of the Seas is open 10.00am-8.00pm
in Pilgrimage season. Services: Saturday
Vigil 6.00pm, Sunday 10.00am, 12.00 noon;
weekdays 10.00am
Open in summer 9.00am-8.00pm, winter 9.00am-4.00pm
ROMAN CATHOLIC   🦽 📶 ⊘ 💻 (in Pilgrimage Centre)

ST FRANCIS XAVIER
CHURCH, CARFIN

684 ST ALOYSIUS, CHAPELHALL

NS 7829 6257

Main Street, Chapelhall
Opened in 1894, built to a design by Pugin and Pugin. Sanctuary completely
renewed 1941-52. Marble reredos with gold mosaic panels depicting scenes from
the life of St Aloysius. Stained glass
installed in rose window 1984, by
Shonna McInnes of Orkney who also
designed the remaining four windows
in the Sanctuary, installed in 1994 to
celebrate the church centenary.
Beautiful gardens behind the church
with excellent presbytery house
designed by McInally.
Services: Saturday Vigil 6.30pm;
Sunday 10.00am, 12.00 noon
and 5.30pm
Open daily 9.00am-7.30pm
ROMAN CATHOLIC   🦽 📶 ⊘ 📖

ST ALOYSIUS, CHAPELHALL

685 ST PATRICK, COATBRIDGE

NS 733 651
Main Street, Coatbridge
Church website:
www.stpatricks-online.com
Built for the many Irish labourers
fleeing the potato famine, and
dispossessed Highlanders. Designed
by Pugin and Pugin 1896, in elegant
Gothic with a finely composed gable
frontage. Services: weekdays
10.00am; Saturday Vigil 6.00pm;
Sunday 10.00am, 12.00 noon and
6.00pm; holidays 10.00am, 1.00pm,
5.30pm (Vigil) and 7.30pm
Open 10.00am-4.30pm
ROMAN CATHOLIC
🦽 wc ② 🕯 📖 ☕ **B**

ST PATRICK, COATBRIDGE

686 ST PATRICK'S, KILSYTH

NS 720 777
30 Low Craigends, Kilsyth
Large-scale one-box brick structure surmounted by a clerestory and unusual roof
by Gillespie, Kidd & Coia 1965. One of only four Gillespie, Kidd & Coia churches
with all its original features intact. Fully restored 2000. Services: Saturday Vigil
6.30pm; Sunday 9.30am and 12.00 noon; weekdays 10.00am
Open by arrangement with the Parish Priest, telephone 01236 822136
ROMAN CATHOLIC 🦽 wc ② **A**

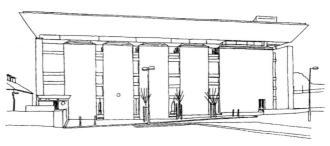

ST PATRICK'S, KILSYTH

687 DALZIEL ST ANDREW'S, MOTHERWELL

NS 752 571

Motherwell Cross

Union of the former Dalziel and St Andrew's
Church of Scotland congregations in 1996. The
parish of Dalziel has a history stretching back to
the 12th century, while St Andrew's was a
daughter church of Dalziel. Erected in 1874, the
building houses an organ by the German firm of
Walcker dated 1900, recently restored. Worship is
a sensitive mixture of traditional and modern with
a warm welcome for all ages. Sunday Services:
11.00am in the Main Sanctuary; evening worship
6.30pm (except July and August)

Open Saturday 10.00am-12.00 noon, or by arrangement
with the Church Officer, telephone 01698 266 284

CHURCH OF SCOTLAND   🦽 📶 ⊘ 🚹 📖 ☕

DALZIEL ST ANDREW'S, MOTHERWELL

688 ST LUKE'S, MOTHERWELL

NS 746 599

Davaar Drive, Motherwell

A recently renovated church whose intimate setting serves well the Liturgy of the
Second Vatican Council. Services: Saturday 9.30am, 5.15pm; Sunday 10.30am,
5.15pm; weekdays 9.30am

Open by arrangement with Chapel House, telephone 01698 230402

ROMAN CATHOLIC   🦽 📶 ⊘

689 OVERTOWN PARISH CHURCH

NS 801 527

Main Street, Overtown, by Wishaw

Church website: www.overtownparishchurch.org.uk

Village church built in 1876. Near picturesque
Clyde Valley, Strathclyde Country Park and
many other places of interest. A71, Edinburgh
to Kilmarnock (35 miles from Edinburgh), just
off M74 (20 miles from Glasgow)

Open early May for sale of plants, with guided tours
and café, 3rd Saturday in September –
Church Open Day, guided tours and café

CHURCH OF SCOTLAND   📶 ⊘ 🚹 ☕

OVERTOWN PARISH CHURCH

690   ST PATRICK, SHOTTS

NS 876 599

84 Station Road, Shotts
Church website: www.saintpatrick.org.uk
The church, designed by P P Pugin,
is a classic example of his work.
White Carrara marble altars and
reredos added 1930s. Stained glass
depicts Crucifixion and scenes of
the local pits and iron works, as well
as St Barbara (patron saint of
miners), St Joseph, St Cecilia, St
John Ogilvie and the Baptism of
The Lord. Stations of the Cross are
from Germany. The church has been
adapted to changing liturgical
practice while retaining its original

ST PATRICK, SHOTTS

character and quality. Services: Saturday 9.30am, 6.30pm Vigil; Sunday 10.45am
Sung Mass with Choir 6.00pm; Monday to Friday 10.00am
Open Monday to Thursday 9.00am-1.00pm, Friday 9.00am-6.00pm
ROMAN CATHOLIC ♿ wc ⊘

691   STEPPS PARISH CHURCH

NS 657 686

17 Whitehill Avenue, Stepps
Fine example of the neo-Gothic style favoured by ecclesiastical architect
P MacGregor Chalmers 1900. Designed to reflect scale and simplicity of a village
church. Interesting stained glass including works by Stephen Adam 1900. Pipe
organ, Joseph Brook 1884, rebuilt James MacKenzie 1976. On rail and bus routes
Glasgow–Cumbernauld. Sunday Service: 10.00am mid June to mid August,
11.00am mid August to mid June
Open Tuesday, Thursday 10.00am-12.00 noon all year. Other times, telephone 0141 779 9556
CHURCH OF SCOTLAND ♿ wc ⊘ 🗋

692 ST IGNATIUS OF LOYOLA, WISHAW

NS 799 551
74 Young Street
Church website:
www.saintignatiuswishaw.org.uk
Designed by George Goldie and
opened in 1865, enlarged by Bruce
& Hay 1883. Built in Basilica form
with two aisles and a bell tower
which is the most prominent
landmark in Wishaw. The tower
houses a bell (tone E) which is rung
every day at 12.00 noon and 6.00pm
for the Angelus prayer and also 30
minutes before the main Sunday
services and during weekday
services. Stained glass windows
based on paintings by Jessie

ST IGNATIUS OF LOYOLA, WISHAW

McGeechan of Coatbridge. Services: Sunday 10.15am, 12.00 noon, 6.00pm;
Saturday Vigil 5.30pm; Monday-Friday 9.30am; Saturday 10.00am
Open Sunday 9.30am-1.30pm and 5.30-7.30pm, Monday-Friday 8.30am-1.30pm
(Thursday 4.30pm), Saturday 9.00am-12.00 noon and 5.00-7.00pm
ROMAN CATHOLIC   ♿   WC   ⊘   **A**

693 ST ANDREW'S PARISH CHURCH, COATBRIDGE

NS 733 653
Church Street
Church website: www.saintandrewscoatbridge.org
This red sandstone Gothic revival church with steeple and clock tower, architects
Scott Stephen & Gale of Glasgow, was opened in 1839 as Gartsherrie Parish
Church for the benefit of the workers employed by Wm Baird & Co, Ironmasters,
and their families. It occupies a commanding site with a large graveyard just a short
walk uphill from the town centre. In 1993 it became St Andrew's following a union
with nearby Dunbeth and Maxwell Churches. Very fine organ by Willis 1870,
thoroughly renovated in 1937 with some additional stops. Stained glass by Alfred
Webster 1912 in the entrance vestibule. Sunday Service: 11.00am
Open by arrangement, telephone 01236 424553
CHURCH OF SCOTLAND   ♿   WC   ⊘   **B**

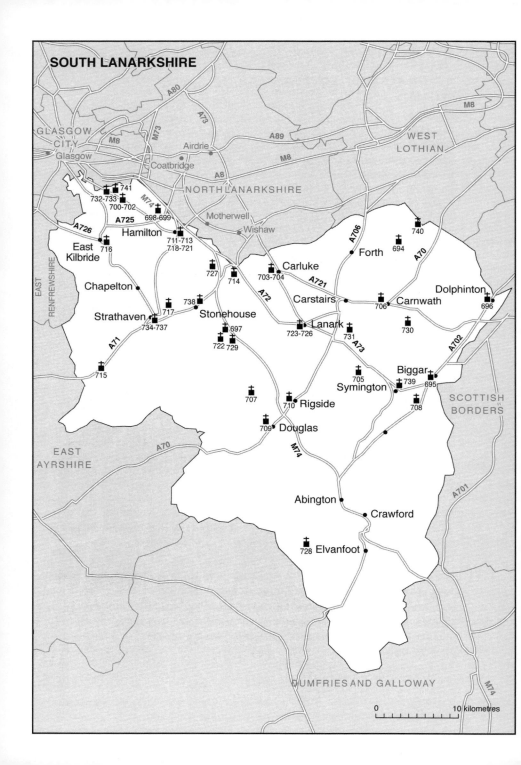

SOUTH LANARKSHIRE

Local Representative: Mr Sandy Gilchrist, 11 Mercat Loan, Biggar
(*telephone* 01899 221350)

694 AUCHENGRAY CHURCH

NS 995 540
Auchengray, 3 miles west of A70
The front of this church of 1863 by F T Pilkington with characteristic stone
carving and a fine rose window is described as an architectural gem. The building
and grounds are undergoing a programme of restoration and upgrading to ensure
an ongoing welcome at the heart of the community.
Sunday Service: 6.30pm September-June, usually on the 1st Sunday of the
month, no services July and August
Open by arrangement, 01501 785267 or 01501 785351. Craft and flower show in September
CHURCH OF SCOTLAND ♿ 🚻 **B**

695 BIGGAR KIRK

NT 040 379
Kirkstyle, Biggar
Rebuilt 1546, the last collegiate church to be founded before the Reformation in
Scotland. A cruciform building with fine stained glass, including work by William
Wilson and Crear McCartney. In the kirkyard are memorials to the forebears of
William Ewart Gladstone and also Thomas Blackwood Murray, the Scottish motor
pioneer of 'Albion'. Sunday Services: 11.00am; also 9.30am June, July and August
Open daily June, July and August 10.00am-4.00pm.
Rest of the year key from Gilespie Centre (across the street)
CHURCH OF SCOTLAND 👂 **B**

BIGGAR KIRK

696 BLACK MOUNT PARISH CHURCH

NT 101 464

Just off A702 at Dolphinton
(turning signposted to Dunsyre)

Originally a parsonage in the 13th century, it
appears to have always occupied the same site,
undergoing a complete rebuild in 1789, with
late 19th-century additions. A typical T-plan
church, built so the preacher has the light
behind him and the congregation can hear him.
The bell dates from *c.*1800. Sunday Service:
9.30am, 10.45am and 12.00 noon on a quarterly
rotation with Culter and Libberton

Open by arrangement, telephone Mrs E Dickson 01968 682265
CHURCH OF SCOTLAND   🔊 wc

BLACK MOUNT
PARISH CHURCH

697 OUR LADY AND ST JOHN, BLACKWOOD

NS 790 439

Carlisle Road, Blackwood, Kirkmuirhill

Stone building in Gothic style, opened 1880.
The grounds for the church were donated by
the Hope-Vere family. Sanctuary extended in
1881 to accommodate the altar donated by
Mrs Lancaster. Stained glass windows were
also added at this time. The first two parish
priests were Benedictines from Ampleforth.
Services: Saturday 6.00pm; Sunday 10.00am
and 6.00pm

Open by arrangement, telephone 01555 893459
ROMAN CATHOLIC ⑦

OUR LADY AND ST JOHN, BLACKWOOD

698 BOTHWELL PARISH CHURCH

NS 705 586

Main Street, Bothwell (off A725)

Scotland's oldest collegiate church still in use for worship, dedicated to St Bride,
occupies the site of a former 6th-century church. Medieval choir. Nave and tower
1833, David Hamilton, altered 1933. Monuments to the Earls of Douglas and the
Duke of Hamilton. Stained glass by Gordon Webster, Douglas Strachan and Sir
Edward Burne-Jones. Fascinating tales of an outstanding royal wedding and link
with Bothwell Castle. Graveyard. Sunday Service: 10.30am

Open daily Easter to September. Bus parties welcome by arrangement, telephone 01698 853189
CHURCH OF SCOTLAND 🔊 wc ⑦ 🍴 📖 ☕A

699 ST BRIDE'S, BOTHWELL

NS 706 550

Fallside Road, Bothwell

This impressive and striking building was
opened in 1973. The concrete block walls
are rendered externally to harmonise with
the surrounding buildings. The red knotty
pine ceiling and quarry tile floor bring
warmth to the interior and coloured blocks
of glass have been used to contrast with
the white walls. Superb pipe organ,
striking modern statue of Mary, and a

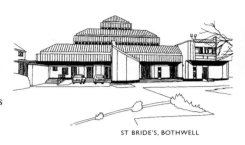

ST BRIDE'S, BOTHWELL

modern sculpture of the Last Supper. Convent of Poor Clares next door to church
can also be visited. Masses: Monday-Friday 9.30am; Saturday Vigil 5.30pm; Sunday
10.00am, 12.00 noon and 6.00pm; Advent and Lent Prayer Service at 5.15pm

Open Tuesday and Wednesday 10.00am-8.00pm or by arrangement with the Housekeeper,
Parish House, Fallside Road

ROMAN CATHOLIC & ? ▭ 📖 **B**

700 CAMBUSLANG OLD PARISH CHURCH

NS 646 600

3 Cairns Road, Kirkhill, Cambuslang (near Greenlees
Road, B759)

Church website: www.cambuslang-old-parish-church.com

St Cadoc is believed to have had a holy site here
AD *c.*550, and early buildings have been recorded
from the 12th century. The present building is by
David Cousin 1841. Steeple with clock and bell.
The chancel is by P MacGregor Chalmers 1922.
Stained glass and tapestries by Sadie McLellan
1957. Millennium wall-hanging in vestibule 2001.
Heraldic shields of heritors decorate the ceiling.
Interesting gravestones in churchyard including
one to Rev William McCulloch, Minister at
Scotland's largest ever revival 'The Cambuslang
Wark' in 1742. Sunday Services: September to
June 11.00am and 6.30pm, July and
August 9.30am and 11.00am

Open by arrangement, telephone
Mrs F McQueen 0141 641 4845

CHURCH OF SCOTLAND & wc ? **B**

CAMBUSLANG OLD PARISH CHURCH

701 ST BRIDE'S, CAMBUSLANG

NS 643 604

21 Greenlees Road, Cambuslang
(opposite police station)
The church, which opened in 1900, has a
Crucifixion window, an example of the early
work of stained glass artist Gordon M Webster,
and another free-standing window also by
Webster. Services: Saturday Vigil 5.30pm;
Sunday 10.00am, 12.00 noon and 6.00pm
Open 7.00am-8.00pm every day
ROMAN CATHOLIC ♿ wc ⊘

ST BRIDE'S, CAMBUSLANG

702 ST CUTHBERT'S, CAMBUSLANG

NS 643 604

3 Brownside Road, Cambuslang
Towards the end of the 19th century Cambuslang became an increasingly
residential area and the need arose for an Episcopal church. In 1899, Bishop W T
Harrison opened a hall on Bushley Hill for worship dedicated to St Cuthbert.
Subsequently, the Duke of Hamilton offered land and the present church was
dedicated in 1909, the architect being W D Walton of Glasgow. Services: Sunday
9.30am (Sung Eucharist), Wednesday 10.00am (Said Eucharist)
Open every morning during term-time, otherwise key in Rectory next door
SCOTTISH EPISCOPAL wc

703 ST ANDREW'S PARISH CHURCH, CARLUKE

NS 843 508

Mount Stewart Street, Carluke
The original church was replaced by the present building
in 1799 following designs by Henry Bell (of the
steamship 'Comet' fame). The tower of the old church
has been retained as a monument in its original site in
the old graveyard at the bottom of the town. Within the
church are an organ made by H Willis and Sons and
installed in 1903, stained glass windows including one
made by Gordon McWhirter Webster 1932 and a pulpit
fall and companion communion table runner by
Marilyn E W McGregor DA 1999. Memorial garden
'Garden of Hope' 2001. Sunday Service: 11.00am
Open by arrangement, telephone
Mrs Jennifer Johnstone 01555 750155
CHURCH OF SCOTLAND ♿ wc ⊘ 📖 **B**

ST ANDREW'S PARISH
CHURCH, CARLUKE

704 ST ATHANASIUS, CARLUKE

NS 844 508

21 Mount Stewart Street, Carluke

The present church was erected in 1857, but a
larger building was required by the 1980s when
the building was extended as far as the grounds
allowed. The marriage of old and new buildings
in 1984 has given a modern and attractive church
while still retaining much of the original
character. The architects were Cullen, Lochhead
and Brown. Services: Saturday Vigil 6.00pm;
Sunday 9.00am and 11.15am; weekdays 10.00am
Open 9.00am-4.00pm daily
ROMAN CATHOLIC 🦽 wc ✏

ST ATHANASIUS, CARLUKE

705 CAIRNGRYFFE KIRK

NS 923 384

Carmichael Crossroads, Carmichael

Known as 'The Little Cathedral of the Upper
Ward', due to the quality of the decoration,
this church was built 1750 and extensively
remodelled 1904 by Sir Robert Lorimer. The
staircase to the gallery and several headstones
were brought from the site of the 12th-century
church a mile away. Magnificent stained glass
window 1904. Other glass by Crear McCartney.
Many memorials to the Carmichael family and

CAIRNGRYFFE KIRK

clan. Sunday Service: 9.30 or 11.00am as indicated on notice board
Open Sundays before Christmas and Easter, 2.00-4.00pm with floral displays,
otherwise by arrangement, telephone the Minister 01899 308838
CHURCH OF SCOTLAND 🦽 wc ✏ ☕ 📖 **B**

706 CARNWATH PARISH CHURCH (ST MARY'S)

NS 976 465

At west end of Carnwath Village on A70

St Mary's is the third building to have been constructed on the site. The architect was
David Bryce and it was built 1864-7. The seating capacity is over 1,000. The roof is
modelled on that of Parliament Hall in Edinburgh and the pulpit is a long wall
pulpit. Sunday Service: 12.00 noon September to June; 11.00am July and August
Open by arrangement with Minister, telephone 01555 840259.
Please note, key for St Mary's Aisle (beside the church) available from the Estate Office adjacent
CHURCH OF SCOTLAND 🦽 wc **B** (St Mary's aisle **A**)

707 COALBURN PARISH CHURCH

NS 813 345

25/1 Bellfield Road

Built as a Mission Station in 1893, becoming a fully
sanctioned charge 1895. Totally destroyed by fire
1918 and rebuilt 1922. Linked with Lesmahagow
1998. Church renovated and reordered 2001 to
become all-purpose. Six Ministers have served
during the 110 years. Sunday Service: 12.00 noon
Open by arrangement, telephone Miss Lundie
01555 820730 or Mrs Nicol 01555 820647
CHURCH OF SCOTLAND ♿ wc ☕ (by arrangement)

COALBURN PARISH CHURCH

708 CULTER PARISH CHURCH, COULTER

NT 027 342

200 yards off Birthwood Road, Coulter

Appropriated by Kelso Abbey in 1170, the church is
dedicated to St Michael. Rebuilt about 1810, being
made shorter and wider. The interior was recast
1910, two of the galleries being removed, leaving
only the west one. Refurnished 1938. Ornamental
gates. Chancel burial ground for Culter Allers and
Culter Mains. Bertram (of Nisbet) burial aisle next
to vestry. Sunday Service: 9.30am, 10.45am and
12.00 noon on a quarterly rotation with Black
Mount and Libberton
Open by arrangement, telephone Mr E Cosh 01899 220221
CHURCH OF SCOTLAND wc ◠ **B**

CULTER PARISH CHURCH, COULTER

709 ST BRIDE'S, DOUGLAS

NS 835 310

In centre of Douglas, on A70

Church website: www.douglasvalleychurch.org

St Bride's was built 1781-2 to replace the nearby medieval building which had
become ruinous (the refurbished chancel and clocktower still stand). The church
was substantially altered in 1868 and 1878. The side drums and pipe banner of the
Cameronian Regiment are kept in the church and the raising of the regiment is
commemorated on the second Sunday of May. Sunday Service: 10.00am, in
summer and on holiday Sundays jointly with Douglas Water & Rigside
Open Tuesday to Thursday 2.00-5.00pm or by arrangement, telephone 01555 851387
CHURCH OF SCOTLAND ♿ wc

710 DOUGLAS WATER & RIGSIDE CHURCH

NS 873 347

Ayr Road, Rigside. Follow signs to golf course
Church website: www.douglasvalleychurch.org
The church was built in 1885-6 as Douglas Water Free Church on land gifted by
Lord Home. The sanctuary was refurbished in 1939. The building originally had a
small belfry, now demolished, and the bell now hangs on a frame beside the
church. Sunday Service: 12.00 noon, in summer and on holiday Sundays jointly
with Douglas Water & Rigside
Open by arrangement, telephone 01555 851213
CHURCH OF SCOTLAND ♿ wc

711 CADZOW PARISH CHURCH, HAMILTON

NS 723 550

Woodside Walk, Hamilton
This Gothic style church, designed by R A Bryden,
was opened in 1877 for coal miners and their families.
Halls designed by Cullen, Lochhead and Brown
added in 1925 and 1961. Pipe organ by Forster and
Andrew of Hull installed in 1889. Communion table,
chairs and eagle lectern are by Thomas Wilson of
Glasgow. Stained glass windows by Stephen Adam,
Douglas Hamilton, John Blyth and Sadie McLellan.
There is a Mission Church in Ferniegair Village.
Sunday Services: 9.30am and 10.45am June to August;
10.45am and 6.30pm September to May
Open by arrangement with Session Clerk, telephone 01698 425512
CHURCH OF SCOTLAND wc ⊘ c

CADZOW PARISH CHURCH, HAMILTON

712 ST JOHN'S CHURCH, HAMILTON

NS 724 523

Top Cross, Duke Street, Hamilton (opposite Marks & Spencer)
Church website: www.stjohnshamilton.org.uk
Idiosyncratic classical building (originally a chapel of ease) 1835. The interior was
renovated in 1971 by Cullen, Lochhead & Brown incorporating the former St John's
Grammar School of 1836 and the Centenary Hall of 1934. Refurbished and extended
2000 (Cullen, Lochhead & Brown). Two works in stained glass by Susan Bradbury
feature in the St John's Centre: in the Chapel ('Wings') and in the coffee room ('Giving
and Receiving'). Sunday Services: 10.45am and 6.30pm (summer 10.00am and 9.00pm)
St John's Centre open to the public Monday to Friday 10.00am-12.00 noon and
2.00-4.00pm; Saturday 10.00am-4.00pm
CHURCH OF SCOTLAND ♿ ⊘ ⌷ ⬒ ☕ c

ST JOHN'S CHURCH, HAMILTON

DALSERF PARISH CHURCH

713 ST MARY'S, HAMILTON

NS 720 557

120 Cadzow Street, Hamilton

Built in 1846 in Early English style, this is the second-oldest Catholic Church in Lanarkshire after St Margaret's, Airdrie. St Mary's is a much-loved building with the parishioners. The beautiful stained glass and woodwork provide a tranquil setting for the celebration of the church's liturgy. Services: Sunday 10.00, 11.30am, 6.30pm; weekdays 10.00am

Open weekdays 9.30am-2.00pm

ROMAN CATHOLIC   ⬚ ⬚ **B**

714 DALSERF PARISH CHURCH

NS 800 507

Off A72 between Garrion Bridge and Rosebank

Built 1655, centre transept added 1892. Oblong building with pulpit on long side. Outside stairs to three galleries. Belfry. Two large memorial windows on either side of pulpit by Douglas Hogg. The graveyard contains a pre-Norman hogback stone and an outstanding Covenanting memorial 1753, to Rev John MacMillan, first minister and principal founder of the Reformed Presbyterian Church.

Sunday Service: 12.00 noon

Open by arrangement, telephone the Church Officer, Mr W Knox 01698 883770

CHURCH OF SCOTLAND   ⬚ ⬚ ⬚ ⬚ **A**

715 DRUMCLOG MEMORIAL KIRK

NS 640 389
A71, 5 miles west on Darvel road
Church website: www.avendale-drumclog.com
J McLellan Fairley 1912. The church has
strong associations with the covenanters. Part
of Avendale Old Church. Sunday Service:
9.30am; all-age communion on the 3rd
Sunday of each month, except July and
August. There is also an open-air Conventicle
Service at the Battle of Drumclog Monument
on the 1st Sunday of June. Details of special
services to be found on church website
Open by arrangement, telephone Church office
01354 529748 (9.00am-12.00 noon)
CHURCH OF SCOTLAND

DRUMCLOG MEMORIAL KIRK

716 ST BRIDE, EAST KILBRIDE

NS 641 544
Whitemoss Avenue, East Kilbride
Built 1963-4 by Gillespie, Kidd & Coia to a radical modernist design. The original
150-ft campanile had to be demolished in 1966 due to the deterioration of the
brickwork. This is one of the busiest churches in South Lanarkshire with a congre-
gation of over 8,000. Services: Sunday 9.00am, 10.30am, 12.00 noon, 6.00pm;
Monday-Friday 10.00am and 1.00pm; Saturday 10.00am and 6.00pm
Open by arrangement with Father Ryan, telephone 01355 220005
ROMAN CATHOLIC ♿ WC ? 💬 (afternoon Mass on Sunday and
10.00am Mass Monday-Thursday) **A**

717 GLASFORD PARISH CHURCH, GLASSFORD

NS 726 470
Jackson Street, Glassford
Built 1820. Memorial stained glass windows to
Rev Gavin Lang, grandfather of Cosmo Lang,
Archbishop of Canterbury. Ruins of 1633
church and Covenanter's stone. Linked with
Strathaven East. Sunday Service: 10.00am
Open by arrangement, telephone
Rev W Stewart 01357 521138
CHURCH OF SCOTLAND ♿ WC 📖 **B**

GLASFORD PARISH CHURCH, GLASSFORD

718 HAMILTON OLD PARISH CHURCH

NS 723 555
Strathmore Road, Hamilton
Church website: www.hopc.fsnet.co.uk
The present building is a Georgian
gem. The only church designed
and built by William Adam, 1734.
Samples from the roof timbers
found to be full of lead shot –
Adam used wood from an old
man-of-war! Chancel furnishings
include embroidery by Hannah
Frew Paterson. Exceptionally
detailed engraved glass windows

HAMILTON OLD PARISH CHURCH

by Anita Pate depict the history of the church back to the 6th century. Memorial
stained glass window of African animals to John Stevenson Hamilton, founder of
Kruger National Park. Eleventh-century Netherton Cross and Covenanting
memorials in graveyard. In centre of town. Sunday Service: 10.45am
Open Monday to Friday, 10.30am-3.30pm, or by arrangement, telephone 01698 281905,
Monday to Friday 9.00am-2.00pm. Easter Sunday, church decorated with thousands of
daffodils
CHURCH OF SCOTLAND [wc] ⊘ 🯄 📖 🯄 ☕ (by arrangement on weekdays) **A**

719 HAMILTON WEST PARISH CHURCH

NS 712 558
Peacock Cross, Burnbank Road, Hamilton
The church was originally founded in 1874 as
the 'Burnbank Mission Station' of St John's Free
Church. Having been raised to full status in
1875, the church was rebuilt 1880, architect John
Hutchison whose design exhibits many features
in the 13th-century Gothic style. The interior has
one of the best examples in Scotland of a
wooden hammerbeam roof. The organ by Hill &
Son of London 1902 is still in use today. The
exterior is floodlit, highlighting the stonework
which was restored in 1988. Sunday Service:
10.45am, except July 10.00am
Open by arrangement, telephone
Mr James Murdie 01698 425237
CHURCH OF SCOTLAND [wc] ⊘ **B**

HAMILTON WEST PARISH CHURCH

720 ST MARY THE VIRGIN, HAMILTON

NS 721 567

Auchingramont Road, Hamilton
Church website:
www.stmarysepiscopalhamilton.co.uk
The building designed by John
Henderson was opened for worship
in 1847 and is Early English in style.
Chancel ceiling panels were painted
by Mabel Royds (1874-1941). There
are fine stained glass commemorative
windows with several memorials in

ST MARY THE VIRGIN, HAMILTON

marble and stone reflecting the links with the town's military history. Organ, Foster
& Andrews 1890. Sunday Services: 8.30 and 10.00am, first and third Sunday
6.00pm; Wednesday 10.00am
Open daily during March to September (key at Rectory)
SCOTTISH EPISCOPAL wc) ⓘ **B**

721 HILLHOUSE PARISH CHURCH

NS 696 554

Clarkwell Road, Hamilton
Church website: www.hillhousechurch.co.uk
Established 1955, the church has warmly welcomed many visitors from this country
and abroad during its relatively short history. Sanctuary enhanced by stained glass
designed by children from local primary schools. We are a lively, go-ahead church,
who believe in challenging people with
the Gospel of Christ in a way that is
relevant today. We promise you one thing,
whatever your age, you won't be bored in
Hillhouse. Events are intimated on the
website. Sunday Services: 10.45am and
7.00pm September to April; 10.45am
May to August
Open by arrangement with the Session
Clerk, telephone 01698 425194
CHURCH OF SCOTLAND

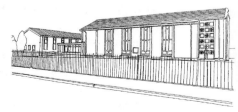

HILLHOUSE PARISH CHURCH

♿ wc) ☕ (by arrangement) ⓘ (by arrangement)

722 KIRKMUIRHILL PARISH CHURCH

NS 799 429

Carlisle Road, Kirkmuirhill

Built in 1868 by the United Presyterian
Church, architect Robert Baldie. Early English
Gothic Revival style, the most prominent
feature being the spire which dominates the
surroundings. Four stained glass windows by
Robert Paterson 1941, Douglas Hamilton 1954,
and Linda Fraser 1986. Embroidered pew and
chair cushions designed by Pat Hodgson of
Hawksland Lesmahagow and worked by
members of the congregation. Sunday
Services: 11.00am and 6.30pm
Open by arrangement with Session Clerk,
telephone 01555 892305
CHURCH OF SCOTLAND   ♿   wc   ⟨⟩   📖

KIRKMUIRHILL PARISH CHURCH

723 GREYFRIARS PARISH CHURCH, LANARK

NS 880 437

Bloomgate, Lanark

Church website: www.webartz.com / greyfriars

William Leiper designed this, his smallest church,
in 1875 for the Bloomgate United Presbyterian
Congregation. Its simple gothic interior is
enlivened by a slender bellcote inspired by Andrew
Heiton's Findlater Church in Dublin.
2-manual pipe organ by Ingram, recently fully
refurbished. Pulpit fall and welcome banner by
local artist Myra Gibson. Sunday Service: 11.00am
Open by arrangement with the Minister,
telephone 01555 663363
CHURCH OF SCOTLAND   ♿   wc   ⟨⟩   B

GREYFRIARS PARISH CHURCH, LANARK

724 CHRIST CHURCH, LANARK

NS 881 439

Hope Street, Lanark

Gothic church of a simple rectangle with aisles of 1853 by John Henderson. Carving
by Major General Stevenson. Modern stained glass by Pauline Payne, art teacher of
Lanark Grammar School in the 1960s and 1970s. Sunday Service: 10.30am
Open by arrangement with the Minister, telephone 01555 663065
SCOTTISH EPISCOPAL   ♿   ⟨⟩   ☕   B

725 ST MARY'S, LANARK

NS 886 435

70 Bannatyne Street, Lanark

Gothic Revival cruciform church by Dublin
architects Ashlin & Coleman 1908. Graceful
144-ft spire. Remarkable interior decoration
including imposing reredos of Caen stone and
marble, statues of St Mungo, St Margaret and
St Columba and fine stained glass. Services:
weekdays 9.30am; Saturday Vigil 6.30pm;
Sunday 9.30am, 11.00am and 6.30pm
Open during daylight hours
ROMAN CATHOLIC [&] [wc] [wc] ⓐ 𝗒 **A**

ST MARY'S, LANARK

726 ST NICHOLAS PARISH CHURCH, LANARK

NS 881 437

The Cross, Lanark

By John Reid of Nemphlar 1774. Stained glass,
baptismal font in Caen stone. Fine pipe organ.
Services: Sunday 11.00am; Wednesday 10.15am
*Open during Doors Open Day and by arrangement,
telephone 01555 662600.*
CHURCH OF SCOTLAND [&] [wc] 𝗒 ⧉ ⓐ **B**

ST NICHOLAS PARISH CHURCH, LANARK

727 ST MARY'S, LARKHALL

NS 757 509

Raploch Road, Larkhall

Founded as a mission in 1861, the
present church was built 1872.
Rectangular Free-style church with
over-hanging eaves and harled walls
with painted surrounds to doors and
windows. Inside, pointed arches divide
the nave from the aisles. Services:
Saturday Mass 6.30pm;
Sunday 8.00am, 10.45am, 4.30pm
(winter), 6.00pm (summer)
*Open by arrangement,
telephone 01698 882564*
ROMAN CATHOLIC [&] [wc] (hall) **C**

ST MARY'S, LARKHALL

728 LOWTHER PARISH CHURCH, LEADHILLS

NS 885 148

On B797 near south end of village

Built in 1883 as the United Free
Church, it amalgamated with the Parish
Church in 1937. Double manual pedal
organ and an electronic organ.
Memorial window depicting 'Dorcas'.
Sunday Service: 11.30am

Open 1st Sunday or by arrangement,
telephone 01659 74326

CHURCH OF SCOTLAND [wc]

LOWTHER PARISH CHURCH, LEADHILLS

729 LESMAHAGOW OLD PARISH CHURCH

NS 814 399

M74, 23 miles south of Glasgow
Church website: www.lopc.org.uk

King David I granted a church and lands to the Tironensian monks in 1144. He
also granted the right of sanctuary, violated in 1335 when the church was burned,
with villagers inside, by John Eltham, brother of Edward I of England. The
present church was built in 1803 and
the apse added in the 1890s. Pipe
organ 1889. Several stained glass
windows including one whose central
panel, 'The Descent from the Cross', is
a copy of the painting by Rubens in
Antwerp Cathedral. The bell is dated
1625. Display in the Chapter House.
Sunday Service: 10.00am

Open by arrangement, telephone Rev Sheila
Mitchell 01555 892425 or Church Officer
Mr Alex McInnes 01555 892697

CHURCH OF SCOTLAND [&] [wc]

LESMAHAGOW OLD PARISH CHURCH

730 LIBBERTON & QUOTHQUAN PARISH CHURCH

NS 992 428

On B7016 from Biggar to Carnwath

Carnwath was separated from Libberton in 1186 and Quothquan Parish was joined to Libberton in 1660. Quothquan Church (about 2 miles from Libberton) is now a ruin; its aisle is the burial place of the Chancellor family. The new church was built on an ancient site of worship at Libberton in 1812, and restored in 1902. It has fine woodwork and memorials of distinction. Sunday Service: 9.30am, 10.45am and 12.00 noon on a quarterly rotation with Black Mount and Culter

Open by arrangement, telephone
Miss J Gibson 01899 308107

CHURCH OF SCOTLAND ♿ wc **B**

LIBBERTON & QUOTHQUAN PARISH CHURCH

731 PETTINAIN CHURCH

NS 955 429

7 miles east of Lanark, between A73 and A70
Church website: www.srct.org.uk

Fine example of a rural parish kirk, with outstanding views across open countryside. The site has been a place of worship since the early 12th century when David I established the chapel of 'Pedynane'. The present church dates principally from the 18th century with an earlier belfry of 1692 and an incised cross slab re-used as a relieving lintel. Interesting walled burial ground. Acquired by the Scottish Redundant Churches Trust in 2000 with the generous support of local people.

Services: occasional, with weddings and funerals by arrangement

Open July and August, Sundays, 1.00-4.00pm or by arrangement with the SRCT, telephone 01334 472032

FORMER CHURCH OF SCOTLAND ♿ ⛽ **B**

PETTINAIN CHURCH

732 RUTHERGLEN OLD PARISH CHURCH

NS 613 617

Main Street x Queen Street, Rutherglen

Church website: www.rutherglen.clara.co.uk/index.htm

The present church was designed by the architect J J Burnet 1902 in Gothic style, the fourth on this site since the original foundation in the 6th century. The gable end of an 11th-century church still stands in the graveyard supporting St Mary's steeple (15th century). It contains the church bell 1635. Stained glass including a First World War memorial. Communion cups dated 1665 are still in use. The churchyard occupies an ancient site, at its gateway two stone offertory shelters, and a sundial set above its entrance dated 1679.

Sunday Service: 11.00am

Open 2nd Saturday of each month,
10.00am-12.00 noon

CHURCH OF SCOTLAND [wc] ⊘ ☕ **B**

RUTHERGLEN OLD PARISH CHURCH

733 ST COLUMBKILLE'S CHURCH, RUTHERGLEN

NS 614 616

Main Street, Rutherglen

Magnificent church, Coia 1940, replacing original church founded in 1851. Modern adaptation of an Italian basilica. Between A724 and A731. Trains and city buses.

Services: Sunday Masses 9.00am, 10.30am, 12.00 noon and 7.00pm;

Vigil Mass Saturday 5.30pm

Open Monday to Thursday 9.00am-
5.00pm, Friday 9.00am-2.00pm

ROMAN CATHOLIC [♿] [wc] ⊘ 📖 ☕

ST COLUMBKILLE'S CHURCH, RUTHERGLEN

734 AVENDALE OLD PARISH CHURCH, STRATHAVEN

NS 701 443

59a Kirk Street, Strathaven
Church website: www.avendale-drumclog.com
Records show a church in Strathaven in 1288.
This church was built in 1772 and the interior
renovated 1879. The centre section of the south
gallery was reserved for the family and tenants of
the Duke of Hamilton and is known as 'The
Duke's Gallery'. Stained glass window of The
Last Supper', Crear McCartney 1996. Sunday
Service: 11.00am. All-age communion is celebrated
at the 11.00am service on the 3rd Sunday of each
month, except July and August. Details of
evening services to be found on church website
Open Monday to Friday 9.00am-12.00 noon
(not school holidays). Other times, telephone the Session
Office 01354 529748 (9.00am-12.00 noon)
CHURCH OF SCOTLAND 🦽 wc ⊘ 📖 👤 **B**

AVENDALE OLD PARISH CHURCH,
STRATHAVEN

735 STRATHAVEN EAST PARISH CHURCH

NS 702 446

Green Street, Strathaven
The building, with its tall tower and spire, is a
local landmark. Built 1777 with clock tower
added 1843. Major rebuilding 1877. Prominent
pulpit and memorial windows. Linked with
Glasford Church. Sunday Service: 11.30am
Open by arrangement, telephone
Rev W Stewart 01357 521138
CHURCH OF SCOTLAND wc ⊘ **A** (tower) **B** (church)

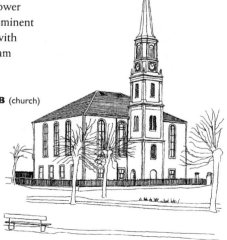

STRATHAVEN EAST PARISH CHURCH

736 STRATHAVEN WEST

NS 700 444

Townhead Street, Strathhaven

Originally a Relief Church out of Strathaven East,
dedicated 1835, it was conceived with enthusiasm,
built and dedicated within nine months. Design based
on Carluke Church. Pipe organ 1930. Two major
refurbishments, for centenary and sesquicentenary,
resulting in a surprising warm, attractive interior.
War memorial in vestibule. Two memorial stained
glass windows. Sunday Service: 11.00am

Open by arrangement, telephone the Minister 01357 529086

CHURCH OF SCOTLAND [♿] [wc] [👂] [☕] [📖] B

STRATHAVEN WEST

737 ST PATRICK'S CHURCH, STRATHAVEN

NS 70 44 (this number does not look complete)

52 Stonehouse Road, Strathhaven

Built 1901 and paid for by Archbishop Charles Eyre
of Glasgow. Sanctuary extension and porch were
added 1953. It was built to serve the growing
Catholic population of Strathaven following
immigration from Ireland and the Highlands. The
original smaller church, built 1853, stands besides
the church and is now a parish hall. Services:
Monday-Friday 9.30am; Saturday 10.00am, Vigil
6.00pm; Sunday 9.00am and 11.00am

Open by arrangement, telephone 01357 520104

ROMAN CATHOLIC [♿] [wc] [👂]

ST PATRICK'S CHURCH, STRATHAVEN

738 PATERSON CHURCH, STONEHOUSE

NS 755 469

Lawrie Street, Stonehouse

The current building, named for the Rev Henry
Angus Paterson who ministered to the congregation for over 60 years, dates from 1879.
Remained a United Free Church at the Union of
1929. Refurbished following a fire in 1977. Fine
collection of stained glass windows by Crear
McCartney. Sunday Service: 10.00am

*Open Tuesday mid-June to end of August
10.00am-12.00 noon*

UNITED FREE [👂] [☕] [📖]

PATERSON CHURCH, STONEHOUSE

739 SYMINGTON KIRK

NS 999 352
Kirk Bauk
The original church was established *c.*1160. The
present building is largely 18th and 19th century
and the belfry is 1734. Watchtower in graveyard. A
feature of the interior is the scissorbeam roof.
Sunday Service: 9.30am or 11.00am as indicated
on notice board; Communion 1st Sunday of
November, March and June
Open by arrangement with the Minister,
telephone 01899 308838
CHURCH OF SCOTLAND ♿ wc (in hall)) **B**

SYMINGTON KIRK

740 TARBRAX CHURCH

NT 025 549
Tarbrax Road, Tarbrax, 1½ miles west of A70
Attractively simple church built in 1919 to serve the mining community of that
time. The mine has long since gone but the church continues, with a surprisingly
cosmopolitan congregation. Sunday Service: September to June, 10.30am, no
services July and August
Open by arrangement, 01501 785234 or 01501 785413
CHURCH OF SCOTLAND ♿ wc)

741 ST ANDREW'S, UDDINGSTON

NS 697 601
4 Bothwell Road, Uddingston
Built 1890, architect Miles Septimus Gibson, the foundation stone laid by Lady
Mary Alice Douglas Home, aunt of the later Prime Minister Sir Alec Douglas
Home. After a fire in 1993 the chancel was restored by Alex Braidwood of
Blantyre. Stained glass by J T & C E
Stewart of Glasgow and Peter Berry
of Malmesbury. The Blackett &
Howden pipe organ, damaged in the
fire, awaits restoration. Painting of
Bothwell Castle by architect and
local historian J Jeffrey Waddell.
Sunday Service: 11.15am
Open by arrangement, telephone
Miss Lyth 01698 812536
SCOTTISH EPISCOPAL wc

ST ANDREW'S, UDDINGSTON

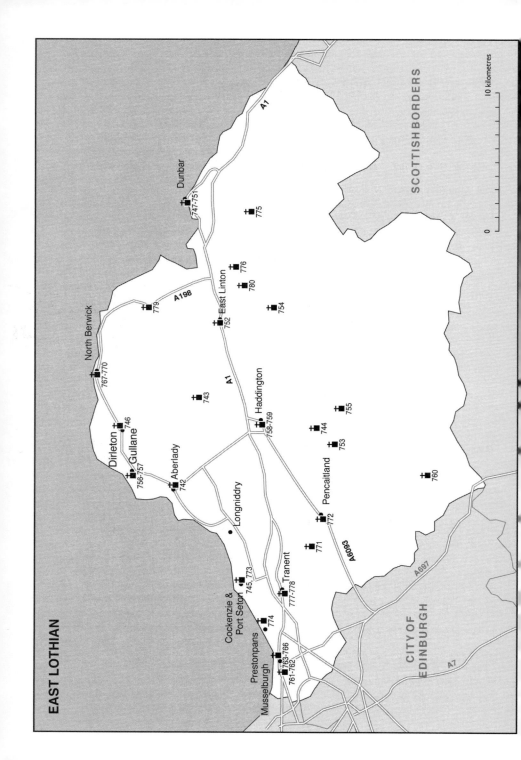

EAST LOTHIAN

SCOTTISH BORDERS

CITY OF EDINBURGH

Dunbar
747-751
775

East Linton
776
780
752
754

North Berwick
767-770
779
A198

Dirleton
746
Gullane
756-757
743
A1

Aberlady
742
Haddington
758-759
744
755
753

Longniddry
Pencaitland
772
760

Cockenzie &
Port Seton
745, 773
771
A6093

Tranent
777-778
774

Prestonpans
763-766
761-762

Musselburgh

A697
A7

0   10 kilometres

EAST LOTHIAN

Local Representative: Mrs Margaret Beveridge, St Andrews, Duns Road, Gifford EH41 4QW (*telephone* 01620 810694)

742 ABERLADY PARISH CHURCH

NT 462 799
Main Street, Aberlady
A198 Edinburgh to North Berwick
Fifteenth-century tower, the body of the church recast in 1886 by William Young. Stained glass by Edward Frampton, London 1889. Eighth-century cross. Marble monument attributed to Canova. Tour guide boards in English, French, German, Spanish, Swedish. Sunday Service: 11.15am
Open 1 May to 30 September, 8.00am to dusk.
Other times, telephone B White 01875 853137
or F Burnett, 14 Rig Street, Aberlady 01875 870237
CHURCH OF SCOTLAND ⑦ 📖 **A**

ABERLADY PARISH CHURCH

743 ATHELSTANEFORD PARISH CHURCH

NT 533 774
Athelstaneford, from A1, B1347
The original church, 'Ecclesia de Elstaneford', on this site is said to have been founded in 1176 by the Countess Ada, mother of William the Lion. The present church dates from 1780. Cruciform design with central aisle, transepts and semi-octagonal chancel. Bellcote on the west gable. Three stained glass windows by C E Kempe. Doocote 1583. Church has historic link with the Scottish Saltire: commemorative plaque and Saltire floodlit. Heritage Centre to rear of church opened in 1997 with audio visual display (entry free). Sunday Service: 10.00am
Open daily, dawn to dusk
CHURCH OF SCOTLAND ♿ 🚾 📖 **B**

ATHELSTANEFORD PARISH CHURCH

744 BOLTON PARISH CHURCH

NT 507 701

Bolton, B6368 from Haddington

Church website: http://ndhm.org.uk

There has been a church on this site since before 1244.
The present building dates from 1809 and has
remained structurally unchanged since that time. The
architect was probably Archibald Elliot. The interior is
plain and unspoiled, complete with carpenter's Gothic
pulpit, and gallery on clustered iron posts. Robert
Burns's mother, brother and sisters are buried in the
churchyard. Graveguard and other items dating from
the time of the 'Resurrection Men' displayed in the
porch. Linked with Saltoun, Humbie and Yester.
Sunday Service: 10.00am, alternating with Saltoun
Open daily
CHURCH OF SCOTLAND 📖 **B**

BOLTON PARISH CHURCH

745 COCKENZIE METHODIST CHURCH

NT 398 756

28 Edinburgh Road, Cockenzie

The third of East Lothian's three Primitive
Methodist Chapels, 1878. Simple and attractive.
Original interior. South side of main road at
west end of village. Sunday Service: 2.30pm
Open by arrangement, telephone Christine Thomson
01875 811137
METHODIST ♿

COCKENZIE METHODIST CHURCH

746 DIRLETON KIRK

NT 513 842

Attractive stone building erected in 1612 to
replace 12th-century kirk in Gullane which was
'continewallie overblawin with sand'. Archerfield
Aisle added 1650, first example of neo-classical
design in Scotland. Tower crowned with Gothic
pinnacles 1836. Interesting examples of stained
glass, including 'St Francis and the Animals',
Margaret Chilton 1936. Sunday Service: 11.30am
*Open daily 10.00am to dusk. Light lunches and
snacks in adjacent Dirleton Gallery*
CHURCH OF SCOTLAND ♿ wc ⓐ 📖 ☕ **A**

DIRLETON KIRK

747 CHURCH OF OUR LADY OF THE WAVES, DUNBAR

NT 678 791

Westgate, Dunbar

Built in 1877, the church has stained glass
behind the altar and wood carvings showing
the Way of the Cross. Services: Sunday
10.30am; Saturday Vigil: 6.30pm; Mass:
Monday, Tuesday, Wednesday and Friday
9.30am and on Thursday 7.00am

Open by arrangement, telephone 01368 862701

ROMAN CATHOLIC

CHURCH OF OUR LADY OF THE WAVES, DUNBAR

748 DUNBAR METHODIST CHURCH

NT 679 791

10 Victoria Street, Dunbar

Scotland's oldest Methodist Church, built in
1764. John and Charles Wesley were trustees
and John often preached here. Enlarged 1857,
renovated 1890. Fine interior, unexpected
from plain exterior. Oak pulpit. Stained glass
windows from St Giles, Edinburgh. South
side of road leading from High Street to
Harbour. Sunday Service: 11.00am

Open by arrangement, telephone David Hancock 01368 862052

METHODIST **A**

DUNBAR METHODIST CHURCH

749 DUNBAR PARISH CHURCH

NT 682 786

Queen's Road, Dunbar. 200 yards south of the High Street

The building, designed by Gillespie Graham in 1821,
has been beautifully reconstructed by Campbell &
Arnott 1990 following a devastating fire in 1987.
The colourful and modern interior includes the early
17th-century monument to the Earl of Dunbar and
some fine stained glass by Shona McInnes and
Douglas Hogg 1990. Intercity trains to Dunbar.
Sunday Service: 11.00am

Open daily 2.00-4.00pm Wednesday and Friday,
June to September, or telephone Mrs D Brunton
01368 862903. Various exhibitions during season

CHURCH OF SCOTLAND **A**

DUNBAR PARISH CHURCH

750 BELHAVEN PARISH CHURCH, DUNBAR

NT 668 787

Edinburgh Road, Dunbar

Church website: www.belhavenparishchurch.org.uk

Built 1838-40 in red whinstone with sandstone dressings and tower, the church occupies a prominent position, with halls to the rear in extensive community use. Chancel windows depict angels of Peace, Faith, Hope and Sacrifice. Pipe organ by Forster & Andrews. Seasonal banners are displayed. A warm welcome to all visitors. Sunday Service: 11.30am

Open by arrangement telephone 01368 863098. Church fête 2nd Saturday in June

CHURCH OF SCOTLAND   🦽 wc 🔔 **B**

751 ST ANNE'S CHURCH, DUNBAR

NT 678 791

Westgate, Dunbar (north end of High Street)
The church is by H M Wardrop and Sir
R Rowand Anderson 1890. Built in the
Gothic Revival style and decorated with
some Scots detail. Carved oak furnishings,
Henry Willis organ, stained glass by
Ballantine & Gardiner, Heaton, Butler &
Bayne, and the Abbey Studio. Sunday
Service: 9.15am (except 1st Sunday of
month) and 10.30am; Thursday 10.30am

ST ANNE'S CHURCH, DUNBAR

Open by arrangement, telephone Rev P Allen 01368 865711 or S Bunyan 01368 863335

SCOTTISH EPISCOPAL 🦽 wc 🔔 📖 **B**

752 PARISH OF TRAPRAIN, PRESTONKIRK, EAST LINTON

NT 592 778

Preston Road, East Linton. Off A1 follow signs to
Preston Mill
Dedicated to St Baldred, the church possesses
in its former chancel the best fragment of 13th-
century church architecture in East Lothian. The
tower dates from 1631; the main building from
1770, enlarged 1824, redesigned internally 1892
by James Jerdan and refurbished 2004. Organ
by Vincent of Sutherland overhauled in 2004.
St Baldred window 1959 and two Second World
War memorial windows by William Wilson.
Among the gravestones are those of Andrew

PARISH OF TRAPRAIN, PRESTONKIRK,
EAST LINTON

Meikle, inventor of the threshing machine, and George Rennie, agriculturalist and brother of John Rennie, the civil engineer. Sunday Service: 11.00am; 25 December 10.00am. Please note times of services may be changed

Open by arrangement, telephone 01620 860598

CHURCH OF SCOTLAND   🚻 (in Church Hall)   ♪   🕯 (by arrangement) 📖 **A**

753   SALTOUN PARISH CHURCH, EAST SALTOUN

NT 474 678

Church website: http://ndhm.org.uk

There has been a church on this site since before 1244. The present building is a T-plan Gothic kirk of 1805 which John Fletcher Campbell built 'as a monument to the virtues of his ancestors'. The actual designer is most likely to have been Robert Burn. The interior was recast in 1885; the architect was John Lessels. Beneath the church lies the Fletcher Vault, containing the remains of Andrew Fletcher, 'The Patriot', and members of his family. Linked with Bolton, Humbie and Yester. Sunday Service: 10.00am, alternating with Bolton

Open daily

CHURCH OF SCOTLAND   🚻 📖 **A**

SALTOUN PARISH
CHURCH, EAST SALTOUN

754   NUNRAW ABBEY

NT 593 700

Garvald, by Haddington

Church website: www.nunraw.org

Modern Monastery of Cistercian Monks built 1952-70 (but unfinished), architect Peter Whiston. Nunraw House is an historic building and functions as the Abbey guest house where people may stay for a few days of retreat in the monastic atmosphere. Sunday Services: Mass 11.00am, Vespers 4pm, Compline 7.30pm; weekday Services: Lauds and Mass 6.45am, Vespers 6.00pm, Compline 7.30pm

Reception area and abbey
open at all times

ROMAN CATHOLIC   🚻 🚻   ♪ 🕯 📖

NUNRAW ABBEY

755 YESTER PARISH CHURCH, GIFFORD

NT 535 681

Main Street, Gifford. B6369 from Haddington
By James Smith, finished 1710. A white
harled T-plan church with square staged
tower and slated spire. Weather vane in
the form of a heron, William Brown,
Edinburgh 1709. Church bell from the
old Church of Bothans 1492. Pulpit 17th-
century with bracket for baptismal basin.

YESTER PARISH CHURCH, GIFFORD

Memorial in village wall opposite to Rev John Witherspoon, son of the Manse,
who signed the American Declaration of Independence 1784.
Sunday Service: 11.30am
Open daily, 9.00am to sunset April to October. Village gala day June. Flower show August
CHURCH OF SCOTLAND [wc] (?) 🛈 **A**

756 GULLANE PARISH CHURCH (ST ANDREW'S)

NT 480 827

East Links Road, Gullane. A198 to North Berwick
The church, designed by Glasgow architect John
Honeyman and completed in 1888, replaced an
earlier 12th-century building vacated in 1612
when the congregation was rehoused in a new
kirk at Dirleton. The Kirk Session of Dirleton
decided to build the present parish church for
the benefit of 'the large number of summer
visitors annually residing in the village'. Simple Norman style with east apse. The

GULLANE PARISH CHURCH (ST ANDREW'S)

zig-zagged chancel arch is derived from the old parish church, as is the south
doorway whose tympanum has a low relief of St Andrew. Sunday Service: 9.45am
Open daily all year. Coffee on Tuesdays 10.00-11.30am
CHURCH OF SCOTLAND [♿] (?) 🛈 🛈 **A**

757 ST ADRIAN'S CHURCH, GULLANE

NT 480 838

Sandy Loan, Gullane
A simple aisleless church in Arts & Crafts style by Reginald Fairlie 1926. Built of
stone from the Rattlebag quarry, with a low tower and slated pyramidal spire.
Three-light chancel window by Douglas Strachan 1934. Sandy Loan is the beach
road at the west end of the village. Sunday Services: Sung Eucharist 9.30;
Said Eucharist 1st and 3rd Sundays 8.00am
Open 10.00am-5.00pm, April to September
SCOTTISH EPISCOPAL [♿] (?) 🛈 **B**

ST ADRIAN'S CHURCH, GULLANE   HOLY TRINITY CHURCH, HADDINGTON

758   HOLY TRINITY CHURCH, HADDINGTON

NT 518 739

Church Street, Haddington

Built 1770 on site of original 'Lamp of Lothian'. Chancel added 1930. 'Stations of
the Cross', Bowman. 'Christ Crucified', Sutherland. Medieval walls of former
priory and town defences. Services: Sunday 8.30am, Sung Eucharist 10.00am,
Evensong 6.00pm (except July and August); Wednesday Eucharist 10.00am
Open Wednesday 10.00am-4.00pm, and in summer Saturday 10.00am-4.00pm.
Other times, contact the Rectory adjacent or office in church halls

SCOTTISH EPISCOPAL   📖 wc ♿ **B**

759   ST MARY'S PARISH CHURCH, HADDINGTON

NT 519 736

Sidegate, Haddington

Church website: www.kylemore.btinternet.co.uk/stmarys.htm

Dating back to the 14th century, one of the three great pre-Reformation churches of
the Lothians, known as 'The Lamp of Lothian', it is the longest parish church in
Scotland, with fascinating history. Nave repaired for John Knox and the Reformers
after Siege of Haddington 1548 and used as the parish church for almost 400 years.
Transepts and choir restored, Ian G Lindsay & Partners 1973. Lauderdale Aisle, now
the Chapel of the Three Kings, in regular ecumenical use. Fine stone carvings,
especially west door. Notable stained glass by Sir Edward Burne-Jones and Sax
Shaw. Modern tapestries. Fine pipe organ by Lammermuir Pipe Organs 1990. A peal
of eight bells installed in the tower (and dedicated by the Moderator) in 1999.
Sunday Services: All Age Worship 9.30am and Worship 11.00am
Open Good Friday to 30 September daily, 11.00am-4.00pm, Sunday 2.00-4.30pm.
Annual ecumenical Whitekirk/Haddington Pilgrimage 2nd Saturday in May.
Regular concerts and recitals of international repute

CHURCH OF SCOTLAND   ♿ wc ♿ 🍴 📖 ⚲ ☕ **A**

ST MARY'S PARISH CHURCH, HADDINGTON

HUMBIE KIRK

760   HUMBIE KIRK

NT 461 637

On the site of a pre-Reformation church, set in an ox-bow of Humbie Burn, a T-plan Gothic church by James Tod dated 1800. Vestry added 1846, and alterations by David Bryce 1866. The chancel added 1930, probably W J Walker Todd. Open scissor-braced timber roof. East window stained glass by Douglas Strachan. Organ c.1850, probably the work of an Edinburgh builder with decorative Gothic dark wood case, from the Norwegian Seamen's Chapel at Granton. Fine gravestones with classical detail dating from earlier church. Two plaques for the united parishes of Humbie and Keith which have had only 25 ministers since 1590.

Sunday Service: 10.00am

Open daily

CHURCH OF SCOTLAND   **B**

761   PARISH CHURCH OF ST MICHAEL'S, INVERESK

NT 344 721

Musselburgh

There has been a church on the site since the 6th century. The present church was built in 1805 to the design of Robert Nisbet; the steeple by William Sibbald. The interior was reorientated and remodelled in 1893 by J MacIntyre Henry and again in 2002 by Simpson & Brown. Known as the 'Visible Kirk' because of its prominent position, it stands on the site of a Roman praetorium and replaces a medieval church. Fine Adam-style ceiling and some excellent stained glass. Magnificent pipe organ by Lewis 1892, originally built with early form of electric action. Graveyard with many interesting old stones. Sunday Service: 11.15am

Open by arrangement, telephone Mr G Burnet 0131 665 2689

CHURCH OF SCOTLAND   ♿ (ramp) ⓦ🄲 ⊘ 📖 ⛪ **A**

PARISH CHURCH OF ST MICHAEL'S, INVERESK

NORTH ESK PARISH CHURCH, INVERESK

762 NORTH ESK PARISH CHURCH, INVERESK

NT 340 727

Bridge Street, Musselburgh (opposite Brunton Hall)

Opened in 1838, this simple, stone-fronted building was designed by William Burn. Inside there is an all-round horseshoe gallery under a high vaulted ceiling. Noteworthy are seven stained glass windows (one by Ballantine and Gardiner, 1892); a World War One memorial plaque; a pink alabaster font and a fine brass eagle lectern. Behind the central pulpit and fronted by a carved pine screen is a recently refurnished Abbot and Smith 2-manual pipe organ of 1904.

Sunday Service: 11.00am

Open on Saturday mornings 10.00am-12.00 noon February to mid-December, or by arrangement with the Session Clerk 0131 665 7109

CHURCH OF SCOTLAND 🔿 wc 🔿 🔿 (Saturday mornings) **B**

763 ST ANDREWS HIGH CHURCH, MUSSELBURGH

NT 345 727

70 Millhill, Musselburgh

St Andrews High is the successful voluntary union in 1985 of the previous St Andrews Church (itself a union of two former UP congregations) and Musselburgh High Church (a former Free congregation). The building was redeveloped and refurbished in 1990/91. The church complex comprises a sanctuary with moveable furniture, reception area, small room and large hall upstairs. Sunday Service: 10.30am

Open every Saturday 9.00am-12.00 noon and Sunday 10.30am-12.30pm

CHURCH OF SCOTLAND 🔿 wc 🔿

ST ANDREWS HIGH
CHURCH, MUSSELBURGH

ST PETER'S EPISCOPAL, MUSSELBURGH

OUR LADY OF LORETTO
AND ST MICHAEL, MUSSELBURGH

764 ST PETER'S EPISCOPAL, MUSSELBURGH

NT 348 723

High Street, Musselburgh

Anglican church near the site of the Battle of Pinkie (1547), in a traditional French
Gothic style by Paterson & Shiells 1865. Narrow chancel and semi-circular apse
and steeply pitched roof. Fine, older stained glass windows and 17th-century
character wooden panelling in St Michael's Chapel. Sunday Services follow biblical
themes and are friendly, relaxed and relevant. Kids' club during services. Sunday
11.15am; Wednesday 10.00am

Open by arrangement with Mr Alan Stevens, telephone 0131 665 6697

SCOTTISH EPISCOPAL ♿ wc ② **B**

765 OUR LADY OF LORETTO AND
ST MICHAEL, MUSSELBURGH

NT 346 753

17 Newbigging, Musselburgh

Stone building opened in 1905. Sanctuary recently modernised. All windows are of
stained glass and the walls of the sanctuary are covered in fine artwork, in gold leaf,
depicting the events in the life of our Lord, corresponding to the Joyful Mysteries
of the Rosary. Sunday Services: 9.00 and 11.30 am; Saturday Vigil 6.00pm

Open daily

ROMAN CATHOLIC ♿ ② 📖 **B**

MUSSELBURGH CONGREGATIONAL CHURCH

ABBEY CHURCH, NORTH BERWICK

766 MUSSELBURGH CONGREGATIONAL CHURCH

NT 341 729

6 Links Street, Musselburgh

Church website: www.musselburghcongregational.co.uk

Simple but charming Georgian building completed in 1801, built with stone carried by fishermen and sailors from the shores of the Forth at Fisherrow. Oldest church in Musselburgh and one of first congregational churches in Scotland. Pipe organ is a fine example of the work of George Holdich, built 1860 for St Michael's, Appleby. Rebuilt for Musselburgh Congregational Church 1977. Church sits behind Brunton Hall. Sunday Service: 11.00am

Open by arrangement, telephone Mrs Doris Brown, 11 Links Street 0131 665 3768

CONGREGATIONAL   ♿   🚻   📖   ⚱   **c**

767 ABBEY CHURCH, NORTH BERWICK

NT 551 853

High Street, North Berwick

Built 1868 as United Presbyterian by Robert R Raeburn in Early English style. A complete early 20th-century scheme of stained glass with, superimposed on one window, an arrangement of suspended planes representing an ascent of doves, by Sax Shaw 1972. Sunday Services: 10.00am and 6.00pm

Open 9.00am-6.00pm, Mondays to Fridays, July and August

CHURCH OF SCOTLAND   ♿   🚻   ☕   📖

768 ST ANDREW BLACKADDER, NORTH BERWICK

NT 553 853
High Street, High Street
Church website: www.standrewblackadder.org.uk
Gothic Revival church by Robert Rowand Anderson 1882, with hall and tower
added 1907 by Henry & MacLennan. Prominent feature of North Berwick, the
clock tower visible for many miles. Stained glass by J Ballantine, Abbey Studio,
William Wilson. Organ by Foster & Andrews 1886, rebuilt and enlarged by Ingram
& Co, 1914. The Sanctuary was divided horizontally 2000 to create meeting rooms
with excellent facilities which are used seven days a week by community groups.
Traditional and modern worship and a warm welcome to visitors.
Sunday services: Traditional 9.30am, All-age 10.30am, 6.00pm
Open July and August 12.00 noon-4.00pm (Saturdays 10.00am-4.00pm),
Easter and September holiday weekends, 10.00am-4.00pm
CHURCH OF SCOTLAND ♿ 🚻 ⊘ 🕯 ☕ **B**

769 CHURCH OF OUR LADY STAR OF THE SEA, NORTH BERWICK

NT 553 850
Law Road, North Berwick
Church website: www.nbstar.org.uk
Simple Victorian church 1879, by
Dunn & Hansom with seating for
200 people. The chancel was added
by Basil Champreys in 1889 and the
Lady Chapel by Sir Robert Lorimer
in 1901. The interior contains a
number of pictures after Benozzo
Gozzoli and Botticelli and
a Della Robbia (probably a copy).
Services: Monday to Friday 10.00am;
Saturday Vigil 6.00pm;
Sunday 10.00am
Open daily, 8.00am to dusk
ROMAN CATHOLIC ♿ ⊘ **B**

CHURCH OF OUR LADY STAR
OF THE SEA, NORTH BERWICK

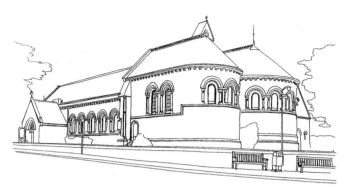

ST BALDRED'S CHURCH, NORTH BERWICK

770 ST BALDRED'S CHURCH, NORTH BERWICK

NT 556 853

Dirleton Avenue, North Berwick

The original Norman-style church by John Henderson 1861 was cleverly extended in 1863 incorporating the old masonry by Seymour & Kinross, who also designed the altar. The porch with its magnificent carved doors was added by Robert Lorimer in 1916. Choir stalls by H O Tarbolton, porch doors by Mrs Meredith-Williams. Stained glass by Ballantine & Son. Convenient for North Berwick railway station. Sunday Services: Sung Eucharist 11.00am; Said Eucharist 2nd and 4th Sunday, 8.00am

Open all year, 10.00am-4.00pm

SCOTTISH EPISCOPAL 🦽 ⍨ 📖 ⚱ **B**

771 ORMISTON PARISH CHURCH

NT 414 693

Main Street, Ormiston

Church website: www.ormistonvillage.com

The first Presybterian Minister was appointed to Ormiston in 1568. The present Arts & Crafts building, consecrated 1938, was designed by T Aikman Swan incorporating a cruciform shape and gallery. Carved stone font and wood-panelled pulpit. Three stained glass windows from the original parish church, depicting Moses, St Paul and the Christ. Sunday Service: 11.30am

Open by arrangement with the Minister, telephone 01875 612031

or Mrs Purves 01875 611423

CHURCH OF SCOTLAND 🦽 wc ⍨ **B**

772 PENCAITLAND PARISH CHURCH

NT 443 690

Church website: www.ppclink.co.uk

A1 from Edinburgh to Tranent, B6355 to Pencaitland

Consecrated in 1242, the earliest part of the church dates
from the 12th century. The present building consists of
nave, with a gallery at the west end, and two aisles on the
north side, the older called the Winton Aisle and the other
the Saltoun Aisle. Churchyard with many interesting
gravestones, offering houses, renovated carriage house,
stables, harness room and cottage. Coffee shop on
Thursdays from 2.00-4.00pm in Carriage House, except the
first Thursday of the month. Sunday Service: 10.00am;
Sunday Evening Service 6.30pm, every fortnight

*Open by arrangement, telephone Rev Mark Malcolm 01875
340208, or e-mail: minister@ppclink.co.uk*

CHURCH OF SCOTLAND [&] [wc] ♟ ♟ □ ▢ **A**

PENCAITLAND PARISH CHURCH

773 CHALMERS MEMORIAL CHURCH, PORT SETON

NT 403 757

Edinburgh Road, Port Seton

Built to a design by Sydney Mitchell for
the United Free Church, the foundation
stone was laid in 1904. It has a very
elegant spire and bell-tower and unique
stencilled interior. Stained glass
windows by Margaret Chilton and
Marjorie Kemp 1924-50. Sunday
Services: 11.15am and 6.15pm

*The Church is open to visitors and for coffee
at the end of both services every Sunday*

CHURCH OF SCOTLAND
[&] [wc] ▢ □ ▢ **A**

CHALMERS MEMORIAL CHURCH, PORT SETON

774 ST ANDREW'S EPISCOPAL, PRESTONPANS

NT 392 749

West Loan, Prestonpans

Stone-built simple hall church, built as a Free
Kirk in 1843, with slender cast-iron columns
supporting the roof. Light, spacious interior.
Former gallery now enclosed to form upper
room over kitchen and toilets. Fine stained glass
including a recent window by Sax Shaw.
Sunday Service: Sung Eucharist 9.30am
Open by arrangement with Mr John Busby,
telephone 01875 340512
SCOTTISH EPISCOPAL   🦽   wc

ST ANDREW'S EPISCOPAL, PRESTONPANS

775 SPOTT PARISH CHURCH

NT 673 755

In middle of Spott village, 2 miles south of Dunbar

A little T-plan harled kirk of 1790 and 1809, incorporating the 17th century Hay
aisle. The old jougs are hung outside the east door, dating from the 17th century
when witch burning was recorded in the church records. Simple box pews and an
elaborate pulpit with Corinthian columns supporting the sounding board.
Sunday Service: 10.00am
Open at all times
CHURCH OF SCOTLAND   🦽   **A**

776 STENTON PARISH CHURCH

NT 641 753

Off A1, follow signs. Main Street, Stenton

By William Burn 1829, a T-plan kirk with a
splendid east tower. Redesigned internally
by James Jerdan in 1892. Stained glass by
E C Kempe and Ballantine & Gardiner.
In the graveyard is a fragment of the
16th-century kirk and a fine selection of
monuments. Rood well in village.
Sunday Service: 9.30am. Please note
time of service may be changed
Open daily dawn to dusk
CHURCH OF SCOTLAND
wc (only available at services) 🎧 **B**

STENTON PARISH CHURCH

ST MARTIN OF TOURS, TRANENT

777 ST MARTIN OF TOURS, TRANENT

NT 410 727

East end of High Street (opposite supermarket), Tranent

This is the third church building on the site in one hundred years and was built in 1969 in an octagonal shape using the Scandinavian compressed timber girder design. Contains two rough stained glass windows and an early 20th-century Italian crucifix above the altar. Irish limestone statue of classical design of St Martin as a Roman soldier and an original icon of St Martin in orthodox style. Services: Saturday Vigil 6.00pm; Sunday Mass 10.30am; weekdays, Tuesday to Friday 9.00am; other Masses and Services advertised in the weekly newsletter

Open by arrangement, telephone 01875 610232

ROMAN CATHOLIC   🚹 wc ⌲ 🕯 ☕ 🍽

778 TRANENT METHODIST CHURCH

NT 405 728

Tranent Day Centre, 3 Church Street

The Methodist congregation of Tranent now worships in Tranent Day Centre and remains rooted in its distinctive traditional community. Church Street runs north from Tranent High Street as the B6371. The Day Centre also hosts many youth and community groups. Sunday Service: 11.00am

Day Centre open daily

METHODIST 🚹 wc

779 ST MARY'S PARISH CHURCH, WHITEKIRK

NT 596 815

Whitekirk, on A198

Dating from 12th century, the original building was reconstructed during the 15th century starting with the vaulted stone choir, built in 1439 by Adam Hepburn of Hailes. In medieval times Whitekirk was an important place of pilgrimage. The church was set on fire in 1914 by suffragettes. Restored by

ST MARY'S PARISH CHURCH, WHITEKIRK

Robert Lorimer. Ceiled wagon roof over nave and transepts, communion table, pulpit, lectern and font all by Lorimer. Stained glass by C E Kempe 1889 and Karl Parsons 1916. Tithe barn and historic graveyard. Sunday Service: 11.30am

Open daily dawn to dusk

CHURCH OF SCOTLAND [wc] [] **A**

780 WHITTINGEHAME PARISH CHURCH

NT 603 737

Off A1, follow signs to Whittingehame

Spiky battlemented Gothic T-plan church built 1722, and added to by Barclay and Lamb in 1820 for James Balfour, grandfather of A J Balfour, Prime Minister 1902-05. Eighteenth-century burial enclosure of Buchan Sydserfs of Ruchlaw and good late 17th-century headstones show that there was an earlier church on the site. No regular Services

Open by arrangement, telephone 01620 860598

CHURCH OF SCOTLAND [♿] **B**

WHITTINGEHAME PARISH CHURCH

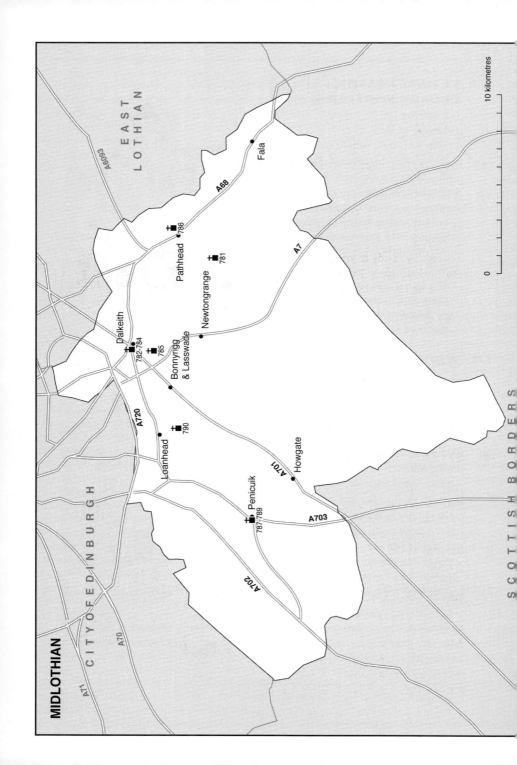

MIDLOTHIAN

Local Representative: Mrs Deirdre Howie, 41a Fountainhall Road, Edinburgh
(*telephone* 0131 667 8836)

781 CRICHTON COLLEGIATE CHURCH
NT 381 616
Crichton, Pathhead
Collegiate church rebuilt in
1449 by William Crichton, Lord
Chancellor of Scotland.
Restored by Hardy & White
1898 and Benjamin Tindall
1998. Fine pointed barrel vaults
over choir and transepts and
splendid square tower over
crossing. Organ by Joseph
Brook & Co. Magnificent

CRICHTON COLLEGIATE CHURCH

position at head of Tyne valley close to Crichton Castle. Programme available of
occasional services and concerts in summer months
Open Sunday 2.00-5.00pm May to September, or by appointment,
telephone Mrs Tindall 01875 320341. Crichton Castle open 1 May to 30 September
NON-DENOMINATIONAL   A

782 ST MARY'S CHURCH, DALKEITH
NT 335 677
Dalkeith Country Park, Dalkeith
Built as the chapel for Dalkeith Palace in 1843
by William Burn and David Bryce. Early
English style with splendid features: double
hammerbeam roof, stained glass windows,
heraldic floor tiles by Minton, and water-
powered organ by David Hamilton of
Edinburgh, installed 1845.
Sunday Service: 9.45am
Open on Saturday and Sunday 2.00-4.00pm
July and August; or by arrangement,
telephone Mrs Grieve 0131 663 4817.
Summer Brass Band concert
SCOTTISH EPISCOPAL   A

ST MARY'S CHURCH, DALKEITH

783 ST DAVID'S, DALKEITH

NT 328 669

Eskbank Road, Dalkeith

Designed by J A Hansom and built 1853-4, the site and church paid for by the
Marchioness of Lothian. Early English Gothic church with superbly decorated
interior. Gorgeously stencilled coffered ceilings by C H Goldie. Mural of
'Coronation of the Virgin' by Miss Gibsone over chancel arch. Stained glass of
various dates. Organ by Hamilton. Services: Saturday 6.00pm Sunday; 10.30am
Open by arrangement, telephone the Parish Priest 0131 663 4286
ROMAN CATHOLIC   🔕 ⑦ **A**

784 ST NICHOLAS BUCCLEUCH PARISH CHURCH, DALKEITH

NT 333 674

121 High Street, Dalkeith. 200 yards east of A68/A6094 junction
Church website: www.stnicholasbuccleugh.org.uk

Medieval church, became collegiate in 1406. Nave and transepts 1854 by David
Bryce. James, 1st Earl of Morton, and his wife Princess Joanna (the profoundly deaf
third daughter of James I) are buried within the choir, *c*.1498. Memorial monument
with their effigies mark the burial site. Organ by Binns 1906. Sunday Services:
Family Worship 9.30am, Parish Worship 11.00am
Open 14 April to 30 September, Monday to Saturday 10.00am-4.00pm
CHURCH OF SCOTLAND   🔕 wc ⑦ 🕯 📖 ⚱ ☕ **A**

ST NICHOLAS BUCCLEUCH PARISH CHURCH, DALKEITH

785 NEWBATTLE CHURCH

NT 331 661

Newbattle Road, Newbattle

Harled, T-plan church with belfry by Alexander
McGill 1727. Two galleries added 1851.
A remarkable number of the original fittings
survive including the upper part of the 17th-
century pulpit and the pilastered wooden frame
of the Lothian Loft. Organ by Eustace Ingram,
1895. Good 17th-century gravestones including
the amazing, ornamented Welsh family
monument. Sunday Service: 10.00am

Open by arrangement, telephone

Mr Iain McCarter 0131 663 3896

CHURCH OF SCOTLAND wc ☺ ▯ B

NEWBATTLE CHURCH

786 CRANSTOUN CHURCH, PATHHEAD

NT 386 656

On A168, ½ mile north of Pathhead

This charming country church stands in the grounds of Oxenfoord Castle, twelve
miles south-east of Edinburgh. It was built by the Architect Richard Dickson. In
the past it was destroyed twice by fire and is now a beautiful, warm and
welcoming church. Sunday Service: 10.45am

Open Sundays in July and August, 2.00-4.00pm

CHURCH OF SCOTLAND ♿ wc ☺ ▯ ☕ B

787 PENICUIK SOUTH CHURCH

NT 236 595

Peebles Road, Penicuik

Church website: http://come.to.penicuiksouthkirk

Designed in 1863 by Frederick T Pilkington.
Open timber roof. Stained glass. Organ by C & F
Hamilton 1901. Fully restored 1991. Short history
available. Sunday Services: 11.15am and 7.00pm

Open by arrangement, telephone 01968 674692

or 01968 674276

CHURCH OF SCOTLAND ♿ wc ☺ ▯ B

PENICUIK SOUTH CHURCH

788 ST JAMES SCOTTISH EPISCOPAL CHURCH, PENICUIK

NT 232 597

Broomhill Road, Penicuik

The original church which now
forms the nave was designed by H
Seymour of Seymour & Kinross
1882. The chancel, vestries, tower
and bell were added by H O
Tarbolton 1899. Excellent stained
glass, including one light by
Shrigley & Hunt of Lancaster and
four magnificent lights by C E
Kempe. Rood screen designed by
Tarbolton and carved by T Good;

ST JAMES SCOTTISH EPISCOPAL CHURCH, PENICUIK

communion rails also designed by Tarbolton and carved by Scott Morton & Co.
Reredos designed and executed by Mrs Meredith-Williams 1921. Sunday Services:
8.00am and 10.15am; first Sundays Choral Evensong 6.30pm

Open by arrangement, telephone the Rector 01968 672862

SCOTTISH EPISCOPAL 🚹 wc ⊘ 🍴 ⚲ ☕ **B**

789 CHURCH OF THE SACRED HEART, PENICUIK

NT 234 601

56 Crown Street

Built in a plain Gothic style in 1882 as a chapel school; it may be the only
(Catholic) chapel school still in use. Extended 1982 by Gilbert Gray, the ceiling
connecting the old and new is quite a feature. Original Stations of the Cross by
Vampoulles. Services: Saturday Vigil 6.00pm; Sunday 10.30am; also weekday
services

Open daily 8.30am-8.00pm

ROMAN CATHOLIC 🚹 wc ⊘

CHURCH OF THE SACRED HEART, PENICUIK

790 ROSSLYN CHAPEL (ST MATTHEW'S)

NT 275 631

Chapel Loan, Roslin

Built 1450 as the church of a college established by William Sinclair, 3rd Earl of Orkney. Intended to be cruciform but only the choir was completed. Famous for its decorative stone carving that covers almost every part of the building. The 'Prentice Pillar' has spectacular decoration. Sunday Services: 10.30am and 4.45pm

Open all year, Monday to Saturday 10.00am–5.00pm, Sunday 12.00 noon–4.45pm

SCOTTISH EPISCOPAL   ♿ 🕯 📖 🖥 [WC] **A**

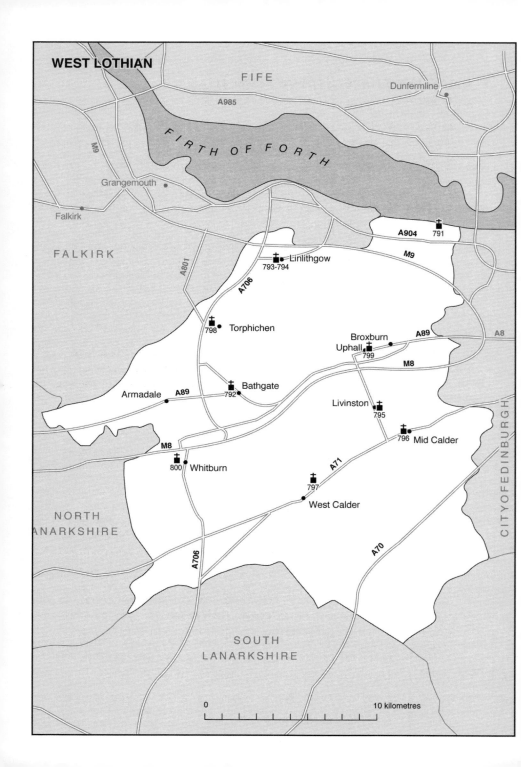

WEST LOTHIAN

Local Representative: Mr Robert Tait, 18 Polmont Park, Polmont
(*telephone* 01324 713746)

791 ABERCORN KIRK

NT 082 792

½ mile east of Hopetoun House
The kirk probably occupies the
site of a 7th-century monastery
founded by Lindisfarne Priory.
The building dates from 11th
century and has a fine 12th-
century south door. The
Duddingston burial aisle 1603,
Binns aisle 1618, Philipstoun
burial enclosure 1723 and

ABERCORN KIRK

Hopetoun aisle 1707 have fine mural monuments. Interior remodelled by Peter
McGregor Chalmers 1893, except for the splendid Hopetoun Loft of 1707
designed by William Bruce with carving by William Eizat and a heraldic ceiling by
Richard Waitt. Sunday Service 10.00am
Open at all times
CHURCH OF SCOTLAND [♿] [wc] **A**

792 ST COLUMBA'S, BATHGATE

NS 967 688

79 Glasgow Road, Bathgate
Church website: www.stcolumbasbathgate.co.uk
Design by W J Walker Todd and Millar in 1915, the church is of rectangular plan
with reduced chancel with organ recess off. The principal elevation is a pitched roof
swept down over ancillary accommodation. Square tower over the vestry and a stone
gabled and arched entrance to the west. Alterations and extension 1998. Triptych in
the apse by local artist Mabel Dawson, said to be presented by Lady Baillie.
Sunday Service: 11.15am. Café last Saturday of the month 12.00 noon-2.00pm
Open Wednesday mornings 10.00am-12.00 noon or by arrangement,
telephone the Priest-in-Charge 01506 842384
SCOTTISH EPISCOPAL [♿] [wc] [☕]

793 ST MICHAEL'S PARISH CHURCH, LINLITHGOW

NT 002 773

Kirkgate, Linlithgow

Church website: www.stmichaels-parish.org.uk

One of the finest examples of a large medieval burgh church. Consecrated in 1242 on the site of an earlier church, most of the present building dates from the 15th century with some 19th- and 20th-century restoration. Situated beside Linlithgow Palace, its history is intertwined with that of the royal house of Stewart. The modern aluminium crown, 1964, symbolises the

ST MICHAEL'S PARISH CHURCH, LINLITHGOW

Church's continuing witness to Christ's Kingship. Window commemorating 750th anniversary of the church 1992 by Crear McCartney. Carving of Queen Elizabeth II by John Donaldson added to Queen's Pulpit in 2003. New organ installed by Matthew Copley 2001 from Queen Ethelburga's College, Harrogate. The Peel, Linlithgow Palace and Loch adjacent. Sunday Services: 9.30am and 11.00am

Open all year, May to September, Monday to Saturday 10.00am-4.00pm;

Sunday 12.30pm-4.00pm; October to April, Monday to Friday 10.00am-3.00pm

CHURCH OF SCOTLAND   ⊘   ⛶ (on request)   ⧠   **A**

794 ST PETER'S EPISCOPAL CHURCH, LINLITHGOW

NS 000 770

153 High Street, Linlithgow

Church website: www.stpeterslinlithgow.co.uk

Built in 1928 as a memorial to George Walpole, Bishop of Edinburgh and his wife Mildred, with assistance from missions in England and USA. Design by J Walker Todd of Dick Peddie & Todd is a Byzantine basilica with a 'cross in the square' plan form, a high central dome and half dome over the sanctuary apse. It is a small church located on south side of High Street, and is popular as a refuge from the main shopping area. Services: Sunday Sung Eucaharist 9.30am; Tuesday Said Eucharist 10.30am

Open Tuesday and Saturday, from May to September 2.00-4.00pm, or by arrangement with the Priest-in-Charge 01506 842384

SCOTTISH EPISCOPAL   wc   ⛶   ⧠

ST PETER'S EPISCOPAL CHURCH, LINLITHGOW

795 LIVINGSTON VILLAGE KIRK

NT 037 669

Kirk Lane, Livingston

Church website: www.livoldpar.org.uk

There has been a church on the site since 12th century. The present building was rebuilt 1732. Late 18th-century pews and pulpit with Gothic sounding board and a pretty stair. Pewter communion vessels and old collecting shovels on display. Plaque in entrance commemorates Covenanters from village who were drowned off Orkney. Kirkyard has some fine monuments from 17th and 18th centuries, including some

LIVINGSTON VILLAGE KIRK

lively headstones featuring phoenixes and leafy cartouches. Close to Heritage Centre. Sunday Service: 10.00am. Other services as advertised on notice board

Open by arrangement, telephone the Minister 01506 420227

CHURCH OF SCOTLAND   🚻 📶 ② **B**

796 KIRK OF CALDER, MID CALDER

NT 074 673

Main Street, Mid Calder

Church website: www.kirkofcalder.com

This 16th-century parish church, recently restored, won the West Lothian Award for Conservation in 1992. John Knox, James 'Paraffin' Young, David Livingstone and Frederick Chopin have visited here – we look forward to meeting you too! Admission free, donations welcome. Organ by James Conacher 1888. Restoration of stained glass windows 1995.

Sunday Service: 10.30am

Open May to September, Sunday 2.00- 4.00pm. Near to Almondell Country Park. Open all year

CHURCH OF SCOTLAND

🚻 📶 ② 🍴 📖 ☕ **A**

KIRK OF CALDER, MID CALDER

797 POLBETH HARWOOD PARISH CHURCH

NT 017 628

Chapelton Drive, Polbeth, West Calder

The congregation was formed in 1795 and the church completed in 1796 as Burgher Kirk. Congregation translated from West Calder to Polbeth in 1962. Fifteen minutes' walk from West Calder station.

Sunday Service: 11.00am

Open Monday and Wednesday during school term time, 10.00am-12.00 noon; Thursday 6.00-8.00pm during summer

CHURCH OF SCOTLAND ♿ ☕

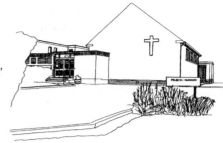

POLBETH HARWOOD PARISH CHURCH

798 TORPHICHEN KIRK

NS 969 725

The Bowyett, Torphichen

Built in 1756 on the site of the nave of the 12th-century preceptory, it is a T-shaped building with three galleries including a laird's loft. Two centre pews can be tipped back to form extended communion tables. Sanctuary stone in the graveyard. Preceptory church adjoining in the care of Historic Scotland. Sunday Services: 11.15am and 7.00pm, 2nd Sunday

Open parish church and preceptory Easter to end October, Saturday 11.00am-5.00pm, Sunday 2.00-5.00pm. Exhibition. Charge for entry to preceptory

CHURCH OF SCOTLAND wc 📖 🧴 **A**

TORPHICHEN KIRK

799 ST NICHOLAS, UPHALL

NT 060 722

Ecclesmachan Road, Uphall

Church website: www.strathbrockparish.net

Tower and nave with Romanesque doorway of
1187, Buchan stairs of the 17th century, aisles
added 1590 and 1878. A picture shows the
balconies that existed before the restoration of
1938. Buried in the tower are Erskines, Earls of
Buchan and sons. Mixture of old and modern
stained glass windows. The bell, one of the
oldest in West Lothian, is inscribed '*in onore sancte*
nicolae campana ecclegie de strabork anno dni mviii'.
'Judas' Bible of 1613. Sunday Service: 11.00am
Open by arrangement, telephone the
Minister 01506 852550

CHURCH OF SCOTLAND   👤 🚻 ⊘ 📖 **B**

ST NICHOLAS, UPHALL

800 WHITBURN SOUTH PARISH CHURCH

NS 947 646

Manse Road, Whitburn

In its present form dating from 1729, the walls house a modern interior of the
1950s, the result of a fire. Cruciform and typically Georgian, though some earlier
architectural features are evident. The graveyard is host to several local notables

and is the last resting place of
Robert Burns's eldest daughter,
Elizabeth Paton (dear 'Bought'
Bess) who married John Bishop,
the overseer at Polkemmet Estate.
Sunday Service: 11.00am all year;
1st Sunday September to May
6.00pm; 1st Sunday in June
3.00pm; Christmas Day 10.00am,
Maundy Thursday 7.00pm
Open by arrangement with the Church
Officer, telephone Mr John Tennant
01501 741627

CHURCH OF SCOTLAND   👤 🚻 ⊘ **B**

WHITBURN SOUTH PARISH CHURCH

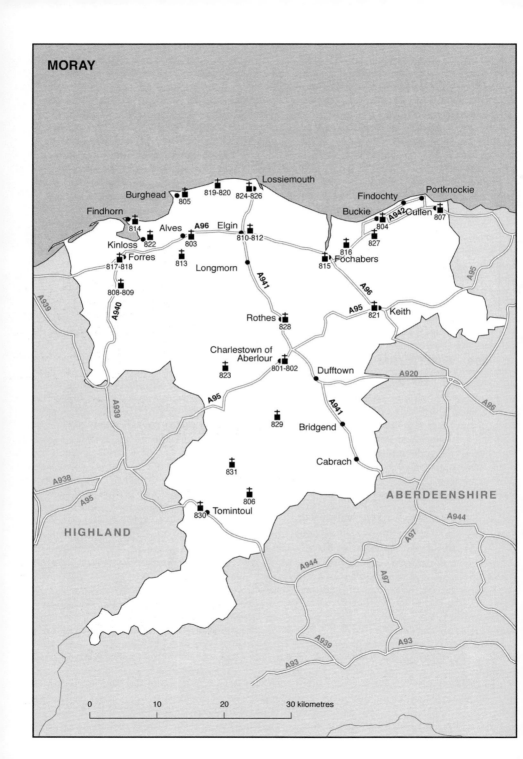

MORAY

Local Representative: Mrs Elizabeth Beaton, 28 St Peter's Road, Duffus, Elgin (*telephone* 01343 830301)

801 ABERLOUR PARISH CHURCH

NJ 264 428

The Square, Aberlour

Originally dedicated to St Drostan, the church was built in 1812. The neo-Norman tower 1840 by William Robertson, architect, Elgin, was the sole survivor of a disastrous fire in 1861. George Petrie, architect, rebuilt the church in neo-Norman style. Choir added 1933 by J Wittet in memory of Sir James Ritchie Findlay. First organ by Brindley & Foster 1900, rebuilt by Ernest Lawton 1932, and present organ rebuilt by Sandy Edmonstone 1991. Sunday Service: 11.00am

Key available, telephone 01340 871027

CHURCH OF SCOTLAND   🦽 📶 🔊 **B**

ABERLOUR PARISH CHURCH

802 ST MARGARET OF SCOTLAND, ABERLOUR

NJ 272 431

High Street, Aberlour

Designed by Alexander Ross and consecrated in 1879, the tall Gothic church retains its splendid original interior. Built for local Episcopal congregation and the orphanage 120 years ago, the feet of hundreds of children have worn down the Victorian tiled floor. Lovely carvings of flowers, birds and squirrels on pillar capitals and screen arch. Organ originally built by Harrison 1879.

Sunday Services: 11.00am, 1st Sunday in each month; 9.15am other Sundays

Key from Aberlour Hotel (must be signed for)

SCOTTISH EPISCOPAL 🦽 📖 **A**

ST MARGARET OF SCOTLAND, ABERLOUR

803 ALVES CHURCH

NJ 125 616

Just south of A96, 1 mile west of Alves

Built 1845 to a design by Thomas Mackenzie of Elgin but only completed in 1878
by architects A & W Reid & Melvin, Elgin. United with the North Church in 1931.
An imposing symmetrical building with round-headed windows and a square
tower capped by a balustrade and urns. Alves Parish Church was originally a
prebend held by the Chantor of Elgin Cathedral. Sunday Service: 11.30am, 1st
Sunday of each month

Open by arrangement telephone 01343 850209

CHURCH OF SCOTLAND [⟨wheelchair⟩] [wc] ⟨?⟩ **B**

804 ST PETER'S CHURCH, BUCKIE

NJ 419 653

St Andrew's Square, Buckie

Church website: www.stpetersbuckie.eboard.com

To plans donated by Bishop Kyle and supervised
by A and W Reid of Elgin. Dedicated on a site
donated by Sir William Gordon. Rose window.
Recent artwork includes six murals of excellent
quality in church hall and two canvases in the
church of David and Saul and of the 'Death of
St Joseph', by local artist Lynn Thain. High altar
of Italian marble surrounded by murals depicting

ST PETER'S CHURCH, BUCKIE

'The Calming of the Storm' and 'The Walking on the Water'. Reredos and baptistry,
C J Menart 1907. Statue of Our Lady of Aberdeen, copy of original in Brussels.
Organ originally by Bryceson 1875, recently installed here from Fort Augustus
Abbey. Services: Saturday Vigil Mass 6.30pm; Sunday 10.00am; weekdays 9.30am

Open daily, 9.00am-6.00pm

ROMAN CATHOLIC [📖] ⟨♟⟩ **A**

805 BURGHEAD CHURCH

NJ 114 688

Grant Street, Burghead

Built as the United Free church by Mr Anderson of Hopeman in 1861, extended
and gallery added 1908. The parish church began as a Chapel of Ease of Duffus
Kirk in 1823 and a successor church opened in 1902. After the Union of 1929, the
United Free church was used. Stained glass by Father Giles Connacher of
Pluscarden Abbey using *dalles de verre* technique. Bell from original Chapel of Ease.
Sunday Service: 11.30am

Open by arrangement, telephone 01343 830932

CHURCH OF SCOTLAND [⟨wheelchair⟩] [wc] ⟨?⟩

806 OUR LADY OF PERPETUAL SUCCOUR, CHAPELTOWN, BRAES OF GLENLIVET

NJ 242 210

3 miles east of B9008, turn off at Auchnarrow

Pink granite Scottish Romanesque church with tower. Built 1896-7 in farmland setting encircled by hills, designed by well-known late Victorian/Edwardian architect John Kinross of Edinburgh, replacing an earlier building of 1828. Vivid stencil decoration illuminates the interior. The finely carved chancel rails, pulpit and canopied reredos are of high quality, while angels with musical instruments in five gilded panels decorate the altar front. Sunday Service: 11.00am every 3rd Sunday in rotation with Tomintoul and Tombae

Open by arrangement, telephone 01807 580226

ROMAN CATHOLIC [♿] **A**

807 OLD KIRK OF CULLEN

NJ 507 664

Old Cullen, ¾ mile south-west of Cullen town centre

This 13th-century church was originally dedicated to St Mary the Virgin and is the burial place of the 'interior parts' of Queen Elizabeth de Burgh 1327. A chaplainry was endowed here by Robert I in 1327 and the church acquired collegiate status in 1543. Later additions include the St Anne's Aisle of 1539, while there is a fine example of a laird's loft 1602. Other features include a pre-Reformation aumbry or sacrament house, tombs and monuments including one to James, 1st Earl of Seafield, Chancellor of Scotland at the Treaty of Union of 1707, and 17th-century box pews. The churchyard has many interesting and imposing tombs, monuments and gravestones. Sunday Service: 10.30am

Open summer 2.00-4.00pm Tuesday and Friday and by arrangement,

telephone the Minister 01542 841851

CHURCH OF SCOTLAND [♿] [wc] [📖] [👤] **A**

OLD KIRK OF CULLEN

808 EDINKILLIE PARISH CHURCH

NJ 020 466

Edinkillie, Dunphail, 9 miles south of Forres
Small church built 1741 in traditional 18th-
century style. Central pulpit and galleries on
three sides. Fine pipe organ. Beautifully
situated on the banks of the River Divie.
Linked with Dyke.
Sunday Service: 12.00 noon
Open by arrangement, telephone
Mr C J Falconer (Beadle) 01309 611220 or
Mr W Reid 01309 611279
CHURCH OF SCOTLAND 🧑‍🦽 wc

EDINKILLIE PARISH CHURCH

809 DYKE PARISH CHURCH

NH 990 584

Dyke, near Forres, Moray
Built 1781 in centre of village. Interesting
crypt and triple pulpit (one of the only
two in Scotland). Follow road to Brodie
Castle, turning right to village before
castle entrance. Linked with Edinkillie.
Sunday Service: 10.30am
Open by arrangement, key in village,
telephone 01309 641257
CHURCH OF SCOTLAND 🧑‍🦽 ⊙ 🚻 **A**

DYKE PARISH CHURCH

810 GREYFRIARS CONVENT OF MERCY, ELGIN

NJ 219 628

Abbey Street, Elgin
Beautiful and careful restoration, 1891-1908, by architect John Kinross for the 3rd
Marquess of Bute, of a 15th-century Franciscan friary. Magnificently carved oak
screen divides the choir from the nave and a splendid barrel-vaulted ceiling
stretches unbroken to the stained glass window above the altar. Fine cloister with
original medieval well. Services: Masses Tuesday 10.00am and Friday 7.00pm
Open by arrangement with the Sisters of Mercy, telephone 01343 547806.
Rose garden open May to September (entrance in Institution Road)
ROMAN CATHOLIC wc 📖 **A**

GREYFRIARS CONVENT OF MERCY, ELGIN

HOLY TRINITY, ELGIN

811 HOLY TRINITY, ELGIN

NJ 214 630

Trinity Place, Elgin

Gothic style on a Greek cross ground-plan to a design by William Robertson 1826. The crenellated and pinacled south entrance gable intended as an architectural feature visible from the High Street is now blocked by the ring-road. Chancel added 1852 and interior recast; nave lengthened 1879. Plain dignified interior with late 19th-century stained glass. Services: Sunday Holy Communion 8.00am, Family Eucharist 11.00am, Evensong 6.30pm; Monday Holy Communion 5.45pm, Tuesday 9.00am, Wednesday 8.00am and Friday 11.00am

Open 9.00am-5.00pm

SCOTTISH EPISCOPAL ☒ ☺ **B**

812 ST SYLVESTER'S, ELGIN

NJ 219 626

Institution Road, Elgin

The church and presbytery were designed and completed in 1844, architect Thomas Mackenzie of Elgin. Dedication in recognition of the financial support by the younger brother of Sir William Drummond of Grantully who took the name Sylvester on converting to Catholicism. Lady Altar 1915, by R B Pratt. Sanctuary altered 1968 in keeping with the new liturgy. Major alterations to church and adjoining school 2000 to form sacristy and meeting rooms, by Ashley Bartlam Partnership. Large cross by the monks of Pluscarden. Services: Saturday Vigil 6.00pm; Sunday 11.15am

Open 9.00am-8.00pm daily except Tuesdays

ROMAN CATHOLIC ♿ ☒ ☺ **B**

PLUSCARDEN ABBEY, ELGIN

813 PLUSCARDEN ABBEY, ELGIN

NJ 143 576

Pluscarden, near Elgin

Church website: www.pluscardenabbey.org

Founded in 1230 by Alexander II for Valiscaulian monks, it became Benedictine in 1454. Following the Reformation it was the property of various local families, culminating in the Dukes of Fife from whom it was bought by the Marquess of Bute, and whose son, Lord Colum, gave it to the monks in 1943. The buildings were eventually re-occupied in 1948. There are a number of interesting works by prominent artists and architects following the restoration. Member of Moray Church trail. The abbey offers retreat accommodation for men and women. Full details of this, together with services and opening times, may be obtained by telephoning 01343 890257 (fax 01343 890258)

Annual Pluscarden Pentecost lectures: Tuesday, Wednesday and Thursday after Pentecost.

Open daily 4.45am-8.45pm

ROMAN CATHOLIC 🚹 🚾 🛈 📖 **A**

814 FINDHORN CHURCH

NJ 042 642

On Main Street of Findhorn village

This is the third Findhorn village, the site of the previous two now lying under the sea. Findhorn consists of rows of fishermen's cottages, gable-end to the water in the local manner. The church was built as Kinloss Free Church in 1843 to a design by John Urquhart of Forres. A handsome building in stone with a pretty tower and lunette windows along the sides. The congregation united with Kinloss in 1930. Sunday Service: 10.00am alternating with Kinloss.

Open by arrangement, telephone 01309 691861

CHURCH OF SCOTLAND 🚹 🚾

GORDON CHAPEL, FOCHABERS

ST NINIAN'S, TYNET

815 GORDON CHAPEL, FOCHABERS

NJ 346 589

Castle Street, Fochabers

Church website: www.gordonchapel.org.uk

Built in 1834 to a design by Archibald Simpson, restored in 1874. Stained glass includes designs by Sir Edward Burne-Jones. Fine organ by Hill 1874. The church is upstairs with the rectory (originally a school) below. Services: Sunday 10.30am Eucharist with hymns; 1st Sunday of the month 6.30pm Sung Evensong

Open daily during daylight hours

SCOTTISH EPISCOPAL [wc] 📖 **A**

816 ST NINIAN'S, TYNET

NJ 379 613

Mill of Tynet, Fochabers

The oldest post-Reformation Catholic church still in use in Scotland. At the request of the Duke of Gordon 1755, built to resemble a sheep-cot in days when it was still an offence to celebrate Mass. Renovated 1957, Ian Lindsay, architect, the long low whitewashed building is still 'a church in disguise'. Sunday Service: 8.30am

Open by arrangement, key from 'Golar', Newlands of Tynet (opposite church)

ROMAN CATHOLIC **A**

817 ST LAURENCE PARISH CHURCH, FORRES

NJ 035 588

High Street, Forres

Built on a site of Christian worship dating from mid-13th century, today's neo-Gothic building – designed by John Robertson and dedicated in 1906 – is a fine example of the stonemason's craft. The stained glass windows by Douglas Strachan and Percy Bacon help to create the special atmosphere of peace and beauty. Font replica of one in Dryburgh Abbey. Information leaflets in English, French, German, Spanish and Italian are free. Sunday Service: 10.00am

Open May to September, Monday to Friday 10.00am-12.00 noon, 2.00-4.00pm. Other times by arrangement, telephone 01309 672260

CHURCH OF SCOTLAND   [ ][wc][⊘][⌇][⌂] **B**

818 ST JOHN'S CHURCH, FORRES

NJ 041 592

Victoria Road, Forres

Built 1830-40, to an italianate design by Patrick Wilson, remodelled and enlarged by Thomas Mackenzie, 1844. The building has been beautified over the years including the laying of mosaic tiles throughout the chancel and aisles. The frontage is adorned with a wheel window, the entrance sheltered by an arcaded logia and flanked by a campanile. A large canvas in the apse 1906 and mural behind the font, 1911, are the work of William Hole RSA.

Sunday Services: 8.00am, 10.00am

Open daylight hours (or key at Rectory)

SCOTTISH EPISCOPAL [ ][⊘][⌂] **A**

ST JOHN'S CHURCH, FORRES

819 THE MICHAEL KIRK, GORDONSTOUN

NJ 193 689

Duffus, by Elgin

Church website: www.gordonstoun.org.uk

Reached by footpath from Gordonstoun (the 'silent' walk), this dignified little church was built in 1705 as a mausoleum for 'the Wizard Laird', Sir Robert Gordon, on the site of the ancient Kirk of Ogstoun. Roofed, furnished and fitted by John Kinross in 1900 for Lady Gordon-Cumming. Remarkable window tracery enhanced by flower carvings. Services: Holy Communion 8.40am most Sundays during the academic year; candlelit Compline 9.00pm, Thursdays during winter term

Open by arrangement with School Reception, telephone 01343 835804

INTERDENOMINATIONAL [⌂] (school shop) **A**

THE MICHAEL KIRK, GORDONSTOUN

ST THOMAS' CHURCH, KEITH

820 ST CHRISTOPHER'S, GORDONSTOUN

NJ 184 690
Duffus, by Elgin
Church website: www.gordonstoun.org.uk

Gordonstoun School was founded in 1934 by Kurt Hahn, with the aim of encouraging self-reliance and independence. St Christopher's is the main school chapel, built 1965-6 to designs by former pupil Patrick Huggins, to complement the Michael Kirk (see above). Seating is 'gathered about the lectern pulpit and the Communion Table' whose positions emphasise the equal importance of Word and Sacrament, while giving space for orchestral or dramatic performances.
Main school service: Sunday 10.45am during term time
Open by arrangement with School Reception, telephone 01343 835804
INTERDENOMINATIONAL ♿ wc 📖 (school shop)

821 ST THOMAS' CHURCH, KEITH

NJ 430 502
Chapel Street, Keith

Built 1831, architect William Robertson of Elgin. Successor to 1785 chapel and cottage at Kempcairn, following planning and fundraising by Father Lovi. Roman Doric pilastered exterior and 'plain' interior with nave and sanctuary. Enlarged with copper-clad dome, altar, communion rails, pulpit and oak pews 1915. Altar piece painting 'The Incredulity of St Thomas', commissioned by Charles X of France 1828. Fine stained glass windows 1970s. St John Ogilvie Chapel commemorating saint born nearby. Extensive restoration 1996
Open daily, dawn to dusk
ROMAN CATHOLIC ♿ 🎧 📖 wc A

822 KINLOSS CHURCH

NJ 063 617

At west end of Kinloss, on B9011

The present church, built 1765, is an elegant rectangle. The crenellated tower was added and the interior remodelled by A & W Reid of Elgin 1863. Before the mid-17th century the congregation met in the chapter house of Kinloss Abbey (founded 1151), of which only ruins remain. Money raised from the sale of stones from the abbey was used to build the first parish church, in use before 1657.

Sunday Service: 10.00am alternating with Findhorn

Open by arrangement telephone 01309 691288

CHURCH OF SCOTLAND   B

823 KNOCKANDO PARISH CHURCH

NJ 186 429

turn off B9102 at Cardhu

Award-winning design for new church by the Law & Dunbar-Nasmith Partnership 1993 on the site of an earlier building destroyed by fire in 1990. Sympathetic with the building which it has replaced. The Creation is symbolised in a new stained glass window by Andrew Lawson-Johnson. Watch-house in the kirkyard. Sunday Service: 10.30am

Open Wednesday only, 2.00pm-4.00pm July and August

CHURCH OF SCOTLAND

KNOCKANDO PARISH CHURCH

824 ST COLUMBA'S, LOSSIEMOUTH

NJ 232 711

Union Street, Lossiemouth

Small church in the shape of a Latin Cross, designed by Arthur Harrison of Stockton-on-Tees and paid for by the Bute family. The building materials were all shipped from Teesside. The sanctuary lamp is in the form of a ship's lamp. Stained glass window by Fr Ninian Sloan of 'Our Lady Star of the Sea' dedicated to the memory of the Royal and Allied navies stationed at Lossiemouth 1946-72 and donated by them. Sunday Mass: 6.30pm

Open by arrangement, telephone Mrs Margaret Kinnaird 01343 813539

ROMAN CATHOLIC   WC

825 ST GERARDINE'S HIGH, LOSSIEMOUTH

NJ 233 706

St Gerardine's Road, Lossiemouth

The foundation stone was laid in 1898 and the building is of Norman design by Sir J J Burnet. The plainness of the Norman Tower, white harled walls and red roof belie the magnificent interior. The features include many items of stained glass depicting various biblical themes. Sunday Services: 11.00am and 6.00pm

Open by arrangement, telephone the Minister 01343 813146,

or Mr James Cumming 01343 812194

CHURCH OF SCOTLAND ♿ ⑦ 📖 **B**

826 ST MARGARET OF SCOTLAND, LOSSIEMOUTH

NJ 227 706

Stotfield Road, Lossiemouth

Small church of 1922 with Gothic detailing built to a design by Alexander Ross of Inverness, responsible for Episcopal churches great and small throughout the north, including Inverness Cathedral. Simple interior with open timber vaulted ceiling. Services: Sunday Parish Eucharist 9.30am; Thursday Eucharist 10.00am and Eventide Prayer 5.30pm

Open May to September,

Fridays 2.00pm–5.00pm

SCOTTISH EPISCOPAL 📿

ST MARGARET OF SCOTLAND, LOSSIEMOUTH

827 ST GREGORY'S CHURCH, PRESHOME

NJ 409 615

Preshome, Clochan

Built in 1788. A wide rectangular church with harled walls and freestone dressing. The church is adorned with urn finials; its west end is a charming product of 18th-century taste, in which Italian Baroque has been skilfully naturalised to a Banffshire setting. Copy of a painting of St Gregory the Great by Annibale Caracci. Oustanding survival of pipe organ by James Bruce of Edinburgh 1820, with carved Gothic case. Two holy water stoups of Portsoy marble. Sunday Service: Mass occasionally at 6.00pm

Open by arrangement, telephone Mr G Gordon, St Gregory's Chapel House

ROMAN CATHOLIC **A**

ST GREGORY'S CHURCH, PRESHOME

ROTHES PARISH CHURCH

828 ROTHES PARISH CHURCH

NJ 278 492

High Street / Seafield Square, Rothes

Built in 1781 with a steeple added in 1870. A traditional Scottish design of the
Reformed tradition with the pulpit on the long wall, a three-sided gallery and an
apse. Linked with Knockando. Sunday Service: 12.00 noon

Open July to August, Tuesday to Thursday 2.00-4.00pm

CHURCH OF SCOTLAND 🔖 📖 ⚲

829 OLD SEMINARY, SCALAN

NJ 246 195

Braes of Glenlivet, Ballindalloch, Banffshire (turn off B9008 at Pole Inn)

Scalan (Gaelic for hut), probably turf shelter serving sheiling during summer
grazing. First home for remote, recusant Catholic seminary established in 1716 for
the education of boys intended for the priesthood. The improved college was built
1762-7, becoming a farmhouse after the Seminary moved to Aquhorthies,
Aberdeenshire in 1799. Services: Annual Mass, 1st Sunday July 4.00pm

Open all year

ROMAN CATHOLIC **A**

OLD SEMINARY, SCALAN

830 ST MICHAEL'S, TOMINTOUL

NJ 169 185

At south end of main street in Tomintoul

Church website: www.saintmikes.co.uk

St Michael's was built in 1837 to a design by George Mathewson of Dundee, replacing a small chapel on the outskirts of the village. The cruciform church, lit by narrow Gothic windows, has a bellcote crowning the west gable. The east transept has been adapted as the Presbytery. The interior was remodelled in the 1930s and is now largely decorated with art-work from adjoining St Michael's Youth Centre. The Youth Centre is a residential centre operated by the Diocese of Abderdeen in a former convent for those on retreat or visiting the Grampian Highlands. Sunday Service: 11.00am every 3rd Sunday in rotation with Tombae and Chapeltown

Open at all times

ROMAN CATHOLIC 🦽 B

831 CHURCH OF THE INCARNATION, TOMBAE, TOMNAVOULIN

NJ 217 256

1 mile south-east of Tomnavoulin

Designed by John Gall of Aberdeen, 1827-9, but completed in 1844 by Bishop James Kyle, replacing a simple 'mass-house' further upstream. The scenic rural site overlooks the River Livet, farmland and hills, now scantily populated. Gothic Revival church with pinnacled west front and lofty, elegant vaulted interior lit by large traceried windows. The former chancel served as Presbytery until 1862 when replaced by neighbouring house, and then as a school until 1903. Sunday Service: 11.00am every 3rd Sunday in rotation with Tomintoul and Chapeltown

Open by arrangement, telephone 01807 580226

ROMAN CATHOLIC 🦽 B

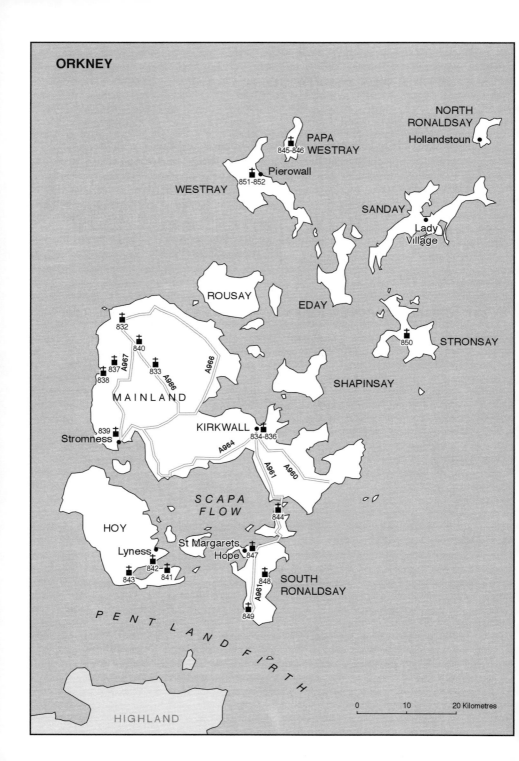

ORKNEY

Local Representative: Mr R L B Cormack, Westness House, Rousay, Orkney (*telephone* 01856 821286)

832 ST MAGNUS CHURCH, BIRSAY

HY 248 277
Across the road from the Earl's Palace
Church website:
www.birsay.org.uk / stmagnus.htm
The original church was built by Earl
Thorfinn *c.*1060 and has been altered
and restored several times, most recently
in 1986. Stained glass window by Alex
Strachan showing scenes from the life of
St Magnus. Inside the church are two
16th- and 17th-century tombstones.

ST MAGNUS CHURCH, BIRSAY

Seventeenth-century belfry. Small gallery. The Mons Bellus stone is probably from
the nearby Bishop's Palace. The church is now maintained by the St Magnus
Church Birsay Trust. Services: occasional details locally
Open daily, April to September. Key available all year from village shop.
Note – due to close for part of 2006 for refurbishment
NON-DENOMINATIONAL [wc] (nearby) ⌂ **B**

833 ST MICHAEL'S, HARRAY

HY 314 179
Mainland
Plain white rendered church of 1836 with Caithness slate roof and round-headed
windows. Pulpit with sounding board with pews and galleries round three sides.
Five stained glass windows.
Refurbished 1980s and extension of
1984 houses the vestry, meeting room,
kitchen and toilets. The bell, dated
1724, was gifted by the Earl of
Morton. Services 11.00am every 3rd
Sunday in rotation with Quoyloo and
Twatt; check locally
Open by arrangement, telephone
Mary Bichan, 01856 771273
CHURCH OF SCOTLAND [♿] [wc] ⏰ **B**

ST MICHAEL'S, HARRAY

834 ST MAGNUS CATHEDRAL, KIRKWALL

HY 449 108
Broad Street, Kirkwall
Church website:
www.orkney.gov.uk/heritage
The Cathedral Church of St Magnus
the Martyr was founded in 1137 by Earl
Rognvald Kolson and dedicated to his
uncle, Earl Magnus Erlendson.
Completed *c.*1500. It contains many
items of interest and ranks as one of
the finest cathedrals in Scotland. Organ
by Willis 1926. Owned and maintained
by Orkney Islands Council. St Magnus
Centre in Palace Road open Monday to
Saturday 8.30am-6.30pm. Sunday 1.30-

ST MAGNUS CATHEDRAL, KIRKWALL

6.30pm (reduced hours in winter); heritage centre, study library, refreshments and
souvenirs; free entry, disabled access/toilets. Sunday Service: 11.15am
Open April to September, Monday to Saturday 9.00am-6.00pm, Sunday 2.00-6.00pm;
October to March, Monday to Saturday 9.00am-1.00pm and 2.00-5.00pm.
Closed public holidays and Christmas festive season, except for Church Services.
Tours on application; tours of upper floors and tower must be booked. £5 per person
CHURCH OF SCOTLAND
♿ (side entrance) ♿ ♿ ♿ (braille and audio tape versions of guidebook available) **A**

835 KIRKWALL EAST CHURCH

HY 451 110
King Street
Church website: www.orkneycommunities.co.uk/kirkwalleastchurch
Built 1892, Architect S Blaikie Jr. In 2002 the interior was completely renovated to
provide a functional suite of rooms on two floors for church and community use.
Services are held in the Upper Room in a bright and friendly atmosphere.
Furnishings by Sui Generis, Eday, Orkney. Eustace Ingram organ.
Sunday Service: 11.15am
Open by arrangement with the Minister, telephone 01856 875469
CHURCH OF SCOTLAND ♿ ♿ ♿ ♿ **C**

836 ST OLAF'S, KIRKWALL

HY 452 106

Dundas Crescent

St Olaf's was opened by Bishop Suthers on St Olaf's Day (29 July) 1876. It is an imposing building of dressed stone, compact and with high timbered ceilings like a ship. Complete scheme of stained glass with windows by Heaton, Butler & Bayne, James Ballantine & Son and Ballantine & Gardiner, with the east window of the Ascension being the centrepiece. Stone credence and aumbry taken from the first St Olaf's church built in the 9th century. Organ by G M Holdich 1881. Services: Sunday Family Communion 9.30am; Wednesday Holy Communion 10.30am

Open in summer 10.00am–5.00pm; at other times by arrangement with the Priest in charge, telephone 01856 872024

SCOTTISH EPISCOPAL wc ⊑ (after service)

837 QUOYLOO CHURCH

HY 246 207

Mainland

Built in 1828 as a United Free Church and united with St Peter's in 1935. New hall, built mainly by voluntary labour, completed 1994. Wall hangings made by Guild and helpers, one for union of Harray and Sandwick in 1997. Photographs of previous Ministers. Services 11.00am every 3rd Sunday in rotation with Harray and Twatt; check locally

Open at all times

CHURCH OF SCOTLAND ♿ wc ⊘ ⊑ (after service)

QUOYLOO CHURCH

838 ST PETER'S, SANDWICK

HY 235 199
One mile north of Skara Brae, Mainland
Church website: www.srct.org.uk
A rare survival of a quite exceptional
unaltered Scots Parish Kirk of 1836.
Situated on a rugged and exposed site,
commanding views over the Bay of Skaill
with Skara Brae in the distance. Dominated
by a towering pulpit reaching to gallery
height, the austere interior powerfully
evokes the experience of Presbyterian
worship in the 19th century when over 500 packed the building – each allowed a
mere 18 inches of pew. Acquired by the Scottish Redundant Churches Trust in
1998 and restored in 2002-03. Europa Nostra award 2004
Open April to October 10.00am-6.00pm, November to March by arrangement with SRCT.
For events and service arrangements, telephone the SRCT 01334 472032
FORMER CHURCH OF SCOTLAND & **A**

ST PETER'S, SANDWICK

839 ST MARY'S, STROMNESS

HY 253 091
Church Road
Established as a mission church in July 1885, St Mary's became an independent
charge, moving into the present building, in 1888. The font and ciborium were
given by the Earl of Zetland. Joined with St Olaf's in Kirkwall in 1943. Two
beautiful modern stained glass windows. Services: Sunday 11.30am Family
Communion, Thursday 11.00am Holy Communion
Open by arrangement with Mr George Walker, Tostigan, Downies Lane,
Stromness, telephone 01856 850534
SCOTTISH EPISCOPAL wc ☕

840 TWATT CHURCH

HY 268 244
Mainland
Tall stone United Free Church of 1874 with front elevation of dressed local stone
with freestone corners and window facings. Inside, a gallery occupies three walls.
In the vestibule a memorial tablet commemorates the first Minister, John Garson.
Extension of 1974. The building is also used as the local Post Office. Services
11.00am every 3rd Sunday in rotation with Quoyloo and Harray; check locally
Open by arrangement with the Minister, telephone 01856 771803
CHURCH OF SCOTLAND & wc ♿ ☕ (after service)

TWATT CHURCH

841 ST COLUMBA'S, LONGHOPE, HOY

ND 312 908

At east end of Longhope

Built 1832 with windows on the south wall and the pulpit in the middle of the wall. Pews and gallery on three sides of pulpit. Communion table of carved oak by local tradesmen, gifted by Guild, 1924. Sandstone font sculpted by local mason to a design by W R Lethaby, architect of Melsetter House. Panels above vestry from the Spanish Armada. Sunday Service: 11.15am

Open at all times (entry through vestry door)

CHURCH OF SCOTLAND ⌖ ☐ **C**

842 ST JOHN'S, NORTH WALLS, HOY

ND 297 916

On B9047, 2 miles south of Lyness

A Mission Kirk, built in 1883 as a counter-attraction to the nearby Free Kirk. It was built by public subscription and often referred to as 'The Fisher Kirk' owing to the esteem in which its longest serving missionary, Mr Fisher, was held. Except for gas heating, all the fittings (pews, oil lamps, etc) are original. Service times variable

Open by arrangement with keyholders, telephone 01856 792234 or 01856 791226

CHURCH OF SCOTLAND **C**

843 CHAPEL OF ST COLM & MARGARET, MELSETTER, HOY

ND 270 893

On B9047 at south end of Hoy

Originally the Episcopal chapel for Melsetter House, William Richard Lethaby's Arts & Crafts 1900 masterwork. The chapel was his first experiment with concrete as a structural material. The theme for the chapel draws on the resonance between ship and Church in the early days on Christianity (Hebrews 6:19). Stained glass by Morris, Whall and Burne-Jones. Hanging by William Morris. Occasional concerts. Variable Services

House and chapel open by arrangement, telephone 01856 791352

ECUMENICAL ⌖ ☐ ⍟ **A**

THE ITALIAN CHAPEL

844   THE ITALIAN CHAPEL

HY 488 006

Lambholm, Orkney

All that remains of the Italian Prisoner of War Camp 60, the famous Italian Chapel was created from two Nissen huts in 1943, using material from sunken blockships in Scapa Flow. Wonderful testimony to the artistic skills of Domenico Chiocchetti and his fellow prisoners who were on Orkney to work on the construction of the Churchill Barriers. Beautifully designed chancel, altar, altar-rail and Holy water stoup. Painted glass windows depicting St Francis of Assisi and St Catherine of Siena. Restored 1960. A Preservation Committee is dedicated to the upkeep of the chapel. Sunday Service: 1st Sunday of summer months 3.00pm

Open daily

ROMAN CATHOLIC   🦽 📖 **B**

845   ST ANN'S, PAPA WESTRAY

HY 496 516

Next to school in centre of island

Built in 1842, this was the first kirk in Scotland to be given to the Free Church by the proprietor. Rectangular building with rubble masonry walls and harled exterior. Restoration 2001 by Orkney Islands Council, Health Board and congregation, St Ann's is now home to the Island's surgery, a small flat and community facilities. Several beautiful locally made felt hangings. Sunday Service: 2.30pm

Open at all times

CHURCH OF SCOTLAND 🦽 🚾 📖 ☕ **C**

846 ST BONIFACE, PAPA WESTRAY

HY 488 527

Kirkhouse, Papa Westray

Two Pictish cross-slabs found in kirkyard (one now in Orkney Museum, Kirkwall, the other in NMS) indicate that there was an 8th- century church here. The present building dates from 12th century, enlarged early 1700s and furnished with box pews, gallery and high pulpit. Restored 1993. Norse period hog-backed tombstone in the kirkyard. Occasional weekday services in summer and at Christmas and Easter

Open at all times

NON-DENOMINATIONAL   🚻 🗋

ST BONIFACE, PAPA WESTRAY

847 ST MARGARET'S, SOUTH RONALDSAY

HY 449 934

Church Road, St Margaret's Hope

Opened 1856 by the United Presbyterian Church and enlarged 1870. Its central location in the village of St Margaret's Hope led to it being deignated as the principal place of worship for the Parish of South Ronaldsay & Burray. Typical UP layout with central pulpit. Communion table and font from former St Lawrence's Church, Burray. Sunday Service: 11.00am (except June and August)

Open by arrangement with the Minister, telephone 01856 831288

CHURCH OF SCOTLAND

848 ST PETER'S, EASTSIDE, SOUTH RONALDSAY

HY 472 908

Formerly the North Parish Church for the island, the present oblong harled building, with Caithness slates in its churchyard, was constructed in 18th century and renovated in 1801 and 1967. Features a pulpit with sounding board on the long wall and a long central communion table (believed to be unique in Orkney). All pews are thought to be made from driftwood. The oil lamps have been converted to electricity. Sunday Service: 11.00am (June and August only), other occasional services as intimated

Open by arrangement, telephone Mrs M Laughton 01856 831233

CHURCH OF SCOTLAND **B**

849 OLD ST MARY'S CHURCH, BURWICK, SOUTH RONALDSAY

HY 441 843

Built on what is often claimed to be the earliest Christian site in Orkney, the former South Kirk was erected 1599. The present building, set in a small graveyard, overlooking the ayre of Burwick, was constructed 1790. The interior was renovated 1860. Contains what is now believed to be a Pictish coronation stone.
No regular services

Open by arrangement, telephone Mrs Y Nicholson 01856 831212

FORMER CHURCH OF SCOTLAND **B**

850 MONCUR MEMORIAL CHURCH, STRONSAY

HY 654 252

In centre of Stronsay

Stronsay's only church, built in 1955 to a design by Edinburgh architect Leslie Grahame MacDougall using a legacy from jute manufacturer Alexander Moncur whose maternal grandfather was Minister in Stronsay 1825-60. A large, harled, cruciform building, retaining many traditional Orcadian features in its construction. Red sandstone and blue whinstone blend with the wooden floor and large roof trusses to give a quiet, dignified appearance. Beautiful stained glass window of 'Christ as the Good Shepherd' by Marjorie Kemp 1935 enhances the chancel.
Sunday Service: Sunday 11.00am

Open daily 9.00am-9.00pm May to September; at other times by arrangement with the Minister 01857 616311

CHURCH OF SCOTLAND

851 WESTRAY PARISH KIRK

HY 457 462

Kirkbrae, Westray

Oblong barn-style building, built 1846, with part-piended roof of local flagstone slates. Original pulpit with canopy, topped by a dove. Whole building refurbished in 2002/03. Renewable energy (ground-source heat pump and wind turbine) to meet energy needs. Pipe organ by Solway Organs 1967. Sunday Service: 11.30am; Evening Services shared with Baptist and United Free Kirks; see local notices

Open at all times

CHURCH OF SCOTLAND **c**

WESTRAY PARISH KIRK

852 WESTRAY UNITED FREE CHURCH (NEW KIRK)

NY 446 473

The first minister, the Rev George Reid, did pioneering work of education, both sacred and secular, of the young people of Westray and the adjacent islands (which then worshipped in a much smaller building). The present church was built 1866-7 to seat 550. In 1899 the Reid Memorial Hall was erected, seating 200-300. This is now used for worship since, with a dwindling population, the church is now too big. Sunday Services 11.30am; Evening as advertised locally

Open by arrangement with the Minister, telephone 01857 677232

UNITED FREE [WC] 🚻 🖥 (after services) **C**

WESTRAY UNITED FREE CHURCH (NEW KIRK)

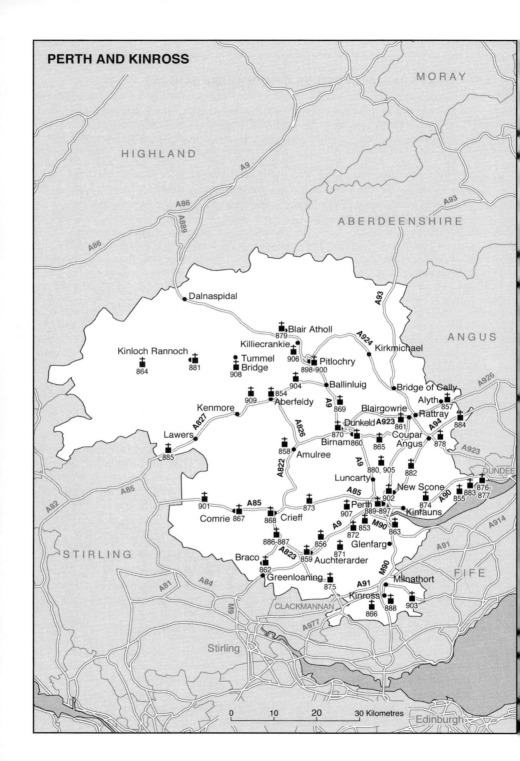

PERTH & KINROSS

853 ABERDALGIE AND DUPPLIN CHURCH

NO 064 194

Aberdalgie, off B9112

Nestling in the Earn Valley on a site of
enduring worship for centuries, the
present church was built by the Earl of
Kinnoull in 1773. A T-plan church of
local sandstone features a fine laird's loft
and Georgian retiring room.
Fourteenth-century Tournai marble
Oliphant monument. Sir Robert
Lorimer remodelled the interior in
1929. Extensive use of Austrian oak
gives the church a sense of peace and
simple dignity. Renovations 1994. One
of the four churches of the Stewartry
of Strathearn. Sunday Service: 11.15am
Open by arrangement, telephone
Rev Colin Williamson 01738 625854
CHURCH OF SCOTLAND [wc] **B**

ABERDALGIE AND DUPPLIN CHURCH

854 ABERFELDY PARISH CHURCH

NN 854 491

Taybridge Road

Church website: www.aberfeldypc.co.uk

Built in 1843 as a Free Church, the galleries were removed, the floor area reduced
and the roof lowered when it was made a church hall after a union of congregations in the 1960s. Reopened 2005 after major alterations with worship resuming
in a sanctuary extended back to its previous floor area, and a new extension added
to the east. With welcome area, crèche, halls and catering facilities the complex
serves as a church centre for the community.
Sunday Services: 11.15am and 6.30pm
Open by arrangement, telephone the Minister 01887 820656
CHURCH OF SCOTLAND [♿] [wc] (🔊) (☕) (after services) **C**

855 ABERNYTE PARISH CHURCH

NO 267 311

Abernyte, by Inchture

The present church was built in 1736 to replace a
building of pre-1400, although there may have
been a Celtic church here much earlier. Major
renovations in 1837 when the present cruciform
shape was established. Intricate beams, stained glass
and a modern wall hanging of 1992. Signposted
from village. Linked with Longforgan and
Inchture with Kinnaird. Sunday Service: 11.00am
Open during daylight hours
CHURCH OF SCOTLAND **B**

ABERNYTE PARISH CHURCH

856 ABERUTHVEN CHURCH

NN 979 155

2 miles from Auchterarder on A824

The present modest church was built in 1991.
The remains of the medieval parish church
of St Kattan are to the west of the village
with the beautifully detailed classical
Montrose Mausoleum of the 1730s by
William Adam. Services: Sunday 12.00 noon
Open by arrangement, telephone
Mrs Lockhart 01764 662204
CHURCH OF SCOTLAND 🦽 Montrose Mausoleum **A**

ABERUTHVEN CHURCH

857 ALYTH PARISH CHURCH

NO 243 488

Kirk Brae, Alyth

In a prominent position overlooking the town, Alyth
Parish Church was completed in 1839 to a design by
Thomas Hamilton. Gothic, with Romanesque influences,
and an unusually high spire. Eighth or 9th century
Pictish stone stands four feet high in the vestibule. All
windows are stained glass and include work by Alf
Webster. Large funeral escutcheon marks the death of Sir
George Ramsay in a duel in 1790. Three-manual organ
by Harrison & Harrison 1890. Sunday Service: 11.00am
Open July and August, Saturday 10.00am-12.00 noon,
Sunday 2.00-4.00pm
CHURCH OF SCOTLAND 🦽 wc wc ⊚ 🍴 📖 **B**

ALYTH PARISH CHURCH

858 AMULREE KIRK

NN 899 366

On A822 Crieff to Dunkeld road

Built in 1743, the setting of this white-washed building in a scantily populated area reminds us of the large numbers who emigrated to Canada, as commemorated in copies of old records available for inspection in the church. The beams from the Black Wood of Rannoch were first used in the construction of Wade's bridge over the Tay in Aberfeldy. Attractive stained glass window of Faith, Hope and Love. Sunday Service: 2.15pm fortnightly

Open all year

CHURCH OF SCOTLAND 🚫 wc ⊘ 🔥 ☕ (after services) **C**

859 ST KESSOG'S CHURCH, AUCHTERARDER

NN 942 128

High Street, Auchterarder

Built 1897, architect Alexander Ross of Inverness. Beautiful altar and reredos of Caen stone, both richly decorated with Florentine mosaic. Rood screen of white stone. East and west windows by Kempe of London. In quiet grounds and garden 50 yards off High Street. Linked with St James, Muthill. Sunday Service: January to June 9.30am, July to December 11.00am

Open July and August, Monday to Friday 2.00-4.00pm, or by arrangement, telephone the Very Rev Randal MacAlister 01764 662525

SCOTTISH EPISCOPAL 🚫 wc ⊘ 🔥 **C**

ST KESSOG'S CHURCH, AUCHTERARDER

860 ST MARY'S CHURCH, BIRNAM

NO 032 418

Perth Road, Birnam (in centre of village)

The main church and clock tower to a design by William Slater 1858, with north aisle by Norman & Beddoe 1883. Slater font and cover, Kempe east window, William Morris windows to Burne-Jones designs. Organ originally by Foster & Andrews 1874. Three-bell chime, clock by James Ramsay of Dundee 1882. Beautifully kept churchyard. Services: Sunday 9.45am; Wednesday 9.30am

Open by arrangement, telephone 01350 727329

SCOTTISH EPISCOPAL 🚫 (via Rectory) wc 📖 **B**

861   BLAIRGOWRIE PARISH CHURCH

NO 177 454

James Street, Blairgowrie

The present building was completed in 1904 in Early
English Gothic style with transepts, aisles, apse and
a small back gallery. Five stained glass windows in
the apse depict scenes from the life of Moses.
Norman & Beard organ 1907, rebuilt 1989 by
Mr A F Edmondstone. The first Free Church of
Blairgowrie 1843 is now the hall and back vestibule.
Sunday Service: 11.00am

Open by arrangement with the Minister,
telephone 01250 872146

CHURCH OF SCOTLAND wc ② ᛁ

BLAIRGOWRIE PARISH CHURCH

862   ARDOCH PARISH CHURCH, BRACO

NO 839 098

Feddal Road, Braco (B8033 Braco-Kinbuck)

Officially opened for worship in 1781 as a
'chapel of ease', the church was originally a
rectangular building. The bellcote was added in
1836 and a chancel built on the east end by
William Simpson of Stirling in 1890. The most
recent addition is the church hall, built 1985.
Ardoch Church sits close by the famous Roman
camp. Sunday Service: 11.30am in 2006

Open by arrangement, telephone 01786 880589

CHURCH OF SCOTLAND ♿ wc ② c

ARDOCH PARISH CHURCH, BRACO

863   DUNBARNEY PARISH CHURCH, BRIDGE OF EARN

NO 130 185

Manse Road, Bridge of Earn (off main street)

Built 1787. Pedimented bellcote added,
interior recast and other alterations 1880.
Rectangular plan with bow-ended west
porch. Sunday Service: 9.30am

Open June to August by arrangement,
telephone 01738 812463. Annual Flower Festival,
last weekend in September (Friday, Saturday
and Sunday)

CHURCH OF SCOTLAND wc ② c

DUNBARNEY PARISH CHURCH,
BRIDGE OF EARN

864 BRAES OF RANNOCH PARISH CHURCH, BRIDGE OF GAUR

NN 507 566

South Loch Road, Bridge of Gaur

Built in 1907, Peter MacGregor Chalmers. The
bellcote is from an earlier building of 1776 and
also borne by a church built in 1855 on this site.
Granite-walled interior, unusual chancel and lovely
woodwork give a special atmosphere of peace and
beauty. Rothwell pipe organ from Urquhart Church,
Elgin, rebuilt 1991 David Loosley. This was the
only charge of Rev Archibald Eneas Robertson
(1907-20), first ascender of all 'Munros' in Scotland
(283 peaks over 3000ft). Sunday Service: 9.45am
Open daily
CHURCH OF SCOTLAND 📖 **B**

BRAES OF RANNOCH PARISH CHURCH,
BRIDGE OF GAUR

865 CAPUTH PARISH CHURCH

NO 088 401

Caputh 4 miles east of Dunkeld on A984

Now into its 3rd century, Caputh Church was
built in 1798. There has been a church in Caputh
since the 9th century, the present one being a fine
stone building. The interior has oak furnishings,
stained glass windows. Organ by James Bruce of
Edinburgh, c.1830. Sunday Service: 11.15am
Open by arrangement, telephone
Mrs Easton 01738 710389
CHURCH OF SCOTLAND 🚾 ⍰

CAPUTH PARISH CHURCH

866 CLEISH CHURCH

NT 095 981

2 miles from M90 Exit 5

Built on 13th-century site in 1832 with additions
1897. Organ and lights from St Giles, Edinburgh.
The hymn 'Jesus, tender Shepherd, hear me' was
written by former Minister's wife in the Manse.
Interesting wall chart and graveyard.
Sunday Service: 11.15am
Open daily, 10.00am-5.00pm
CHURCH OF SCOTLAND ⍰ **B**

CLEISH CHURCH

867 COMRIE PARISH CHURCH

NN 770 221

Burrell Street, Comrie

Designed and built in 1881 by George T
Ewing on a site surrounded by attractive
grounds overlooking the River Earn.
Organ by T C Lewis, built 1910 for the
London Exhibition. Regular bus service
from Perth. Linked with Dundurn.
Sunday Service: 10.00am June to
September; 10.30am October to May
Open daily
CHURCH OF SCOTLAND [⌾] [wc] ② [] **C**

COMRIE PARISH CHURCH

868 CRIEFF PARISH CHURCH

NN 867 219

Strathearn Terrace

Church website: www.crieffparishchurch.org

St Michael's tall saddle-backed tower dominates the skyline of Crieff. Designed
by local architect George T Ewing and built of Alloa stone. The organ, originally
1882 by Forster & Andrews, was reconstructed 1964. Brilliant stained glass
windows including some by Alfred Webster and Stephen Adam.
Sunday Services: Informal Service with church band 9.30am; Morning Worship
11.00am; Evening Worship 6.30pm
Open by arrangement with the Minister, telephone 01764 653907
CHURCH OF SCOTLAND [⌾] [wc] ② **B**

869 ST ANNE'S, DOWALLY

NO 001 480

A9, 3½ miles north of Dunkeld

Church website: www.dunkeldcathedral.org.uk

Built in 1818 on the site of a 16th-century building, St Anne's is a small country
church with a bright interior. The designer was probably John Stewart, although
the church has been much altered since. Dates on the bell (which is still in use) and
belfry suggest that they came from the earlier church. The chancel has carved
screens which were originally in Dunkeld Cathedral. One of the memorials is to
John Robb, a minister of the parish who perished in the shipwreck in which Grace
Darling became a national heroine. Sunday Service: 2.00pm, 2nd, 4th and 5th
Sundays of the month
Open by arrangement, telephone Mrs Jim Kirk 01796 482407
CHURCH OF SCOTLAND **B**

870 DUNKELD CATHEDRAL

NO 024 426

Cathedral Street, Dunkeld

Church website: www.dunkeldcathedral.org.uk

The cathedral lies in a superb setting on the banks of the Tay. The restored choir, now used as the parish church, was completed in 1350. Chapter house 1469, adjacent to choir, contains a small museum. The choir, completely renovated 1907, contains a Lorimer screen, the tomb of the Wolf of Badenoch, the Scottish Horse Regimental Roll of Honour and Black Watch colours and memorial. The tower, ruined nave and south porch are in the care of Historic Scotland. Just off A9, at west end of Dunkeld. Sunday Services: Easter to Remembrance Sunday, 10.00am and 11.00am

Open daily, summer 9.30am-7.00pm, winter 9.30am-4.00pm,
or by appointment 01350 727792. Flower Festival 25-27 May 2006,
Concerts at 3.00pm Sundays in July 2006

CHURCH OF SCOTLAND [⅚] ⓐ 🛏 ⓘ (July and August) ⓘ **A**

871 DUNNING CHURCH

NO 019 145

Perth Road

Built for the United Free Church in plain Gothic style, the foundation stone was laid in 1908. The church became Church of Scotland in 1929, replacing the old St Serf's. The church features an open timber roof and a chancel and has simple well-crafted furnishings. Fine stained glass, including the west window of the Evangelists and a new window to mark the second Christian Millennium. Services: Sunday 10.30am

Open by arrangement, telephone R Nicol 01764
684203 (Monday to Saturday 7.00am-5.00pm)

CHURCH OF SCOTLAND [⅚] [wc] ⓐ 🍵

DUNNING CHURCH

872   FORTEVIOT CHURCH (ST ANDREW'S), FORTEVIOT

NO 050 174

In an area of historical importance – in the 9th
century Kenneth MacAlpin had his palace here, and a
basilica existed from the first half of the 8th century
– this church, the third, was erected in 1778. It was
remodelled in the mid-19th century. Celtic bell dated
AD 900, one of five Scottish bronze bells. Medieval
carved stones. The font is from the pre-Reformation
church of Muckersie united with Forteviot in 1618.
Organ by Hamilton of Edinburgh. Extensively
renovated 1994. One of the four churches of the
Stewartry of Strathearn. Sunday Service: 10.00am
Open by arrangement, telephone
Rev C Williamson 01738 625854
CHURCH OF SCOTLAND **C**

FORTEVIOT CHURCH
(ST ANDREW'S), FORTEVIOT

873   FOWLIS WESTER PARISH CHURCH

NN 928 241

The church is a 13th-century building renovated in
1927 by Jeffrey Waddell of Glasgow with much
Celtic ornament. It retains many of the original
features including a 'lepers' squint'. The Pictish cross
under the north wall is evidence of over 1,000 years
of Christian worship in the area. Turn off A85,
five miles from Crieff to Fowlis Wester (signed).
Sunday Service: 11.30am in 2006
Open by arrangement, telephone Mrs McColl 01764 683205
CHURCH OF SCOTLAND ♿ ② **B**

FOWLIS WESTER PARISH CHURCH

874   ST MADOES AND KINFAUNS CHURCH, GLENCARSE

NO 167 223

Glencarse, near Perth

Built 1799 on the site of earlier churches and refurbished in
1923. T-plan church with laird's gallery. New vestry and entrance
hall by David Murdoch of Methven 1996. Interesting historic
graveyard with 18th-century gravestones of sculptural merit.
Pictish St Madoes Stone now on display in Perth Museum and
Art Gallery. Contemporary embroidered pulpit falls. Sunday
Service: September to May 11.00am; June to August 10.00am
Open 1st Sunday of month, June to September 1.00-4.00pm
CHURCH OF SCOTLAND ♿ wc ② ⛪ **B**

ST MADOES AND KINFAUNS
CHURCH, GLENCARSE

875 GLENDEVON PARISH CHURCH

NN 979 051

West side of A823, one mile north of Tormaukin Hotel
Seventeenth-century church with large stained
glass window by Alf Webster of Glasgow 1913
and small stained glass window in memory of
Rev Alexander Taylor 1872-1949. Various
memorial plaques. Pulpit and Communion table
and chair carved by Mr Philips of Tormaukin.
Large gravestone to Jane Rutherford. Sunday
Service: 11.15am
Open at all times
CHURCH OF SCOTLAND [wc] **B**

GLENDEVON PARISH CHURCH

876 ALL SOULS' CHURCH, INVERGOWRIE

NO 347 303

59 Main Street, Invergowrie
Church website: http://allsouls.webspace.fish.co.uk
Red sandstone church with 140-ft spire, designed by
Hippolyte Blanc 1890. High altar has beautiful Italian
marble reredos and crucifix. Lady Chapel contains altar
from Rossie Priory Chapel. Sculptured Stations of the
Cross. Embroidered wall-hanging to celebrate centenary
of consecration 1996. Church hall used for community
activities. Services: Sunday Sung Eucharist 10.00am;
Wednesday Said Eucharist 10.15am
Open weekdays during school terms, 9.00am-4.00pm (approx)
SCOTTISH EPISCOPAL [wc] (only available if hall is in use) **A**

ALL SOULS'
CHURCH, INVERGOWRIE

877 INVERGOWRIE PARISH CHURCH

NO 346 304

Main Street, Invergowrie
Church website: www.invergowrie.f9.co.uk
Building opened 1909. Architect John Robertson. Early Gothic with square tower
and fine open timber roof. Pulpit and Communion Table of Austrian oak with
carvings by local branch of YWCA. War memorial bell 1924. Stained glass
window depicting Disruption minister Rev R S Walker conducting open-air
Communion. Sunday Service: 11.00am
Open Wednesdays in July and August, 2.00-4.00pm or 7.00-8.00pm with half-hour
musical recitals. Details from Mrs Grant, telephone 01382 562251
CHURCH OF SCOTLAND [wc] ⌾ 🕯 **B**

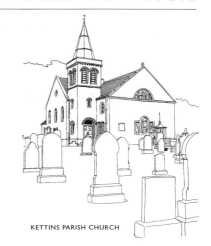

INVERGOWRIE PARISH CHURCH

KETTINS PARISH CHURCH

878 KETTINS PARISH CHURCH

NO 238 390

Kettins, by Coupar Angus (off A923, 1¼ miles south-east of Couper)

On the site of one of six chapels established by a nearby Columban monastery, the present church dates from 1768, with the north wing added in 1870 and the tower in 1891. Sixteen stained glass windows dating from 1878 onwards. Belgian bell of 1519 now rests, complete with belfry, close to the west gable it once surmounted. Celtic stone. Linked with Meigle. Sunday Service: 11.30am

Open by arrangement, telephone 01828 640278

CHURCH OF SCOTLAND   ♿ ⊘ 🍴 **B**

879 KILMAVEONAIG CHURCH

NN 874 658

Kilmaveonaig, Blair Atholl (opposite Tilt Hotel)

An Episcopal Chapel rebuilt in 1794 by John Stewart on the site of the old parish church of Kilmaveonaig 1591, and having belonged to the Episcopal Communion without a break since the Revolution. Enlarged 1899. Lorimer reredos added 1912. Old bell 1629, from Little Dunkeld church. Sunday Service: 10.00am; spring and summer Evensong, 1st Sunday of the month April to September 6.30pm

Open by arrangement, key available from Tilt Hotel

SCOTTISH EPISCOPAL ♿ **B**

KILMAVEONAIG CHURCH

880 KINCLAVEN PARISH CHURCH

NO 151 385

By Stanley, near Perth

Built 1848 on site of previous church. Mixed
Romanesque and Tudor with a narthex at the
west end and bellcote at the east end.
Churchyard contains the war memorial lychgate
1919 by Reginald Fairlie, and some table tombs
of the 17th century and later. Built into the
churchyard wall is the monument to Alexander
Cabel (Campbell), Bishop of Brechin 1608.
Sunday Service: 9.45am
Open by arrangement, telephone
Mr Gordon 01738 710548
CHURCH OF SCOTLAND [wc] [wc] ⊘ ⃞ ⃟ **B**

KINCLAVEN PARISH CHURCH

881 THE OLD CHURCH OF RANNOCH, KINLOCH RANNOCH

NN 663 585

South Loch Road, Kinloch Rannoch

A Thomas Telford church of 1829, extensively
altered and enlarged 1893. Wooden beamed
roof, stained glass window, hour-glass by
pulpit. Sunday Service: 11.30am
Open daily 10.00am-dusk. Other times,
key from Mrs D MacDonald, Bridgend Cottage,
telephone 01882 632359
CHURCH OF SCOTLAND [♿] [wc] ⊘ ⃞ **C**

THE OLD CHURCH OF
RANNOCH, KINLOCH RANNOCH

882 COLLACE PARISH CHURCH, KINROSSIE

NO 197 320

Kinrossie, by Perth (signposted from village
smithy)

Early 19th century on site of an earlier
church dedicated in 1242. Stained glass
window 1919. Remains of medieval
building. Important 17th- and 18th-century
gravestones. Sunday Service: 11.15am
Open by arrangement, contact Miss E Miller
01821 650236 or Mr W Ewing 01821 650235
CHURCH OF SCOTLAND [wc] ⊘ ⃟ ⃞ **B**

COLLACE PARISH CHURCH, KINROSSIE

883 LONGFORGAN PARISH CHURCH

NO 309 300

Main Street, Longforgan

There has been a church on this site for at
least 900 years. The tower is dated 1690
and has eight-sided steeple and unusual
clock. The main building dates from 1795,
the apse from 1900. Windows from 1900-
2003, wood carving by Sir Robert Lorimer,
a unique pipe organ and the remains of a
medieval font. Several interesting tomb
stones from 12th century are preserved in
the church. Sunday Service: 11.30am

Open Wednesdays 2.00-4.00pm May to
August, or by arrangement, telephone
Mrs Hulbert 01382 360294

CHURCH OF SCOTLAND 🚹 wc ⊘ 🚹 📖 **B**

LONGFORGAN PARISH CHURCH

884 MEIGLE PARISH CHURCH

NO 287 446

The Square, Meigle

Re-built in 1870 by John Carver after fire
destroyed the pre-Reformation stone church of
1431. Stands on the ancient site of a turf church
erected by Columban missionaries around AD
606. Fine stone font. Interesting graveyard.
Pictish stones in adjacent museum (Historic
Scotland). Linked with Kettins.

Sunday Service: 10.00am

Open by arrangement, telephone 01828 640278

CHURCH OF SCOTLAND 🚹 wc ⊘ 🚹 **B**

MEIGLE PARISH CHURCH

885 MORENISH CHAPEL

NO 607 356

On A827 Killin–Kenmore

Built in 1902 by Aline White Todd in memory of her daughter Elvira who died in
childbirth. The central piece of the chapel is the magnificent east window by
Tiffany in heavily leaded tracery, and sumptuous stained glass showing Moses
receiving the ten commandments on Mount Sinai. Served by Killin and Ardeonaig.

Sunday Service: 3.00pm, 1st Sunday of month during the summer

CHURCH OF SCOTLAND

886 MUTHILL PARISH CHURCH

NN 868 171

Station Road, Muthill, 3 miles south of Crieff on A822
Replacing the 12th-century church (still existing). Built
in 1826 in Gothic style to a design by Gillespie Graham,
nicknamed 'Pinnacle' Graham by those less enthusiastic
for the sprockets of 19th-century Gothic. Pulpit canopy
similarly sprocketed. Buses from Stirling to Crieff.
Sunday Service: 11.30am (coffee 11.00am)
Open 1st Sunday in August. Coincides with opening of nearby
Drummond Castle Gardens (Scotland's Gardens Scheme)
CHURCH OF SCOTLAND 👤 🚹 **B**

MUTHILL PARISH CHURCH

887 ST JAMES CHURCH, MUTHILL

NN 869 170

Station Road, Muthill
Built 1836, designed by R & R Dickson of
Edinburgh. Oldest Episcopal church in the area.
Numerous family crests of historic interest and
memorial tablets. Fifty yards from village centre
opposite primary school. Linked with St Kessog's,
Auchterarder. Sunday Service: 11.00am January to
June; 9.30am July to December
Open by arrangement, telephone the
Very Rev Randal MacAlister 01764 662525
SCOTTISH EPISCOPAL 👤 🚾 ⊘ **B**

ST JAMES CHURCH, MUTHILL

888 ORWELL PARISH CHURCH

NO 121 051

Church constructed 1729 using stone from the Old
Kirk of Orwell on the banks of Loch Leven. The roof
was raised and the present windows, floor and seating
installed and galleries added in 1769. The interior is
enhanced by embroidered banners and kneelers crafted
by members of the Church. Number of interesting
gravestones in the graveyard. Sunday Services:
11.30am, 9.00am July and August; 7.00pm on 3rd
Sunday January to June and September to November
Open by arrangement with keyholder
Mr Foley, telephone 01577 863397
CHURCH OF SCOTLAND 👤 🚾 ⊘ **B**

ORWELL PARISH CHURCH

889   ST JOHN'S KIRK OF PERTH

NO 119 235
St John Place, Perth
Church website: www.st-johns-kirk.co.uk
Burgh Church of Perth dedicated to
John the Baptist and consecrated in
1242 on site of earlier church. Divided
into three churches after the
Reformation and restored 1923-6 by
Sir Robert Lorimer. Good examples of
modern stained glass including
window of Knox Chapel by Douglas
Strachan. Statue of John the Baptist by
Indian sculptor Fanindra Bose, and
tapestry by Archie Brennan of

ST JOHN'S KIRK OF PERTH

Dovecote Studios Edinburgh. Nave with barrel vaulting has carvings of events in
the life of Christ. Glass screen at west door installed 1988. Organ by Rothwell
1926, rebuilt 1986 by Edmonstone. Sunday Services: 9.30am and 11.00am
Open May to September, 10.00am-4.00pm weekdays, 12.00-2.00pm Sundays; October to
April, when Church Officer is present, usually Wednesday to Saturday from 10.00am. Guided
tours by arrangement, telephone Mrs M Howat 01738 626520
CHURCH OF SCOTLAND   ♿ ☣ 🚻 **A**

890   ST NINIAN'S CATHEDRAL, PERTH

NO 116 237
North Methven Street
First cathedral to be built after the Reformation, being consecrated in 1850. The
architect was William Butterfield. Baldachino in Cornish granite, fine wooden statue
of the Risen Christ and interesting
stained glass. Founder's window, the
font and one of the banners by Sir
Ninian Comper. Services: Sunday
Holy Communion 8.00am, Sung
Eucharist 11.00am; Monday to
Friday Morning Prayer 9.00am;
Wednesday Holy Communion
11.00am; Thursday Holy
Communion 9.00am
Open Monday to Friday
9.00am-5.00pm
SCOTTISH EPISCOPAL   ♿ ☣ **B**

ST NINIAN'S CATHEDRAL, PERTH

891 NORTH CHURCH, PERTH

NO 116 237
Mill Street, Perth
Church website: www.northchurch.org.uk
A pleasant city-centre church built in 1880
by T L Watson of Glasgow in Italian
Romanesque style. Sunday Services: 9.30am,
11.00am and 6.30pm; Thursday
lunchtime 1.00pm
Open by arrangement, telephone
Mr G Weaks 01738 444033
CHURCH OF SCOTLAND [wc] ⓓ ☕ **B**

NORTH CHURCH, PERTH

892 ST LEONARD'S-IN-THE-FIELDS & TRINITY, PERTH

NO 117 232
Marshall Place, Perth
Fine example of the late Gothic revival by
John L Stevenson of London, opened in
1885. Outstanding architectural features are
the crown tower and the heavy buttresses.
The organ, Bryceson 1881, which came
from North Morningside Church in
Edinburgh, was installed in the centenary
year 1985. Sunday Service: 11.00am
Open on Doors Open Day (September)
CHURCH OF SCOTLAND **A**

ST LEONARD'S-IN-THE-FIELDS & TRINITY, PERTH

893 ST MATTHEW'S, PERTH

NO 112 231
Tay Street
Church website: www.perthpresbytery.org.uk
Early English Gothic by John Honeyman 1871. Its impressive steeple is a much-
photographed landmark of Perth. Organ by J W Walker. In 1965, after the union
of four churches, stained glass windows, plaques and memorial tablets from the
four churches were incorporated in the existing West Church, now St Matthews.
Sunday Service: 11.00am
Open daily 9.00am-12.00 noon
CHURCH OF SCOTLAND [♿] [wc] ⓓ **B**

894 KINNOULL PARISH CHURCH, PERTH

NO 118 233

Dundee Road

Church website: www.kinnoullparishchurch.org.uk

Kinnoull Parish Church opened in 1827 and was designed by the Edinburgh architect William Burn in a neo-perpendicular style with crisply detailed buttresses and pinnacles. The glory of the interior is the stained glass, especially the east window based on a series of paintings of the Parables of Our Lord by Sir John Everett Millais. Three other windows by Douglas Strachan.

Sunday Service: 10.30am

Open 1st Sunday of each month May to September 2.00-4.30pm or
by arrangement, telephone 01738 634785

CHURCH OF SCOTLAND ♿ 🚾 ⓘ 🍽 📖 **B**

895 ST JOHN'S EPISCOPAL, PERTH

NO 119 233

Princes Street, Perth

The present site has been used for worship since 1800. Present building designed by John Hay of Liverpool 1850-1. Many stained glass windows, sculptures by Miss Mary Grant, chancel arch carved by Heiton. Fine Harrison & Harrison organ 1971.

Services: Sunday Holy Communion 8.00am, Sung Eucharist 10.30am; Thursday Holy Communion 11.00am

Open by arrangement, telephone Mr T Mason
01738 627870

SCOTTISH EPISCOPAL 🚾 ⓘ 📖 **B**

ST JOHN'S EPISCOPAL, PERTH

896 ST JOHN THE BAPTIST, PERTH

NO 114 241

20 Melville Street (near main Police Station)

Traditional building of 1832, enlarged, 1896 by Andrew Heiton. Presbytery 1932 by Reginald Fairlie. Church renovated 1967 for new liturgy by Peter Whiston of Edinburgh and many previous accretions removed.

Services: Saturday 6.30pm; Sunday 9.00am, 11.00am and 6.30pm

Open 8.00am-dusk

ROMAN CATHOLIC ♿ 🚾 **C**

897 ST MARY MAGDALENE, PERTH

NO 113 226

Glenearn Road

Modern building (1959), attractive in its simplicity, designed by Peter Whiston of Edinburgh. Very interesting window by William Wilson and crucifix by Benno Schotz. Sunday Service: 10.00am

Open for daily Mass 8.00am or by arrangement with Parish Priest 01738 622241

ROMAN CATHOLIC 🚾

898 PITLOCHRY CHURCH

NO 942 581

Church Road, Pitlochry

Church website: www.pitlochrychurchofscotland.co.uk

Built in 1884 by C & L Ower, Dundee. The porch was added in 1995, built of stone from Pitlochry East Church, the East and West congregations having united in 1992. Seating arranged in a part circle around the communion table. Monument to Alexander Duff, 19th-century missionary. Identifiable as 'the church with the clock' 100 yards from main street. Sunday Services: All Age Worship 9.30am, and Traditional form of service 11.00am

Open mid-June to mid-September,

Monday to Friday 10.00am–12.00 noon

CHURCH OF SCOTLAND 🚾 **B**

PITLOCHRY CHURCH

899 HOLY TRINITY EPISCOPAL, PITLOCHRY

NN 946 578

Atholl Road

Opened 1858, architect C Buckeridge of Oxford, nave extended 1890. Organ by Hele (1903). Reredos by Sir Ninian Comper, pulpit panels by pupils of Miss Kinderslay of Cliffe, Dorchester. Stained glass windows by various artists including E Kempe, donated between 1877 and 1956. Lychgate built about 1923. Services: Sunday Holy Communion 8.00am; 1st and 3rd Sundays Holy Communion 11.30am with hymns; 2nd and 4th Sundays Matins 11.30am; 5th Sunday see notice in church porch

Open by arrangement, telephone 01796 472176, or see notice in church porch

SCOTTISH EPISCOPAL 🚾 **B**

HOLY TRINITY EPISCOPAL, PITLOCHRY

900　PITLOCHRY BAPTIST CHURCH

NO 942 580

Atholl Road, next to Tourist Information Centre
Church website: www.pitlochrybaptistchurch.org
Founded 1878 and originally meeting in a
joiner's shop, the Pitlochry Fellowship built
this church in 1884 to a design by Crombie of
Edinburgh. Today's congregation welcomes
visitors from across the world all year round.
Sunday Services: 11.00am and 6.30pm
Open by arrangement with Atholl Centre,
a Christian holiday and conference centre,
situated behind church, telephone 01796 473044
BAPTIST 🚽 wc ✒ (Christian bookshop in adjoining Atholl Centre) **C**

PITLOCHRY
BAPTIST CHURCH

901　DUNDURN PARISH CHURCH, ST FILLANS

NN 697 241

Built 1878. Of particular interest is the
medieval stone font. Oak panelling, pulpit and
communion table with Celtic knotwork. Set in
grounds with striking view across Loch Earn.
Linked with Comrie Parish Church.
Sunday Service: 11.30am June to September;
12.00 noon October to May
Open daily, Easter to October
CHURCH OF SCOTLAND ✒ 📖

DUNDURN PARISH CHURCH, ST FILLANS

902　SCONE OLD PARISH CHURCH

NO 134 256

Burnside, Scone
Church built in 1286 near to Scone Palace.
Moved to present site in 1806 using stone
from original building. Mansfield pew
presented by Queen Anne of Denmark 1615.
Memorial to David Douglas, botanist, in
graveyard. Number 7 bus from Perth.
Sunday Service: 11.00am
Open various Saturdays in 2004, 10.00am–
12.00 noon. For details, telephone Mr Moir
01738 551549
CHURCH OF SCOTLAND 🚽 wc 📖 ☕ **B**

SCONE OLD PARISH CHURCH

903 PORTMOAK PARISH CHURCH, SCOTLANDWELL

NO 183 019

1 mile west of Scotlandwell

The present building, dated 1832, is the third on the site. The bell is dated 1642 and the Celtic crosses are of the 10th or 11th centuries. Memorial stone in the graveyard to Michael Bruce (1746-67), author of several of the scripture paraphrases used in Church of Scotland worship. Annual commemorative service in evening of first Sunday in July. Sunday Service: 10.00am

Open by arrangement with Mrs Crighton, telephone 01592 840550

CHURCH OF SCOTLAND ♿ ⊘ **B**

PORTMOAK PARISH CHURCH,
SCOTLANDWELL

904 ST ANDREW'S CHURCH, STRATHTAY

NN 910 534

On A827 between Ballinluig and Aberfeldy

The chancel was built in 1888 and the nave added in 1919. A vestibule and hall were added in 1982. Heavily carved woodwork on pulpit, lectern and priest's prayer desk. Lovely stained glass. A free-standing belfry was provided in 1995. Linked with St Mary's, Birnam. Sunday Service: 11.30am

Open by arrangement. Key from village shop

SCOTTISH EPISCOPAL ⓦⓒ 📖 **A**

905 STANLEY PARISH CHURCH

NO 108 330

Built in 1828 by local mill owners the Buchanan family for mill workers, the church seated 1,000. It was adapted in 1962 and incorporated a new pew arrangement. The halls which are below the sanctuary were refurbished in 1997. The vestibule houses the war memorial. The site is floodlit by night and the extensive church grounds hold an annual outdoor fête on the first Saturday of September. Sunday Service: 11.30am

CHURCH OF SCOTLAND ♿ ⊘ **B**

STANLEY PARISH CHURCH

906 TENANDRY CHURCH

NN 911 615

Tenandry, Pitlochry

Church website: www.geocities.com/atholkirks

Small country church built in 1836 of stone
and slate and of traditional design. Fine view
of the Pass of Killiecrankie from the road
above the church. North from B8019 at Garry
Bridge 2 miles north of Pitlochry (signed).

Sunday Service: 10.00am

Open daily

CHURCH OF SCOTLAND 🦽 wc 📖 **B**

TENANDRY CHURCH

907 TIBBERMORE CHURCH

NO 052 234

¼ mile south of Tibbermore crossroads

Church website: www.srct.org.uk

The present church dates from 1632, though the site has been a place of worship
from the Middle Ages onwards. The church was remodelled and enlarged in 1789
to designs by James Scobie, made T-plan in 1808 and the interior refurnished in
1874. The present interior is little altered since that date. The graveyard contains
many monuments of interest, in particular the exceptional memorial to James
Ritchie, displaying his curling equipment and the recumbent figure of his bull.
Transferred to the ownership of the Scottish Redundant Churches Trust in 2001.

For opening and service arrangements contact the SRCT, telephone 01334 472032

FORMER CHURCH OF SCOTLAND 🦽 **B**

TIBBERMORE CHURCH

908 FOSS KIRK, TUMMEL BRIDGE

NN 790 581

South Loch Tummel Road, Foss

Founded AD 625 by St Chad and used until the Reformation. Fell into disrepair 1580, restored 1821. Perth bell 1824. Ancient graveyard behind the church with view of Loch Tummel. Linked with Braes of Rannoch and Rannoch. Sunday Services: May to September, 1st and 3rd Sundays 7.00pm; October to April, 1st Sunday 2.30pm

Open daily

CHURCH OF SCOTLAND 📖 **C**

FOSS KIRK, TUMMEL BRIDGE

909 WEEM CHURCH

NN 844 497

1 mile north of Aberfeldy on B846

The style of this beautiful stone building indicates its origin as an Episcopal church of the late 19th century; the ancient former church of Dull and Weem being 3 miles west. Interesting organ. A small hall was added to the north in 1990, during the construction of which the ancient well of Weem was discovered.

Sunday Service: 10.00am

Often open, but if locked, contact the Minister 01887 820656

CHURCH OF SCOTLAND ♿ 🚾 👂 ☕ (after services) **C**

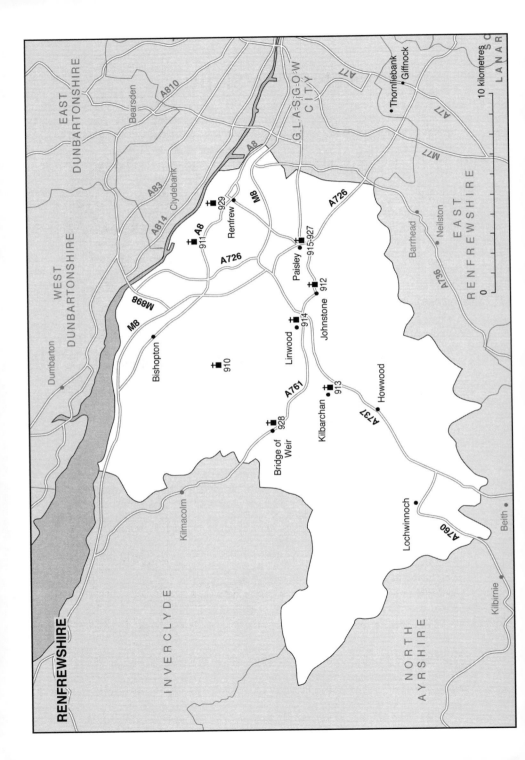

RENFREWSHIRE

Local Representative: Mrs Anne Moohan, 13 Riccartsbar Avenue, Paisley
(*telephone* 0141 889 2074)

910 HOUSTON & KILLELLAN PARISH CHURCH

NS 410 671
Kirk Road, Houston
Church website: www.houstonkirk.org
Gothic, by David Thomson 1874, this
building is the third on this ancient site.
Very good stained glass. Interesting organ.
Between Bridge of Weir and Inchinnan.
Sunday Service: 11.00am
Open Sundays 11.00am-1.00pm.
Kirk Carnival, 2nd Saturday in May
CHURCH OF SCOTLAND **B**

HOUSTON & KILLELLAN PARISH CHURCH

911 INCHINNAN PARISH CHURCH (ST CONVAL'S KIRK)

NS 479 689
Old Greenock Road, Inchinnan
(2 miles west of Renfrew on A8)
Sir R Rowand Anderson's church
of 1904 was razed to make way for
Glasgow Airport, and the present
building by Miller and Black,
consecrated in 1968, incorporates
much of interest and beauty from
the earlier church. Foundation by St
Conval in 597. King David I gave
patronage of first stone church to
Knights Templar, succeeded by
Knights of St John. Celtic and
medieval stones.
Sunday Service: 10.45am
Open Thursday during term-time, 12.00
noon-1.30pm. Light lunches available
CHURCH OF SCOTLAND

INCHINNAN PARISH CHURCH (ST CONVAL'S KIRK)

912 JOHNSTONE HIGH PARISH CHURCH

NS 426 630

Quarry Street, Johnstone

An octagonal building of grey
sandstone built in 1792. Clock tower
with spire. Stained glass. Historic
graveyard. In the town centre, trains
from Glasgow every 15 minutes.
Sunday Service: 11.00am; Songs
of Praise 1st Sunday 6.30pm
*Open Thursday to Saturday 10.00am-
12 noon, all year. Tours by arrangement
at church hall coffee shop*
CHURCH OF SCOTLAND
♿ wc ⊘ 📖 ☕ **B**

JOHNSTONE HIGH PARISH CHURCH

913 KILBARCHAN WEST CHURCH

NS 401 632

Church Street, Kilbarchan, Kilbarchan Cross, (next to NTS Weaver's Cottage)

Hall built as the church in 1724 on the site of an earlier church. Present church
completed 1901, architect W H Howie. Some fine stained glass resited from old
church and glass from early 20th century. Three-manual organ built 1904 by
William Hill & Sons. At Kilbarchan Cross next to NTS Weaver's Cottage.
Services: Sunday 11.00am; Wednesdays 10.30am, October to May
Open by arrangement, telephone 01505 342930
CHURCH OF SCOTLAND ♿ wc ⊘ 🍶 **B**

KILBARCHAN WEST CHURCH

LINWOOD PARISH CHURCH

914 LINWOOD PARISH CHURCH

NS 432 645

Blackwood Avenue, at Clippens Road, Linwood

A spacious red brick building dating from 1965. An earlier church of 1860 existed on another site, demolished in 1976. The furniture and communion silver are from the earlier church. Contemporary artwork includes a large aluminium cross presented by the former Rootes Vehicle Plant. Fine pipe organ 1957.

Sunday Services: 9.30am and 11.00am

Open Friday 11.30am-1.30pm during school term, and by arrangement,
telephone Mrs F Dooley 01505 331 065

CHURCH OF SCOTLAND

915 PAISLEY ABBEY

NS 486 640

Founded in 1163. Early 20th-century restoration of the choir by P MacGregor Chalmers and Lorimer. Medieval architecture, royal tombs of Marjory Bruce and Robert III, the 10th-century Barochan Cross. Exceptionally fine woodwork including organ case by Lorimer, stained glass by Burne-Jones and others. Organ by Cavaille-Coll 1872, rebuilt Walker 1968. Sunday Services: 11.00am, 12.15pm, Holy Communion 6.30pm

Open daily, Monday to Saturday
10.00am-3.30pm. Details of events from
Abbey Office, telephone 0141 889 7654

CHURCH OF SCOTLAND

PAISLEY ABBEY

916 ST MIRIN'S CATHEDRAL, PAISLEY

NS 488 642

Incle Street, Paisley

St Mirin's Cathedral was built in
1931 to replace the old church in
East Buchanan Street. Constituted
Cathedral Church of the Diocese
of Paisley in 1947. The architect
was Thomas Baird and the building
is neo-Romanesque in style with an
airy arched interior. Visitors should
note the sculpted pulpit and Art
Deco Stations of the Cross.
Services: Daily 10.00am and
1.00pm; Saturday Vigil 6.30pm;
Sunday 8.00am, 10.00am, 12.00
noon and 4.00pm
Open daily 8.00am-8.00pm
ROMAN CATHOLIC   🚻 ♿ **B**

ST MIRIN'S CATHEDRAL, PAISLEY

917 CASTLEHEAD PARISH CHURCH, PAISLEY

NS 476 636

Main Road, Castlehead, Paisley (junction with Canal Street)

Built 1781 as the first Relief church in Paisley. Interior renovated 1881. Bishop
organ 1898. Graveyard has graves of Robert Tannahill (local poet), past ministers,
merchants and the mass graves of the cholera epidemic. Sunday Service: 11.00am
Open May to September, Monday, Wednesday and Friday 2.00-4.00pm
CHURCH OF SCOTLAND ♿ 🚻 **B**

CASTLEHEAD PARISH CHURCH, PAISLEY

918 OAKSHAW TRINITY CHURCH, PAISLEY

NS 480 641

Oakshaw Street/Church Hill

Church website: www.oakshawtrinity.org.uk

Former Paisley High Church, built 1756 by John White, the steeple added 1770, renovated and extended during the 19th century. A rectangular classical church with galleried interior, the organ set under the tower. Stained glass by Ballantine & Sons. Outreach at the Wynd Centre, 6 School Wynd, Paisley. Sunday Service: 11.00am

Open by arrangement with Wynd Centre, telephone 0141 887 4647.

Wynd Centre open Monday to Saturday 9.00am-10.00pm; Sunday 12.30-6.30pm

CHURCH OF SCOTLAND   🦽 wc 🎧 **A**

919 MARTYRS' CHURCH, PAISLEY

NS 474 639

Broomlands Street, Paisley

The church is named after the Paisley martyrs who were executed in 1685. Built 1847 with additions and alterations, including tower and south front in neo-Norman style 1905, T G Abercrombie, architect. Inside are galleries on three sides on cast-iron colonnettes. The pulpit, 18ft long, has been likened to the bridge of a ship. Sunday Service: 11.00am

Open Friday 10.00am-1.00pm

CHURCH OF SCOTLAND   wc ☕ **B**

MARTYRS' CHURCH, PAISLEY

920 NEW JERUSALEM CHURCH, PAISLEY

NS 481 637

17 George Street, Paisley
Church website:
www.paisleynewchurch.org.uk
Built for Wesleyan Methodists in
1810, and in use by
Swedenborgians since 1860, this
is an unusual building with halls
on the ground floor and the
church upstairs. Three striking
stained glass windows by W & J J
Keir, including one designed by
Sir Noel Paton. Fine pulpit,
communion table, and ceiling
rose. Sunday Service: 11.00am
Open by arrangement, and on
Doors Open Day, September
11.00am-4.00pm, telephone
Rev Robert Gill 0141 887 4119
SWEDENBORGIAN [wc] (2)

NEW JERUSALEM CHURCH, PAISLEY

921 ST MARY'S (OUR LADY HELP OF CHRISTIANS), PAISLEY

NS 471 636

167 George Street, Paisley
Church website: www.stmaryspaisley.fsnet.co.uk
Designed by Pugin & Pugin in Decorated style and built 1891, the apse was added
1905. Organ by Andrew of Glasgow. Recent refurbishment has included redeco-
ration of the interior. The church contains works of Austrian and Bavarian origin.
Services: daily 9.15am and 9.30am; Saturday Vigil 6.30pm;
Sunday 9.30am and 11.00am
Open daily 8.30am-5.30pm
ROMAN CATHOLIC [&] [wc] (2) [] **B**

922 ST CHARLES, PAISLEY

NS 483 633

5 Union Street, Paisley

The Parish of St Charles was established in 1897 and had three churches, the present occupying the site of the original. Designed by J G Quigley, 1986, it forms a courtyard enclosure with the hall and presbytery. Predominantly top-lit, it has a bright and spacious interior. The altar was built from the altar used by Pope John Paul II at Bellahouston. Services: Saturday Vigil 7.00pm; Sunday 10.30am, 12.00 noon, 7.00pm; weekday: 10.00am

Open daily 9.00am-5.00pm

ROMAN CATHOLIC 🚹 WC ⓟ

923 ST JAMES'S CHURCH, PAISLEY

NS 477 644

Underwood Road, Paisley

Early French Gothic style to a design by Hippolyte Blanc, largely gifted by Sir Peter Coats 1884. Spire 200ft. Full peal of bells, rung every Sunday. 'Father' Willis pipe organ, rebuilt J Walker 1967. Stained glass windows 1904. Landscaped grounds. Sunday Service: 11.00am

Open Monday, Wednesday and Friday, 10.00am-4.00pm. Also Doors Open Day, September 10.00am-4.00pm. Contact day centre at rear of church for access

CHURCH OF SCOTLAND 🚹 WC ⓟ **B**

924 ST PETER'S, PAISLEY

NS 474 613

154 Braehead Road, Paisley

Church website: www.st-peters-paisley.co.uk

The church with its brick tower is a dominant feature on the hill at Glenburn. It was completed in 1958 and a new church hall opened in 2003. The parish celebrated the 50th anniversary of its foundation in 2004. Services: Sunday 10.00am, 12.00 noon (includes a Children's Liturgy), 5.15pm; Saturday 9.30am and Vigil 6.30pm; Monday-Friday 9.30am; Wednesday 7.00pm

Open by arrangement with the Parish Priest, telephone 0141 884 2435

ROMAN CATHOLIC 🚹 WC ⓟ ⚲

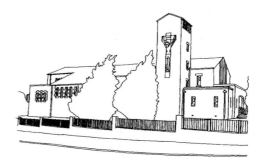

ST PETER'S, PAISLEY

925 THOMAS COATS MEMORIAL BAPTIST CHURCH, PAISLEY

NS 478 640
High Street, Paisley
Church website: www.fenet.co.uk/coats
Built by the Coats Family as a memorial to
Thomas Coats. Hippolyte Blanc Gothic,
opened May 1894. Beautiful interior, 'by far
the grandest of the Paisley churches'
(*Groome's Gazetteer*) with carved marble and
alabaster. Famous Hill 4-manual pipe organ.
On main street going west from Paisley
Cross. Sunday Service: 11.00am
Open by arrangement, telephone
Mr L Irvine 0141 887 2773
BAPTIST 🔧 wc ✍ 🍴 📖 **A**

THOMAS COATS MEMORIAL
BAPTIST CHURCH, PAISLEY

926 WALLNEUK NORTH CHURCH, PAISLEY

NS 486 643
Abercorn Street, Paisley
Church website: www.wallneuknorthchurch.co.uk
Built 1915. Architect T G Abercrombie. Pipe
organ by Abbott & Smith of Leeds 1931,
dedicated to Peter Coats, donor of this
church. Its fine oak case was carved and
built by Wylie & Lochead, Glasgow. Near
town centre. Sunday Service: 11.00am;
Wednesday: 12.30pm
Open Doors Open Day September
CHURCH OF SCOTLAND 🔧 ✍ 🍴 📖 ☕ **A**

WALLNEUK NORTH CHURCH, PAISLEY

927 GLASGOW INTERNATIONAL AIRPORT CHAPEL, PAISLEY

NS 478 663
Second Floor, Terminal Building, Glasgow Airport
A recent addition to Glasgow Airport, open to passengers and staff of all faiths and
creeds. Christian Services are announced 30 minutes in advance by public address.
Open at all times
NON-DENOMINATIONAL 🔧 ☕

928 ST MACHAR'S, RANFURLY

NS 392 653
Kilbarchan Road, Ranfurly, Bridge of Weir
(east end of village)
Church website: www.stmacharsranfurly.org
Early Gothic 1878 by Lewis Shanks, brother
of one of the local millowners. The chancel
was added in 1910 by Alexander Hislop.
Stained glass by J S Melville & J Stewart
1900, Herbert Hendrie 1931, William Wilson
1946, Gordon Webster 1956. Descriptive
booklet by Maurice L Gaine 1996. Sunday
Service: 11.00am (10.30am July and August)
Open Fridays 10.00am-12.00 noon. Bridge of
Weir Gala Week in June
CHURCH OF SCOTLAND [wc] ⊘ 📖 🛈 ☕

ST MACHAR'S, RANFURLY

929 RENFREW OLD PARISH CHURCH

NS 509 676
26 High Street, Renfrew
The Church of Renfrew was bestowed by King David on the Cathedral Church
of Glasgow in 1136. Within the present lancet Gothic 1862 sanctuary are two late
medieval monuments, a hooded vault with
recumbent effigies and an altar tomb.
In Renfrew town centre.
Sunday Services: 11.15am and 6.30pm
Doors Open Day, September
CHURCH OF SCOTLAND [♿] [wc] 🛈 🛈 **B**

RENFREW OLD PARISH CHURCH

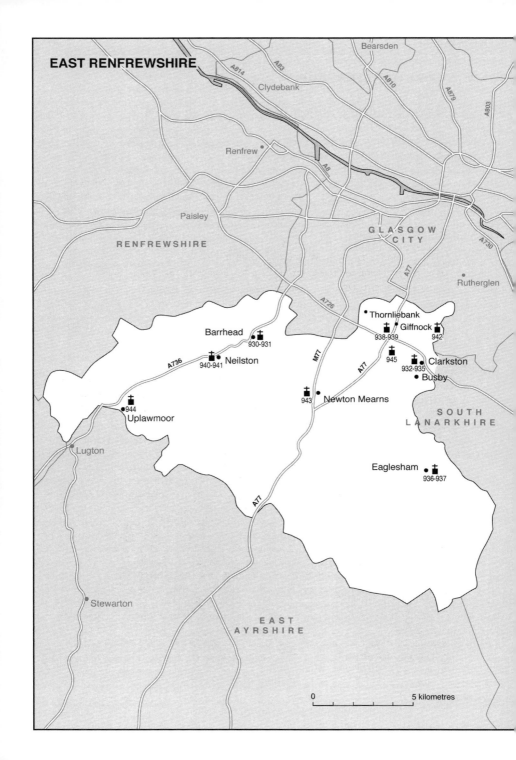

EAST RENFREWSHIRE

930   ARTHURLIE PARISH CHURCH, BARRHEAD

NS 501 588

Ralston Road / Main Street, Barrhead
Church website: www.arthurliechurch.org.uk

Built 1967 to replace the 1796 'whitewashed kirk'. Designed by Honeyman, Jack and Robertson of Glasgow. High roof and long aisles. The open pews, constructed from the same light hardwood (ramin) as the cross, font, lectern and choirstalls, create an understated unity. Stained glass by Gordon Webster in the style 'Dalles de Verre'. The grounds, laid out by Bessie McWhirter, are open to all.
Services: Sunday 11.00am; Wednesday 10.45am
Open by arrangement with the Church Officer, telephone 0141 881 1792
CHURCH OF SCOTLAND ♿ (side entrance) wc 🖉 📖

931   ST JOHN'S, BARRHEAD

NS 508 592

Aurs Road, Barrhead
Church website: www.stjohnsbarrhead.org

Built in 1961, architect Thomas S Cordiner, after the old building was burnt down in 1941, before its centenary Mass. Note the prevalence of Greek iconography over Latin and the recurrence of the motif of St John. Tabernacle door designed by Hew Lorimer and presidential chair by John McLachlan. Rushworth and Dreaper organ. Services: Saturday Vigil 6.30pm; Sunday 10.00am, 12.00 noon and 6.30pm; Exposition of the Blessed Sacrament, in the oratory, Monday to Friday 10.30am to 10.00pm. All welcome for private prayer
Open by arrangement with Presbytery House, telephone 0141 876 1553
ROMAN CATHOLIC
♿ (side door) wc 🖉

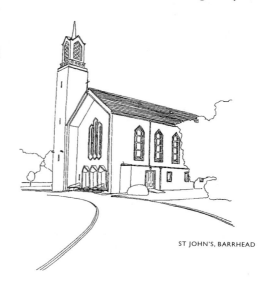

ST JOHN'S, BARRHEAD

932 GREENBANK CHURCH, CLARKSTON

NS 574 568
Eaglesham Road, Clarkston
Church website: www.greenbankglasgow.org.uk
The Church designed by McKissack & Rowan was
opened in 1884. The chancel, furnishings and
stained glass windows (James Ballantine) were
added in 1937. A mural by Alistair Gray in the
transept was completed in 1979. The Centenary
Chapel was opened in 1984.
Sunday Services: 9.30am and 11.00am
Open by arrangement, telephone the
Church Officer 0141 644 2839
CHURCH OF SCOTLAND   ♿   wc   ⓘ

GREENBANK CHURCH, CLARKSTON

933 ST AIDAN'S, CLARKSTON

NS 573 574
Mearns Road, Clarkston
Church website: www.staidans.freeserve.co.uk
Hall Church built 1924 and present church 1951,
architects Noad & Wallace. Building has a steel
frame and brick interior. Red sandstone facing
matches hall. Stained glass including a pair of
windows by Susan Bradbury 1998. Sunday
Services: Holy Communion 8.00am, Sung
Eucharist 10.00am, Evensong/Evening Prayer 6.30
Open Wednesdays 9.00-11.30am
SCOTTISH EPISCOPAL ♿   ⓘ   ☕

ST AIDAN'S, CLARKSTON

934 ST JOSEPH'S, CLARKSTON

NS 575 572
2 Eaglesham Road, Clarkston
First church built also as a school in 1880. Replaced by a modern building on same
site in 1971. Stained glass windows by Shona McInnes and tapestries by Joanna
Kinnersly-Taylor. Services: Saturday
Vigil 6.00pm; Sunday Masses 8.30
am, 10.00 am, 12.00 noon and
6.00pm; weekday Masses 10.00am
and 7.00pm Monday-Friday;
Saturday 10.00am
Open all day
ROMAN CATHOLIC ♿   wc   ⓘ   ☕

ST JOSEPH'S, CLARKSTON

935 STAMPERLAND CHURCH, CLARKSTON

NS 576 581

Stamperland Gardens, Clarkston

Congregation's first service held in an
air raid shelter of a local garage in
1940. Thereafter a local shop was
occupied at 38 Stamperland Crescent
before a hall church was built in 1941
(now hall of church). Present modern
building erected 1964, architect J
Thompson King & Partners. Concrete
bell-tower. Three stained glass
windows by Gordon Webster,

STAMPERLAND CHURCH, CLARKSTON

previously in Woodside Parish Church. Pipe organ 1897 by Lewis & Co of
Brixton and earlier in Regent Place United Presbyterian Church, Dennistoun,
Glasgow. Furnishings include items from 1938 Glasgow Empire Exhibition Church.
Bas-relief of mythical pelican on outside wall. Sunday Services: 9.45am and
11.00am

Open by arrangement, telephone Norman Bolton 0141 638 3502

CHURCH OF SCOTLAND ♿ ⍰

936 EAGLESHAM PARISH CHURCH

NS 572 518

Montgomery Street, Eaglesham

Church website: www.eaglesham-parish-church.com

The present attractive church with clock steeple was designed by Robert
McLachlane and completed in 1790. It
replaced churches on this site since early
times. Former United Free Church is
now the Church Halls and Carswell
United Presbyterian Church refurbished
as 'The Carswell Halls' (both located on
Montgomery Street). 'Father' Willis
organ and fine embroidered pulpit falls
by Kathleen Whyte and Fiona Hamilton.
Covenanter graves in churchyard.

Sunday Service: 11.00am

Open Tuesday and Thursday June to September,
2.00-4.00pm or by arrangement, telephone the
Beadle 01355 303411

CHURCH OF SCOTLAND ♿ wc ⍰ 📖 B

EAGLESHAM PARISH CHURCH

937   ST BRIDGET'S, EAGLESHAM

NS 572 521

12 Polnoon Street, Eaglesham

Built 1858 to provide a local place of worship for Catholic villagers, many of whom had settled as refugees from the Irish potato famine. Land provided by 13th Earl of Eglinton behind 'Mayfield' a house in Polnoon Street, now chapel house. Interior enhanced by Californian redwood beams and a large canvas of the 'Deposition of Christ from the Cross' by de Surne. Statue of Madonna and Child from Ireland. Interior refurbished in 1960s. Sunday Service: 11.00am

Open daylight hours or on request, telephone 01355 303298

ROMAN CATHOLIC [⌨] [wc] ⊇ **C**

938   GIFFNOCK SOUTH PARISH CHURCH

NS 559 582

Greenhill Avenue, Giffnock

Church website: www.glasgowkirks.org.uk

A 'hall church' (now Eglinton Hall) was opened in 1914. The present church was begun in 1921 and dedicated in 1929. It is by Stewart & Paterson in late Gothic style with blonde sandstone. There is a fine collection of stained glass windows,

GIFFNOCK SOUTH PARISH CHURCH

including six by Gordon Webster. There are three recent windows, one by Sadie McLellan and two by Brian Hutchison. Sunday Service: 11.15am

CHURCH OF SCOTLAND [⌨] [wc] ⊘ **B**

939   ORCHARDHILL PARISH CHURCH, GIFFNOCK

NS 563 587

Church Road, Giffnock (east side of Fenwick Road, north of Eastwood Toll)

Church website: www.orchardhill.org.uk

Church and hall built in Gothic Revival style, H E Clifford 1900. Of local stone with a red tiled roof, squat tower with spiral wooden stair and roof turret. Extensions carried out in 1910 and 1935. Stained glass 1936-86 by Webster, McLellan, Wilson and Clark. Wood panelling 1900-35. Two-manual pipe organ, Hill, Norman & Beard. Embroidered pulpit falls 1993. Sunday Services: 10.00am, 11.15am and 6.30pm (part year only)

Open by arrangement, telephone the Church Officer 0141 589 4353 or Secretary 0141 638 3604

CHURCH OF SCOTLAND [⌨] ⊘ **B**

ORCHARDHILL PARISH CHURCH, GIFFNOCK

940 NEILSTON PARISH CHURCH

NS 480 574

Main Street, Neilston

There has been a Christian presence on the site for over 1,000 years. Originally a single-storey building, the church was enlarged 1746-98, including the balcony. Further alterations 1820. An important feature is a Gothic window above the vault of the Mure family of Caldwell. Stained glass by Stephen Adam. Nearby is a memorial to John Robertson, a native of Neilston, who built the engine for the *Comet*, the first steamship on the Clyde. Circular mort-house of 1817.

Sunday Service: 11.00am

Open by arrangement, telephone 0141881 1958

CHURCH OF SCOTLAND ♿ 🚻 ⊘ ☕ 📖 **B**

NEILSTON PARISH CHURCH

941 ST THOMAS'S, NEILSTON

NS 479 573

70 Main Street, Neilston

Built 1861 and dedicated to St Thomas the Apostle as a tribute to the work to make the parish succeed. The tower was added in 1891. Services: Monday-Saturday Mass 10.00am; Saturday Vigil 6.00pm; Sunday 9.00am, 10.00am

Open daily

ROMAN CATHOLIC ♿ 🚻 ☕ 📖

ST THOMAS'S, NEILSTON

NETHERLEE PARISH CHURCH

942   NETHERLEE PARISH CHURCH

NS 557 590

Ormonde Avenue, Netherlee

Built in neo-Gothic style of red Dumfriesshire sandstone by Stewart & Paterson
1934. Oak panelling and furnishings beautifully carved. Lovely stained glass. City
buses via Clarkston Road. Sunday Services: September to May, 11.00am and some
at 6.30pm; June to August 9.30am and 11.00am

Open by arrangement, telephone Mr McVey 0141 637 6853

CHURCH OF SCOTLAND   ⬛ 🚻 ⊘ ⬜ ⬜ ☕ **B**

943   MEARNS PARISH CHURCH, NEWTON MEARNS

NS 551 556

Junction of Eaglesham Road and Mearns Road

Religious settlement and site since AD 800, the
present church dates from 1813 and was extensively
renovated in 1932. Organ originally from Glasgow
City Hall. Stained glass windows by Gordon
Webster and James McPhie. South wall tapestry
donated by the late Lord Goold. A phosphor-
bronze weathercock weighing two and a half cwts
atop the bell-tower was erected in the late 1940s.
Gate posts in the form of sentry boxes date
from the era of the Resurrectionists.
Sunday Services: 9.30 and 11.00am

*Open by arrangement, telephone the
Minister 0141 616 2410*

CHURCH OF SCOTLAND   ⬛ 🚻 ⊘ **B**

MEARNS PARISH CHURCH, NEWTON MEARNS

944 CALDWELL PARISH CHURCH, UPLAWMOOR

NS 435 552
Neilston Road, Uplawmoor
(off B736 Barrhead to Irvine)
Simple country church built 1889 William Ingram. Memorial glass sculpture depicting the Trinity by Ralph Cowan 1989. Garden of Remembrance dedicated 1997. Sunday Service: 11.00am; summer timetable, July to August 10.00am; Wednesday brief act of worship 12.00 noon
Open daily 11.00am-3.00pm. Soup lunch
in hall adjacent October to March,
Friday 12.00 noon-1.30pm
CHURCH OF SCOTLAND [wc] 📖

CALDWELL PARISH CHURCH, UPLAWMOOR

945 WILLIAMWOOD PARISH CHURCH

NS 567 576
Seres Road, Williamwood
Built in 1937 as a church extension charge, the church is a fine example of mid-1930s church architecture. Original and somewhat austere interior upgraded and enriched. Historical and other information available. By rail from Glasgow Central to Williamwood or Clarkston, 10 minutes' walk from both stations. Bus services from Glasgow to Eaglesham, alight at Clarkston. Sunday Service: 11.00am
Open February to June and September to December, weekdays, 9.45am-12.00 noon.
Other information, telephone 0141 638 2091
CHURCH OF SCOTLAND 🚹 ⊘ 🍴 📖 ☕

WILLIAMWOOD PARISH CHURCH

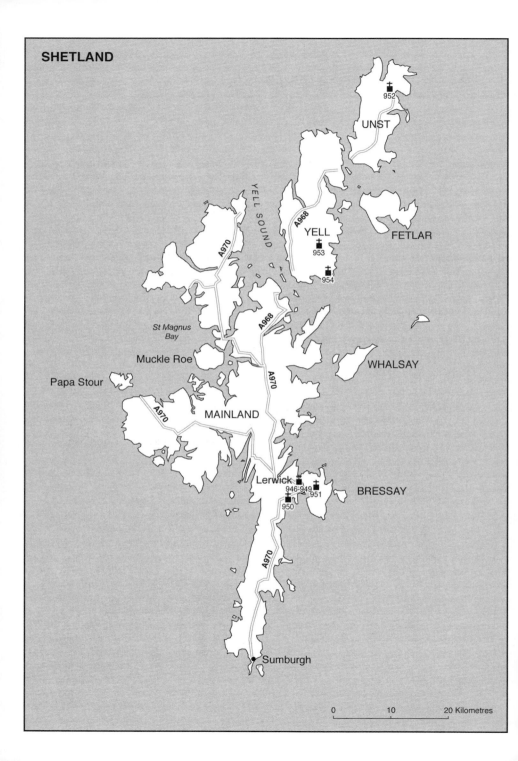

SHETLAND

UNST

952

YELL SOUND

A968

YELL

953

954

FETLAR

A970

St Magnus
Bay

A968

Muckle Roe

A970

WHALSAY

Papa Stour

A970

MAINLAND

Lerwick

946-949

951

BRESSAY

950

A970

Sumburgh

0   10   20 Kilometres

SHETLAND

Local Representative: Dr Ramsay Napier, 4 Sletts Park, Lerwick, ZE1 0LN (*telephone* 01595 693716)

946 ST COLUMBA'S, LERWICK

HU 478 411

1 Greenfield Place, Lerwick

Designed by James Milne of Edinburgh and built 1828 with interior and apse of 1895 by John M Aitken, the church is recognised as a fine example of neo-classical architecture in the north of Scotland. Splendid horse-shoe gallery. Organ by Bryceson Bros of London 1871, one of the earliest in the Church of Scotland. Stained glass window depicting the figure of Jesus by Danish sculptor Thorvaldsen. Sunday Service: 11.15am

Open by arrangement, telephone the Minister 01595 692125

CHURCH OF SCOTLAND   ♿ 🚾 ② 📗 **B**

947 ST MAGNUS EPISCOPAL, LERWICK

HU 479 411

Greenfield Place, Lerwick

Church website: www.stmagnus.org

Designed by Alexander Ellis in Early English style and built 1862-4. Battlemented tower added 1891. Alterations to chancel by Alexander Ross, 1899. Windows by Sir Ninian Comper (moved here from the chapel of the former House of Charity in 1973). Services: Monday to Friday 7.45am and 5.30pm; Sunday Sung Eucharist 10.45am, Evening Prayer 6.30pm, Compline 8.00pm (summer)

Open at all times

SCOTTISH EPISCOPAL   ♿ 🚾 ☕ 📗 **B**

ST MAGNUS EPISCOPAL, LERWICK

948 ST MARGARET'S RC, LERWICK

HU 473 415

Harbour Street / St Olaf Street, Lerwick

When St Margaret's was opened in 1911, it was described as 'the prettiest church in Lerwick'. The architect was James Baikie of Kirkwall. One of the outstanding features is the High Altar, carved out of Belgian oak. The church is dominated by three large stained glass windows by C R Sinclair, 1986, depicting traditional and contemporary life in Shetland as well as some of the wildlife. Well worth a visit! Services: Sunday 10.30am; for other services, check notice board or telephone 01595 692233

Open daily 8.00am-8.00pm

ROMAN CATHOLIC 🔓 🚻 ⟨⟩ **C**

949 ADAM CLARKE MEMORIAL METHODIST CHURCH, LERWICK

HU 475 412

Hillhead, Lerwick

Built 1872 and named after the Rev Adam Clarke (1760-1832), President of the Wesleyan Methodist Conference, who greatly encouraged the development of Methodism in Shetland. Major refurbishment in 1994. Stained glass window in memory of William Goudie, a Shetlander designated President of the Wesleyan Methodist Conference in 1922, who died before taking office.

Sunday Services: 11.00am and 6.15pm

Open by arrangement, key available at adjacent Manse, telephone 01595 692874

METHODIST 🔓 🚻 ⟨⟩

ADAM CLARKE MEMORIAL METHODIST CHURCH, LERWICK

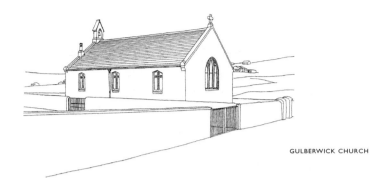

GULBERWICK CHURCH

950 GULBERWICK CHURCH

HU 443 389

2 miles south of Lerwick

A handsome and simple church built in 1898 with Orkney stone facings. The windows behind the pulpit are filled with cathedral squares. Picturesquely situated in the village of Gulberwick with a graveyard overlooking the sea.

Sunday Service: 10.00am

Open by arrangement, telephone the Minister 01595 692125

CHURCH OF SCOTLAND **C**

951 BRESSAY CHURCH

HU 493 410

1 mile from ferry

A typical harled kirk with belfry of the early 19th century, built 1812 to replace an earlier kirk of 1722 which in turn replaced Bressay's three ancient chapels. The church boasts two beautiful stained glass windows 1895 of St Peter and St Paul. At each of the windows are memorial tablets. The church overlooks the bay and its seals. Sunday Service: 3.00pm

Open by arrangement, telephone the Minister 01595 692125

CHURCH OF SCOTLAND **B**

HAROLDSWICK METHODIST CHURCH, UNST

952 HAROLDSWICK METHODIST CHURCH, UNST

HP 646 134

Haroldswick, Unst

The most northerly church in Britain. The present building 1993 was designed by
a Shetland architect, based on a simplified form of a Norwegian wooden stave
kirk. Most of the work was done by local voluntary labour. The interior beams
and panelling are Scandinavian pine and the lightness, warmth and proportion of
the worship area are striking. New bell turret for the 1867 bell has just been
completed. Sunday Service: 11.00am or 6.00pm (alternate Sundays)

Open all the time

METHODIST   🦽   wc

953 EAST YELL METHODIST CHURCH, YELL

HP 517 855

Otterswick, East Yell

Built 1892 to serve the needs of the local community, this lovely 'Chapel in the
Valley' is noted for its simple beauty, warmth of its welcome and ecumenical
nature of its congregation. The chapel has been described as a 'little gem'. Much
admired unique pulpit fall, designed and crafted locally, depicting the Lamb of
God. Sunday Services: 10.45am or 2.45pm (alternate Sundays)

Open all the time

METHODIST   🦽   wc

EAST YELL METHODIST CHURCH, YELL

954 ST COLMAN'S EPISCOPAL, YELL

HU 520 798

Burravoe, Yell

A little rural gem in Arts & Crafts Gothic. Designed by R T N Spier and built 1900. Apsidal end and spirelet. Herring-bone patterned panels to doors, timber choir stalls and pews. Folding Gothic timber chair by Morris & Co and painted front to the timber altar depicting the Worship of Heaven.

Services: Eucharist 3rd Sunday every month 2.45pm, plus 1st Sunday June to September

Summer Flower Festival Service: 1st Sunday in July, 2.45pm. Open at all times

SCOTTISH EPISCOPAL   🚶 wc **B**

ST COLMAN'S EPISCOPAL

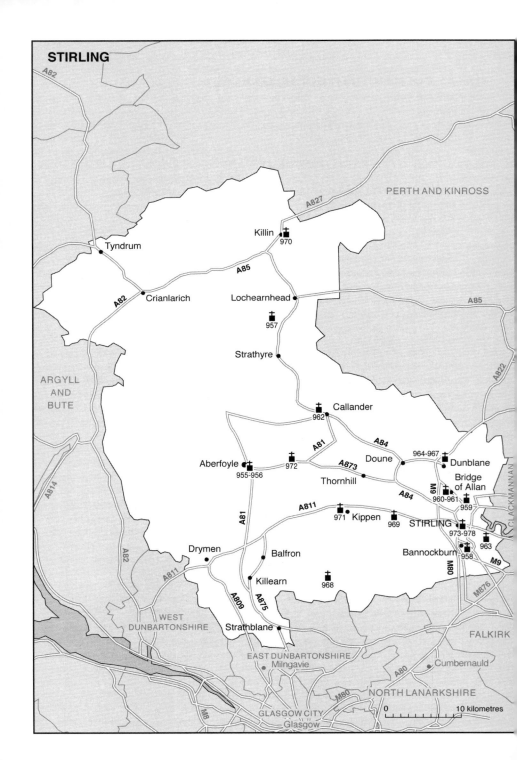

STIRLING

STIRLING

Local Representative: Mr Louis Stott, 10 Trossachs Road, Aberfoyle FK8 3SW (*telephone* 01877 382784)

955 ABERFOYLE PARISH CHURCH

NN 518 005

Loch Ard Road, Aberfoyle. On the B829
John Honeyman designed this church which sits at the foot of Craigmore and on the banks of the River Forth. In early-Gothic style 1870, it replaced the old kirk of Aberfoil on the south bank of the river reached by crossing the hump-backed bridge. The new church was enlarged in 1884 to include transepts. The interior is elegant

ABERFOYLE PARISH CHURCH

with the minimum of ornamentation. Magnificent roof timbers. Stained glass, including a window by Gordon Webster 1974. Two-manual pipe organ 1887 by Bryceson Brothers, London. Linked with Port of Menteith.

Sunday Service: 11.15am

Open July and August, daily 2.00-4.00pm

CHURCH OF SCOTLAND wc ⊘ 📖 B

956 ST MARY'S, ABERFOYLE

NN 524 010

Main Street, Aberfoyle
The church was designed by James Miller, who also designed Gleneagles Hotel. It was built 1892-3 by workers from the local slate quarry. The stone came from Ailsa Craig by railway (free of charge) to test the weight capacity of the new branch railway. Oak panelled reredos. Organ by Henry Willis.

Sunday Service: Sung Eucharist 11.15am

Open by arrangement with Mrs M Johnson, telephone 01877 382611

SCOTTISH EPISCOPAL wc ⊘

ST MARY'S, ABERFOYLE

957   BALQUHIDDER PARISH CHURCH

NN 536 209
A84 at Kinghouse
Handsome parish church in dressed stone, built
1853 by David Bryce. Exhibition of the history of
the church. Bell donated by Rev Robert Kirk
(1644-92), a notable boulder font and the supposed
gravestone of St Angus, possibly 9th century. The
ruins of the old parish church are in the graveyard
where there are many intriguing carved stones,
including that of Rob Roy MacGregor. Linked
with Killin. Sunday Service: 12.00 noon
Open daily. Summer Music Sunday
evenings during summer months
CHURCH OF SCOTLAND   ⌖ ⓦⓒ **B**

BALQUHIDDER PARISH CHURCH

958   OUR LADY & ST NINIAN'S, BANNOCKBURN

NS 813 903
Quakerfield
Archibald Macpherson 1927, in a modified Early Christian style. Built in multi-
coloured bricks with a red tiled roof and a copper spire. Grey brick interior with
wide-arched arcades and open timber ceiling. Stained glass windows. Services:
Sunday 12.00 noon; Tuesday and Thursday 10.00am; Saturday Vigil 6.30pm
Open by arrangement, telephone 01786 812249
ROMAN CATHOLIC ⌖ ⓦⓒ ⓐ ⌣ ⬙ **C**

959   LOGIE KIRK, BY BLAIRLOGIE, STIRLING

NS 829 968
A91, four miles north-east of Stirling
Church website: www.logiekirk.co.uk
The tower, square and pedimented and surmounted by an octagonal belfry, was
designed by William Stirling of Dunblane 1805. The remainder of the church is an
elegant whinstone box, by McLuckie & Walter of Stirling 1901. Stained glass
windows include one by C E Kempe and two modern windows by John Blyth.
Fourteen oak panels depicting scenes from the Bible enclose the chancel and
pulpit. The ruined Old Kirk of Logie, with its good selection of 17th and 18th-
century gravestones, is nearby. In idyllic rural setting at foot of Dumyat and in the
shadow of the Wallace Monument. Sunday Service: 11.00am
Open Sundays, July and August 2.00-5.00pm or by appointment,
telephone 01786 475414. Check website for events
CHURCH OF SCOTLAND ⌖ ⓦⓒ ⓐ ⬙ ⬙ ⓘ ⌣ **B**

LOGIE KIRK, BY BLAIRLOGIE, STIRLING

BRIDGE OF ALLAN PARISH CHURCH

960 BRIDGE OF ALLAN PARISH CHURCH

NS 791 974

Keir Street, Bridge of Allan (on corner of Fountain Road)
Church website: www.bridgeofallanparishchurch.org.uk
Built in 1860 and enlarged later, the church contains chancel furnishings designed in 1904 by the eminent Scottish architect, Charles Rennie Mackintosh. The church has an attractive timber roof and excellent stained glass windows by Kempe family, Ballantine and Adam. Organ by Lewis, 1884, with additions. Bus service from Stirling to Royal Hotel, one block. Rail service to Bridge of Allan Station, 10 minutes' walk. Sunday Service: 11.00am
Open June to August, Saturdays 10.00am-4.00pm or
by arrangement telephone 01786 834155
CHURCH OF SCOTLAND 🚻 wc ② 🕯 📖 B

961 ST SAVIOUR'S CHURCH, BRIDGE OF ALLAN

NS 792 973

Keir Street, Bridge of Allan
(On corner with Fountain Road)
Church adjacent to rectory 1857, architect John Henderson, and later enlarged 1871-2 by Alexander Ross. Halls added to rectory 1893. Vestry added 1928. West window by Robert Anning Bell, Stephen Adam Studio, 1922. Pipe organ, Forster & Andrews 1872. By road, bus and rail services from Stirling. Sunday Services: Said Eucharist 8.00am, Sung Eucharist and Sermon 10.00am
Open generally 10.00am-5.00pm
SCOTTISH EPISCOPAL 🚻 B

ST SAVIOUR'S CHURCH, BRIDGE OF ALLAN

962 ST ANDREW'S, CALLANDER

NS 624 080

Leny Road, Callandar

Sheltered by a magnificent cedar of Lebanon,
this pretty little church was consecrated in
1857. The architects were either J, J W & W
H Hay or 'the stonemason at Stronvar' who
worked on the parish church at Balquhidder
for David Bryce in 1853. Enlarged by the
addition of transepts in 1886. Organ by
Abbot and Smith of Leeds 1898. Services:
Sunday 10.00am; Wednesday 10.00am

ST ANDREW'S, CALLANDER

Open by arrangement, telephone Ms Gunkel 01877 330798

SCOTTISH EPISCOPAL 🔵 wc wc ⦾ **B**

963 SACRED HEART, COWIE

NS 836 890

Main Street, Cowie

In a rural hilltop setting, a red brick church by Reginald Fairlie, 1937. A pyramid-
slated octagon with projecting porch and sanctuary. Inside, steel lattices support the
roof structure. Sanctuary floor and altars in variegated marbles. Services: Sunday
10.30am; Monday and Friday 10.00am

Open by arrangement with Parish Priest telephone 01786 812249

ROMAN CATHOLIC 🔵 wc ⦾ ⯊ **B**

964 DUNBLANE CATHEDRAL

NN 782 014

The Cross, Dunblane

Church website: www.dunblanecathedral.org.uk

One of Scotland's noblest medieval churches, the lower part of the tower is
Romanesque, but the larger part of the building is of the 13th century. Six late
15th-century choir stalls survive. The Cathedral was restored by Sir Robert Rowand
Anderson between 1889 and 1893. Screen, pulpit, lectern and font by Anderson.
Choir stalls and organ case by Sir Robert Lorimer. Important ensemble of stained
glass by Clayton & Bell, Gordon Webster, Douglas Strachan, C E Kempe. The six
magnificent choir windows are by Louis Davis. Sunday Services: 9.15am and
10.30am (winter); 9.15am only (summer)

Open April to September, Monday to Saturday 9.30am-6.30pm; Sunday 1.30pm-6.30pm
October to March, Monday to Wednesday 9.30am-4.30pm; Thursday 9.30am-12.30pm;
Saturday 9.30am-4.30pm; Sunday 2.00pm-4.30pm

CHURCH OF SCOTLAND 🔵 ⦾ ⯊ **A**

965 ST BLANE'S CHURCH, DUNBLANE

NN 783 014

High Street/Sinclairs Street Lane, Dunblane
Open 1854 as Free Church which through
unions became East United Free Church and
East Church of Scotland. United with
former Leighton Church in 1952 to become
St Blane's Church. Stained glass includes
windows from Leighton Church, other
windows by Roland Mitton. Interesting
tapestries in vestibule including a
reproduction of 'The Light of the World'
by Holman Hunt. Pipe organ 1860 by Peter

ST BLANE'S CHURCH, DUNBLANE

Conacher, perhaps the earliest example of his work in Scotland.
Sunday Services: 11.15am (10.15am June to August), and 6.30pm
Open by arrangement, telephone the Minister 01786 822268, Dr Duncan 01786 822657,
or Mr Cattan 01786 822142
CHURCH OF SCOTLAND [wc] (2) [] **B**

966 CHURCH OF THE HOLY FAMILY, DUNBLANE

NN 780 006

Claredon Place, Dunblane
Designed by Reginald Fairley, this church was erected in 1934 by the Honourable
Mrs Margaret Striling in memory of her husband, General Archibald Stirling of
Keir. Stained glass windows by Shona McInnes in memory of the victims of the
Dunblane School Incident in 1996.
Services: Saturday Vigil 5.00pm, Sunday 11.00am, daily 10.00am
Open daily 10.00am-5.00pm
ROMAN CATHOLIC [&] [wc] (2) **C**

967 SCOTTISH CHURCHES HOUSE CHAPEL, DUNBLANE

NN 783 014

Kirk Street, Dunblane, opposite cathedral
Church website: www.scottishchurcheshouse.org
Uncovered in 1961 during restoration of buildings which became Scottish
Churches House. Medieval in origin, possibly a chapel of one of several ecclesias-
tical residences which then surrounded the cathedral. Fine barrel-vaulted roof.
Restored for use as the chapel of Scottish Churches House, an ecumenical
conference house and retreat centre. Programme of events, and retreats available
from the warden. Daily House Prayers: 9.00am
Open at all times
ECUMENICAL [wc] (2) [] **B**

968 FINTRY KIRK

NS 627 862

Fintry Village

The present church, built in 1823, was
constructed around the original kirk of
1642, and the congregation continued to
worship in the old sanctuary while
building went on around them! On
completion, the inner church was
demolished. The bell was transferred from
old to new and is still in use today. Early
20th-century stained glass, including a First
World War memorial window. Session
House in the kirkyard added 1992. Linked
with Balfron. Sunday Service: 10.00am
*Open Easter Saturday and Saturdays May to
September, 2.00-4.00pm*
CHURCH OF SCOTLAND ⬚ⓦⓒ ② 🍴 ☕ **B**

FINTRY KIRK

969 GARGUNNOCK PARISH CHURCH

NS 707 943

Manse Brae, Gargunnock (5 miles west of Stirling)

Situated in very beautiful rural location. Village church 1650 on pre-Reformation
foundation, renovated 1774 and 1891. Three individual outside stairs to three
separate lairds' lofts. Two good
20th-century stained glass windows.
War memorial by Lorimer.
Mountain indicator. Graveyard.
Sunday Service: 11.30am in July
and August; joint services with
linked churches, see notice board
*Open by arrangement, telephone 01786
860678 or 01786 860321*
CHURCH OF SCOTLAND ⬚ⓦⓒ 🍴 📖 ♿ **B**

GARGUNNOCK PARISH CHURCH

970 KILLIN AND ARDEONAIG PARISH CHURCH, KILLIN

NN 571 330

Main Street, Killin

Distinctive white-harled octagonal classical church built in 1744 by the mason Thomas Clark to a design by John Douglas of Edinburgh. Inside it has been altered from a 'wide' church to a 'long' church. The Fillan Room, a small chapel for prayer in the tower, was created in 1990. In front of the church is a monument to Rev James Stewart (1701-89), minister of Killin, who first translated the New

KILLIN AND ARDEONAIG PARISH CHURCH, KILLIN

Testament into Scots Gaelic (published 1767). At the eastern end of the village. Serves Morenish Chapel (see Perth & Kinross); linked with Balquhidder. Information about services in Morenish Chapel from Tourist Information by Falls of Dochart in village. Sunday Service: 10.00am

Open May to October during daylight hours

CHURCH OF SCOTLAND [wc] (?) **B**

971 KIPPEN PARISH CHURCH

NS 652 849

Fore Road, Kippen

Built 1827 by William Stirling, extensively redesigned 1924-6 by Reginald Fairlie and Eric Bell. Exceptionally graceful, Latinate in style, and incorporating a splendid and perfectly combined display of (mainly) 20th-century Christian art, including works by Sir Alfred Gilbert, Alfred Hardiman, James Woodford and Henry Wilson, as well as local craftsmen. Stained glass by Herbert Hendrie.

Sunday Service: 11.30am

Open 9.00am-4.30pm (dusk in winter). Times presently under review

CHURCH OF SCOTLAND

 (ramp available for wheel chairs)

[wc] (?) [] **B**

KIPPEN PARISH CHURCH

972 PORT OF MENTEITH CHURCH

NS 583 011

On B8034 beside the Lake Hotel
On the shore of the Lake of
Menteith, a church built in 1878
to designs by John Honeyman on
a site of earlier churches with
medieval connections. Simple
rectangular plan, Gothic style,
with square tower containing
carillon of eight bells. Victorian
pipe organ, probably by Brook.
Surrounded by a graveyard and a
few minutes' walk from the ferry

PORT OF MENTEITH CHURCH

to Inchmahome where the ruined 13th-century Augustinian Priory may be visited.
Linked with Aberfoyle. Sunday Service: 10.00am
Open July and August; Wednesday and Thursday 2.00-4.00pm
CHURCH OF SCOTLAND [wc] 🕑 📖 **B**

973 ALLAN PARK SOUTH CHURCH, STIRLING

NS 755 933

Dumbarton Road, Stirling
Peddie & Kinnear 1886 with the interior modernised for the centenary in 1986 by
Esmé Gordon. Radical change under consideration to bring interior and grounds to
the requirements of the 21st
century. Two large circular and
three smaller stained glass
windows to commemorate the
fallen in the two World Wars,
the ministry of the Rev Alan
Johnston and members of the
Kinross family. Sunday Service:
10.00am January to June,
11.30am July to December
*Open by arrangement, telephone
Church Secretary 01786 471998.
Office hours Tuesday, Wednesday
and Friday 11.30am-2.30pm*
CHURCH OF SCOTLAND [wc] 🕑 **B**

ALLAN PARK SOUTH CHURCH, STIRLING

974 THE CHAPEL ROYAL, STIRLING CASTLE

NS 790 941

There has been a chapel in the castle since at least 1117. It became the Chapel Royal of Scotland in the time of James IV in about 1500. The present building was built in 1594 by James VI for the baptism of Prince Henry. It was redecorated in 1629 in advance of the visit in 1633 of Charles I. After being sub-divided to serve military uses, there was a first phase of restoration in the 1930s, and the

THE CHAPEL ROYAL, STIRLING CASTLE

latest phase of work was completed in 1996. A large rectangular building with Renaissance windows and a central entrance framed by a triumphal arch along its southern front. Notable features include decorative paintings of 1629 by Valentine Jenkin, a modern wagon ceiling reflecting the profile of the original, and modern furnishings including a communion table cover designed by Malcolm Lochead. Services by arrangement

Open April to October 9.30am-6.00pm; November to March 9.30am-5.00pm

NON-DENOMINATIONAL 🔈 ② 🗋 ∏ 🖵 (Castle Restaurant) **A**

975 CHURCH OF THE HOLY RUDE, STIRLING

NS 792 937

St John Street, Stirling

Church website: www.churchoftheholyrude.org.uk

The original parish kirk of Stirling, used for the coronation in 1567 of James VI, at which John Knox preached. Largely built in 15th and 16th centuries. Medieval open-timbered oak roof in nave. Choir and apse added in 1555, the work of John Coutts, one of the greatest master masons of the later Middle Ages. Notable stained glass by Adam & Small, Ballantine, Cottier, W & J J Keir, McCartney, Strachan, Wailes. Largest pipe organ in Scotland, built by Rushworth & Dreaper 1940 and rebuilt 1994. Oak choir stalls and canopies 1965. Historic graveyard. Near to Stirling Castle. On Historic Stirling (open top) bus route.

Sunday Service: 11.30am January to June, 10.00am July to December

Open May to September 11.00am-4.00pm. Venue for many concerts

CHURCH OF SCOTLAND 🔈 wc ② ∏ 🗋 ⓡ **A**

CHURCH OF THE HOLY RUDE, STIRLING

976 HOLY TRINITY CHURCH, STIRLING

NS 793 934

Albert Place, Dumbarton Road, Stirling

One of Sir R Rowand Anderson's most distinctive churches 1878, close to Stirling Castle, old town and shops. Very close to town centre, on Historic Stirling (open top) bus route. Sunday Services: Eucharists 8.30 and 10.30am, Evening Prayer 6.30pm

Open mornings daily

SCOTTISH EPISCOPAL   **B**

977 ST NINIAN'S OLD, STIRLING

NS 797 917

Kirk Wynd, St Ninian's. Stirling

Only the tower and bell of 1734 survive following desecration of the nave by Cromwellian troops and an explosion of munitions stored in the 13th-century church by Jacobites. Present building is of 1751 with remodelling 1937 by A A McMichael. Interior restored and remodelled. Sunday Services: 10.30am and 6.30pm (2nd Sunday in March, June, September and December)

Open by arrangement with Mr Robert Simpson, telephone 01786 813335

CHURCH OF SCOTLAND   **A** (Steeple) **C** (Hall)

ST NINIANS OLD, STIRLING

978 VIEWFIELD PARISH CHURCH, STIRLING

NS 795 938

Irvine Place, Stirling

The present building, seating 600, was erected in 1860 to replace the 1752 meeting house. The congregations have been part of the Secession of 1733, going through United Presbyterian and United Free Churches until joining the Church of Scotland in 1929. Interior largely as constructed, though the window of the creation story behind the pulpit is a modern intervention by Christian Shaw. Sunday Service: 11.00am

Open by arrangement with keyholder
Mr Monteith, telephone 01786 461350

CHURCH OF SCOTLAND

♿ (from Irvine Place) wc ♾

VIEWFIELD PARISH CHURCH, STIRLING

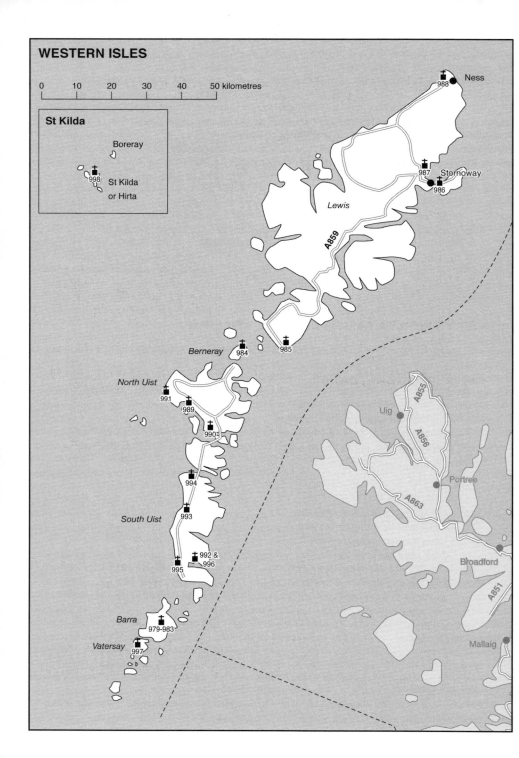

WESTERN ISLES

0   10   20   30   40   50 kilometres

St Kilda

Boreray

St Kilda
or Hirta

998

Ness
988

Lewis

Stornoway
987
986

A859

985

Berneray
984

North Uist
991
989
990

994

South Uist
993

992 &
996
995

Barra
979-983

Vatersay
997

Uig

A855

A856

Portree

A863

Broadford

A851

Mallaig

WESTERN ISLES (EILEAN SIAR)

Local Representative: Atisha McGregor Auld, Ruisgarry, Isle of Berneray, by Lochmaddy, North Uist HS6 5BQ

979 OUR LADY STAR OF THE SEA, BARRA

NL 667 983
Castlebay, Barra
Opened Christmas 1886, architect Woulfe Brenan of Oban. Statue by Dupon of Bruges of Our Lady Star of the Sea. Stained glass of crucifixion in Sanctuary, and of Our Lady Star of the Sea installed as war memorial in early 1950s. Bell in tower; the clock chimes the hour during day and night.
Sunday Service: 11.00am
Open at all times
ROMAN CATHOLIC 🚶 (ramp access available) 👂 **B**

OUR LADY STAR OF THE SEA, BARRA

980 ST BRENDAN, BARRA

NF 657 018
Craigston, Barra
Dating from 1805, the oldest church in the Isles of Barra. Restored 1858. Two etchings (scraperboard white on black) of St Brendan and St Barr, by Fr Calum MacNeill, retired priest of the diocese. Service: Saturday Vigil 7.00pm
Open at all times
ROMAN CATHOLIC 🚶

981 ST VINCENT DE PAUL, EOLIGARRY, BARRA

NF 703 076
Eoligarry, Barra
Built in 1964, the church has a tall roof with swept eaves. Small cemetary at Cille Bharra, burial place of MacNeil chieftains. Sunday Service: Mass 11.00am
Open at all times
ROMAN CATHOLIC

ST VINCENT DE PAUL, BARRA

982 NORTH CHAPEL, BARRA

NF 705 074
Cille Bharra, Eoligarry, Barra
Twelfth-century church built on site of 7th-century foundation dedicated to St Finbarr of Cork, Eire. Re-roofed with help from the Scottish Development Department. Contains notable 12th-century runic stone (original now in the National Museums of Scotland, Edinburgh) and 16th-century grave-slabs with carvings of animals and foliage. Mass on the feasts of the Celtic saints
Open at all times
ROMAN CATHOLIC

983 ST BARR'S

NF 707 031
Northbay, Barra
A simple lancet-windowed building by G Woulfe Brenan 1906, with porch and vestry added 1919. Small bellcote on porch. Services: daily Mass 7.30pm; Sunday 11.00am
Open at all times
ROMAN CATHOLIC

ST BARR'S, BARRA

984 BERNERAY CHURCH, ISLE OF BERNERAY

NL 552 801
Opposite war memorial, Berneray
Built 1887, architect Thomas Binnie of Glasgow, for the United Free Church. By uniting with the Established Church, now in ruins, it became the Church of Scotland and still flourishes as such. HRH the Prince of Wales worshipped here on a private visit in 1991. Berneray is now accessible by a causeway from North Uist across the Sound of Harris. Sunday Services: 12.00 noon in English, 6.00pm in Gaelic
Open by arrangement with Mr MacLean, telephone 01876 540249
CHURCH OF SCOTLAND [wc] Ⓓ Ⓘ

985 ST CLEMENT'S CHURCH, HARRIS

NG 047 831
Rodel, on A859 at southern point of Harris
Church website: www.historic-scotland.gov.uk
A fine 16th-century church built by Alexander MacLeod of Dunvegan and Harris; his richly carved tomb is within the church. St Clement was the third Bishop of Rome after St Peter and was martyred in AD99. The church is in the care of Historic Scotland. No services except by arrangement
Open dawn to dusk all year
NON-DENOMINATIONAL Scheduled Ancient Monument

986 ST COLUMBA'S (OLD PARISH) CHURCH, STORNOWAY, LEWIS

NB 426 330

Lewis Street, Stornoway, Lewis

Successor to St Lennan's Church Stornoway and St Columba's Uidh, the church of 1794 by John Lobban, master mason, was repaired in 1831 and extended in 1885 when stone Y-tracery and leaded glass was added to the windows, and the transept and porch added. Internally, the 1794 roof survives. Caen stone and marble font gifted by Lady Matheson of the Lews. Two-manual pipe organ, Joseph Brooks; rebuilt 1954, Henry Willis & Co. Oak sanctuary furniture and brass eagle lectern gifted by Greyfriars Tolbooth and Highland Kirk, Edinburgh.

Services: Sunday 11.00am and 6.30pm; Thursday 7.30pm

Open by arrangement with Church Officer 01851 704510

CHURCH OF SCOTLAND 🦽 🚾 ⏺ ♀ Gaelic spoken ☕ **B**

987 ST MOLUAG'S COMMUNITY CHURCH, LEWIS

NB 448 366

Opposite Tong School, on B895, Lewis

In 1999 the building, which had formerly been a village shop and Post Office, was converted into a church, opened and dedicated 2000. Sunday Service: Sung Eucharist 11.00am (except 1st Sunday of month from May to September and Easter Day – Service at Eoropaidh)

Open by arrangement, telephone 01851 820559

SCOTTISH EPISCOPAL 🦽 🚾 🚾 ☕ (after Service)

988 ST MOLUAG, LEWIS

NB 519 651

Eoropaidh, Ness, Lewis. 200 yards from B8013 (signposted Eoropaidh from A857)

The building probably dates from the 12th century, but the site is believed to have been consecrated in the 6th century and is probably the place where Christianity was first preached to the people of Lewis. The church was restored in 1912 by Norman Forbes of Stornoway, under the guidance of the architect J S Richardson; the altars date from this restoration. The side chapel is connected to the main church only through a squint. The church has no heating, electricity or water; lighting is by candles and oil lamps. Services: 11.00am Easter Day, and on 1st Sunday of May to September

Open during daylight hours, Easter to last weekend in October. Vehicular access impossible. In wet weather, path to church can be muddy

SCOTTISH EPISCOPAL **A**

ST MOLUAG, LEWIS

989 CARINISH CHURCH, NORTH UIST

NF 820 604

Built as a Mission Church (title deeds dated 1868) for the Church of Scotland. The main feature is that the communion pews run down the length of the church so that those taking communion would sit side-on to the pulpit. They would be invited to come and sit at the table to take communion. Services no longer held

Open by arrangement, telephone 01876 580219

CHURCH OF SCOTLAND wc **B**

990 CLACHAN CHURCH, NORTH UIST

NF 811 638

Clachan na Luib, North Uist

Built 1889 for the Clachan na Luib Free Church, architect Thomas Bennie of Glasgow. Considerable difficulty was experienced procuring the site from Sir William Powlet Campbell Orde, Bart. After lengthy negotiations he reluctantly gave the present site at an annual rental of £3.9s. The congregation became United Free until 1929 when they became part of the Church of Scotland. Sunday Services: 12.00 noon and 6.00pm in English, unless otherwise announced

Open by arrangement, telephone 01876 580219

CHURCH OF SCOTLAND wc (?)

CLACHAN CHURCH, NORTH UIST

991 KILMUIR CHURCH, NORTH UIST

NF 708 706

West side of North Uist, close to Balranald RSPB Reserve

Originally North Uist Parish Church. Gothic T-plan by Alexander Sharp 1892-4. In the south-west inner angle is a 2-stage tower, its battlemented parapet enclosing a slated pyramidal spire. Inside, a wealth of pitch-pine.

One of the few remaining Gaelic-essential charges; during the morning Gaelic service one can hear, and participate in, the precenting of Gaelic psalms. Sunday Services: 10.00am in Gaelic, 6.00pm in English

Open by arrangement, telephone Mr Macbain 01876 510241

CHURCH OF SCOTLAND wc (?)

KILMUIR CHURCH, NORTH UIST

992 DALIBURGH/DALABROG, SOUTH UIST

NF 754 214

Built originally as South Uist Free Church in 1862-3, now Church of Scotland.
Manse completed 1880 and vestry/hall behind low wall added later. All harled.
Church rectangular in plan with three bays with round-headed openings and a
single window in either gable. Door and apex belfry to south gable. Pulpit with
panelled front. Communion table and war memorial based on design of that at
Howmore by Archibald Scott. Sunday Service: 11.00am
Open at all times
CHURCH OF SCOTLAND [wc] ⊘ **B**

993 HOWMORE CHURCH, SOUTH UIST

NF 758 364

Simple austere building by John McDearmid
1858, set in open land overlooking the Atlantic.
Acts as landmark for west-coast fishermen.
One of few churches in Scotland with central
Communion table. Nearby are remains of
13th-century church. Sunday Service: 12.30pm
Open at all times
CHURCH OF SCOTLAND [♿] [wc] **B**

HOWMORE CHURCH, SOUTH UIST

994 IOCHDAR CHURCH, SOUTH UIST

NF 787 463

Eochar, South Uist

Built 1889 as a Mission House by David MacIntosh, it is a small, compact church
with traditional pews and central pulpit. The church particularly lends itself to
quiet prayer and meditation. Sunday Service: 6.00pm 1st Sunday of the month
Open by arrangement, telephone Mrs Stephenson 01870 610401
CHURCH OF SCOTLAND

995 OUR LADY OF SORROWS, SOUTH UIST

NP 758 165

Garrynamonie, South Uist

Built 1965, Architect Richard J McCarson, with a monopitch roof. Above Blessed
Sacrement altar is a ceramic on the theme of the Sacred Heart by David Harding
of Edinburgh who was also responsibile for original mural of Our Lady of
Sorrows at the entrance. This was replaced in 1994 by the present mural reflecting
the sorrows of the contemporary world by Michael Gilfeddar, commissioned by
Canon Galbraith. Service: Saturday Vigil 6.30pm
Open throughout each day
ROMAN CATHOLIC [♿] [wc]

996   ST PETER'S, SOUTH UIST

NF 745 211
Daliburgh, South Uist
Big harled church of 1868 with a birdcage bellcote on the south gable and a tall
concrete hoop bellcote on the 1960s porch. North sanctuary added 1907.
Service: Sunday Mass 11.30am
Open throughout each day
ROMAN CATHOLIC   wc ⟨⟩ c

997   OUR LADY OF THE WAVES & ST JOHN, VATERSAY

NL 646 961
Uidh, Vatersay
Small functional church for celebration of Mass and other church services.
Reached by causeway from Barra. Sunday Service: 3.30pm
Open at all times
ROMAN CATHOLIC   wc

998   CHRIST CHURCH, ST KILDA

NF 100 994
Village Bay, St Kilda
The stimulus for the kirk, designed by Robert Stevenson, came from the Rev Dr
John Macdonald who visited St Kilda several times in the early 19th century. The
church fell into disrepair after evacuation in 1930. Renovated over a period of 20
years since coming into the care of the National Trust for Scotland in 1957.
St Kilda is Scotland's first World Heritage Site. Services by arrangement
Open by arrangement, contact the National Trust for Scotland, telephone 01631 564 710
INTER-DENOMINATIONAL

CHURCHES WITH A
HISTORIC SCOTTISH CONNECTION

999   THE CHURCH OF SCOTLAND IN CARLISLE

NY 403 562

Chapel Street, Carlisle

Built 1834, altered 1979 and extended 1994. A city-centre church, the interior is arranged over two floors with halls and kitchen on the ground floor and sanctuary on the first floor. The extension provides three floors housing ecumenical One World Centre, coffee lounge and Fair Trade shop. Two minutes from main 'Lanes' shopping area and civic centre; five minutes from the cathedral, castle and parks; ten minutes from Tullie House Museum. Two minutes from bus station in Lowther Street.
Sunday Service: 11.00am; also 6.30pm 1st Sunday (except January, July and August)
Open Monday to Friday 10.00am-2.00pm. Coffee lounge and Fair Trade shop,
open Monday to Friday 10.00am-2.00pm
CHURCH OF SCOTLAND   ⓖ ⓦ🄲 ⓓ 🖺A

1000   CROWN COURT, COVENT GARDEN, LONDON

Adjacent to Fortune Theatre, Russell Street
Church website: www.crowncourtchurch.org.uk
Historic London church in the heart of Theatreland. The 'Kirk of the Crown of Scotland' dates from 1909, replacing an earlier church of 1711. Longest established Presbyterian Church in England. Royal arms of George I above communion table. Baptismal font of Iona marble. Superb stained glass. Services: Sunday 11.15 and 6.30pm; Thursday 1.10-1.30pm
Open June to August, 11.30-2.00pm Tuesday, Wednesday and Thursday.
At other times, telephone the Church Secretary 020 7836 5643
CHURCH OF SCOTLAND   ⓖ ⓦ🄲 ⓦ🄲 ⓓ ⓘ 📖

1001   ST COLUMBA'S, LONDON

Pont Street, London
Church website: www.stcolumbas.org.uk
The present building, re-dedicated in 1955, replaced the original building destroyed by incendiary bombs in 1941. The architect was Sir Edward Maufe. Fine rose window, 'The Creative Spirit of God', by Moira Forsyth. The London Scottish Chapel contains the Rolls of Honour of the London Scottish Regiment. The arms of the Scottish Counties, painted in heraldic colours, are carved at the base of the tall windows all round the church. Services: Sunday 11.00am; 6.30pm Holy Communion 1st Sunday of the month; Wednesday 1.00pm
Open 9.30am-5.00pm, Monday to Friday
CHURCH OF SCOTLAND   ⓦ🄲 ⓦ🄲 ⓓ 📖 **Grade II**

SCOTLAND'S CHURCHES SCHEME

ENCOURAGES CHURCHES TO:

- Open their doors with a welcoming presence
- Tell the story of the building, its purpose and the faith which inspired it
- Care for visitors in a sensitive and enriching way
- Work together with others to make the Church the focus of its community

SUPPORTS CHURCHES WITH:

- The publication of its comprehensive guidebook – *Churches to Visit in Scotland*
- Free advice on all aspects of visitor welcome, publicity, interpretation and exhibitions
- A network of local representatives in direct contact with headquarters
- Effective national publicity

SCOTLAND'S CHURCHES SCHEME GRATEFULLY ACKNOWLEDGES SUPPORT FROM:

THE CRUDEN FOUNDATION

THE DULVERTON TRUST

THE EAST-WEST TRUST

THE GARFIELD WESTON FOUNDATION

THE INCHES CARR TRUST

THE MANIFOLD TRUST

THE OPEN CHURCHES TRUST

THE P F CHARITABLE TRUST

THE RUSSELL TRUST

SCOTTISH & NEWCASTLE PLC

THE WEBSTER CHARITABLE TRUST

AND SEVERAL ANONYMOUS PRIVATE BENEFACTORS

DONATIONS

Please consider making a donation to Scotland's Churches Scheme, either in an individual or corporate capacity, so that this guide may become an indispensable part of the Scottish calendar, and the permanent financial future of the Scheme is secured.

Options, including Gift Aid which generates additional monies through the reclaim of tax already paid by donors, are:

[a]   Gift Aid
[b]   Gifts through the Charities Aid Foundation
[c]   Give As You Earn schemes operated by employers, and
[d]   Bequests in a Will, which are exempt from Inheritance Tax

Information and forms for [a] and [b] may be obtained from:

Scotland's Churches Scheme
Dunedin, Holehouse Road
Eaglesham
Glasgow G76 0JF

Telephone: 01355 302416
Fax: 01355 303181
E-mail: fraser@dunedin67.freeserve.co.uk
Website: www.churchesinscotland.co.uk

- ✂

Donation Form

I enclose £ _____ as a donation to Scotland's Churches Scheme

Name _____

Address _____

_____ Postcode _____

CHURCHES TO
VISIT IN SCOTLAND

To:

The Director, *Scotland's Churches Scheme,*
Dunedin, Holehouse Road, Eaglesham, Glasgow
Telephone: 01355 302416
Fax: 01355 303181 *E-mail:* fraser@dunedin67.freeserve.co.uk
Website: www.churchesinscotland.co.uk

Please send me details and an application form for entry in the next guidebook

Name

Address

Postcode

Name of Church

Address of Church

Postcode

Further copies of the current guidebook are available from the above address
at £8.99 paperback (£12.50 including p&p); or contact:

NMS ENTERPRISES LIMITED – PUBLISHING
National Museums of Scotland, Chambers Street, Edinburgh EH1 1JF
Telephone: 0131 247 4026

SCOTLAND'S GARDENS SCHEME

Scotland's Gardens Scheme was founded in 1931 to support the training and pension funds of The Queen's Nursing Institute Scotland and follows much the same procedures as were started all those years ago. In 2006 we are celebrating our 75th birthday, adopting the theme of Gardening for Health. It is our intention to hold various events all around Scotland and The Queen's Nursing Institute is to run a competition to mark its long time association with our Scheme. The competition is open to everyone to create or improve a garden that would benefit people with a health problem. It is open to hospitals, hospices, residential homes, perhaps an attractive church garden, or any area which could be open to the public and fulfill the aims of the competition. Substantial prizes are offered to create or improve a garden and full details can be obtained from the address below.

Look out for our yellow posters on display all around Scotland which give details of all our garden openings, and in 2006 any local events to support our anniversary year. Our garden owners can select any registered charity to which they can donate up to 40% of their gross takings on the opening day, which allowed us to donate to 147 different charities in 2004. Several owners chose their local church and in 2005, 31 churches benefited from individual garden openings.

Remember to look out for our large plant sales. Plants are carefully matured throughout the season and then put on sale at very reasonable prices. Sales staff are also on hand to offer free advice as to what might grow in that awkward spot in your garden and this service has become a major feature of the sales. Our website is now an important feature of our Scheme and attracts many new visitors to our gardens.

We wish Scotland's Churches Scheme yet another successful year, and every success with their most attractive guidebook.

SCOTLAND'S GARDENS SCHEME
22 Rutland Square
Edinburgh EH1 2BB

Telephone: 0131 229 1870
Fax: 0131 229 0443

E-mail: office@sgsgardens.netco.uk
Website: www.gardensofscotland.org

CHURCH RECORDERS

NADFAS

Scottish churches do not immediately promise rich pickings. Most of the present-day buildings are 19th-century replacements of pre-Reformation parish churches or former Free Churches. Consequently we do not expect to find the thumb-print of our ancestors on their bare walls and anonymous furnishings.

The activities of Church Recorders, who are volunteer members of the National Association of Decorative & Fine Arts Societies (NADFAS) show how a closer scrutiny of church interiors can illuminate both past and present. Church Recorders make a comprehensive Record of the furnishings and some of the fabric with text, photographs, drawings and historical research; often much of intrinsic and historical interest is found.

Churches of all denominations are being recorded, and those in the guide are indicated by the above logo. 2005 marks the 10th year of Recording in Scotland, with 19 Records completed or in hand.

Today, there is much vandalism, theft, and loss of precious artefacts. The Records, which are paid for by NADFAS Societies, provide a permanent, detailed inventory invaluable for repairs and insurance.

The Record is of interest to parishioners, visitors, and serious scholars. Guides in churches may obtain information from it, but it must be stressed that the Record is confidential.

One copy is presented to the church, others are lodged with official bodies such as the Church Authority and the Royal Commission for Ancient and Historical Monuments of Scotland.

The Records will provide valuable information now and in the future, when, sadly, some of the churches could face closure.

Further information may be obtained from:

The Church Recorders Scottish Representative
NADFAS HOUSE, 8 Guildford Street, LONDON WC1 1DT

Telephone: 020 7430 0730. *E-mail*: churchrecorders@nadfas.org.uk

THE OPEN CHURCHES TRUST

What Scotland's Churches Scheme is doing in Scotland and this Trust in England and Wales are complementary. The Scheme has huge support and a very impressive list of open churches.

The main work of the Trust at present is to put on roadshows for Diocesan areas, which tackle all the problems of opening a place of worship to the public. There is a huge growth of organisations which are tourist motivated and which lead to the opening of a large number of such places. The North West Multi-Faith Tourism Association operates from Manchester to Dumfries and incorporates synagogues, temples and mosques. With big operations in North Yorkshire, Rotherham, Mid Bedfordshire, Kent, Sussex and Wales, the Open Churches Trust is now working with a mass of friends, all with the same objectives.

I realise that a great many of your churches will be open but without stewards. Our roadshow demonstrates the real value of stewards.

We reckon that a stewarded church attracts double the number an unstewarded church attracts.

The continual growth of the churches in Scotland's Churches Scheme is an inspiration to us all. By our new roadshow we hope to start catching it up on the number of churches open.

We must never forget that the prime purpose of an open church is to allow people to use it. Tens of thousands of people every day pop into an open church for ten minutes of peace, quiet, contemplation and prayer. This is a reflection of the stressful times we live in and the need for a haven. All open churches provide this.

The Trust has just published *The Church Explorer's Handbook*, a pocket-sized reference book which will help anyone going into a church understand what they see. Book available from the Trust at £14.99.

THE OPEN CHURCHES TRUST
c/o The Really Useful Group Ltd, 22 Tower Street, London WC2H 9TW

Telephone: 020 7240 0880
Fax: 020 7240 1204
E-mail: oct@reallyuseful.co.uk
Website: www.openchurchestrust.org.uk

THE SCOTTISH REDUNDANT CHURCHES TRUST

EAST CHURCH, CROMARTY, ROSS-SHIRE

AIMS:

- To take into ownership the best examples of redundant places of worship of all denominations in Scotland
- To preserve and protect their fabric
- To maintain them for the benefit of the local community and the nation
- To provide public access to them

Incorporated as a Charitable Company in 1996, the SRCT owns four redundant churches throughout Scotland: St Peter's Church, Orkney, Cromarty East Church, Ross-shire, Pettinain Church, Lanarkshire and Tibbermore Church, Perthshire. These outstanding examples of our rich ecclesiastical heritage are repaired and preserved as 'sleeping' churches, open to visitors and made use of by local people for occasional worship and community events.

Changes in social and cultural attitudes, the decline in the church-going population and the high cost of maintaining ageing buildings mean that an increasing number of historic churches throughout Scotland are in limited use or have become redundant. The SRCT is the only national body that aims to protect, preserve and care for churches of all denominations whilst maintaining public access to them.

We rely on fundraising, donations and legacies to continue our work and to support the repair projects in the churches we own. If you would like to contribute towards saving Scotland's ecclesiastical heritage, or would like more information about the work of the SRCT and the Friends Groups and events at our churches, please contact: Victoria Collison-Owen, Scottish Redundant Churches Trust, 4 Queen's Gardens, St Andrews KY16 9TA. *Telephone:* 01334 472032; *Fax:* 01334 470767; *E-mail:* contact@srct.org.uk; *Website:* www.srct.org.uk

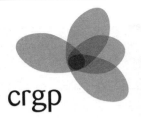

Scottish Churches House

*'Scottish Churches House is a pearl of
great value – a house of hospitality ...'*

'... the warm heart of ecumenism in Scotland.'

This House, which was established by the Scottish
churches and dedicated by the World Council of
Churches in 1960 in Dunblane, is a Conference Centre
and Retreat House with 50 beds, a dining room and
meeting rooms which can accommodate up to 85. In
beautiful surroundings, the main building is made of
renovated 18th-century cottages on the Cathedral
Square. A 16th-century stone chapel in the gardens
behind (p.427, No. 967) is available for small weddings,
with the option of receptions in the House.

For further information including details of
the House Programme:
SCOTTISH CHURCHES HOUSE
Kirk Street, Dunblane FK15 0AJ

Telephone: 01786 823 588
E-mail: reservations@scottishchurcheshouse.org
Website: www.scottishchurcheshouse.org

INDEX OF ARTISTS

Number refers to church entry, not page

INDEX OF CHURCHES

Number refers to church entry, not page